Bullying in schools

Bullying in schools: How successful can interventions be? is the first comparative account of the major intervention projects against school bullying that have been carried out by educationalists and researchers since the 1980s, across Europe, North America, and Australasia. Bullying in schools has become an international focus for concern. It can adversely affect pupils and in extreme cases lead to suicide. Schools can take action to reduce bullying and several programmes are available but do they work? In fact, success rates have been very varied. This book surveys thirteen studies and eleven countries. Working on the principle that we can learn from both successes and failures, it examines the processes as well as the outcomes, and critically assesses the likely reasons for success or failure. With contributions from leading researchers in the field, *Bullying in schools* is an important addition to the current debate on tackling school bullying.

PETER K. SMITH is Professor of Psychology and Head of the Unit for School and Family Studies at Goldsmiths College, University of London. He is the editor of *Violence in schools: The response in Europe* (2003) and co-editor of several other books on bullying in schools, including *The nature of school bullying: A cross-national perspective* (1999).

DEBRA PEPLER is Professor of Psychology at York University, Toronto, Canada, and Senior Research Associate at the Hospital for Sick Children. She is co-editor of *The development and treatment of childhood aggression* and the recent volume *The development and treatment of girlhood aggression*.

KEN RIGBY is Adjunct Associate Professor of Social Psychology at the School of Education, University of South Australia. He is the author of *Bullying in schools and what to do about it* (1997), *Stop the bullying: A handbook for schools* (2001), and *New perspectives on bullying* (2002).

Bullying in schools: how successful can interventions be?

Edited by

Peter K. Smith, Debra Pepler, and Ken Rigby

CAMBRIDGE
UNIVERSITY PRESS

PUBLISHED BY THE PRESS SYNDICATE OF THE UNIVERSITY OF CAMBRIDGE
The Pitt Building, Trumpington Street, Cambridge, United Kingdom

CAMBRIDGE UNIVERSITY PRESS
The Edinburgh Building, Cambridge CB2 2RU, UK
40 West 20th Street, New York, NY 10011–4211, USA
477 Williamstown Road, Port Melbourne, VIC 3207, Australia
Ruiz de Alarcón 13, 28014 Madrid, Spain
Dock House, The Waterfront, Cape Town 8001, South Africa

http://www.cambridge.org

First published 2004

Printed in the United Kingdom at the University Press, Cambridge

Typefaces Plantin 10/12 pt.   *System* LaTeX 2$_\varepsilon$ [TB]

A catalogue record for this book is available from the British Library

Library of Congress Cataloging in Publication data
Bullying in schools : how successful can interventions be? / edited by Peter K.
Smith, Debra Pepler, and Ken Rigby.
    p.   cm.
Includes bibliographical references (p.   ) and index.
ISBN 0 521 82119 3 – ISBN 0 521 52803 8 (pb.)
1. Bullying in schools–Prevention–Cross-cultural studies.   I. Smith, Peter K.
II. Pepler, D. J. (Debra J.)   III. Rigby, Ken.
LB3013.3.B815   2004   2004045190

ISBN 0 521 82119 3 hardback
ISBN 0 521 52803 8 paperback

Contents

Figures

Tables

Notes on contributors

FRANÇOISE ALSAKER is at the Department of Psychology, University of Berne, Muesmattstrasse 45, CH – 3000 Berne 9, Switzerland. francoise.alsaker@psy.unibe.ch

RONA ATLAS is at the LaMarsh Centre for Research on Violence and Conflict Resolution, York University, Canada.

ILSE DE BOURDEAUDHUIJ is at Ghent University, Faculty of Medicine and Health Sciences, Department of Movement and Sport Sciences, B-9000 Ghent, Belgium. ilse.debourdeaudhuij@rug.ac.be

ALICE CHARACH is at the Hospital for Sick Children, 555 University Avenue, Toronto, Ontario, Canada M5G 1X8.

WENDY CRAIG is at the Department of Psychology, Queen's University, Kingston, Ontario, Canada. craigw@queensu.ca

DONNA CROSS is at the Western Australian Centre for Health Promotion Research, School of Public Health, Curtin University of Technology, GPO Box U1987, Perth, Western Australia 6845. d.cross@curtin.edu.au or dscross@bigpond.com

ERIN ERCEG is at the Western Australian Centre for Health Promotion Research, School of Public Health, Curtin University of Technology, GPO Box U1987, Perth, Western Australia 6845. e.erceg@curtin.edu.au

MIKE ESLEA is at the Department of Psychology, University of Central Lancashire, Preston, England. mjeslea@uclan.ac.uk

VICKY FLERX is at the University of South Carolina, USA.

DAVID GALLOWAY is at the School of Education, University of Durham, Leazes Road, Durham DH1 1TA. D.M.Galloway@durham.ac.uk

MARGARET HALL is at the Centre for Public Health, School of Nursing and Public Health, Edith Cowan University, 100 Joondalup Drive, Joondalup, Western Australia 6027. m.hall@ecu.edu.au

GREG HAMILTON is at the Western Australian Centre for Health Promotion Research, School of Public Health, Curtin University of Technology, GPO Box U1987, Perth, Western Australia 6845. g.hamilton@curtin.edu.au

REINER HANEWINKEL is at IFT-Nord, Institute for Therapy and Health Research, Düsternbrooker Weg 2, 24105 Kiel, Germany. hanewinkel@ift-nord.de

ARI KAUKIAINEN is at the Centre for Learning Research, University of Turku, FIN-20014 Turku, Finland.

MAILA KOIVISTO is at Konttitie 29, FIN-90440 Kempele, Finland. maila.koivisto@pp.inet.fi

SUSAN P. LIMBER is at the Institute on Family and Neighborhood Life, Clemson University, 158 Poole Agricultural Center, Clemson, SC 29634, USA. slimber@clemson.edu

GARY B. MELTON is at Clemson University, USA.

STEPHEN JAMES MINTON is at the Department of Education, Trinity College, Dublin, Ireland. sjminton@hotmail.com

JOAQUÍN A. MORA-MERCHÁN is at the Department of Developmental and Educational Psychology, University of Seville, Spain. merchan@us.es

MAURY NATION is at the University of North Florida, USA.

PAUL O'CONNELL is at the LaMarsh Centre for Research on Violence and Conflict Resolution, York University, Canada.

DAN OLWEUS is at the Research Center for Health promotion (HEMIL), University of Bergen, Norway. Dan.Olweus@psych.uib.no

MONA O'MOORE is at the Anti-bullying Research and Resource Centre, Education Department, Trinity College, Dublin, Ireland. momoore@tcd.ie

PAULETTE VAN OOST is at Ghent University, Research Group Health and Behaviour, H. Dunantlaan 2, B-9000 Ghent, Belgium. paulette.vanoost@rug.ac.be

ROSARIO ORTEGA is at the Faculty Science of Education, Av S. Alberto Magno s/n, 14004 Cordoba, Spain. ed1orrur@uco.es

DEBRA PEPLER is at the LaMarsh Centre for Research on Violence and Conflict Resolution, York University, 4700 Keele Street, Toronto, Ontario, Canada M3J 1P3. pepler@yorku.ca

YOLANDA PINTABONA is at the School of Psychology, Curtin University of Technology, GPO Box U1987, Perth, Western Australia 6845. y.pintabona@curtin.edu.au

ROSARIO DEL REY is at the Department of Developmental and Educational Psychology, University of Seville, Spain. delrey@us.es

KEN RIGBY is at the Faculty of Humanities and Social Sciences, University of South Australia, Underdale Campus, Holbrooks Road, Underdale, Adelaide 5032, Australia. Ken.Rigby@unisa.edu.au

ERLING ROLAND is at the Center for Behavioral Research, Stavanger University College, POB 8002, N-4068 Stavanger, Norway. erling.roland@saf.his.no

BARRI ROSENBLUTH is at SafePlace, PO Box 19454, Austin, TX 78760, USA. Brosenbluth@austin-safeplace.org

CHRISTINA SALMIVALLI is at the Department of Psychology, University of Turku, FIN-20014 Turku, Finland. tiina.salmivalli@utu.fi

ELLEN SANCHEZ is at Safeplace, PO Box 19454, Austin, TX 78760, USA.

SONIA SHARP is at Educationleeds, 10th floor east, Merrion House, 110 Merrion Centre, Leeds LS2 8DT, England. sonia.sharp@educationleeds.co.uk

MIRVA SINISAMMAL is at Ahven Lammen Kuja 8, FIN-42100 Jämsä, Finland.

PETER K. SMITH is at the Department of Psychology, Goldsmiths College, New Cross, London SE14 6NW, England. p.smith@gold.ac.uk

VEERLE STEVENS is at the Flemish Institute for Health Promotion, G. Schildknechtstraat 9, B-1020 Brussels, Belgium. veerle.stevens@vig.be

DAVID THOMPSON is at the Division of Education, University of Sheffield, Sheffield S10 2TN, England.
D.A.Thompson@sheffield.ac.uk

ALLISON TRACY is at Wellesley College, USA.

LINDA ANNE VALLE is at the Centers for Disease Control and Prevention, 4770 Buford Highway, Mailstop K-60, Atlanta, GA 30341, USA.

MARINUS VOETEN is at the Department of Educational Sciences, University of Nijmegen, PO Box 9104, 6500 HE Nijmegen, The Netherlands.

DANIEL J. WHITAKER is at the Centers for Disease Control and Prevention, 4770 Buford Highway, Mailstop K-60, Atlanta, GA 30341, USA.

Preface

For some two decades now, bullying in schools has been widely recognised as a societal problem, which can seriously and negatively affect the lives and career paths of many schoolchildren. Following the work of Olweus in Norway in the 1980s, educationists and researchers have been inspired to try out programmes of intervention against bullying in schools. An appreciable number of such interventions have now taken place, in Europe, North America, and Australasia. This is an opportune moment to take stock of what has been achieved, and critically to evaluate these interventions so as to pass on advice to the next generation of educational practitioners and researchers.

There have been some successes, but also some less successful studies. Working on the principle that we can learn from both successes and failures, this book for the first time compiles a detailed account of the major intervention projects against school bullying. It examines the processes as well as the outcomes, and critically assesses the likely reasons for success or failure.

Criteria for inclusion were that a project should have intervened against bullying in more than one school; that there should be a description of the process of intervention; and that there should be some evaluation of the outcome, including some quantitative data on pupil experiences and/or on actual reported incidences of bullying.

The opening chapter summarises the history of research on bullying and makes the case for why interventions are important. We follow this with a new chapter from Dan Olweus, the 'father' of bullying research; this is succeeded by another thirteen chapters of accounts of independent intervention studies; we have encouraged authors to follow a standard format here, describing first the impetus for the intervention, and early stages of planning and funding; then the selection of schools, and the characteristics of schools and students; the components of the intervention programme; evaluation framework and procedures; and then, crucially, what actually happened – the achievements and difficulties in implementing the intervention; this is followed by the results of the evaluation; any longer term effects or evaluation of the programme; and any dissemination and impact beyond the programme schools. These thirteen chapters cover three continents and eleven countries.

In our final chapter, we try to summarise the main lessons we have learned from this now substantial body of research. What advice can we give now to teachers, schools, education authorities, regional and national governments? What help can we give to pupils involved in victimisation at school? We do not know all the answers, but we do believe that our knowledge is advancing – as always, through failures as well as successes, so long as we learn from them. Our hope is that this book will carry forward the current debate on ways of best tackling school bullying, and contribute to this gradual but cumulative process of applying empirical research to one important area of human experience.

1 Working to prevent school bullying: key issues

Ken Rigby, Peter K. Smith, and Debra Pepler

A brief historical background

Over the last two decades, bullying in schools has become an issue of widespread concern (Smith, Morita, Junger-Tas, Olweus, Catalano and Slee, 1999). This is not to say that in earlier times bullying in schools was ignored. There was much animated public discussion of bullying in English private schools in the mid-nineteenth century following the publication of the famous novel *Tom Brown's school days* (Hughes, 1857). This book evoked strong expressions of abhorrence towards, and condemnation of, the practice of bullying, and various suggestions were made on how it could be countered (see Rigby, 1997). However, the systematic examination of the nature and prevalence of school bullying only began with the work of Olweus in the 1970s in Scandinavia.

The volume of research since then has clarified much about the nature of bullying, and the suffering it can cause (see Rigby, 2002; Smith, 2004). Certain pupils are clearly more at risk of being involved as bullies or victims, or sometimes both (bully/victims), by virtue of personality, family background factors, characteristics such as disability, and the nature and quality of friendships and peer-group reputation. Also, there is considerable evidence that the experience of being a victim can exacerbate outcomes such as low self-esteem, anxiety, depression, mistrust of others, psychosomatic symptoms, and school refusal (Hawker and Boulton, 2000). In addition, a career as a bully in school predicts increased risks of violence and abuse in later life. There is now a clear moral imperative on teachers and educators to act to reduce bullying in schools; and a moral imperative on researchers to try to give the most informed advice in this respect.

The most tragic outcome of victimisation is suicide. It was the suicide, within a short interval, of three boys in Norway that led in 1983 to the first major anti-bullying intervention by schools, at a national level. The reports of an evaluation of this intervention in Bergen, with supplementation by the developing Olweus Bullying Prevention programme (see chapter 2; and Olweus, 1993, 1999), indicated reductions of 50% in bullying and alerted many educationists to the possibility that interventions to counter bullying could be effective. However, the evaluation of the national Norwegian programme in Stavanger produced near-zero results (Roland, 1989). Since then there have been numerous attempts in many countries to demonstrate that intervention programmes to counter bullying can result in significant reductions in bullying behaviour. On the whole, evaluative reports (written by researchers largely responsible for the anti-bullying programmes) have indicated some consequent improvement in children's peer relations, but generally much less than the reduction of 50% in Bergen (Olweus, 1993); this includes some programmes based on the Bergen project (chapters 4 and 5). Some interventions have been much less successful or even failed to show any significant improvement.

What can explain this diversity of outcomes? These programmes have typically contained some common and some distinctively different elements. Hence, it is difficult at this stage to identify the crucial elements in the anti-bullying programmes or to say which programmes are the most effective. Most of the programmes to counter bullying have resulted in a degree of success, at least on some outcome measures. This is encouraging. But the task of describing what is 'the best practice' for schools to follow on the basis of evaluative studies of interventions remains.

The nature of programmes to counter bullying: general features

Anti-bullying programmes generally contain some common elements. They recognise the need for the school community and especially the teaching staff to be aware of the prevalence and seriousness of the problem of bullying in schools. To this end, time is spent discussing these matters with teachers and in some cases with parents and students.

It is widely accepted that countering bullying requires a 'whole school approach' in which the elements and initiatives in a programme are carefully co-ordinated. Co-ordinated action, it is often said, is needed at different levels: namely, the school, the classroom, and the individual student. How this is to be done is typically incorporated in a school anti-bullying policy that describes the stand that is being taken against bullying and the procedures and actions that are to be taken in its implementation. This is sometimes described as the indispensable core feature of an anti-bullying policy. The policy may also provide guidelines on how bullying behaviour is to be discouraged and how victims of school bullying can be helped.

Variations in anti-bullying programmes

There have been considerable variations in anti-bullying policies in what is actually included and what is most emphasised. In some programmes a great deal of attention has focused upon motivating teachers to address the problem of bullying and providing them with relevant training. Given that relatively little (if any) content about bullying is included in the pre-training of teachers (Nicolaides, Toda, and Smith, 2002), addressing the problem through 'in-servicing' prior to implementing a programme is regarded as essential, and may include numerous sessions conducted by those directing the programme. Some programmes make use of anonymous questionnaires completed by students (and sometimes also by teachers and parents) to provide reliable data on the prevalence and nature of the bullying that has been taking place in the school. Discussing such data is seen as a preliminary step to engaging in the development of a well-supported anti-bullying policy.

Programmes typically include both preventative and interventive procedures. However, the emphasis on one or the other may vary widely. Some programmes place major emphasis upon developing a positive classroom climate on the assumption that, if classrooms are characterised by positive relations between teachers and students and among students, children will not be inclined to engage in bullying (Roland and Galloway, 2002; and chapter 3). Curriculum work plays a major part in some anti-bullying programmes. This may include providing information about what constitutes bullying, the harm it does to victims, and the help children can receive from their school if they are victimised. In some programmes, emphasis has been placed on countering social prejudice and undesirable attitudes such as racism and sexism. Specific techniques thought to be relevant to countering bullying may be taught, such as assertiveness, anger management, and helpful bystander behaviour (Rigby, 2003). Discussions may be encouraged among students, leading to them formulating rules about how they believe they should behave in relating to each other (Olweus, 1993). Literature, film, and role plays may be used to develop more empathic and insightful ways of interacting with each other.

Emphasis may also be placed upon surveillance and monitoring of student behaviour outside classrooms. It is known that most bullying occurs during breaks from lessons and that bullying tends to be lower when there is more supervision by adults. Peer support programmes such as befriending are becoming common. Some programmes involve students who have been trained as peer mediators to assist in identifying and resolving conflicts. Such involvement is, however, controversial with some educators maintaining that in cases of bullying, adult authority is needed.

Dealing with cases of bullying

The area in which there is most variation between programmes is that of working with students who have been identified as bullies. The most commonly used procedure employs rules against bullying and consequences for breaking them. These may take the form of non-physical penalties or sanctions, such as the withdrawal of privileges or, in extreme cases, suspension from school. Parents of the bullies may be asked to come to the school to discuss how the bully's behaviour can be changed. This approach has been incorporated into anti-bullying programmes adopted in a number of European countries and in North America. In some programmes responsibility for investigating charges of bullying and recommending sanctions has been delegated to students who function as members of so-called bully courts (Mahdavi and Smith, 2002). Such punitive measures are seen by some as not only likely to discourage bullying behaviour but also to 'send a message' to deter others who might otherwise engage in bullying. However, it is often difficult to devise and apply clear rules relating to some forms of bullying such as excluding individuals from groups and rumour spreading. A miscarriage of justice resulting in resentment on the part of the bully may lead to a redoubling of efforts to continue the bullying in less detectable but equally damaging ways.

In cases of extreme bullying, community conferences are sometimes held. Victims are encouraged to express their grievances in the presence of those who had bullied them, and also with the relatives, friends, or supporters of those involved in the bullying incidents in attendance. Here the aim is to evoke in the perpetrator(s) a sense of shame about what they had done; but to do so in circumstances in which they feel accepted as persons by their supporters and can be effectively reintegrated into a caring community (Hyndman, Thorsborn, and Wood, 1996).

In contrast to methods that, in varying degrees, employ a punitive approach, some anti-bullying policies promote non-punitive problem-solving approaches. These include the use of mediation between students in conflict, conducted either by staff or appropriately trained students. Where there is a notable imbalance of power between the individuals in conflict, it is frequently argued that mediation is of limited value, since the mediator cannot reasonably act in a neutral manner.

Some programmes make use of the No-Blame approach developed by Robinson and Maines (1997). The teacher or person conducting the intervention first meets with the person who has been victimised and obtains a vivid picture of how the victim has been harmed. Subsequently a meeting is convened which includes the bullies and the victim, and also other students who are expected to influence the outcome of the meeting in a positive way. The teacher explains to the group how the victim has been hurt by the bullying and seeks proposals on how the situation can be improved. Responsibility for solving the problem is then left to the students; the outcomes, however, are carefully monitored.

A more complex process for dealing with bully/victim cases, especially among adolescent students, is that of the Shared Concern Method devised by Pikas (1989, 2002). Directed towards resolving problems of group bullying, this approach seeks initially through meetings with individual bullies to communicate and elicit a concern for the plight of the victim and also to acknowledge that each member of a bullying group is, to some degree, concerned that other members might turn on him or her. Further meetings are conducted, first with the victim, then with the bullying group, and finally with the bullying group together with the victim to ensure that acceptable relations are established. Although there is some evidence of its effectiveness (Smith and Sharp, 1994), this approach requires that its practitioners are thoroughly trained in its application and in some quarters it remains controversial (Ross, 1996, 2002).

Other approaches aimed at effecting positive behavioural changes in students involved in bully/victim problems include providing training in social skills and anger management, and actions directed towards raising self-esteem. To date there is little evidence that such measures can reform bullies; however, training aimed at developing assertiveness skills among victims appear to have greater chances of reducing the victimisation of some students (Field, 1999).

Measuring bullying and related phenomena

Defining bullying

There is no universally agreed definition of bullying. Some authorities have viewed bullying as essentially the *desire* to hurt or put someone under pressure (Tattum, 1993). However, increasingly researchers have come to agree that bullying involves negative or hurtful *behaviour* (Olweus, 1993); and the majority add that – as distinct from wider definitions of aggression or violence – bullying must also involve an imbalance of power with the less-powerful person or group being repeatedly and unfairly attacked (Rigby, 2002; Ross, 2002). This could be summarised as 'the systematic abuse of power' (Smith and Sharp, 1994).

It is common to distinguish between physical, verbal, and indirect forms of bullying. Examples of the latter category include deliberate exclusion and rumour spreading that is intended to damage someone. Sexual and racial harassment are sometimes viewed as types of bullying.

Outcome measures to assess the effects of interventions

In evaluating interventions, researchers are generally most interested in changes in bullying behaviour. Sometimes global indicators encompassing physical, verbal, and indirect forms have been employed. More commonly, separate indices have been created, and it has been reported at times that significant changes occur in one type of bullying but not another. Data from which measures are derived may come from a variety of sources. These include self-reports from students answering questionnaires anonymously or (less commonly) elicited in face-to-face interviews.

Further information may be obtained through teacher and/or parent ratings of individual students. Students are sometimes asked to nominate which of their peers are most involved in bullying others and/or being targeted as victims. Finally, direct observational methods may be used to assess the prevalence of bullying behaviour in a school; in some cases video recordings have been used (Pepler and Craig, 1995).

Some degree of standardisation in the use of questionnaires has been established, for example using the Olweus questionnaire, although there is still much variation in the questions being asked by different researchers. Some favour the use of single-item measures whilst others employ reliable multi-item scales (Petersen and Rigby, 1999). Typically, the severity of the bullying is assessed by questions that require students to report the frequency with which they have bullied others and/or have been victimised by others, using such categories as daily, weekly, monthly, or never, and also the period over which the victimisation has occurred. In addition to behavioural indicators, use has also been made of measures of attitude, for example, feelings towards victims and readiness to intervene as bystanders when bullying occurs (Sanchez et al., 2001).

Research design

Different methods have been used to infer the effects of interventions, and again some variety is present in the chapters in this book. Most commonly, researchers have used a basic *pre-test, post-test* design and have assessed the direction and degree of changes that occurred over the period when the intervention programme was applied.

It is recognised that changes could be due to extraneous factors, such as the effect of the pre-testing (increasing awarenesss of bullying), the maturation of students over the period of intervention (rendering them more inclined or less inclined to becoming involved in bully/victim problems), and historical events that could influence bullying behaviour (such as an anti-bullying media campaign or a highly publicised suicide due to bullying). Accordingly, many studies have made use of *control groups* to take into account such effects (see Cook and Campbell, 1979). Selecting suitable control schools equivalent to the intervention schools presents difficulties because researchers can normally only draw upon schools that opt to be in the study.

There have been two main methods used in comparing pupil outcomes before and after an intervention. One is the more obvious: this is a *longitudinal* study, following the same pupils over the course of the intervention. A major issue in interpreting such data is that age-related changes can occur, independently of the intervention. Large-scale surveys based on self-report questionnaires consistently show that reports of being bullied decline rather steadily over the late primary and secondary age ranges (Smith, Madsen, and Moody, 1999). Thus, simple main effects for the intervention group over time are difficult to interpret. However, if it is possible to use well-matched control groups, then differential changes over time between the intervention and control groups should clarify what are intervention effects.

The other research procedure that has some practical advantages (not requiring control groups from other schools) is the *cohort time-lagged design*, or *selection cohorts design*, in which data for children who have experienced an intervention are compared with data from 'untreated' children who were in the same age/year group as them at an earlier time (see Olweus, 1993; and chapter 2). This quasi-experimental design has the disadvantage of comparing children who may have been subjected to different historical events. However, it does control for age-related changes in victimisation.

Designs sometimes differ in the time period over which measurements are taken; some studies have used repeated measures to assess both short- and longer term effects. Some studies have utilised retrospective reports, for example, students and teachers have been asked to give their judgements of what changes they have noticed in student behaviour and attitudes, and to what causes the changes may be ascribed. Clearly, this procedure relies on subjective impressions and has questionable reliability. Finally, studies have differed according to the number of schools included in the intervention programme and whether analyses have been conducted based on results from individual schools or pooled data from all the involved schools.

In this book, we have included only relatively large-scale studies in preference to studies using data from one or two schools; at the same time, it is acknowledged that some useful small-scale evaluations have been conducted. We mention briefly here four examples.

Some smaller scale evaluation studies

Styria, Austria

This small-scale programme took place for ten weeks in Austria between February and April 1997 (Singer, 1998; Spiel, 2000). Four classes from two different schools participated; out of these, 2 acted as the experimental (intervention) group and 2 as controls. A total of 97 pupils aged 12 and 14 years participated.

The intervention was a shortened version of the Olweus programme, with measures at school, class, and individual level, mostly focusing on the class level (setting up class rules) because of the short time scale of the programme and because only two classes from each school participated (Singer, personal communication). A German version of the Olweus questionnaire was used for data collection before and after the implementation of the programme. Outcomes for victimisation, and for bullying, showed no reduction in the intervention schools; also there were no significant differences in either victimisation or bullying rates between intervention and control schools. The authors suggest the short duration of the programme and the low level of commitment on the part of some of the participants as possible reasons for the programme's lack of effectiveness.

Kansas, USA

This study took place in 2 inner-city elementary schools (1 intervention, 1 control) over 3 school years from 1995 to 1998 (Twemlow et al., 2001). Matched age groups of third graders (numbers from 26 to 64) were compared over successive years on disciplinary referrals and suspension rates. The programme had 4 components: zero tolerance for behavioural disturbances such as bullying; a discipline plan for modelling appropriate behaviour; a physical education plan designed to teach self-regulation skills; and a mentoring programme for adults and children to avoid involvement in bullying and violence.

There were significant drops in disciplinary referrals, and for suspensions, in the intervention school, compared to little change in the control school. Teacher reports and academic results in the intervention school were also encouraging. A larger scale randomised study of elementary schools in Kansas is in progress.

New South Wales, Australia

A small-scale intervention aimed at reducing bullying in a single co-educational high school in New South Wales, Australia, was conducted between 1995 and 1997 (Petersen and Rigby, 1999). Students from years 7, 9, 10, and 11 participated, there being 758 students in 1995 and 657 students in the same years in 1997.

The programme emphasised student participation in an anti-bullying committee which advised upon and implemented a range of anti-bullying initiatives. In addition, cases of bullying were addressed using a non-punitive method of dealing with bullying problems: the Method of Shared Concern of Pikas (1989). A pre-test/post-test design was employed without a control group. The programme was evaluated using the Peer Relations Questionnaire (PRQ) self-report measure (Rigby and Slee, 1995), and by retrospective reports from students who rated the effectiveness of specified components of the intervention. The results indicated that, while there was no overall reduction in bullying in 1997, there was a significantly lower proportion of year 7 students reporting being bullied by peers than previously. Student evaluations of the effectiveness of the methods indicated that the activities of the student anti-bullying committee were rated highest, especially the work of the 'school welcomers programme' for new enrolments.

Evaluations of school interventions in Italy

Menesini has reported on a number of interventions to reduce bullying in Italian schools (Menesini and Modiano, 2002). An example is a small-scale study conducted with third-grade students at an elementary school in Modena over one school year. The participants consisted of 101 children in an experimental group and 76 in a control group. Emphasis was placed on curricular activities, which included the discussion and sharing of personal experiences, role-playing activities, and the use of literature, video, and movie stimuli. An adapted Olweus questionnaire was used to assess changes in 'being bullied'. As is common, there was an increase in the control group in reportedly being bullied by others over time; by contrast, the proportion of students reporting being bullied in the experimental group decreased over the same time period. There were corresponding positive findings for reports of bullying others.

A further study conducted in two middle schools in Tuscany over a 6-year period included the creation of a school counselling service and a whole school policy against bullying (Menesini, 2000). A sharp decline in being bullied was reported between 1993 and 1996 and thereafter a levelling off. No significant change was found in the level of bullying others before 1996, but a significant decline in bullying others did occur between 1996 and 1999.

A more recent study has been carried out between 1999 and 2002 in schools in Venice (Menesini, 2003; Menesini et al., 2003). Teacher training, curricular work, and peer support in 2 primary and 4 middle schools produced some decline in being bullied in experimental relative to control classes. In three secondary schools the emphasis was on enhancing good communication between teachers and students about bullying and relational problems. Student ratings (N = 263) of the presence of bullying at each of the three schools was lower in each school after this intervention.

Plan of the book

In this book we attempt to take forward the process of understanding best practice, by including reports from 13 major intervention projects – in Norway, Finland, England, Ireland, Canada, Belgium, Switzerland, Germany, the United States, Spain, and Australia. These provide an array of different projects, methods, and outcomes, in different countries, but with a common objective: to reduce or prevent school bullying. It is important to learn from both their successes and their less-successful outcomes. In our final chapter, we summarise what might be learned and suggest important themes for future research and practice.

References

Cook, T. D. and Campbell, D. T. (1979). *Quasi-experimentation*. Chicago: Rand McNally.

Field, E. M. (1999). *Bully busting*. Lane Cove, NSW: Finch Publishing.

Hawker, D. S. J. and Boulton, M. J. (2000). Twenty years research on peer victimization and psychosocial maladjustment: A meta-analytic review of cross-sectional studies. *Journal of Child Psychiatry and Psychiatry*, 41, 441–55.

Hughes, T. (1857). *Tom Brown's School Days*. 1968 edn: New York: Airmont Publishing Co.

Hyndman, M., Thorsborn, M., and Wood, S. (1996). *Community accountability conferencing: Trial report*. Brisbane: Education Queensland.

Mahdavi, J. and Smith, P. K. (2002). The operation of a bully court and perceptions of its success: A case study. *School Psychology International*, 23, 327–41.

Menesini, E., Codecasa, E., Benelli, B., and Cowie, H. (2003). Enhancing children's responsibility to take action against bullying: Evaluation of a befriending intervention in Italian middle schools. *Aggressive Behavior*, 29, 1–14.

Menesini, E. (2000). *Bullismo: che fare? Prevenzione e strategie di intervento nella scuola*. Firenze: Giunti.

Menesini, E. (ed) (2003). *Il bullismo: le azioni efficaci della scuola*. Trento: Erickson Edizioni.

Menesini, E. and Modiano, R. (2002). A multi-faceted reality: A report from Italy. In P. K. Smith (ed.), *Violence in schools: The response in Europe*. London: Routledge Falmer, pp. 153–68.

Nicolaides, S., Toda, Y., and Smith, P. K. (2002). Knowledge and attitudes about school bullying in trainee teachers. *British Journal of Educational Psychology*, 72, 105–18.

Olweus, D. (1993). *Bullying at school: What we know and what we can do*. Oxford: Blackwell.

(1999). Sweden. In P. K. Smith, Y. Morita, J. Junger-Tas, D. Olweus, R. Catalano, and P. Slee (eds.), *The nature of school bullying: A cross-national perspective*. London: Routledge, (pp. 7–27).

Pepler, D. J. and Craig, W. M. (1995). A peek behind the fence: Naturalistic observations of aggressive children with remote audiovisual recording. *Developmental Psychology*, 31, 548–53.

Petersen, L. and Rigby, K. (1999). Countering bullying at an Australian secondary school. *Journal of Adolescence*, 22, 481–92.

Pikas, A. (1989). The Common Concern Method for the treatment of mobbing. In E. Roland and E. Munthe (eds.). *Bullying: An international perspective*. London: David Fulton, pp. 91–104.

(2002). New developments of the Shared Concern Method. *School Psychology International*, 23, 307–26.

Rigby, K. (1997). Reflections on Tom Brown's Schooldays and the problem of bullying today. *Australian Journal of Social Science*, 4, 85–96.

(2002). *New perspectives on bullying*. London: Jessica Kingsley.

(2003). *Stop the bullying: A handbook for schools*. Melbourne: Australian Council for Educational Research.

Rigby, K. and Slee, P. T. (1995). *The Peer Relations Questionnaire*: (PRQ). Point Lonsdale, Australia: The Professional Reading Guide.

Robinson, B. and Maines, G. (1997). *Crying for help: The No Blame approach to bullying*. Bristol: Lucky Duck Publishing.

Roland, E. (1989). Bullying: The Scandinavian research tradition. In D. P. Tattum and D. A. Lane (eds.), *Bullying in schools*. Stoke-on-Trent: Trentham, (pp. 21–32).

Roland, E. and Galloway, D. (2002). Classroom influences on bullying. *Educational Research*, 44, 299–312.

Ross, D. M. (1996, 2nd edn. 2002). *Childhood bullying and teasing: what school personnel, other professionals and parents can do*. Alexandria, NA: American Counselling Association.

Sanchez, E., Robertson, T. R., Lewis, C. M., Rosenbluth, B., Bohman, T., and Casey, D. M. (2001). Preventing bullying and sexual harassment in elementary schools: The Expect Respect model. *Journal of Emotional Abuse*, 2, 157–80.

Singer, M. (1998). Anwendung des Anti-Aggressionsprogramms nach Dan Olweus an österreichischen Schulen. Zusammenhänge zwischen Aggression, Klassen- und Familienklima. Unpublished M.Phil dissertation. Karl-Franzens-Universität, Graz, Austria.

Smith, P. K. (2004). Bullying – recent developments. *Child and Adolescent Mental Health*, 9, 98–103.

Smith, P. K., Madsen, K. C., and Moody, J. C. (1999). What causes the age decline in reports of being bullied at school? Towards a developmental analysis of risks of being bullied. *Educational Research*, 41, 276–85.

Smith, P. K. and Sharp, S. (eds.) (1994). *School bullying: Insights and perspectives.* London: Routledge.

Smith, P. K., Morita, Y., Junger-Tas, J., Olweus, D., Catalano, R., and Slee, P. (eds.) (1999). *The nature of school bullying: A cross-national perspective.* London: Routledge.

Spiel, C. (2000). Gewalt in der Schule: Täter – Opfer, Prävention – Intervention. In E. Tatzer, S. Pflanzer, and R. Kirsch (eds.), *Schlimm verletzt. Schwierige Kinder und Jugendliche in Theorie und Praxis.* Vienna: Krammer.

Tattum, D. P. (1993). What is bullying? In D. Tattum (ed.), *Understanding and managing bullying.* London: Heinemann.

Twemlow, S. W., Fonagy, P., Sacco, F. C., Gies, M. L., Evans, R., and Ewbank, R. (2001). Creating a peaceful school learning environment: A controlled study of an elementary school intervention to reduce violence. *American Journal of Psychiatry*, 158, 808–10.

2 The Olweus Bullying Prevention Programme: design and implementation issues and a new national initiative in Norway

Dan Olweus

The need for evidence-based intervention programmes

As bully/victim problems have gradually been placed on the official school agenda in many countries, a number of suggestions about their handling and prevention have been proposed. Some of these suggestions and approaches seem ill-conceived or maybe even counter-productive, such as an excessive focus on changing the victims' behaviour to make them less vulnerable to bullying. Others appear meaningful and potentially useful. A key problem, however, is that most of them have either failed to document positive results or have never been subjected to systematic research evaluation. Therefore it is difficult to know which programmes or measures actually work and which do not. Yet it is the results with the students that count, not how adults might feel about using the programme (user satisfaction).

The situation is well illustrated by the following facts. Recently, a US expert committee under the leadership of a respected criminologist, Professor Delbert Elliott, made a systematic evaluation of more than 400 presumably violence- (or problem-behaviour) preventing programmes according to certain minimum-level criteria (Elliott, 1999). These criteria were:

- that the programme had had positive effects on relevant target groups (students in this case) in a relatively rigorous scientific evaluation;
- that the effects had lasted for at least one year; and,
- that the programme had produced positive results in at least one site beyond the original one.

Only ten of the programmes (four of which are school-based and only one focusing on bully/victim problems) satisfied the specified criteria. These so-called 'Blueprint', or evidence-based or model, programmes are now being implemented in a number of sites with financial support from the US Department of Justice (OJJDP) and other sources.

A similar evaluation by an officially appointed, departmental committee was recently made in Norway. In this case, 56 programmes designed

13

to counteract and/or prevent 'problem behavior' and in use in Norwegian schools were evaluated (Rapport, 2000). Only one programme was recommended for further use without reservations.

The Olweus Bullying Prevention Programme is one of the 10 (now 11) Blueprint programmes (Olweus and Limber, 1999), and was the programme selected by the Norwegian committee. This is likely to be an important background for the recent government-funded national initiative in Norway, described at the end of the chapter.

Before presenting this initiative, I outline and discuss a design for evaluating the effects of an intervention programme, for example against bullying, that may be useful both for researchers and practitioners. This design was used in the first evaluation of the Olweus Bullying Prevention Programme and the same design has been employed in three recent evaluations of the programme, in one of them with some modifications. As it has become more and more clear to me that the effects of an intervention are to a great extent dependent on the quality and fidelity of programme implementation, I later present some recent research on teacher- and school-level factors that affect implementation of the Olweus Bullying Prevention Programme. This research gains particular importance due to the fact that little research has been conducted on such issues.

A useful evaluation design

A researcher or practitioner interested in evaluating the effects of an intervention programme is very often faced with a situation where it is not possible or desirable to use a traditional experimental design. This means that the observational units such as students or classes/schools are not randomly assigned to the various treatment conditions (intervention versus no intervention/control, or various degrees of intervention versus no intervention/control). In such situations, the investigator usually must turn to what is called a quasi-experimental design. How can the investigator then evaluate the effects of an intervention in a reasonably rigorous way?

There is a large literature on various quasi-experimental designs (see Cook and Campbell, 1979, and a number of standard textbooks in design and statistics), the strengths and weaknesses of which will not be discussed in the present context. However, here I will focus brief attention on one design that I have found particularly useful and which is relatively easy to use, also for investigators who are not primarily researchers. The general structure of this design, sometimes called a *selection cohorts design*, is described in Cook and Campbell's classic book (1979); but there are few examples of it in the literature, in particular not the 'extended' version of the design (below) that I recommend and have used in several intervention studies. Important aspects of this variant of the design are that it consists of several *adjacent or contiguous cohorts* and that there is a *one-year* (or possibly, two-year) *interval between measurement occasions*.

A concrete illustration

I will give a brief description of this extended design version as it was used in the 'First Bergen Project Against Bullying' (Olweus, 1991, 1993a, 1994). Since this project was part of a nationwide campaign against bullying, it was not possible to set up a strictly experimental study with random allocation of schools or classes to treatment and control/comparison conditions.

Evaluation of the effects of the intervention programme was based on data from approximately 2,500 students who were followed over a period of two and a half years. The students originally (at Time 1, below) belonged to 112 grade 4–7 classes (corresponding to grades 5–8 in the new grade system) in 42 primary and junior high schools in Bergen. Each of the four grade/age cohorts (with modal ages of 11, 12, 13, and 14 years, respectively, at Time 1) consisted of 600–700 students with a roughly equal distribution of boys and girls. In the present context, the students belonged to a 'cohort' in the sense that they were joined together in distinct classes within a particular grade level and were approximately the same age. The first time of data collection (Time 1) was in May/June 1983, approximately four months before the intervention programme was introduced, in October. New measurements were taken in May 1984 (Time 2) and May 1985 (Time 3). The intervention programme was (more or less) in place for the whole 20-month period from October 1983, until May/June 1985. The basic structure of the design is shown in fig. 2.1 (for ease of exposition and understanding, the figure uses fictitious and idealised data which to some extent reflect the general trends of the empirical findings for 'being bullied'; however, with regard to 'involvement in antisocial behaviour', for example, the expected developmental curves would go upwards).

For three of the cohorts (C5, C6, and C7), data collected at Time 1 were used as a baseline with which data for age-equivalent cohorts at Time 2 could be compared. The latter groups had then been exposed to the intervention programme for about 8 months. To exemplify, the data for the grade 5 cohort at Time 1 (modal age 12 years) were compared with the Time 2 data for the grade 4 cohort, which at that time had reached approximately the same age as the baseline group. The same kind of comparisons were made between the grade 6 cohort at Time 1

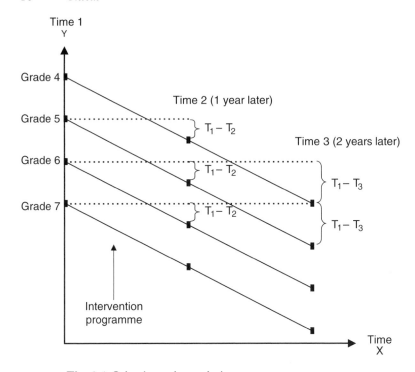

Fig. 2.1 Selection cohorts design.

and the grade 5 cohort at Time 2, and between the grade 7 cohort at Time 1 and the grade 6 cohort at Time 2.

Comparison of data collected at Time 1 and Time 3 permitted an assessment of the persistence or possible decline or enhancement of the effects over a longer time span. For these comparisons data for only two of the cohorts could be used as a baseline: those of the grade 6 and grade 7 cohorts, which were contrasted with data collected at Time 3 on the grade 4 and grade 5 cohorts, respectively. The latter groups had been exposed to the intervention programme during approximately 20 months at that time.

Additional characteristics of the design

In any study designed to establish or make probable the effects of some factor such as an intervention programme, it is mandatory that the investigator examines, and ideally is able to rule out, most or all alternative explanations of the findings in terms of possible confounding, 'irrelevant' factors. This is true whether the study is experimental or quasi-experimental, although some alternative interpretations can be more easily eliminated if the units of sampling have been allocated to the various conditions by a random procedure. Accordingly, it is very important to be aware of common possible 'threats to the internal validity' (Cook and Campbell, 1979) of any design, and to examine to what extent and in what ways such threats or sources of confounding can be eliminated or counteracted. Here I only give a brief discussion of these issues in relation to the present design; for more detailed and technical discussions of certain aspects, see Olweus and Alsaker (1991) and Olweus (1991).

A key aspect of this design is that the relevant groups or cohorts compared are the same age. This is necessary in order to take care of, or rule out, explanations of the results in terms of differences in age or 'maturation'. It is well documented that changes in bully/victim problems occur as a function of age (Olweus, 1993a; Smith, Madsen, and Moody, 1999; Solberg and Olweus, 2003). Such developmental changes must be 'controlled', and this is done by comparison of age-equivalent groups at various time points.

By controlling for age in this way, the time of the year when the outcome or dependent variable(s) is being measured is also 'held constant'. In some areas such as bully/victim problems, this may be important in order to control for possible seasonal variations due to the amount and nature of outdoor activities, typical interaction patterns, and the like.

A major problem in many quasi-experimental studies relates to the fact that the *intervention group(s) and control or comparison groups may differ in known or partly unknown ways* in important aspects, before the intervention is introduced. As has been pointed out in the statistical literature (Pedhazur, 1982; Porter and Raudenbush, 1987), the common strategy of using Analysis of Covariance (ANCOVA) to control for initial differences among pre-existing groups is often an inappropriate or risky enterprise. It is a great advantage if the investigator can get hold of naturally occurring groups that are reasonably similar or equivalent with regard to the outcome variable (and dimensions related to the outcome variable), *before* the intervention is administered to one or more of the groups.

When the groups to be compared belong to the same schools (for example, the grade 5 cohort at Time 1, with no intervention, compared with the grade 4 cohort at Time 2, with 8 months of intervention, recruited from the same schools), there are often good grounds for assuming that one cohort differs in only minor ways from its contiguous cohort(s). Usually, the majority of the members in the various grade cohorts have been recruited from the same relatively stable populations and have also been students in the same schools for several years. In some cases, in particular in more research-oriented studies, it may be possible actually to check out the similarity of the groups compared with regard to presumably important dimensions.

In spite of the fact that cohorts selected from the same schools can often be assumed to be reasonably equivalent in important respects, it is possible that some kind of *selection bias* can occur. Such bias could be the result of inadvertent changes in the recruitment of students to the various cohorts, so that the cohorts, in fact, represent populations with partly different characteristics, including different growth rates. If present, such bias complicates interpretation of the time-lagged comparisons.

The extended selection cohorts design with adjacent cohorts does, however, provide partial protection against such selection bias, due to the fact that several of the cohorts serve as a baseline group in one set of comparisons and as an intervention group in another. This is the case, for example, with the grade 5 cohort at Time 1, the data for which are used as a baseline in comparison with the grade 4 cohort data collected at Time 2 (after 8 months of intervention; see fig. 2.1). At the same time, the grade 5 cohort data obtained at Time 2 serve to evaluate the possible effects of 8 months of intervention when they are compared with the data for grade 6 cohort at Time 1. The same situation applies to grade 6 cohort in comparisons with grade 5 and 7 cohorts, respectively.

The considerable advantage of this aspect of the design is that a possible bias in the composition of the cohorts would operate in opposite directions in the two sets of comparisons, thus making it difficult to obtain apparent 'intervention effects' across cohorts as a consequence of such selection bias. This feature of the design also provides protection against faulty conclusions in case the baseline data for one or both of these cohorts were unusually high or low simply as a function of chance. The protection against selection bias is partial in the sense that both the youngest and the oldest cohort, in the present illustration the grade 4 cohort and the grade 7 cohort, serve only as an intervention group (grade 4 cohort at Time 2) or a baseline group (grade 7 cohort at Time 1) with regard to the Time 1–Time 2 comparisons.

Sometimes conclusions may be erroneous due to *possible selective attrition*; for example, more extreme or deviant individuals may be more likely to drop out in longitudinal studies. To safeguard against this, analyses can be restricted to students for whom there are valid data at both time points in a particular comparison (given that the identity of the participants is secured).

In addition, it should be mentioned that selection of groups/subjects in this design is typically not based on some kind of extreme score criterion.

Accordingly, the problem with *regression toward the mean*, which looms large in many evaluation studies, is not at issue here.

Possible effects of repeated measurement and history

There are two other potential confounds to be considered. One relates to possible *'testing' or repeated measurement effects*. As evident from fig. 2.1, the scores for the baseline (Time 1) data usually represent a first-time measurement, whereas the Time 2 data come from a second wave of measurement. Although it may not appear very likely that a second measurement, separated by a whole year from the first measurement occasion, would result in some kind of systematic change in the students' responses, it may, as a precaution, be valuable to examine whether such changes have occurred and in what directions they might go. If such (non-trivial) effects were found, this might complicate interpretation of the results. One way of examining such effects would be to let half of the students/classes in the youngest cohort skip the first measurement occasion, and then compare the two halves of this cohort at Time 2. In the First Bergen Project Against Bullying, the possibility of repeated measurement effects was investigated in a slightly different way (Olweus, 1991: 442) and such effects were found to be small and non-systematic.

With a selection cohorts design, one has also to be aware of the possibility that registered changes in the outcome variable are a consequence of some *'irrelevant' factor concomitant to the intervention programme*, implying that the results may be given a *'history' interpretation* (see Cook and Campbell, 1979). For example, the intervention groups may have been exposed, in addition to the intervention programme, to some kind of changes in the educational, administrative, or other school routines that affected their behaviour and response at Time 2. It may be important for the investigator to examine if such parallel changes have occurred during the intervention period(s) and, if so, whether they can be meaningfully linked to systematic changes in the outcome variable(s).

A similar argument can be made with regard to *general time trends* in the outcome variable or related dimensions, that is, historical societal changes, often due to unknown causes, which happened to coincide with the intervention (Olweus, 1994b: 120–21). Although such 'history explanations' frequently appear fairly unlikely, particularly in consideration of the relative abruptness of the changes often observed, the investigator can get additional help in ruling out, or possibly incorporating, such interpretations if he or she can include in the design some equivalent units (schools/classes) without any intervention at all, that is, some control units.

Although this extended selection cohorts design has many attractive features, there are also some limitations that deserve mention. First, some of the collected data cannot be used in the evaluation of the programme effects. This is true of the grade 4 cohort data at Time 1 and the grade 7 cohort data at Time 2, for example, with regard to the Time 1–Time 2 comparisons. Also, although the design is longitudinal, this aspect cannot be taken into account in the statistical analyses. Therefore, the advantage of having repeated measurements on the same subjects is not translated into a reduced error term. Accordingly, the design is likely to have less statistical power or precision than if a repeated-measures design had been used. However, these two concerns may not be very important in the context of a selection cohorts design where large amounts of data can often be collected without great effort.

These possible alternative explanations, in addition to potential under- and over-reporting of the systematic reductions in bully/victim problems and related behaviour patterns, were carefully examined in the First Bergen Project Against Bullying, and generally found to be deficient in explaining the results obtained (Olweus, 1991, 1993a; Olweus and Alsaker, 1991).

Some of the arguments presented above may appear somewhat subtle and technical. They are, however, important to consider in a research study, whether experimental or quasi-experimental, aiming to document the possible effects of an intervention programme. In addition, for an adequate statistical treatment, the hierarchical or 'nested' nature of the data must be taken into account (Olweus, 1991; Olweus and Alsaker, 1991). The extended selection cohorts design has a number of attractive features and built-in safeguards which should facilitate interpretation of the results.

Practitioners such as the school leadership or the school board can probably take most of the validity concerns discussed fairly lightly, provided that the intervention situation is reasonably 'clean'. By this I mean that preferably no other intervention programmes or similar activities or events are introduced in the participating schools in the same time period that the programme at issue is being evaluated. (In preparation of possible implementation of the Olweus Bullying Prevention Programme at a particular school, we very strongly advise the school leadership not to start implementation of some other programme at the same time, because of the necessary time and energy resources, possible negative interactions among programmes, and likely ambiguities with regard to interpretation of possible 'intervention effects'. In case the school concerned already has in place a programme which in any way is in conflict with the principles and general approach of the Olweus programme, the school leadership is strongly recommended to postpone implementation of the Olweus Programme to a later point in time.)

Summing up, with use of an extended selection cohorts design, chances are good that conclusions about the effects or non-effects of an intervention programme will be roughly correct in most cases. This easy-to-use design is a natural step in the monitoring of what goes on in schools involved in anti-bullying work. The design can prove useful for practitioners and researchers alike, and in my view, it is clearly underused. Nevertheless, the many positive aspects of the design cannot exempt us from the responsibility of using other available data, and our heads, in making a balanced evaluation of the results obtained.

Components of the Olweus Bullying Prevention Programme

The programme has been fully described in several previous publications (Olweus, 1993a, 2001b; Olweus and Limber, 1999). The intervention package consists of the book *Bullying at school – what we know and what we can do* (Olweus, 1993a), *Olweus' core program against bullying and antisocial behavior: A teacher handbook* (Olweus, 2001b), the 'Revised Olweus Bully/Victim Questionnaire' (Olweus, 1996) with accompanying PC-program, the publication *Blueprint: Bullying prevention program* (Olweus and Limber, 1999) and the video cassette *Bullying* (see Olweus and Limber, 1999). An overview of the programme is presented in table 2.1 (see also the note at the end of chapter).

Evaluation of the effects of the Olweus Bullying Prevention Programme

As described above, an extended selection cohorts design was used to evaluate the effects of the intervention programme in the First Bergen Project Against Bullying, running from 1983 to 1985. Variants of the same design have also been used in three more recent evaluation projects, two of which will be briefly described here. (Detailed results for the third evaluation project, running from 2002 to 2003, are not yet available.)

The New Bergen Project Against Bullying ran from 1997 to 1998. It comprised some 3,200 students in grades 5–7 and grade 9 (modal ages 11–13, and 15 years) from 14 intervention and 16 comparison schools (Olweus, 1999a). The label 'comparison schools' does not in any way imply a lack of intervention work against bullying; such work is actually expected from all schools in present-day Norway; however, they were not

Table 2.1. *Overview of the Olweus
Bullying Prevention Programme*

General prerequisites
Awareness and involvement on the part of adults

Measures at the school level
Questionnaire survey
School conference day
Effective supervision during break times
Establishment of staff discussion groups
Formation of co-ordinating group

Measures at the class level
Class rules against bullying
Class meetings with students
Meetings with parents of the class

Measures at the individual level
Serious talks with bullies and victims
Serious talks with parents of involved students
Development of individual intervention plans

part of the intervention project involving the Olweus Bullying Prevention Programme.

The Oslo Project Against Bullying ran from 1999 to 2000. Oslo is the capital of Norway with about 500,000 inhabitants. Some of the schools in the Oslo area have large percentages of children of immigrant backgrounds. In this project there were 10 intervention schools with a total of some 2,300 students in grades 5–7 and 9 (Olweus, 2001a). (There were no comparison schools in this project.)

Here I will give only a brief summary of the results from these three projects. For the two recent projects, I restrict the reporting to data from the elementary grades (5–7), where important components of the programme were more fully implemented.

First Bergen Project Against Bullying

The main results from this project can be summarised as follows (and see Olweus, 1991, 1993a; Olweus and Alsaker, 1991):
- There were marked (and statistically highly significant) reductions – by 50% or more – in self-reported bully/victim problems for the periods studied, with 8 and 20 months of intervention, respectively. By and large, the results applied to both boys and girls, and to students from all grades studied. Similar results were obtained for a kind of aggregated

peer-rating variables and teacher ratings. However, the effects were somewhat weaker for the teacher ratings.

- There were also clear reductions in general antisocial behaviour such as vandalism, fighting with the police, pilfering, drunkenness, and truancy.
- In addition, there was marked improvement in various aspects of the 'social climate' of the class: improved order and discipline, more positive social relationships, and a more positive attitude to schoolwork and the school. Also, there was an increase in student satisfaction with school life.

In the majority of comparisons for which reductions were reported above, the differences between baseline and intervention groups were quite marked and highly significant. Detailed analyses of the quality of the data and the possibility of alternative interpretations of the findings led to the general conclusions that it is very difficult to explain the results obtained as a consequence of (a) under-reporting by the students; (b) gradual changes in the students' attitudes to bully/victim problems; (c) repeated measurement; and (d) concomitant changes in other factors, including general time trends (Olweus, 1991).

In addition, a clear 'dosage-response' relationship ($r = .51, N = 80$) was established in analyses at the class level (the natural unit of analysis in this case). Those teachers/classes that had larger reductions in bully/victim problems had implemented three presumably essential components of the intervention programme (including establishment of class rules against bullying and use of regular class meetings) to a greater extent than had those with smaller changes. This finding provides corroborating evidence for the hypothesis that the changes observed were a consequence of the intervention programme and not of some other 'irrelevant' factor.

Stevens, de Bourdeaudhuij, and Van Oost (2000, and this book) have raised the question of whether the positive results of the First Bergen Project Against Bullying could be a so-called Hawthorne effect: a consequence of general attention from the media and the general public rather than an effect of the intervention programme itself. As detailed in a publication written in Swedish (Olweus, 2002), I argue that this hypothesis is highly unlikely to be true, the main reasons focusing on (a) the timing of the media attention to the project; (b) the interpretation of allegedly contradictory results from a study by Roland (1989; Olweus, 1999b); (c) the nature of a possible Hawthorne effect; (d) the breadth of the programme effects; and (e) the documentation of a dosage-response relationship mentioned above. Their hypothesis is further contradicted by the positive results from the two recent intervention studies, on which there was no media attention at all, until the results of the interventions were reported to the media.

New Bergen Project Against Bullying

In this project (1997–98), we again found clear reductions with regard to bully/victim problems in the intervention schools; but the effects were somewhat weaker than those in the first project, with averages varying between 21% and 38%. However, the intervention programme had been in place for only 6 months or less when the second measurement was made (at Time 2). In addition, this particular year (1997–98) was a very turbulent one for the teachers, with the introduction of a new national curriculum which made heavy demands on their time and emotional resources.

For the comparison schools, there were very small or no changes in 'being bullied' and actually a 35% *increase* in the level of 'bullying other students'. Before having analysed the questionnaire information obtained from the teachers in the comparison schools, we are not prepared to give a detailed explanation of this result. However, it is certainly consistent with other findings of 'negative' effects of interventions intended to counteract delinquent and antisocial behaviour (Dishion, McCord, and Poulin, 1999; Gottfredson, 1987; Lipsey, 1992).

Oslo Project Against Bullying

In this project, we found an average reduction across the three grade levels of some 40% for 'being bullied' and about 50% for 'bullying other students'. These results are shown in figs. 2.2 and 2.3.

Similar, though somewhat weaker, results have been obtained in partial replications in the USA, Germany, and the UK (Olweus and Limber, 1999; Smith and Sharp, 1994; and chapters 4, 5, and 6).

Factors affecting implementation of the programme

The programme effects described above represent a kind of aggregate result, reflecting the overall effects of an intervention package with several different components. To get more detailed information about the nature and mechanisms of these effects, there are several *key issues* that need to be pursued and researched in more detail.

One of these issues concerns *differences or variability in implementation* of the programme. As preliminary analyses of our implementation data for the 'First Bergen Project Against Bullying' showed, most of the teachers participating in the project had actually put some part of the programme into practice. However, the degree of implementation varied considerably both among teachers and schools. What, then, were the characteristics of the teachers and schools that could predict or explain these differences

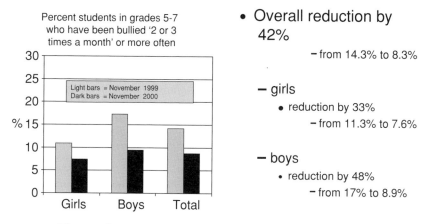

Fig. 2.2 Oslo project: per cent victims 1999 and 2000.

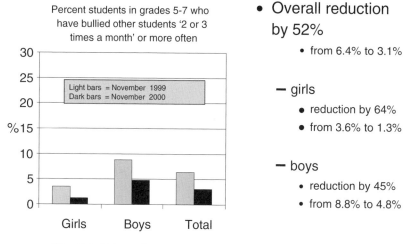

Fig. 2.3 Oslo project: per cent bullies 1999 and 2000.

in implementation of the Olweus Bullying Prevention programme? This was the main focus of a study that one of my doctoral students, Jan Helge Kallestad, and I have recently reported on (Kallestad and Olweus, 2003).

To the best of our knowledge, empirical, quantitative research on factors affecting differences in implementation of a circumscribed intervention programme in the personal/social-development area is very scarce. However, systematic research on this issue can be very useful, helping improve implementation of a programme and thereby making it more effective. Such knowledge may also contribute to the establishment and development of a 'science of effective implementation'. As emphasised by Biglan (1995: 15): 'the adoption of an effective practice is itself a behavior in need of scientific research'.

The data on which our analyses were based came from 89 teachers who responded to comprehensive questionnaires at two time points, October–November 1983 and May–June 1984. The teachers were distributed across 37 schools. Two measures of implementation were constructed, but I present here results mainly for one of them, the *Classroom Intervention Measures* index. This is an additive index consisting of seven specific intervention measures, such as establishment of classroom rules against bullying; use of regular classroom meetings and role plays; showing and discussing a video about bullying, etc. There were also three questions about the degree to which the individual teacher, in his or her own view, had involved himself/herself, the students in the class, and their parents in counteracting bullying during the past spring term (4–5 months in the Norwegian school system).

For the main statistical analyses, we used multi-level techniques (Bryk and Raudenbush, 1992; Goldstein, 1987) because of the hierarchical structure of the data and our interest in identifying factors related to implementation both at the teacher/classroom and the school levels. The major results for the *Classroom Intervention Measures* index are summarised in figs. 2.4 and 2.5, where the figures close to the arrows are standardised beta coefficients. I want to stress the importance of using adequate statistical models such as multilevel techniques for these kinds of issues and data. They may help in shaping the questions addressed and, in particular, will definitely affect the answers obtained.

Teacher-level predictors

The five predictors shown in fig. 2.4 account for a substantial 53% of the variance in implementation. The strongest predictor was *Perceived staff importance*, with a standardised beta coefficient of .47. This finding implies that teachers who saw themselves, their colleagues, and the schools as important agents of change for counteracting bully/victim problems among their students were more likely to involve themselves in anti-bullying efforts and to introduce specific classroom measures. This is clearly in line with previous research concerning 'teacher efficacy' (Smylie, 1990; Kallestad and Olweus, 2003). This result may also imply a belief on the part of teachers that it was actually possible to reduce the level of such problems through systematic classroom and school activities.

Perceived staff importance may not only measure teachers' perceived influence but probably also reflects their perceived responsibility for doing

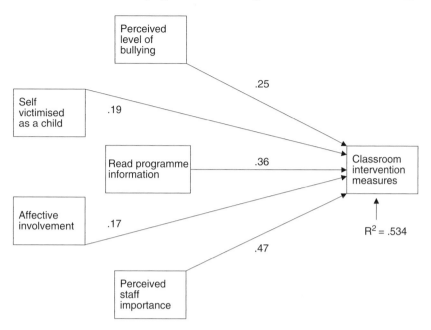

Fig. 2.4 Teacher-level factors predicting implementation of classroom intervention measures (within-school model). Numbers close to arrows are standardised regression coefficients.

something about bullying in their own classrooms. With such an interpretation, this result also implies that teachers who saw it as their own, and the school's, task and professional responsibility to counteract bully/victim problems among their students were more likely to involve themselves in anti-bullying efforts and to introduce specific classroom measures. Forceful legislation in this area, with responsibility for preventing and counteracting bullying problems being clearly placed with the teachers and the school leadership, is certainly one of several worth-while means of increasing teachers' perceived importance and responsibility on this point (Smith, Morita, Junger-Tas, Olweus, Catalano and Slee, 1999; Olweus, 1999c).

Another important predictor of *Classroom Intervention Measures* was the variable *Read programme information*, with a standardised beta coefficient of .36. The informational materials, the teacher booklet and the parent folder, had two key aims: to provide some research-based knowledge about bully/victim problems; and to give guidelines for how to deal with such problems. A straightforward interpretation of this finding is that teachers who read more of the programme information became more motivated to do something about the problem and, in particular, acquired more knowledge about how to counteract the problems through suggested classroom activities. It is, however, also possible that teachers who were highly involved and motivated at the outset read more of the programme materials, and were likely to implement proposed classroom activities to a greater extent than were less-motivated colleagues. If the second interpretation is also true (for some teachers), the possible implicated mechanisms are likely to be more complex and may involve reciprocal causal processes between the *Read programme information* and the unmeasured motivation variable. Nonetheless, and irrespective of the underlying mechanisms, having read the available programme materials and acquired knowledge about the various programme components can be seen as an important general prerequisite to implementation of the programme.

The information about the programme and its components provided to the teachers can, in principle, be made more or less stringent and directive with regard to guidelines and other requirements. Teachers' general attitude to 'experts' and highly structured programmes seems to vary across time periods (Cochran-Smith and Lytle, 1999; Fullan, 1982, 1998). The relative lack of detailed advice and how-to-do-it information was probably an advantage for the project at the time when it was initiated in the first half of the 1980s. The *Zeitgeist* has changed markedly over the past 15–20 years, however, and nowadays teachers ask for more detailed instructions, guidelines, and ready-made work materials to be able to fit a new programme or educational innovation into their busy work schedules.

Following up on this change in overall climate, a new teacher manual (Olweus, 1999a, 2001b), which elaborates the essential components of the programme and gives a good deal of practical advice and guidelines, has been developed for our recent intervention projects (Olweus, 1999b, 2001a; Olweus and Limber, 1999). Also, in order to secure better understanding and knowledge of the programme and its implementation, we usually establish staff discussion groups at each intervention school, under the leadership of teachers who have received special training about the programme. These groups are expected to meet regularly for 1.5 hours at a fixed time, for example every other week, for review and discussion of the core elements of programme on the basis of the new teacher handbook (Olweus, 2001b) and the book *Bullying at school* (Olweus, 1993a).

These activities and other quality control measures are likely to enhance programme fidelity, resulting in more uniform implementation of the programme. There should then be less teacher and school variability in implementation, which is probably considered a desirable goal by most designers of intervention programmes for our time, and is certainly my own position.

Degree of implementation was also predicted by the variable *Perceived level of bullying* (in own class), with a standardised beta weight of .25. It is quite understandable that teachers who perceived bullying problems among their own students were more likely to introduce various classroom measures to counteract and prevent escalation as compared with teachers who did not (or did not want to) see such problems in their own classrooms. In a sense, the demand characteristics of the classroom situation in this respect, as perceived by the teacher, likely influenced their readiness to address the problems.

As seen in the uppermost part of the programme overview in table 2.1, awareness and involvement on the part of adults are seen as important general prerequisites to effective implementation of the programme. In our recent intervention work, systematic use of the *Olweus Bully/Victim Questionnaire* (Olweus, 1996, 2004; Solberg and Olweus, 2003) with the associated PC program for processing the data, is considered an important vehicle for raising awareness and involving the adults at school, in particular. To assess the level of problems, we strongly recommend that schools carry out a survey with the questionnaire in an early phase as part of the intervention package. This survey will give teachers a reasonably realistic picture of the situation with regard to bully/victim problems in their own school and thereby increase their readiness to engage in anti-bullying work, where needed (which is actually needed in most schools, as of today). We also recommend schools to administer the questionnaire one year after the first assessment (and at regular intervals thereafter) to find out what may have been achieved or not achieved, and what needs continuing or new efforts.

The two remaining predictors of *Classroom Intervention Measures* were *Affective involvement* and *Self-victimised as a child*. These variables concern the teacher's general emotional responsiveness and empathic identification with victims of bullying. Teachers with a high score on *Affective involvement* reported feeling upset and uncomfortable about bullying among students, and such reactions seem to have resulted in implementation of more intervention measures in their own classrooms. Also, teachers who reported having been bullied themselves as children were more likely to implement suggested classroom intervention measures. Very naturally, such an experience will make it easier for a teacher to identify in an empathic way with victims of bullying, and increase their motivation to counteract the problem in their own classrooms. Although the relationship of these two variables with *Classroom Intervention*

Measures was somewhat weaker than was the case with the three predictors discussed above, the results point to the importance of the teachers' affective involvement for a successful result, here defined as a relatively high degree of implementation of the programme.

This finding may have some implications for teachers who reported weak emotional reactions to bullying among students. Judging from reports by parents, it seems reasonable to believe that at least some teachers see victims of bullying in a fairly negative light as a kind of 'nuisance', just creating problems and giving them extra work. It is important to try to change such detached or even hostile views of victims, if present. Research results on the typical characteristics of victims may be of some help in giving the teachers a more realistic picture of the degrading and distressing situation of most victims and the long-term consequences of persistent victimisation (Olweus, 1993a,b). Maybe even more important, use of detailed real-life or literary case descriptions or a well-designed video (such as the Norwegian *Bullying: Scenes from the everyday lives of two bullied children* from 1983 or its American counterpart *Bullying* from 1996) may increase empathic responding and help teachers (and students) to see the situation at least in part from the perspective of the victim. As suggested by our empirical analyses, such affective involvement is likely to increase the teachers' readiness to counteract bullying in their own classrooms.

School-level predictors

Our school-level analyses focused primarily on work-related aspects of the school climate (Kallestad, Olweus, and Alsaker, 1998) and the schools' attention to bully/victim problems. The three predictors shown in fig. 2.5 account for almost 50% of the variance in school-level implementation. A major finding was that schools with a higher degree of *Openness in communication* among the teachers, implemented more of the *Classroom Intervention Measures* (with a standardised beta-coefficient of .49). Also, considering the zero-order correlations, the climate variable *Orientation to change* was substantially related to the *Classroom Intervention Measures* variable ($r = .48$); much of the variance predicted by *Orientation to change*, however, was also predicted by the *Openness in communication* variable, thereby reducing the contribution of the *Orientation to change* variable to a non-significant level in the between-school model. Due to the sizeable correlation between these two school climate predictors ($r = .52$), we found it reasonable to extend the previous conclusion to the effect that schools characterised by openness in communication among staff and a generally positive attitude to change were particularly likely to implement the programme (see Kallestad and Olweus, 2003, for details).

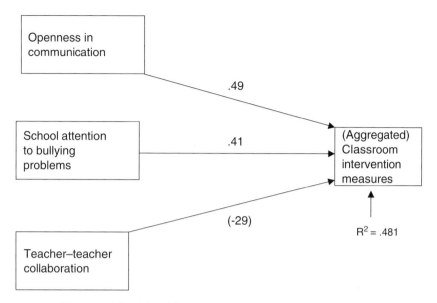

Fig. 2.5 School-level factors predicting implementation of (aggregated) classroom intervention measures (between-school model). Numbers close to arrows are standardised regression coefficients.

An interesting between-school finding was the negative relationship between the *Teacher–teacher collaboration* variable and degree of implementation (although the negative regression coefficient was nonsignificant due to the small number degrees of freedom, there was a zero-order correlation of −.34). This result implies that schools characterised by 'good collaboration' among the teachers actually tended to implement *less* of the intervention programme. High general satisfaction with the working relationships with other teachers may not always promote an active approach to problems and new challenges; it may even be the other way around as the negative relationship suggests, implying that teachers actually try to avoid changes in schools where the collegial collaboration is 'particularly good'. Such an interpretation is strengthened by the negative correlation of −.40 between *Teacher–teacher collaboration* and (positive) *Orientation to change*.

Although somewhat unexpected, these results are actually consistent with statements made by educational researchers such as Little (1990: 524): 'to promote increased teacher-to-teacher contact may be to intensify norms unfavorable to children'. Similar views can be found in Hargreaves' (1994) description of 'individualistic' school cultures. At the very least, our findings do not support the common view that improvement of the situation for the students in a school must start by creating a better quality of working relationships among the teachers.

Based on earlier research, we expected to find a relationship between principal leadership and implementation. Thus, we were somewhat surprised to find that *Teacher-leadership collaboration* did not predict implementation of the programme. However, this climate variable was based on items formulated in fairly general terms, so we had very little information in this study about the degree of support or relative lack of support of the programme provided by the principal/leadership group. It is reasonable to believe that the role of the principal/leadership group would have been more prominent in our prediction models if such more specific information had been available and included among the predictors.

The third school predictor in the between-school model was *School attention to bullying problems* (with a standardised beta-weight of .41; fig. 2.5). It appears that schools with more bullying-related activities for all or most of the staff generated an interest in the programme and increased motivation among the teachers to implement key programme components. This interpretation is based on the likely assumption that most of the activities included in this index took place in the early stages of the implementation process.

Relating to the previous discussion of the role of the principal, the positive relationship between *School attention to bullying problems* and the outcome variable may be an indirect indication of the principal's influence on teacher implementation of the intervention programme. A principal can influence staff attitudes and behaviour by putting anti-bullying work on the school's official agenda, initiating plenary meetings with staff and parents, and providing clear guidelines about the organisation of the supervisory system during break periods, for example. For anti-bullying work to get official recognition, it is also important that the principal allocates time and financial resources to such activities, in addition to giving psychological support.

In summary, the results from our study indicate that the teachers were undoubtedly the key agents of change with regard to adoption and implementation of the Olweus Bullying Prevention Programme in school. Substantial amounts of variance in implementation could be predicted on the basis of our teacher- and school-level variables. Generally, we think our study has shed light on several factors of importance and contributed to a better understanding of the process of programme implementation. The empirical results have also suggested ways in which implementation of the programme can be improved, and several of these amendments have already been incorporated in the programme and its dissemination (Olweus, 2001b, 2004).

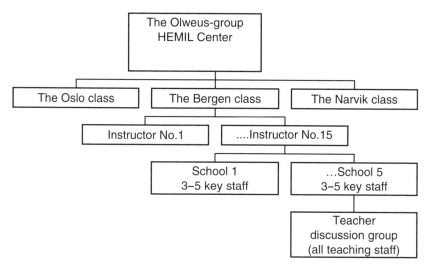

Fig. 2.6 Training of instructors.

Dissemination and impact beyond the programme schools

A new national initiative against bullying in Norway

Against the background described in the introductory section, the Ministry of Education and Research (UFD) and the Ministry of Children and Family Affairs (BFD) decided in late 2000 that the Olweus Bullying Prevention programme was to be offered on a large-scale basis to Norwegian elementary and junior high schools over a period of years. In building up the organisation and infrastructure for this national initiative, we use a four-level strategy of dissemination, a kind of 'train-the-trainer' model. The Olweus Group Against Bullying at the HEMIL-center at the University of Bergen trains and supervises specially selected *instructor candidates* who each train and supervise 'key persons' from several schools (typically five schools or less). The key persons are then responsible for leading recurrent *staff discussion groups* at each participating school (see above). The basic structure of the model is shown in fig. 2.6.

The training of the instructor candidates consists of 10–11 whole-day assemblies distributed over a period of some 16 months. Between these meetings the instructor candidates receive ongoing consultation via telephone or e-mail with members of my group. In implementing this 'train-the trainer' model in the USA, some modifications have been made to accommodate cultural differences and practical constraints. In particular, the number of whole-day assemblies have been reduced to four or five, and the 'Bullying Prevention Co-ordinating Committees' at the individual schools have been accorded somewhat greater responsibility than in Norway.

Up to now, some 120 instructor candidates have been trained or are in training, and more than 375 schools from all over Norway participate in the programme. In late 2001, the government decided to increase the funding of the whole enterprise in order to enable us to offer the programme to a greater number of schools from 2003. We perceive all of this as a breakthrough for the systematic, long-term, and research-based work against bully/victim problems in school and hope to see similar developments in other countries.

Acknowledgement

The research programme reported on in this article was supported by grants from the Ministry for Children and Family Affairs (BFD), the Research Council of Norway (NFR, NAVF), the Norwegian Foundation for Health and Rehabilitation, the National Association for Public Health, and, in earlier phases, from the Ministry of Education and Research (UFD), which is gratefully acknowledged.

NOTE

More information about the intervention programme and how to order it can be obtained from one of the following e-mail addresses: nobully@clemson.edu or Olweus@psyhp.uib.no. Also see www.clemson.edu/Olweus

References

Biglan, A. (1995). *Changing cultural practices: A contextualist framework for intervention research.* Reno, Nev.: Context Press.

Bryk, A. S. and Raudenbush, S. W. (1992). *Hierarchical linear models: Applications and data analysis methods.* London: Sage.

Cochran-Smith, M. and Lytle, S. L. (1999). The teacher research movement: A decade later. *Educational Researcher*, 28, 15–25.

Cook, T. D. and Campbell, D. T. (1979). *Quasi-experimentation.* Chicago: Rand McNally.

Dishion, T. J., McCord, J., and Poulin, F. (1999). When interventions harm: Peer groups and problem behavior. *American Psychologist*, 54, 755–64.

Elliott, D. (1999). Editor's introduction. In D. Olweus and S. Limber, *Blueprints for violence prevention: Bullying Prevention Program.* Institute of Behavioral Science, University of Colorado, Boulder, USA.

Fullan, M. (1982). *The meaning of educational change.* New York: Teachers College.

   (1998). The meaning of educational change: A quarter of a century of learning. In A. Hargreaves, A. Lieberman, M. Fullan, and D. Hopkins (eds.), *International handbook of educational change.* London: Kluwer.

Goldstein, H. I. (1987). *Multilevel models in educational and social research.* London: Oxford University Press.

Gottfredson, G. D. (1987). Peer group interventions to reduce the risk of delinquent behavior: A selective review and a new evaluation. *Criminology*, 25, 671–714.

Hargreaves, A. (1994). *Changing teachers, changing times – teachers' work and culture in the postmodern age.* London: Cassell.

Kallestad, J. H. and Olweus, D. (2003). Predicting teachers' and schools' implementation of the Olweus Bullying Prevention Program: A multilevel study. *Prevention and Treatment*, 6, Article 21. Available on the World Wide Web: http://www.journals.apa.org/prevention/volume6/pre0060021a.html

Kallestad, J. H., Olweus, D., and Alsaker, F. (1998). School climate reports from Norwegian teachers: A methodological and substantive study. *School Effectiveness and School Improvement*, 9, 70–94.

Lipsey, M. W. (1992). Juvenile delinquency treatment: A meta-analytic inquiry into the variability of effects. In T. D. Cook, H. Cooper, D. S. Corday, H. Hartman, L. V. Hedges, R. J. Light, T. A. Louis, and F. Mosteller (eds.) *Meta-analysis for explanation: A casebook.* New York: Russell Sage, pp. 83–125.

Little, J. W. (1990). The persistence of privacy: Autonomy and initiative in teachers' professional relations. *Teachers College Record*, 91, 509–36.

Olweus D. (1991). Bully/victim problems among schoolchildren: Basic facts and effects of a school based intervention program. In D. Pepler and K. Rubin (eds.) *The development and treatment of childhood aggression* Hillsdale, NJ: Erlbaum, pp. 411–48.

(1993a). *Bullying at school: What we know and what we can do.* Oxford: Blackwell.

(1993b). Victimization by peers: Antecedents and long-term outcomes. In K. H. Rubin and J. B. Asendorf (eds.), *Social withdrawal, inhibition, and shyness in childhood.* Hillsdale, NJ: Erlbaum, pp. 315–42.

(1994). Annotation: Bullying at school: Basic facts and effects of a school based intervention program. *Journal of Child Psychology and Psychiatry*, 35, 1171–90.

(1996). The Revised Olweus Bully/Victim Questionnaire. Mimeo. Bergen, Norway: Research Center for Health Promotion, University of Bergen.

(1999a). Noen hovedresultater fra Det nye Bergensprosjektet mot mobbing og antisosial atferd. [Some key results from The New Bergen Project against Bullying and Antisocial Behaviour.] MS. HEMIL-senteret, Universitetet i Bergen.

(1999b). Norway. In P. K. Smith, Y. Morita, J. Junger-Tas, D. Olweus, R. Catalano, and P. Slee (eds.), *The nature of school bullying: A cross-national perspective.* London: Routledge, pp. 28–48.

(1999c). Sweden. In P. K. Smith, Y. Morita, J. Junger-Tas, D. Olweus, R. Catalano, and P. Slee (eds.), *The nature of school bullying: A cross-national perspective.* London: Routledge, pp. 7–27.

(2001a). Antimobbingsprosjekt i Oslo-skoler med meget gode resultater [Anti-bullying project in Oslo schools with quite positive results]. MS. HEMIL Center, University of Bergen.

(2001b). Olweus' core program against bullying and antisocial behavior: A teacher handbook. Research Center for Health Promotion Bergen, Norway.

(2002). Efterskrift (Postscript). In E. Menckel (Ed.), *Vänskap vinner: Om mobbning ock kränkande behandling i skolan* (Friendship wins: About bullying and insulting treatment in school). Halmstad, Sweden: Högskolan i Halmstad., pp. 55–59.

(2004). Bullying at school: Prevalence estimation, a useful evaluation design, and a new national initiative in Norway. In D. Galloway (ed.), *Occasional Paper No. 23, Bullying in Schools.* London: Association for Child Psychology and Psychiatry.

Olweus, D. and Alsaker, F. D. (1991). Assessing change in a cohort longitudinal study with hierarchical data. In D. Magnusson, L. R. Bergman, G. Rudinger, and B. Törestad (eds.), *Problems and methods in longitudinal research.* New York: Cambridge University Press, pp. 107–32.

Olweus, D. and Limber, S. (1999). *Blueprints for violence prevention: Bullying Prevention Program.* Institute of Behavioral Science, University of Colorado, Boulder, USA; see also www.colorado.edu/cspv/blueprints

Pedhazur, E. (1982). *Multiple regression in behavioral research.* 2nd edn. New York: Holt, Rinehart and Winston.

Porter, A. C. and Raudenbush, S. W. (1987). Analysis of covariance: Its model and use in psychological research. *Journal of Counseling Psychology*, 34, 383–92.

Rapport 2000. (2000). *Vurdering av program og tiltak for å redusere problematferd og utvikle sosial kompetanse.* [Evaluation of programs and measures to reduce problem behavior and develop social competence.] Oslo, Norway: Kirke-, undervisnings-, og forskningsdepartementet.

Roland, E. (1989). Bullying: The Scandinavian research tradition. In D. P. Tattum and D. A. Lane (eds.), *Bullying in schools.* Stoke-on-Trent: Trentham, pp. 21–32.

Smith, P. K., Madsen, K. C., and Moody, J. C. (1999). What causes the age decline in reports of being bullied at school? Towards a developmental analysis of risks of being bullied. *Educational Research*, 41, 267–85.

Smith, P. K. and Sharp, S. (eds.) (1994). *School bullying: Insights and perspectives.* London: Routledge.

Smith, P. K., Morita, Y., Junger-Tas, J., Olweus, D., Catalano, R., and Slee, P. (1999) (eds.). *The nature of school bullying: A cross-national perspective.* London: Routledge.

Smylie, M. A. (1990). Teacher efficacy at work. In P. Reyes (ed.), *Teachers and their workplace.* London: Sage, pp. 48–66.

Solberg, M. and Olweus, D. (2003). Prevalence estimation of school bullying with the Olweus Bully/Victim Questionnaire. *Aggressive Behavior*, 29, 239–68.

Stevens, V., de Bourdeaudhuij, I., and Van Oost, P. (2000). Bullying in Flemish schools: An evaluation of anti-bullying intervention in primary and secondary schools. *British Journal of Educational Psychology*, 70, 195–210.

3   Is the direct approach to reducing bullying always the best?

David Galloway and Erling Roland

Introduction

Projects to reduce bullying have had some notable successes, both at local level (e.g. Smith and Sharp, 1994) and in local evaluations of national programmes (e.g. Olweus, 1993, Roland, 2000; Roland and Munthe, 1997). However, the gains have often been short term. When they have been maintained at two-year follow-up, as in the project in Bergen, Norway, it seems probable that progress was maintained by the researchers visiting schools in the follow-up period to give them feedback and to discuss further work with staff (Olweus, 1991, 1993; Roland, 2000; Roland and Munthe, 1997). While adopting a range of procedures, the primary focus of these projects was on bullying as a psychosocial problem. They sought to raise awareness of it among pupils and teachers, to convince everyone in the school community that it was unacceptable, and to describe methods to stop ongoing bullying. The 1996–97 project in Norway (Roland, 2000; Roland and Munthe, 1997) broadened the scope to emphasise the quality of day-to-day classroom management.

The mainly bullying-focused approach described above is consistent with a large body of literature, which has investigated characteristics of bullies and their victims. Thus Olweus (1993) argued that bullying results from adverse home conditions, which create a stable aggressive trait within some pupils. Crick and Dodge (1994) saw a social-skills deficit as the origin of bullying. In contrast, Sutton, Smith, and Swettenham (1999) found empirical evidence that bullies are socially skilled and competent manipulators; this is consistent with other evidence that school bullies are not necessarily unpopular with their peers (Olweus, 1993). The common theme is that the dominant variables relate to relatively stable aspects of personality and/or family circumstances (Olweus, 1980, 1993; Roland and Idsøe, 2001).

We believe that some redirection of focus may be desirable for three related reasons. First, bullying, in common with all other behaviour, is likely to be influenced by the quality of the social and educational climate of the school and classroom. It may be that the best way to raise teachers' awareness of bullying is to raise their knowledge and understanding of the full range of problem behaviours and their own role in responding to problems. Second, attempts to reduce bullying should be based on an explicit theory of professional development. Third, they should also be based on an explicit theory of pedagogy and school improvement. We describe a small-scale pilot project based on our argument that some redirection of focus may be profitable. Finally, we discuss the possible implications of our results.

Impetus for the intervention

School influences on bullying

The case for programmes to reduce bullying is simple: the emotional and educational damage to victims is enormous; the patterns of bullying behaviour which start at school often become ingrained and associated with serious social problems in adult life (Olweus, 1993). Clearly, everything possible should be done to reduce bullying. We agree, but argue that the direct bullying-focused approach is not necessarily the most effective in the long term. It is not clear that an explicit focus on bullying can address all the factors that may contribute to the problem. For example, the behaviour of bullies and victims may be influenced by aspects of school and classroom management that appear at first sight unrelated to bullying. Thus, erratic and inconsistent marking of students' work is not directly related to bullying but may contribute to a climate that makes it more likely to occur. A more holistic approach is needed.

The classroom behaviours consistently reported by teachers as most troublesome are not bullying but talking out of turn and hindering other children's progress (Wheldall and Glynn, 1989; Gray and Sime, 1989). Surprisingly, bullying seldom seems to attract attention in surveys of problem behaviour at school. That is a powerful argument for campaigns to raise teachers' awareness of bullying and its damaging effects. Numerous studies have identified bullying as the hidden behaviour problem, frequently unrecognised by teachers (Olweus, 1993; Roland, 1998). However, agreement on the often hidden nature of bullying and on its destructive impact does not necessarily lead to the conclusion that high profile, bullying-focused campaigns are the best way to reduce it. Before reaching such a conclusion we have to ask two questions. First, are we convinced that bullying is independent of weaknesses in general school or classroom management? If not, the long-term outlook for a bullying-focused programme would not be good, since the underlying causes would remain unresolved. Second, how much can teachers reasonably be expected to do? At a time of increasing pressure to demonstrate higher standards, how much extra will they be willing or able to take on? We return to this second question in the section on professional development.

If, as suggested by a large body of literature, the origins of bullying lie in family background and personality, we should expect to find the prevalence of bullying fairly evenly distributed across schools. We might find bullying to be more frequent in certain areas, for example in areas of social disadvantage, but among schools in such areas the distribution should be reasonably even. Unfortunately there is not a lot of research testing this hypothesis. It is clear, though, at least in Norway, that differences between schools in levels of bullying exist and are independent of the degree of urbanisation and of school size (Olweus, 1993; Roland, 1989). At classroom level, too, they are independent of size. Moreover, substantial school and classroom level differences remain after controlling for family issues (Roland, 1998; Roland and Galloway, 2002). In Sheffield, UK, Whitney, Rivers, Smith, and Sharp (1994) reported evidence of significant differences between schools in the amount of bullying reported by pupils, with a modest relationship to social deprivation. However, none of these studies reported sufficiently detailed evidence on the backgrounds of pupils in schools with differential rates of bullying to justify firm conclusions. Within primary schools in Norway, Roland and Galloway (2002) found evidence that aspects of classroom management, as perceived by pupils, had a direct effect on the frequency of bullying, and also exerted an indirect effect via their impact on the social structure of the class. We return to this point later, but note here that in this study family relations were not associated with bullying. Neither the size nor the location of the schools were considered, but these variables have not been linked to bullying in previous research in Norway.

Regarding bullying as one aspect of troublesome behaviour in school, albeit a particularly disturbing and often unrecognised one, opens up a number of possibilities. There is clear evidence of substantial differences between schools in the proportion of pupils showing significant behaviour problems. The most comprehensive data on pupil behaviour were gathered in the classic study of Rutter, Maughan, Mortimore, and Ouston (1979). As well as large differences between London secondary schools, they also found clear evidence that behaviour on entry to these schools at age 11 did not predict behaviour at age 14. Moreover, the correlation between behaviour at school and parents' occupation was very low, close to zero. The explanation of the differences lay within the schools themselves and not in the pupils or their family backgrounds. In their study of London primary schools, Mortimore, Sammons, Stoll, Lewis, and Ecob

(1988) also found significant school influences, though not as strong as in the secondary-school study. The more notable result in the primary study was that teachers rated about 30% of pupils as showing significant behaviour problems in each of three consecutive years, but only 3% were so rated in all three years. The pupils and their families had not changed, but they had a different class teacher each year, implying that, although there is overall agreement on the proportion considered troublesome, teachers do not agree nearly as well on *which* children are disruptive.

School influences on the most extreme minority of pupils whose behaviour results in exclusion appear just as important. Galloway, Ball, Blomfield, and Seyd (1982) found that excluded pupils were a highly vulnerable group on cognitive, educational, family, and constitutional grounds. A large majority had a low IQ, were educationally backward, came from stressful families, and were much more likely to have a history of serious illnesses and/or accidents than the norm. Yet they were unevenly distributed across the city's secondary schools and an exhaustive search failed to find any demographic factors to explain the school differences (Galloway, Martin, and Wilcox, 1985). Again, the explanation seemed to lie in the schools.

Probably due to the preoccupation of many governments and funding agencies with literacy and numeracy, most of the recent school effectiveness studies have neglected the school's impact on pupils' psychosocial development. Indeed, they have largely overlooked behaviour in general, let alone bullying as an example of deviant or aggressive behaviour. The case for regarding bullying within the overall context of such behaviour, and hence as being as susceptible to the school's influence as other problem behaviour, is nevertheless strong.

We have traced no evidence from school effectiveness studies that teachers in schools with the lowest rates of problem behaviour are more likely to have undergone training in behaviour management, let alone that they are more likely to have taken part in anti-bullying programmes. Rather, it seems likely that teachers demand such programmes when the social climate permits widespread problem behaviour and impedes pupils' educational progress. The problem is that many programmes which aim to change behaviour, including anti-bullying programmes, tend to regard the problem behaviour as the primary problem: deal with this and everything else will be all right.

Yet the evidence suggests that school effectiveness and classroom management are infinitely more complex than eliminating or reducing problem behaviour. Certainly that is important, but it cannot sensibly be seen in isolation from school organisation and management, nor from the quality of teaching in the class. In other words, a more holistic approach is needed. Rutter et al. (1979) drew on the important, though slippery, concept of school climate to describe the interactions among pupils and teachers, among teachers, and among pupils that explained why some schools had such widely varying rates of problem behaviour. Others have used the equally nebulous concept of the hidden curriculum (Galloway, 1990). The point is that school climate affects the quality of teaching and learning, as well as the quality of relationships in the classroom and in other parts of the school. So how can teachers create this climate?

A basis for professional development

No one doubts the importance of professional development. It is needed to keep abreast of advances in technology, knowledge, and ideas. It is also needed to respond positively to changes in public expectations, whether in safety standards or in the educational standards that pupils should be expected to reach by a certain age. Teachers' jobs are complex and they have to address many problems besides bullying. Epidemiological studies have made it clear that teachers face a wide range of problem behaviour in the classroom (Rutter, Tizard, and Whitmore, 1970). Other problems also have a valid claim on teachers' time and, arguably, are even more explicitly linked to educational under-achievement. Boys' poor educational progress relative to that of girls, for example, is a source of international concern and seems to be linked to their attitudes towards education (Myhill, 2002; Arnot, David, and Weiner, 1996). Similarly, anxious or withdrawn children are less likely to be noticed by teachers than are pupils who are disruptive, though they are not less likely to be a source of concern to their parents (Rutter et al., 1970). Perhaps there should be a campaign to raise awareness of these pupils too.

Given the range of tasks facing teachers, perhaps it is unsurprising that agreement on a rational basis for professional development remains elusive. In England, the government's preferred approach has been to identify priorities, for example literacy, link them to targets, prescribe a long list of 'standards' that teachers are required to demonstrate in order to attain a target, provide money for professional development, and finally draw up accountability procedures with draconian penalties for non-compliance. Few educational concerns illustrate better than bullying why this approach is intellectually vacuous in theory and ineffective in practice. There are two problems.

First, the word 'development' in professional development implies the importance of building on existing practice with an existing knowledge base. The core tasks of teaching are to create a social climate which pupils value and in which they want to learn, and to create an educational climate which enhances pupils' learning. Hargreaves (2001) has sum-marised these core tasks as enhancing social and cognitive capital. Suc-cess is evaluated against outputs, namely evidence about the quality of teaching and learning and about the school as a social community. The latter, of course, includes the quality of relationships and is therefore directly relevant to bullying. A sound basis for any professional develop-ment must, therefore, include both the social and the cognitive aspects of teachers' work.

Second, the interrelated professional development tasks of enhancing the quality of learning and the quality of the class and school as a social community are not helped by the apparent government policy, at least in England, of 'management by new initiative'. The tendency of ministers to rush breathlessly from conference to conference, announcing a new major initiative at each one, betrays a deep indifference to how knowledge is acquired and professional practice changed. The plethora of initiatives has had an entirely predictable effect. Local education authorities and headteachers concentrate on the most high profile initiative, in which the consequences of non-compliance are most severe. Usually, these involve targets in literacy or numeracy, or, in secondary schools, improvement in public examination results. Targets in the social aspects of schooling are harder to set. Preoccupied with the high-stakes cognitive targets, a headteacher's solution for all other educational issues, including bullying, is to produce a policy statement, which will satisfy inspectors. To be absolutely safe, a junior member of staff can be allocated the task of recording 'evidence' about the policy's implementation.

This solution is not entirely cynical. Most initiatives, including those on bullying, are perceived by teachers and often presented by ministers, perhaps unintentionally, as 'add-on extras', rather than as an integral part of the teachers' work. Most teachers, however, are already working hard, and indeed many are close to exhaustion. This feature of teaching was eloquently described by Hargreaves (1982) in his observation that while other professionals get tired, teachers get exhausted. Too often, the core aspects of the job are all consuming. Teachers can take on something extra for a short time, but are unlikely to be able to sustain the increased load in the long term. The challenge for professional development is to find ways 'to work smarter, not harder' (Hargreaves, 2001).

The prescriptive approach linking professional development to whichever initiative a minister currently favours leads to another prob-lem. Management by initiative and by accountability produces a climate of fear. Fear elicits compliance but the compliance is based on anxiety and underlying resentment. The chances of beneficial changes in children's classroom experience are minimal. Nowhere is this better illustrated than

		Output quality/quantity	
		Low	High
Energy input	High	Frustration and/or exhaustion	Short-term effectiveness but unsustainable due to burn-out
	Low	Cynicism and apathy	High leverage

Fig. 3.1 Energy input and quality and quantity of output (adapted from Hargreaves, 2001).

in Hargreaves' (2001) model showing the impact of high- and low-energy inputs when introducing a new initiative (fig. 3.1). The quantity and quality of output can be high or low, but if the initiative has a high-profile (high-energy) input, high-quantity and quality output will be unsustainable due to burnout. Only a low-profile (low-energy) input when introducing a new initiative has the potential for 'high leverage', i.e. for levering up standards through sustainable change. This model is unlikely to find favour with government ministers, nor with enthusiasts for any particular project. Yet it illustrates vividly why teachers cannot successfully be bullied into implementing a new initiative, whether on bullying or on anything else. (They *can*, of course, be bullied, but the impact will be short term at best.)

Pedagogy and school improvement

We have argued that the core tasks of teaching are to increase social and cognitive capital. Few things are more destructive of social relationships than bullying. Necessarily short-term programmes to tackle behaviour problems, whether bullying or talking out of turn in the classroom, though, do not usually achieve supportive relationships between pupils. They are more likely to be achieved by improving teachers' competence in the classroom, including their understanding of interactions between pupils. Bullying should be addressed, and addressed explicitly, but within the wider context of social interaction and the learning tasks of the classroom.

The precise focus will vary from programme to programme, but we can identify four common themes. First, the programme should build on teachers' existing knowledge and skills. Second, it should be seen by teachers as helping them to work more effectively and efficiently; in other words it should help them to work smarter not harder. Third, it should result in demonstrable change in the classroom. Fourth, the emphasis should be on improving the quality of teaching and social relationships rather than on complying with some externally imposed directive.

These four criteria are consistent with well-known work on school improvement. Fitz-Gibbon (1996) emphasises the importance of regular monitoring in order to identify change in the classroom. She also draws attention to the negative consequences of policy decisions that are imposed on teachers without negotiation. She is scathing about much current practice in educational management, contrasting it with the experience of Max Perutz, a Nobel prize winning scientist who describes how 'the MRC [Medical Research Council in the UK] still operates a system in which individual researchers are in contact with individual administrators who become familiar with their work and "do everything possible to help them with their research"' (Fitz-Gibbon 1996: 184).

Priorities will inevitably vary from country to country and from school to school. Nevertheless, it is possible to identify aspects of teaching methods and classroom improvement which are of particular relevance to bullying. In planning research on class-level effects on bullying, Roland and Galloway (2002) identified four potential influences on bullying. First, teachers provide a model for pupils in the quality of care they show for them as individuals. Pupils who believe that their teacher has a caring attitude towards them are less likely to bully others. Second, the way in which teachers implement routines for task-oriented work sends a powerful indirect message about their control of the class as well as an explicit one about their expectations of the class's success in the task. Pupils who recognise their teacher's competence and feel secure in their ability to succeed may be less likely to bully. Third, children are quick to notice how the teacher monitors their progress in curriculum tasks and their social relationships. From the teacher's skill in monitoring their work and their social interactions, students learn what is expected of them, socially as well as intellectually. Fourth, the manner and effectiveness of interventions when problems occur, whether bullying or other behaviour problems, not only maintains learning but also shows the teacher's ability to generate a climate of security and maintain constructive social relationships in the face of obstacles.

A notable feature of these four aspects of a potential school improvement programme is that each can be as relevant to bullying as to other aspects of classroom life. Hence, any initiative to reduce bullying can be multi-dimensional, and we would argue that it should be. School improvement implies improvement in the social and cognitive aspects of teachers' work. As an example of damaging social relations, bullying cannot be seen in isolation from the core tasks of teaching. The benefit of such an holistic approach is not only that the quality of teaching may be raised across subject areas through a programme to reduce bullying; in addition, it may be possible to incorporate explicit attention to bullying in programmes whose primary focus is on the cognitive aspects of teaching.

A pilot project

Planning and funding   The implications of the argument presented above are that attempts to reduce bullying can, and should, form an integral part of wider ranging attempts to improve the quality of teaching and learning. Teachers should perceive an anti-bullying initiative as assisting them in their core work, from which they derive their job satisfaction and for which they are rightly held accountable. Anti-bullying strategies should be introduced with a low profile simply because high-profile introduction is likely to divert teachers from their core work, which includes monitoring social interactions among students. In the short term high-profile introduction may have an impact but it is most unlikely to be sustainable beyond the short to medium term. With these considerations in mind, one of us (ER) planned a professional development programme for teachers with the limited aim of investigating its impact on bullying. Funding was provided by the Center for Behavioural Research, University College Stavanger, Norway.

Selection of schools

The project took place in a town in the south of Norway with over 50,000 inhabitants and with 18 primary schools. In 9 of these schools, a professional development programme for teachers was initiated. The schools were chosen independently by an education officer who knew all the schools in the area and agreed to select a representative sample. The remaining 9 were invited to take part in the survey as comparison schools, and 6 of these agreed to do so. A subsequent check revealed no differences between the experimental and the comparison schools in terms of size. The remaining 3 schools refused to take part for various reasons, such as pressure on staff from other projects.

Characteristics of schools and students

The programme took place from 1992 to 1994. Two comparison samples were selected and two experimental samples.

Comparison Sample 1 consisted of first-grade pupils (aged 6–7 years) in 9 primary schools the year before the professional development programme started (year 1 of the programme). None of these pupils or their teachers was subsequently involved in the programme.

Experimental Sample 1 was the following year's intake of first-grade pupils in the same 9 primary schools as Comparison Sample 1. This was year 2 of the programme. The designated class teachers of these pupils, 1 per class, formed the first cohort ($N = 20$) of the professional development programme. (In Norway each primary class may be taught by three or four teachers, one of whom is the designated class teacher and teaches the class for a majority of lessons).

Experimental Sample 2 was the next year's intake of first-grade pupils (year 3 of the programme), at the same 9 primary schools. These pupils' designated class teachers formed the second cohort of the professional development programme ($N = 20$). There was no overlap between teachers in cohorts 1 and 2.

Comparison Sample 2 consisted of first-grade pupils in 6 schools in the same town, which had not taken part in the professional development programme (year 3 of the programme).

Each sample had 300–350 pupils, except Comparison Sample 2, which had 151.

Components of the intervention programme

The professional development programme was based on the argument outlined above that four critical influences on the quality of teaching and learning in a primary school are: the quality of care for individual pupils; implementation of routines for task-oriented work; monitoring children's progress and social interactions; and intervening when problems occur. There were explicit references to the causes and prevention of bullying, but only as part of the wider programme.

For the 20 teachers in each cohort the programme consisted of 4 in-service days over a 9-month period. A handout summarising the content was distributed on each occasion. In addition, there were 15 2-hour peer supervision sessions on lines described by Dalin and Rolft (1993); and Handal (1991). These were held in groups of 6–7 and were led by a colleague trained by the Centre for Behavioural Research. Their aim was to give teachers an opportunity to discuss the practical implications of the theoretical concepts introduced on the in-service days.

Evaluation framework and procedures

An anonymous pupil questionnaire was designed to evaluate the project, with 10 items to answer on a 3- or 4-point scale (the full questionnaire can be obtained from the authors). The first 7 items asked about children's feelings about school and their social behaviour while there, for example, 'Do you help other pupils when they need it?' and 'Do you sometimes not want to go to school?' These were designed to assess the impact of the programme on attitudes and behaviour, which were not directly related to bullying. The eighth, 'Do you feel sad at home?' was included as an item that should not be affected by any change in classroom climate at school; no significant difference between the experimental and comparison samples was expected on this item. A heading 'about bullying' was followed by a standard description of bullying as used in previous studies (Roland and Galloway, 2002): 'It is bullying when a pupil is being hit, kicked or pushed by other pupils. It is also bullying when a pupil is teased a lot by others, or when a pupil is no longer allowed to be with the others, when a pupil is isolated by the others.' The final two items then asked 'Does it happen that you are bullied by other pupils at school?' and 'Does it happen that you take part in bullying other pupils at school?', with response options: never; now and then; weekly; several times a week.

The experimental samples completed the questionnaires towards the end of years 2 and 3, on completion of their teachers' professional development course. The comparison sample completed them towards the end of years 1 and 3. Administration was by the class teacher, who read each item aloud and gave explanations on request.

Because all participants in all four samples were first-grade children, no baseline assessment was practical so there are no pre-test/post-test comparisons. Asking children about their experience of schooling in their first month at school is most unlikely to produce reliable data. The justification for focusing on the first year of schooling was that this has been shown to be a reliable predictor of subsequent progress (Tymms, Merrell, and Henderson, 2000).

What actually happened: achievements and difficulties in implementing the intervention

The programme did not increase the teachers' overall workload. The four in-service days were part of their standard entitlement to time for professional development, as were the peer supervision sessions. In other national school systems, such as the English system, the course would be considered time-intensive. In this sense it could be considered high

Table 3.1. *Mean ratings, number of pupils, t-values, and levels of significance for 10 variables: experimental and control groups*

Variables	Experiment		Control			
	Mean	N	Mean	N	t	p
1. Like it in class	1.48	673	1.40	476	2.36	.01
2. Like subjects	1.63	675	1.45	477	4.70	.00
3. Help other pupils	1.29	673	1.19	476	3.16	.00
4. Not want to go to school	0.61	672	0.77	477	3.14	.00
5. Noise and disruption	1.21	673	1.50	477	6.00	.00
6. Disruptive yourself	0.60	643	0.67	475	1.83	.04
7. Sad at school	0.56	674	0.66	476	2.70	.01
8. Sad at home	0.75	672	0.78	477	0.83	.41
9. Bully others	0.34	672	0.40	475	1.66	.04
10. Being bullied	0.87	675	1.07	475	4.29	.00

profile. On the other hand, no targets were set and the reputation of the teachers and the school did not depend on any stated outcome. The emphasis was solely on professional development. In that sense it was clearly low profile.

Results of the evaluation

Our first task was to compare the results from the two experimental samples and the two comparison samples. T-tests (two tailed) were used to compare the mean ratings on each item. Comparison Samples 1 and 2 differed significantly on only one item, 'helping other pupils', in which Comparison Sample 2 had a higher mean rating. Similarly, Experimental Samples 1 and 2 had significantly different mean ratings on only one item, 'noise and disruption in class', in which Experimental Sample 2 had a higher rating. For all other items, including the two questions about bullying and being bullied, the mean ratings of the two comparison samples were very close, and not significantly different; the same applied to the two experimental samples. We therefore felt justified in merging the two comparison samples into a single sample, and likewise the two experimental samples.

The most interesting analysis involved comparing responses of pupils whose teachers had not taken part in the professional development programme (the merged comparison sample) with those whose teachers had taken part (the merged experimental samples). The results are shown in table 3.1. Here one-tailed t-tests were used, as the hypothesis was that the results would be in favour of the experimental sample; except for item 8, 'sad at home', where a two-tailed test was used. As predicted, the experimental group's ratings were significantly more positive than those of the control samples, except for 'sad at home', for which there was no significant difference. This supported the view that the other items were investigating aspects of children's experience, which had been affected by their class teacher's participation in the professional development programme. The significance levels were consistently high ($p < .01$ on 7 items and $p < .04$ on 2). In relation to the final 2 items on bullying and being bullied, the mean of the experimental group was 15% below that of the comparison group for bullying others, and 18.7% below for being bullied.

Discussion and conclusions

This pilot study was based on our argument that some redirection may be desirable in anti-bullying programmes; specifically, that a more holistic approach to bullying would see it in the context of the range of behaviours that teachers encounter in the classroom, and that intervention should be based on a clear theory of professional development and a clear theory of pedagogy and school improvement. The procedures used to assess bullying were identical to those used in numerous other studies (e.g. Roland and Galloway, 2002). Although the experimental groups reported significantly less bullying, the reduction was less dramatic than in Olweus' (1991, 1993) local evaluation in Bergen of a Norwegian national project, and in the Sheffield project (Smith and Sharp, 1994). It was better, however, than the reduction found in another local evaluation of the national project in Norway (Roland, 2000; Roland and Munthe, 1997). These projects all investigated the effects of campaigns against bullying that focused directly on bullying, even in aspects of the programme that concentrated on prevention rather than on identifying and responding to bullying when it occurred.

Hargreaves' (2001) theory would predict that the reduction in bullying reported here should be more sustainable than reductions resulting from programmes with a more direct focus on the problem. That requires further investigation. Nevertheless, the general picture has been one of considerable difficulty in maintaining the impact of anti-bullying programmes (Roland and Munthe, 1997; Thompson, 2003). If gains are not maintained it may be that programmes have not adopted a sufficiently holistic approach by integrating them into core aspects of teachers' day-to-day work.

A project with first-grade pupils makes baseline data on bullying and other social behaviour impractical, although this does have the disadvantage of not having pre-test/post-test comparisons, which most projects in this field have reported. Within these constraints, we are confident that the comparison between the experimental and control samples was legitimate. There were no grounds for suspecting that extraneous factors such as parental income or socio-economic status could have biased the results in favour of the experimental sample. That said, we were clear about the limitations in what could be achieved in a small-scale pilot study.

The data on bullying were based on similar procedures to those in larger scale projects. Like them, we had to rely on self-report data. It is difficult to see the alternative when investigating a problem that, notoriously, teachers often fail to recognise. In addition, we obtained other data showing that pupils' perceptions of schooling were more positive if their teachers had taken part in the professional development programme. However, we were not able to obtain observational data about pupils' actual behaviour in class. Nor were we able to show whether pupils' improved perceptions were reflected in better educational progress. More information about the reliability of the questionnaire would be desirable, and it would be preferable for someone other than the class teacher to administer it. None of this necessarily invalidates our results. Nevertheless it does provide a powerful argument for larger scale studies that include reduction in bullying in other age groups as part of wider ranging school improvement programmes, and evaluate their impact on a wider range of educational and social variables.

Longer term effects or evaluation of the programme

This was a small-scale pilot project and it has not been possible to follow it up. Hargreaves' (2001) argument suggests that teachers should be more likely to continue using the professional development outlined above than training aimed more narrowly at bullying. Similarly, it would also suggest that bully and victim rates should remain lower than in more narrowly focused programmes. Unfortunately, resources did not allow the kind of follow-up that would have enabled us to test these hypotheses.

Dissemination and impact beyond the programme schools

It has not been possible to follow up this pilot project with a larger scale study with more schools and a wider age range of students. However, together with the ongoing work of Olweus (2003; and chapter 2), it has contributed to awareness of bullying at school level and at political level in

Norway. Evidence of political awareness came in a 2002 announcement by the prime minister of a further national campaign with 'zero tolerance' of bullying. Olweus (2003) has provided a framework for annual monitoring of bullying levels and, with the large sample provided by participation in the national programme, this will undoubtedly make a significant contribution to understanding the impact of large-scale initiatives.

It has to be said, though, that the programmes encouraged by the Norwegian government are focusing very strongly on bullying rather than on the more holistic approach advocated in this chapter. This is true of Olweus' programme and, to a lesser extent, of Roland's programme in Stavanger. While the latter explicitly recognises the importance of school- and class-level variables that may only indirectly be related to bullying, the emphasis is still on bullying as the primary problem. A larger and more rigorous replication of the pilot project reported here remains an urgent priority.

There is one other way in which the programme has had an impact. The Center for Behavioural Research in Stavanger provides numerous short in-service courses to help teachers in the management of problem behaviour (Midthassel and Bru, 2001). Research on school and classroom influences on bullying (Roland and Galloway, 2002), together with the pilot project reported here, has provided a strong indication that problem behaviour in general may be tackled most effectively, and sustainably, by courses which aim to improve the quality of day-to-day classroom teaching (see Galloway, 2003). This approach is a far cry from the narrowly behavioural courses on assertive teacher behaviour that are currently favoured by many authorities, for example in the UK. Yet here, too, there is an urgent need for rigorous studies comparing alternative approaches with long-term follow-up. Until such studies are carried out, teachers will continue to work in the dark.

References

Arnot, M., David, M., and Weiner G. (1996). *Recent research on gender and educational performance.* London: HMSO.

Crick, N. R. and Dodge, K. A. (1994). A review and reformulation of social information-processing mechanisms in children's social adjustment. *Psychological Bulletin*, 115, 74–101.

Dalin, P. and Rolft, H.-G. (1993). *Changing the school culture.* London: Cassell.

Fitz-Gibbon, C. T. (1996). *Monitoring education: Indicators, quality and effectiveness.* London: Cassell.

Galloway, D. (1990). *Teaching and counselling: An approach to personal and social education across the curriculum.* London: Longman.

(2003). School policies on bullying: A problem of competing initiatives? In D. Galloway (ed.), *Occasional Paper No. 23, Bullying in schools*. London: Association for Child Psychology and Psychiatry.

Galloway, D., Ball, T., Blomfield, D., and Seyd, R. (1982). *Schools and disruptive pupils*. London: Longman.

Galloway, D., Martin, R., and Wilcox, B. (1985). Persistent absence from school and exclusion from school: The predictive power of school and community variables. *British Educational Research Journal*, 11, 51–61.

Gray, J. and Sime, N. (1989). Findings from the national survey of teachers in England and Wales. In Department of Education and Science, *Discipline in schools: Report of the committee of inquiry chaired by Lord Elton*. London: HMSO.

Handal, G. (1991). Collective time – collective practice? *The Curriculum Journal*, 2, 317–33.

Hargreaves, D. (1982) *Challenge for the comprehensive school: Curriculum, culture and community*. London: Routledge.

(2001). A capital theory of school of school effectiveness and school improvement. *British Educational Research Journal*, 27, 487–503.

Midthassel, U. V., and Bru, E. (2001). Predictors and gains of teacher involvement in an improvement project on classroom management. Experiences from a Norwegian project in two compulsory schools. *Educational Psychology*, 21, 229–42.

Mortimore, P., Sammons, P., Stoll, L., Lewis, D., and Ecob, R. (1988). *School matters: The junior years*. Wells: Open Books.

Myhill, D. (2002). Bad boys and good girls? Patterns of interaction and response in whole class teaching. *British Educational Research Journal*, 28, 339–52.

Olweus, D. (1980). Familial and temperamental determinants of aggressive behaviour in adolescent boys: A causal analysis. *Developmental Psychology*, 16, 644–60.

(1991). Bully/victim problems among school children: Basic facts and effects of a school-based intervention program. In D. J. Pepler and K. H. Rubin (eds.), *The development and treatment of childhood aggression*. Hillsdale, NJ: Erlbaum.

(1993). *Bullying at school: What we know and what we can do*. Oxford: Blackwell.

(2003). Bullying at school: Prevalence estimation, a useful evaluation design, and a new national initiative in Norway. In D. Galloway (ed.), *Occasional Paper No. 23, Bullying in schools*. London: Association for Child Psychology and Psychiatry.

Roland E. (1989) *Tre år senere*. Stavanger: Senter for Atferdsforskning.

(1998) 'School influences on bullying.' Unpublished Ph.D. thesis, University of Durham, UK.

(2000). Bullying in school: Three national innovations in Norwegian schools in 15 years. *Aggressive Behavior*, 26, 135–43.

Roland, E. and Galloway, D. (2002). Classroom influences on bullying. *Educational Research*, 44, 299–312.

Roland, E. and Idse, T. (2001). Aggression and bullying. *Aggressive Behavior*, 27, 446–62.

Roland, E. and Munthe, E. (1997). The 1996 Norwegian program for preventing and managing bullying in schools. *Irish Journal of Psychology*, 18, 233–47.

Rutter, M., Maughan, B., Mortimore, P., and Ouston, J. (1979). *Fifteen thousand hours: Secondary schools and their effects on pupils*. London: Open Books.

Rutter, M., Tizard, J., and Whitmore, K. (1970). *Education, health and behaviour*. London: Longman.

Smith, P. K. and Sharp, S. (eds.) (1994). *School bullying: Insights and perspectives*. London: Routledge.

Sutton, J., Smith, P. K., and Swettenham, J. (1999). Social cognition and bullying: Social inadequacy or skilled manipulation? *British Journal of Developmental Psychology*, 17, 435–50.

Thompson, D. (2003). Anti-bullying policies: Are they worth the paper they are written on? In D. Galloway (ed.), *Occasional Paper No. 23, Bullying in schools*. London: Association for Child Psychology and Psychiatry.

Tymms, P., Merell, C., and Henderson, B. (2000). Baseline assessment and progress during the first three years at school. *Educational Research and Evaluation*, 6, 105–29.

Wheldall, K. and Glynn, T. (1989). *Effective classroom learning*. Oxford: Blackwell.

Whitney, I., Rivers, I., Smith, P. K., and Sharp, S. (1994). The Sheffield project: Methodology and findings. In P. K. Smith and S. Sharp (eds.), *School bullying: Insights and perspectives*. London: Routledge.

4 Implementation of the Olweus Bullying Prevention programme in the Southeastern United States

Susan P. Limber, Maury Nation, Allison J. Tracy, Gary B. Melton, and Vicki Flerx

Impetus for the intervention study, early stages of planning, and funding

In 1994 the Institute for Families in Society at the University of South Carolina received a grant from the Office of Juvenile Justice and Delinquency Prevention (within the US Department of Justice) to undertake a 3-year project to conduct research related to violence among rural youth. A critical component of this grant was the implementation and evaluation of the Olweus Bullying Prevention Programme in rural schools in South Carolina. Faculty at the Institute for Families in Society were familiar with the success of the programme in Norwegian schools, from reading published summaries of the programme (Olweus, 1991; 1993) and from discussions with Professor Olweus. Recognising that no other violence-prevention programme to date had produced such impressive results, faculty were anxious to test the programme in an American setting.

Early planning and preparation for the implementation of the programme involved the hiring of staff, extensive consultation with Professor Olweus, and the selection and preparation of participating schools. With the receipt of the Justice Department grant, the Institute hired a project director and part-time faculty, staff, and graduate students to support the implementation of the project. The principal university project team consisted of the principal investigator (Melton), a three-quarter time project director (Limber), three part-time PhD-level faculty at the Institute and at the Medical University of South Carolina who were responsible for providing ongoing technical assistance to schools, a part-time consultant for the project's evaluation, and several graduate research assistants to collect, input, and collate data from participating schools.

Several strategies were undertaken to help to ensure that programme staff implemented the Norwegian programme with fidelity. One faculty member attended a several-day workshop provided by Professor Olweus and colleagues in Bergen, Norway. The workshop provided a detailed description of the Olweus programme and its research base. In addition, Professor Olweus was engaged to provide consultation throughout the implementation of the programme. He visited South Carolina in the Spring prior to the implementation of the programme and modelled a day-long training in the programme for local school personnel (whose schools would not be participating in the programme). After viewing this modelled training, programme staff then conducted a trial training for staff members from several additional schools that were not participating in the formal programme. Based upon feedback from training participants and Professor Olweus, programme staff refined their training agenda, materials, and techniques in preparation for the subsequent training of staff from participating schools.

Selection of schools

The intervention was targeted at children in middle schools. The university-based project staff identified six participating school districts based upon the following criteria: (a) school districts were located in non-metropolitan regions of the state; (b) districts were matched with another participating school district in a neighbouring county on the basis of student and community demographics; (c) districts were distributed in various regions of the state; and (d) the school district's superintendent expressed an interest in, and willingness to take part in, the project. In each pair, one school district was selected to receive the intervention for both years of the project (Group A schools). The other school district in each pair served as a comparison group for the first year of the project and received the intervention during the second year (Group B schools).

With the agreement of the superintendent to take part in the project, university-based project staff scheduled meetings with relevant district and school-level administrators (typically the principal from each participating school, the superintendent, and other relevant personnel invited by the superintendent). This meeting provided an opportunity for project staff to describe the programme in detail, answer questions, and make initial plans to conduct the pre-test survey of students. No principals declined participation in the project following these meetings.

Characteristics of schools and students

In all, 18 South Carolina schools were identified to take part in the intervention component of the project. (Several other schools assisted by administering pre-test measures to students in 4th grade but were

Table 4.1. *Sample sizes of students in each group of intervention schools, by year of intervention participation and gender*

	Group A schools		Group B schools	
	Girls	Boys	Girls	Boys
Baseline year	587	526	788	748
One year	625	550	1,056	942
Two years	479	404		

not part of the intervention.) Participating schools included all middle schools in the identified 6 school districts. Although there are no fixed grade ranges for middle schools in South Carolina, most included grades 6, 7, and 8 (approximately, ages 11, 12, and 13 years). During the first year of the project, there were 11 Group A schools identified to implement the programme. During the second year of the project, 7 Group B schools began the programme, and the 11 Group A schools continued the intervention.

For purposes of statistical analysis, we restricted the sample to schools with at least 50 students rated at each of the time points of interest (pre-intervention baseline year and post-tests following each year of participation). The final analysis sample contained data from 12 schools: 6 schools in Group A and 6 in Group B. Table 4.1 shows the number of students in each of these treatment groups by year of participation in the programme and by gender.

School-level demographic data were not available to researchers, but district-wide demographic data indicated that the ethnicity of students ranged from 46% to 95% African-American, and from 4% to 53% White. In 5 of the 6 school districts, the percentage of students receiving free or reduced lunches (a measure of poverty) ranged from 60% to 91%, substantially exceeding the state average of 47%. The percentage of students receiving free or reduced lunches in the sixth district was 47%. All districts were in counties that ranked in the top 15% in the state for rates of juvenile arrest in 1994.

Components of the intervention programme

Like the original Norwegian model, the South Carolina programme embraced an ecological model. Its goal was to reduce bullying and related antisocial behaviour among middle-school children by intervening at multiple levels of a child's environment. The South Carolina programme remained true to the principles of the original Norwegian model, recognising that to reduce bullying, it was critical to create a school atmosphere characterised by

- warmth, caring, and involvement by adults towards students;
- firm limits for unacceptable behaviours; and
- application of non-hostile, non-physical consequences, when rules are violated and/or behaviours are unacceptable.

It was the intent of the planners for the South Carolina project to implement all of the core components of the Olweus programme at the school, classroom, and individual levels (as outlined in Olweus, 1993). Modifications and additional supports were planned, however, to help to ensure that the programme met the needs of our rural, American, middle-school population and to involve the larger community in bullying-prevention activities. Two primary modifications were made to the original Olweus Bullying Prevention Programme model: the development of school-wide rules against bullying (as opposed to classroom rules); and the engagement of the broader community in bullying-prevention activities.

School-wide rules against bullying

A core component of the Norwegian model was the establishment of classroom rules against bullying. Within the American middle-school context, it was decided that it would be preferable to encourage schools to develop school-wide rules against bullying rather than develop rules within each classroom. Of primary consideration in this decision was the fact that American middle-school students usually change classes several times throughout the school day. Unlike their Norwegian counterparts, these students also typically have multiple teachers. Thus, the development of school-wide rules against bullying was thought to encourage uniformity of rules within a school and minimise confusion among students and staff. In recent publications, Olweus (2001), too, has recommended the development of school-wide, as opposed to classroom, rules against bullying.

Community involvement

Olweus' original model focused exclusively on school-level, classroom, and individual interventions (Olweus, 1993). In recognition of the effect that the broader community environment has on children and families, we sought to broaden the focus of our intervention to include efforts targeted at community members, and the programme team planned to encourage members of each school's co-ordinating committee to engage the broader community in bullying-prevention efforts.

Materials

Programme staff planned for the development of several materials to assist with the implementation of the programme, and for personnel support. We also recognised that it was likely that additional materials would need to be developed once the programme was launched and feedback was received. With extensive consultation from Dan Olweus, an English version of Olweus' Bully/Victim Questionnaire was developed (Olweus, 1996). Programme staff also worked with Professor Olweus to develop a questionnaire to assess related antisocial behaviours.

A short video entitled *Bullying* was developed and produced by South Carolina Educational Television (1995), in collaboration with Dan Olweus and project staff. The 11-minute video includes four vignettes featuring middle-school-aged children and their experiences with bullying. Like the Norwegian video after which it was patterned, it was intended to be used to initiate discussions with students. A *Teacher Guide* (Institute for Families in Society, 1995) was developed by programme staff for use with the video. It provides background information about bullying, a suggested framework for showing the video to students, and a variety of classroom activities related to the video (e.g. questions for discussion, ideas for role-play activities, written exercises).

Project staff also developed a brief pamphlet for distribution by participating schools. The tri-fold pamphlet provided background information about the problem of bullying, described the Olweus Bullying Prevention Programme, noted some warning signs of bullying behaviour and bully victimisation, and encouraged parental involvement in the programme.

Ongoing consultation by university-based project staff

Recognising the difficulty of implementing and sustaining a comprehensive prevention programme in schools that already were under-staffed and under-funded, project staff planned to provide ongoing consultation to schools throughout the project.

On-site support from school-based mental health professionals

Since the university-based members of the project team were located some distance from each of the participating schools (2–4 hours distance), we recognised the importance of developing needed personnel support within the schools themselves, which also could help to sustain the programme after its initial grant funding ceased. School-based mental health professionals were hired by local mental health centres, as part of a separate programme developed by the South Carolina Department of Mental Health and the Institute for Families in Society, to provide school-based mental health services to students and families. Staff associated with the Olweus Bullying Prevention Programme planned to meet on several occasions with these mental health professionals to introduce them to the programme and garner their support for the initiative. We envisioned that these individuals would serve as an on-site co-ordinator for the programme and also initiate interventions with children who bullied, with those who were bullied by their peers, and with parents of affected students.

Evaluation framework and procedures

Evaluation procedures and findings will be described only summarily in this chapter, as a detailed description of the evaluation currently is being prepared (Limber et al., in preparation). The evaluation involved surveying students at three time points: March 1995 (pre-test), March 1996, and March 1997. In year 1 (March 1995) students in grades 4, 5, and 6 (modal ages 10–12) were administered the Olweus Bully/Victim Questionnaire (Olweus, 1996) and a questionnaire assessing related antisocial behaviours. In year 2 (March 1996), students in grades, 5, 6, and 7 completed the survey. The final survey was administered during year 3 (March 1997) with students in grades 6, 7, and 8. After restricting the sample to those individuals with complete data on critical variables, the final analysis sample contained data from 5,317 students at baseline, 5,137 during year 2, and 3,855 during year 3.

Participation in the study was entirely voluntary. Letters were sent home to parents to inform them about the anonymous student survey and consent procedures. Parents who did not want their child to participate in the study were asked to notify the school office. No parents asked to exclude their children from the study. Teachers administered the survey to their classes during a single class period. After instructing students that the survey was both voluntary and anonymous, they read aloud the survey instructions, the definition of bullying, and each question in turn. Students followed along in questionnaire booklets and marked answers that best described their feelings or behaviours.

What actually happened; achievements and difficulties in implanting the plan of intervention

With support from programme personnel, schools were encouraged to implement all core components of the Olweus Bullying Prevention programme and to use creativity in developing additional activities consistent with the principles of the programme. Our collective efforts to implement the programme will be described below. Several changes to the planned intervention occurred and also will be discussed.

School-level interventions

School-wide survey The English version of Olweus' Bully/Victim Questionnaire (and a questionnaire to assess related antisocial behaviours) was administered to students the March prior to the implementation of the programme, and for the next two years during the same week in March.

School-wide staff training School-level data from the survey were compiled and presented to school administrators, teachers, and other school staff as part of a training day during August, prior to the start of the school year. One training was held for each of the 6 school districts involved in the project. As the number and size of schools from each district varied significantly, so too did the number of staff at each training. The smallest training included approximately 20 staff from 1 middle school; the largest included approximately 150 staff members from 5 schools. The purpose of the training was to raise awareness about the problems associated with bullying at school, discuss core elements of the programme, and begin to discuss ways of implementing programme elements at each school. Trainings were conducted by 2–3 programme staff, who had observed Dan Olweus in conducting a similar training for school staff.

Bullying Prevention Co-ordinating Committees In order to facilitate the development of each programme, Bullying Prevention Coordinating Committees were formed at each school. Typically, the group comprised 6–8 members and included a school administrator (i.e. a principal or assistant principal), a teacher representative from each grade, a guidance counsellor, a school-based mental health professional (if present within the school), and other staff representatives (e.g. physical education teacher, school attendance officer). This group was encouraged to meet regularly throughout the year (ideally monthly) to plan specific components of the programme and to act as programme liaisons between the university consultants and the entire school staff. A programme consultant from the university typically helped to facilitate the first several meetings of this committee and met periodically with the group throughout the school year. Committees functioned well and met consistently in some schools. Others met fairly inconsistently and/or infrequently.

School-wide events to launch the programme   After the initial planning for the implementation of the programme was completed, schools held a special event to announce formally and explain the new programme to staff and students. In many schools, principals and/or members of the Bullying Prevention Co-ordinating Committee introduced the programme during a school assembly. Several other schools used other means of launching the programme, including announcing it via a student-produced news programme that broadcast information about the Olweus Bullying Prevention Programme throughout the school on closed-circuit television.

Supervision of student behaviour   Increased supervision of students was a key element of schools' efforts. Co-ordinating committees examined data from the school survey regarding the most prevalent locations for bullying within their school. Committees then developed plans to increase monitoring of students in these 'hot spots'. Commonly, committees developed plans for increased supervision during recess, in hallways and bathrooms during the changing of classes, and during the loading and unloading of the school buses.

Development of school rules against bullying   School rules were developed by each school's co-ordinating committee, posted throughout the school (e.g. in classrooms, the cafeteria, hallways), and discussed with students in classroom meetings during the first several weeks of the programme. Although the wording of the rules varied somewhat from school to school, they typically captured the following messages, as proposed by Olweus (1993):
• we will not bully other students;
• we will try to help students who are bullied;
• we will make a point to include students who are easily left out.
    All adults in the school were enlisted to help to enforce the rules. Each co-ordinating committee also was asked to develop a plan for sanctioning students who violated the first school rule (we will not bully other students). Typically, the plans consisted of a graduated system of intervening with children who bullied their peers. Initial bullying incidents frequently were addressed by having individual discussions with students. Subsequent violations commonly were met with the loss of privileges and/or meetings between school personnel, the student, and his or her parents. In some instances, children were referred to the school-based mental health counsellor for more intensive individual or family intervention to address their bullying behaviour.

Reinforcement of pro-social behaviour   Co-ordinating committees also were encouraged to develop plans to reinforce students for prosocial behaviour, such as including students in social activities, standing up for students who were bullied, and being a 'buddy' to younger students. Several schools rewarded students by distributing coupons that could be redeemed at the school store. Others compiled names of students who had been observed engaging in prosocial behaviour and held a monthly drawing for prizes or privileges.

Parent involvement   Parents were notified of the programme through a variety of strategies. Within the first month of the programme, schools distributed informational pamphlets to all parents (as described above). Most schools also highlighted the programme during regular parent–teacher events, such as Parent–Teacher Association meetings, school open-houses, and special violence prevention events. For example, one school convened a special discussion session that included school staff, project personnel, and parents of children who had been bullied.

Classroom interventions

An important component of the Norwegian programme involved holding regular classroom meetings on the topic of bullying. Schools in our programme also were strongly encouraged to schedule classroom meetings (at least once every two weeks for 20–30 minutes per session), during which students and teachers could focus on issues of bullying and peer relations in their school. The co-ordinating committees worked with school administrators to try to ensure that the meetings were scheduled regularly. The actual frequency of meetings varied considerably between schools and within schools.

Early in the programme's implementation, class meetings provided a forum for discussion of the nature and prevalence of bullying at their school, harm caused by bullying, the school's rules against bullying, and sanctions for bullying behaviour. Teachers were encouraged to use the video, *Bullying*, and accompanying *Teacher Guide* as tools to engage children in discussions, role playing, and other activities (e.g. creative writing, artistic expression) to help children to understand the seriousness of bullying, support victims of bullying, and help to prevent bullying at their school.

During the course of the first year of the programme, teachers in participating schools requested additional resources to assist them in holding classroom meetings. Supplemental lesson plans were developed by project staff, together with a resource guide of books, videos, and other resources on bullying.

Individual interventions

Each school was encouraged to develop strategies for intervening with children who bullied other children and for supporting children who were victims of bullying. The goal of interventions with bullies was to end their bullying behaviour by registering immediate awareness of, and disapproval for, their actions and administering appropriate sanctions. The goals of interventions with victims of bullying were to guarantee their protection from harassment by their peers and to enhance their social skills and friendships with peers. Teachers and other staff were encouraged to assume responsibility for intervening in every bullying situation that they were aware of, and to involve school administrators, mental health professionals, counsellors, and parents as needed to resolve the situations and provide ongoing monitoring.

Community interventions

Each school's co-ordinating committee was encouraged to develop plans to engage the broader community in bullying-prevention efforts. The form of these interventions varied from community to community, but typically included efforts: (a) to make the programme known among a wide range of residents in the local community (e.g. convening meetings with community leaders to discuss the school's bullying-prevention programme, encouraging local media coverage of the school's efforts, engaging students in efforts to discuss the school's programme with informal leaders in the community); (b) to engage community members in the school's bullying-prevention activities (e.g. soliciting material assistance from local businesses to support aspects of the programme, involving community members in 'Bully-Free Day' events); and (c) to engage community members, students, and school staff in bullying-prevention efforts within the broader community (e.g. introducing core programme elements into summer church school classes).

Programme support

Approximately half of the schools involved in the project had assistance from a full-time school-based mental health professional (and in several cases, one or more graduate student assistants). Staff associated with the Olweus Bullying Prevention Programme met on several occasions

with these mental health professionals to introduce them to the programme and garner their support for the initiative. Although several of
these school-based mental health professionals were quite supportive of,
and engaged in, the Bullying Prevention programme, as a group, they
were less involved in the preventive aspects of the project than had been
anticipated, largely due to heavy demands on their time and pressures to
bill for their services with identified clients.

In addition to providing initial training to school staff and meeting on
several occasions with school-based mental health professionals, project
staff provided ongoing consultation to schools throughout the project
(one staff member was assigned to each school district). One project
consultant was assigned to each of the three school districts in Group A
schools (those receiving the programme during year one) during the first
year of the project. Consultants provided intensive on-site consultation
during the first two months of the project, holding introductory meetings
with school administrators assisting with initial staff in-services, and facil-
itating early meetings with members of the school's co-ordinating committees. For the remainder of the school year, consultants typically spent
several hours per week at each school, meeting with teachers, school-
based mental health professionals, and administrators; and assisting with
the development of community activities.

During the second year of the project, the three project consultants
were responsible for assisting with the development of programmes in
Group B schools (those beginning the programme in year two), as well as
providing ongoing consultation to all Group A schools. Necessarily, the
time that consultants spent in each school and community during year 2
was significantly less than during the first year of the programme.

Supportive materials

In addition to support provided through ongoing consultation, distribution of several materials had been planned by the project staff, and others
were developed midway through the implementation of the programme,
in response to perceived need of sites. Supportive materials included:
- The yearly surveys of bullying and antisocial behaviour. Written summaries of the school-specific data (including charts and graphs of
  data by grade and gender) were presented annually to staff at each
  school.
- The book, *Bullying at school: What we know and what we can do* (Olweus,
  1993), which describes in detail the elements of the Olweus Bullying Prevention Programme and problems associated with bullying, was
  provided to all staff members at participating schools.

- The educational videotape, *Bullying* (South Carolina Educational Television, 1995) and accompanying *Teacher Guide* (Institute for Families in Society, 1995), was provided.
- The informational pamphlet for parents, which was personalised by each participating school, was distributed to all parents and to selected members of the community.
- Two supplementary lesson guides provided suggestions for numerous classroom and community-based activities to engage children in efforts to reduce bullying and related antisocial behaviours.
- The resource guide of books, videos, and other resources on bullying; this included an annotated bibliography of several hundred resources and was provided to all teachers in participating schools.
- Programme newsletters – a newsletter entitled *Bully-Free Times* was developed and distributed each semester to all staff in participating schools. The newsletter featured creative programme activities in participating schools and communities and described upcoming project activities.

Implementation challenges

Establishing and sustaining a comprehensive, school-wide approach to the prevention of bullying is inherently challenging. Several particular challenges in the implementation of the Olweus Bullying Prevention Programme in middle schools in South Carolina will be discussed.

Commitment of school staff   As Olweus notes (Olweus, 1993; Olweus, Limber, and Mihalic, 1999), a necessary prerequisite to the effective implementation of the Olweus Bullying Prevention Programme is commitment of the school administrator and a majority of the school staff to addressing problems associated with bullying. Although programme staff discussed the programme with district superintendents and principals of participating schools, and although all of these administrators expressed support for the programme, we did not take any further steps during our preparation for the project to assess the interest of teachers and other staff to implement the programme. Had we done so, we likely would have found strong support for the programme among faculty in some schools but more tepid reactions from others. Lack of enthusiasm for implementing the programme among some staff may have reflected a lack of concern regarding problems of bullying at their school (and within society at large), a lack of time and energy on the part of already-stressed staff, and/or a lack of comfort with or understanding of this particular model.

At the time that this programme was introduced to schools, there had been little attention paid to problems of bullying by the American media, educators, health or mental health practitioners, or researchers. As a result, although administrators and their staff commonly expressed concerns about fighting and weapon possession and use among their students, they were less convinced that bullying was a serious issue for their school or for American youth in general. Some were swayed by the findings from their school-level student surveys (e.g. showing that 1 of 4 students reported being bullied 'several times' or more often within a 3-month period), but others remained sceptical about the seriousness of bullying problems at their school. The current national attention to bullying has resulted in significantly heightened awareness among educators of problems associated with bullying. Consequently, teachers and administrators are considerably more receptive to the topic and the programme than was the case in the mid-1990s.

Many staff in participating schools also expressed feeling overwhelmed by the current demands of their jobs and unable to expend the time and energy necessary to implement aspects of the programme. Unlike the adoption of purely curricular or other more narrow approaches to bullying prevention, the adoption of the Olweus Bullying Prevention programme requires a significant and sustained commitment by teachers to read programme materials, prepare for and conduct regular classroom meetings, be vigilant in monitoring students for overt or subtle bullying, intervening consistently and effectively with affected students, and engage parents in bullying-prevention efforts, among other activities.

Project staff noted particular implementation challenges among Group B schools, which appeared, overall, less diligent in implementing the Olweus programme. It is possible that initial enthusiasm for the programme on the part of administrators may have waned in the year during which the Group B schools served as control sites for the Group A schools.

Provision of ongoing consultation   In order to provide support for teachers and other staff in the adoption and institutionalisation of the Olweus programme, university-based programme staff spent considerable time consulting with schools during the first year of the project. Weekly visits by consultants proved important means of sharing particular intervention strategies, problem-solving, and encouraging staff. Moreover, consultants frequently provided the extra 'legwork' needed to engage parents and community members in the school's efforts. The work of the consultants was more critical than originally anticipated, as the school-based mental health professionals were not able to spend as much time as originally anticipated in co-ordinating the programme at several schools, and as commitment to the programme was somewhat lacking in several sites. As a result, consultants were heavily relied upon by staff in several schools to help to guide the work of the co-ordinating committees and keep the programme vital. During the second year of the project, the time that consultants could spend with any given school was essentially reduced by half, as new schools began the project. Some of the new Group B schools likely did not receive sufficient on-site consultation to launch the initiative effectively, and several continuing programmes may have lost momentum without significant ongoing consultation.

Adoption of the Olweus programme as a short-term strategy for bullying prevention   Despite efforts by the programme consultants and a number of school personnel to institutionalise the principles and core elements of the programme within schools, many staff nevertheless viewed the Olweus Bullying Prevention Programme as a year-long curriculum, of sorts. Once the video had been viewed and discussed and once teachers had engaged students in the various anti-bullying activities described in the supplemental resources, many staff felt that they were finished with the programme and were ready, at the start of the next school year, to move on to try other violence-prevention programmes such as conflict resolution programmes and peer mediation strategies.

It is, in fact, quite common in the United States for schools to adopt a *'programme du jour'* approach to violence prevention, whereby they adopt a successive list of prevention programmes or strategies. Unfortunately, not only does such an approach frequently sap the enthusiasm and energy of staff, parents, and students but it fails to take into account that changes in the climate of the school and in norms for behaviour come only with a consistent, sustained, effort on the part of staff.

Conflicts with other approaches to prevention   Another challenge that we encountered in implementing the Olweus programme involved staff members' embracing prevention strategies or philosophies that were contradictory to the Olweus Bullying Prevention Programme. For example, at least one school decided to group children who were identified as 'bullies' within one classroom for educational purposes. Several others grouped children who bullied in therapeutic groups that focused on anger management, skill-building, empathy-building, or the enhancement of bullies' self-esteem. Although well intentioned, such strategies likely are counter-productive, even with skilful teachers and/or adult facilitators, as students in such settings are likely to reinforce each other's bullying and antisocial behaviours (Limber, 2004).

Moreover, therapeutic efforts focused on boosting the self-esteem of children who bully or teaching anger management skills to such children may be somewhat misguided. For example, current research suggests that children who bully typically have average or above-average self-esteem (Olweus, 1993; Rigby and Slee, 1991; Slee and Rigby, 1993; but see Duncan, 1999; O'Moore and Kirkham, 2001). Improving their self-esteem may help to create more-confident bullies but likely will not decrease their bullying behaviour. Anger management training is likely to be equally ineffective, as anger is not a common motivation for children who bully (Olweus, 2001).

Difficulty in holding classroom meetings   One programme component, classroom meetings, created particular *angst* among some teachers, who expressed discomfort in engaging students in discussions about (and other activities related to) bullying. In response, several consultants, counsellors, and school-based mental health professionals offered assistance to teachers in modelling classroom meetings. Programme staff also developed the supplemental lesson plans and annotated resource guide that could be used by teachers to facilitate classroom meetings.

Another challenge for teachers in holding classroom meetings involved carving out a consistent time within the hectic middle-school week to hold the meetings (Limber, 2004). Unlike students in American elementary schools, who have one primary teacher, American middle-school students change classes several times during the course of a day, and commonly have 4 or 5 teachers. Within this structure, their weekly schedules typically are fairly inflexible. Some schools in the South Carolina project held classroom meetings during a student activity period, which occurred once per week; others carved out time from social studies or health classes. Administrative commitment to the classroom meeting concept proved particularly crucial in our middle schools, as the principal needed to approve changes to the students' schedules and actively encourage teachers to hold meetings.

The middle school structure not only makes it more challenging to find a time to discuss issues of bullying and peer relations but it also makes it somewhat more difficult for teachers and students to get to know each other and to develop a supportive classroom community that is vigilant against possible bullying. Teachers frequently are responsible for instructing 80–100 students and cannot be expected to be as intimately familiar with the social relationships of students as elementary school teachers would be, who are responsible for 20–25 students. Within a middle-school setting, effective communication among grade-level teachers becomes critical to the identification of potential bullying problems.

Results of the evaluation

The analysis strategy incorporated a complex sampling frame, in which students were clustered within schools and the assessment of the schools was repeated over three time points. Various analytic techniques have been developed to account for nested designs, such as repeated measures ANOVA and hierarchical linear modelling (HLM). However, since the true level of analysis is the school rather than individual students (i.e. repeated measures are collected from each school without following individual students over time), we did not use these modes of analysis for this application. Since individual students were not uniquely identified from one time to the next, the analysis strategy must aggregate the responses at the lowest level of analysis while accounting for clustering in the sampling strategy and then compare these aggregates across time at a higher level of analysis. We used the Mplus statistical package (Muthén and Muthén, 1998) to estimate the means of students' reports simultaneously for 5 separate groups, representing baseline (year 1 for Group A schools and year 2 for Group B schools), the year 1 follow-up (year 2 for Group A schools and year 3 for Group B schools), and the year 2 follow-up (year 3 for Group A schools only). In these models, the effects of grade level and sampling design on the group means were statistically controlled. These models were fit to the data of female and male students separately.

Analyses focus on 7 key outcome variables: self-reported bullying of others; self-reported victimisation; reporting of victimisation to parents; student isolation; perceptions of bystander engagement; adult responsiveness to bullying (i.e. students' reports of adults addressing individual students who are being bullied or victimised); and student attitudes towards bullying.

Self-reported *bullying* was measured with one question from the Olweus Bully/Victim Questionnaire (1996). Students were asked to consider their experiences and behaviours during the current spring semester (i.e. from the end of winter break until the second week in March) and respond to the question 'How often have you taken part in bullying other students at school?' Self-reported *victimisation* was measured using two questions: one question about students' experiences of being bullied during the semester and students' estimations of the frequency with which they had been bullied in the previous week. We measured students' *reporting of victimisation experiences* using a scale consisting of two questions that assessed the frequency with which students reported their victimisation to teachers and to a parent during the current semester. Student *isolation* was measured by developing a scale consisting of three questions that assessed: (a) the frequency with which students reported being alone at recess or break times; (b) students' perceptions of the frequency with which they felt lonely at school; and (c) the frequency with which they reported feeling less well liked than their classmates. Participants' *perceptions of bystander engagement* were measured using scores from two questions that assessed the frequency with which teachers or other adults try to put a stop to bullying and the frequency with which other students try to stop bullying that they are aware of. *Adult responsiveness to bullying* was assessed using scores from two questions that asked whether staff members had talked with the student about being bullied or about bullying others. Finally, *student attitudes toward bullying* were measured using a scale composed of five items that assessed how participants felt about bullying and children who bully.

Although students also completed a survey assessing related antisocial behaviours (e.g. frequency of engagement in fights, vandalism), these data are not discussed in this chapter. The primary goals of the Olweus Bullying Prevention Programme involve the reduction of bullying behaviour among students (Olweus, 1993). A reduction of related antisocial behaviours is a secondary outcome and discussion of these data was determined to be beyond the scope of this chapter.

The findings presented here focus on Group A schools only. No positive programme effects were observed for Group B schools, which were introduced to the Olweus programme in year 2 of the study. Although the lack of programme effects among Group B schools is not entirely clear, the most likely explanation has to do with a lack of fidelity to the programme among these schools, many of which failed to embrace the Olweus model and resembled 'control schools'. These concerns were noted previously in our discussion of implementation challenges.

The results of the models for Group A schools for the seven key outcome variables are discussed in detail below and several are presented visually in figs. 4.1–4.4. Differences in standardised mean scores were designated as a large effect if they were greater than or equal to 0.8, moderate if they were between 0.5 and 0.8, and small if they were between 0.2 and 0.5.

Bullying others

There was a large decrease in students' reports of bullying others from the baseline to the year 1 follow-up for both boys and girls (see fig. 4.1). The means estimated for the year 2 follow-up were not as low as for the

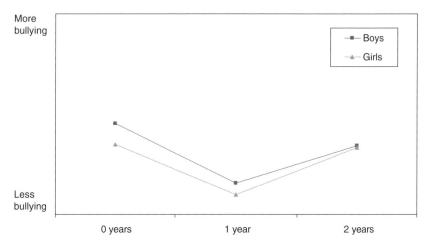

Fig. 4.1 Group-level means of students' reports of bullying others, by years of participation in the intervention programme, and gender.

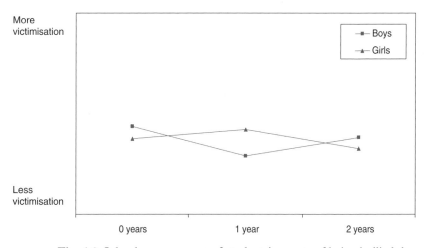

Fig. 4.2 School-group means of students' reports of being bullied, by years of participation in the intervention programme, and gender.

first year of the intervention and were not significantly different from the baseline means, although they were somewhat lower than the baseline levels. As was discussed previously, these findings may reflect the decrease in consultation provided to schools during the second year of implementation and the inherent difficulty of sustaining programmes over time.

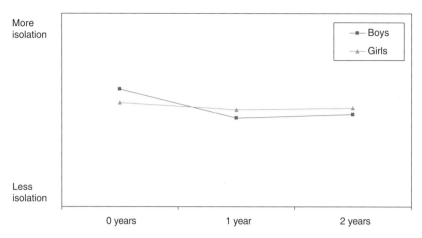

Fig. 4.3 School-group means of student social isolation, by years of participation in the intervention programme, and gender.

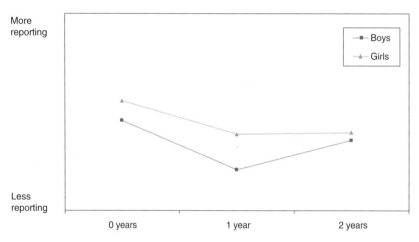

Fig. 4.4 School-group means of students reporting being bullied to a parent, by years of participation in the intervention programme, and gender.

Victimisation

We observed a large significant decrease in boys' reports of having been bullied by the end of year 1 but observed a slight (although not significant) increase among girls (see fig. 4.2). Differences from the baseline means estimated for the year two follow-up were not significant for either boys or girls.

Student isolation

As bullied students are likely to be socially isolated among their peers (Olweus, 1993), we examined students' self-reports of social isolation. We noted a large decrease in boys' reports of isolation from baseline to year 1 (see fig. 4.3). This difference was somewhat attenuated by year 2, although the standardised programme effect was still large and more homogeneous. Reports of isolation decreased only slightly, if at all, among girls across both years of the programme.

It is unclear why decreases in self-reported victimisation and social isolation were observed for boys and not for girls. It is possible that the programme was more effective in reducing some forms of bullying (e.g. overt physical and verbal bullying) than others (e.g. subtle forms of bullying such as exclusion or friendship manipulation) that may have been more commonly experienced by girls in this study. The revised version of the Olweus Bully-Victim Questionnaire (1996), which was not available for use in the present study, now assesses the frequency with which students engage in, and experience, a variety of different forms of bullying. Studies using this revised measure will be able to shed light on this issue by assessing the effectiveness of the programme in reducing various types of bullying.

Reporting bullying incidents to parents

We observed a large decrease in students' reporting of bullying experiences to parents among boys and a moderate decrease among girls after one year of the programme (see fig. 4.4). This initial decrease was attenuated somewhat by the year 2 follow-up among boys. The year 1 decrease remained rather stable through year 2 among girls. Indeed, although the decrease from baseline levels among girls after the first year was not statistically significant, the difference from baseline at year two was clearly significant, indicating a more homogeneous effect across individuals during the second year than during the first.

Plausibly, this decrease in reports of bully victimisation to parents reflects a decrease in actual bullying experiences among students. It is curious, however, that girls reported less bullying to parents after taking part in the Olweus programme, but they did not report reductions in bully victimisation. Future research that examines in more detail the types of bullying that children report that they experience and the types of bullying that they report to parents may help to shed light on this finding.

Bystander intervention

Interestingly, the reported incidence of bystander interventions in bullying behaviour decreased significantly from baseline during year 1 and, to a somewhat lesser extent, during year 2 among both boys and girls. Effect sizes for boys and girls were large. This seemingly counter-intuitive finding may reflect a decrease in the actual number of instances of bullying observed by students and adults. It is interesting to note that the year 2 estimates, while less strong in terms of effect size, increase in statistical significance for both boys and girls, suggesting that there is a more homogeneous effect across students as the programme progresses.

Adult response to bullying

From baseline to the end of year 1, there was a moderate decrease in boys' and girls' reports of adults addressing individual students who were bullying or being victimised. This may be the result of fewer instances of bullying behaviour once the programme had begun. However, this decrease was attenuated to non-significance by year 2 for boys but increased in strength by year 2 for girls.

Attitudes towards bullying

We did not observe statistically significant differences in boys' attitudes towards bullying behaviour during years 1 and 2. Among girls, an initial slight change towards less tolerance of bullying behaviour (albeit non-significant) during the first year yielded to a large increase in tolerance by year 2. It is unclear why girls in year 2 would reflect attitudes of increased tolerance to bullying. It is possible that girls' attitudes reflected a somewhat diminished focus on bullying prevention of Group A schools to the programme during its second year. It also is plausible that the findings reflect a historical effect of exposure to increased violence and bullying in the media. Because we did not have a true control group for year 2 of the project, it could be that the intervention group showed a less sharp attitude change towards tolerance of bullying than they would have if they were not in the programme.

Limitations of the study

Although a detailed discussion of the study's limitations are beyond the scope of this chapter, several are worth highlighting. First, as noted above, students' reports of bullying and bully-victimisation were assessed through global questions about students' experiences. Because the questionnaire did not assess the frequency with which students engaged in, or experienced, different types of bullying, we were unable to note possible differential effects of the programme on various forms of bullying or to explain some gender differences observed.

Second, due to political and logistical considerations, we were not able randomly to assign schools to conditions. As a result, Group A likely included school administrators and staff that were more enthusiastic about, and committed to, implementing a comprehensive bullying-prevention programme. This may help to account for differences observed in the success of Group A and Group B schools.

Third, because we lacked a true control group in this study, we were unable to rule out the possibility that naturally occurring historical change (e.g. increased media attention to violence and bullying in schools, or changes in rates of bullying or school violence over time) may have affected our findings. Future studies that address these issues will be important in our future assessments of the Olweus Bullying Prevention Programme in the USA.

Dissemination and impact beyond the programme schools

In light of some promising findings from the initial evaluation of the programme and increasing attention to the issue of bullying in the USA, there has been a great deal of interest in dissemination of the Olweus Bullying Prevention Programme to elementary and middle schools across the country. The programme has now been implemented in schools in more than a dozen states and many sites are in the process of conducting process and/or outcome evaluations of their efforts. The states of Massachusetts and Pennsylvania showed particular interest in the programme in the late 1990s, and have helped to support dissemination of the model to numerous schools.

Based upon cumulative experiences of the authors, Olweus, and other colleagues in implementing the programme in sites in the USA and in Norway, some additional modifications are now recommended to new schools that are interested in implementing the programme.

Training and ongoing consultation

In the original implementation of the programme in South Carolina, one day of training was provided for all school staff involved in the programme. As some school districts wished to conduct a single training for all participating schools, the number of participants could exceed 150. Experience suggests that such trainings are likely to be less effective than smaller, more personalised, training sessions. In order to help to ensure that a core team at each school receives intensive and effective training as well as ongoing consultation, a modified training and consultation model was developed.

Under the new model of training, a school's Bullying Prevention Co-ordinating Committee receives at least 1.5 days (and preferably 2 full days) of training, during which participants engage in a variety of interactive activities designed to increase their familiarity with research related to the nature and prevalence of bullying, and the philosophy and core components of the Olweus Bullying Prevention Programme (Olweus, Limber, and Mihalic, 1999). During the training, a half day is devoted to developing detailed written plans to implement the various components of the programme at each school (including plans for the co-ordinating committee to introduce the programme to the remainder of the staff at the school). The number of participants at the trainings are limited in order to ensure that the sessions are interactive and personalised (particularly in regard to the development of plans to implement the programme at each school). One to three co-ordinating committees participate in any given training, depending upon the number of trainers present.

In addition to providing initial training, trainers also provide approximately 1 hour per month of telephone consultation to a contact person at each school. Consultants help to ensure fidelity to the programme, assist with solving problems that may arise, and direct school personnel to resources that may be of assistance in the implementation of programmes.

On-site co-ordinator

In recognition of the demands of implementing and sustaining a comprehensive prevention programme, it is strongly recommended that participating sites designate an on-site co-ordinator for the programme (Olweus, Limber, and Mihalic, 1999). Sites with more than three schools are encouraged to employ a full-time co-ordinator; those with fewer schools may employ a part-time co-ordinator. The role of the on-site co-ordinator is to orchestrate the administration of the Bully/Victim Questionnaire and the processing of results; order and maintain a library of necessary and optional programme materials; schedule and take an active role in meetings of the Bullying Prevention Co-ordinating Committee; schedule and assist with the planning of staff trainings, engage in ongoing consultation from a certified programme trainer, assist teachers in conducting effective classroom meetings, lead a staff discussion group (if appropriate), and, with other members of the committee, plan and oversee all interventions. From experience, the on-site co-ordinator fills a critical role in helping to successfully launch and sustain a programme over time. If it is not possible to hire a full- or part-time co-ordinator for the programme, a volunteer co-ordinator or members of the school's co-ordinating committee must assume these duties.

Staff discussion groups

Programme implementers (within South Carolina as well as in other sites in the US and abroad) have been concerned about maintaining programme fidelity over time. The establishment of staff discussion groups is viewed as one important means of doing so, by helping to increase the competence, confidence, and enthusiasm of staff members (Olweus, Limber, and Mihalic, 1999). Staff discussion groups involve relatively small groupings of teachers and other school staff (6–12), who meet regularly to review and discuss core elements of the programme, share challenges and successes in implementing the programme, and co-ordinate their activities. Experience in the US context suggests that, although it can be somewhat challenging for schools to co-ordinate such meetings of their staff on a regular basis, the benefits for individual staff members (and for the programme) can be significant.

Dissemination model

In order to meet effectively the growing demand for the programme in the USA, a national train-the-trainer model has been developed, with some financial assistance from the Center for Substance Abuse Prevention and the Center for Mental Health Services (US Department of Health and Human Services). Trainers receive certification after participating in an initial 3-day intensive training by programme experts, engaging in monthly telephone consultation with programme experts for at least one year, and participating in at least one 2-day booster training. To date, 85 nationally trained trainers from 26 states have received provisional or full certification in the Olweus Bullying Prevention Programme.

The implementation of the Olweus Bullying Prevention Programme in South Carolina and subsequent dissemination of the programme in schools throughout the USA have provided valuable insights into the development of training, supportive materials, and strategies to help ensure that the programme is implemented effectively and sustained over time. Ongoing outcome and process research within the USA will be helpful to assess the success of the programme with a variety of populations and to ascertain those school- and classroom-level factors that best predict positive outcomes.

References

Duncan, R. D. (1999). Peer and sibling aggression: An investigation of intra- and extra-familial bullying. *Journal of Interpersonal Violence*, 14, 871–86.

Institute for Families in Society (1995). *A teachers' guide to accompany the video 'Bullying'*. Columbia, SC.

Limber, S. P. (2002). *Addressing youth bullying behaviors*. Proceedings from the American Medical Association Educational Forum on Adolescent Health: Youth Bullying.

(2004). Implementation of the Olweus Bullying Prevention program in American schools: Lessons learned from the field. In D. L. Espelage and S. M. Swearer (eds.), *Bullying in American schools: a social – ecologiese perspective on prevention and intervention*. Mahwah, NJ: Erlbaum, 11, 351–63.

Melton, G. B., Limber, S. P., Cunningham, P., Osgood, D. W., Chambers, J., Flerx, V. et al. (1998). *Violence among rural youth*. Washington, DC: Office of Juvenile Justice and Delinquency Prevention.

Muthén, L. K. and Muthén, B. (1998). *Mplus user's guide*. Los Angeles, Calif. Muthén and Muthén.

Olweus, D. (1991). Bully/victim problems among schoolchildren: Basic facts and effects of a school based intervention program. In D. J. Pepler and K. H. Rubin (eds.), *The development and treatment of childhood aggression*. Hillsdale, NJ: Erlbaum, pp. 411–48.

(1993). *Bullying at school: What we know and what we can do*. NY: Blackwell.

(1996). *Olweus bully/victim questionnaire*. Available from the author.

(2001). *Olweus' core program against bullying and antisocial behavior: A teacher handbook*. Available from the author.

Olweus, D., Limber, S., and Mihalic, S. (1999). *The Bullying Prevention Program: Blueprints for Violence Prevention*. Boulder, Colo.: Center for the Study and Prevention of Violence.

O'Moore, M. and Kirkham, C. (2001). Self-esteem and its relationship to bullying behaviour. *Aggressive Behavior*, 27, 269–83.

Rigby, K. and Slee, P. T. (1991). Bullying among Australian school children: Reported behaviour and attitudes toward victims. *Journal of Social Psychology*, 131, 33–42.

Slee, P. T. and Rigby, K. (1993). The relationship of Eysenck's personality factors and self-esteem to bully–victim behaviour in Australian schoolboys. *Personality and Individual Differences*, 14, 371–73.

South Carolina Educational Television (1995). *Bullying*. Columbia, SC.

5   Prevention of bullying in German schools: an evaluation of an anti-bullying approach

Reiner Hanewinkel

Impetus for the intervention study, early stages of planning, and funding

Within the last decade several epidemiological studies on school bullying have been carried out nationally as well as internationally (Olweus, 1991; Smith, Morita, Junger-Tas, Olweus, Catalano, and Slee, 1999). In Germany a number of cross-section studies were published (Holtappels, 1987; Tillmann, 1994; Todt and Busch, 1994). However, in contrast to the wide number of descriptive correlational studies on bullying and aggression, there are relatively few longitudinal studies that allow us to assess possible changes in bullying.

This chapter presents the conception, implementation, and evaluation of an intervention study to prevent bullying and aggression in German schools. In 1993 a survey was commissioned by the Ministry of Education of the Land Schleswig-Holstein to assess the extent of bullying and victimisation in schools in Schleswig-Holstein. From the results of the survey, recommendations for school-based violence prevention were derived (Niebel, Hanewinkel, and Ferstl, 1993). The Ministry of Education formed the networking group 'violence prevention in schools' which consisted of school staff, parents, as well as experts from different working areas. The working group decided to adapt and implement an anti-bullying programme in schools in Schleswig-Holstein which is based on the concepts and ideas of Dan Olweus (1993).

Selection of schools

In April 1994, the information brochure 'Prevention of Violence and Aggression in Schools' was distributed to all schools in Schleswig-Holstein (N = 1,055), introducing the idea of, as well as offering participation in, the programme. In total, 47 schools (4.45% of all schools in Schleswig-Holstein) applied for participation in the programme and were included in the study.

Table 5.1. Sample sizes by grade, pre-test and post-test (T1, T2), and gender (per cent female pupils)

| | | Primary | | | Secondary | | | | | | | School grade |
		3	4	5	6	7	8	9	10	11	12
Number of pupils	T1	1,022	966	1,592	1,563	1,681	1,597	1,377	669	292	293
	T2	1,028	982	1,595	1,616	1,638	1,475	1,254	479	304	239
Per cent female	T1	45.5	49.8	48.5	50.0	49.0	49.4	48.2	49.2	52.1	49.5
	T2	46.7	49.5	50.4	47.2	49.6	51.2	50	52.6	49.7	44.3

Characteristics of schools and students

The German school system is quite complex. Each of the 16 Bundesländer (German states) has the right to set up their own school system. In Schleswig-Holstein, primary school is from grades 1 to 4 (around 6–10 years); this is followed by four different types of schools, depending on the intellectual capacity of the students: Hauptschule are from grades 5 to 9 (this is the basic form of education in Germany); Mittelschule (middle school): from grades 5 to 10 (at a slightly higher academic level); and Gymnasium (grammar school) from grades 5 to 13 (leading to university entrance qualifications); the Gesamtschule combines the Hauptschule, the Mittelschule, and the Gymnasium. In addition there are special schools for children with disabilities.

All schools had been informed before the beginning of the project that they would be invited to participate in the first data assessment without having to take part in the intervention and the post-test. The original sample consisted of 14,788 pupils (2,219 in primary school; 12,569 in secondary school). During the implementation phase, 10 schools dropped out from the second data assessment: 3 Hauptschule; 1 combined primary/Hauptschule; 2 Mittelschule; 3 Gymnasia; and 1 special school. The reasons mainly mentioned by schools for not taking part in the post-test were that they had not planned to do so, further, a small number were dissatisfied with the questionnaire. In the final sample 11,052 pupils from 37 schools were assessed at baseline, and this fell to 10,610 at post-test (2,010 in primary school and 8,600 in secondary school).

Of the 37 schools, 6 were primary schools, 14 were Hauptschule (11 combined with a primary school), 8 were Mittelschule (one combined with a Hauptschule; and one combined with a primary school), 6 were Gymnasia, and 3 were Gesamtschule. A full breakdown of numbers at pre-test and post-test, by grade and gender, is given in table 5.1. Grades 3 and 4 (ages 9–10 years) belong to primary school. Secondary schools start at grade 5 and go to up to grade 13 (ages 11–19). With regard to the grades 3–9 the sample size is large, whereas in grade 10, and especially grades 11–12, the sample size is considerably smaller.

Components of the intervention programme

According to Olweus (1991: 413) the term 'bullying' can be defined in the following manner: 'A person is being bullied when he or she is exposed, repeatedly and over time, to negative actions on the part of one or more other persons.'

In this definition negative actions can be carried out by:

- words (threatening, calling nasty names, other forms of verbal harassment)
- physical contact (hitting, punching, kicking, pinching)
- other ways (making faces, dirty gestures, exclusion from the group, refusing to comply with another pupil's wishes).

The term 'bullying' is not used when two pupils who are of approximately the same strength physically or psychologically fight or quarrel. The term 'bullying' is appropriate when there is an imbalance of strength where the one who is exposed to bullying is physically and/or psychologically weaker than her/his opponent.

The targets of the programme are to increase adults' and students' awareness of problems of bullying and victimisation, and to reduce as much as possible existing bully/victim problems in and out of the school setting as well as to prevent the development of new problems. The programme tries to encourage active involvement of adults and peers in resolving bully/victim incidents in school. In so doing it represents a 'whole school policy approach to bullying' (Olweus, 1993). The core element of the programme is to restructure the social environment by implementing clear rules against bullying behaviour so that the positive reinforcement of bullying is reduced while the negative outcomes decrease. Moreover, it enhances the network building with more specialised services outside school.

Four components are crucial for the programme:

(i) general prerequisites: awareness raising and involvement on the part of the adults;
(ii) measures taken at the school level: questionnaire survey; school conference day; supervision during the breaks; meetings of staff and parents of victims and bullies, when bullying occurred;
(iii) measures at class levels: class rules against bullying; class meeting;
(iv) measures at the individual level: serious talks with bullies and victims, serious talks with parents of involved students; teacher and parent use of imagination.

Evaluation framework and procedures

The study had a quasi-experimental field design with a pre-test and post-test. Due to ethical limitations, it was not possible to carry out a control-group study. Questionnaires were administered to all participating schools in 1994 for the pre-measurement.

Data assessment at pupil level

In the present analysis three measures described below were of particular interest, since they illustrate the central aspects of the bully/victim problem. This procedure has also been reported by Olweus (1991) and permits a comparison with surveys of other countries. The following three items in the questionnaire measured indirect victimisation, direct victimisation, and bullying:

(1) How often does it happen that other students don't want to spend recess with you and you end up being alone?
(2) How often have you been bullied in school since last Christmas?
(3) How often have you taken part in bullying of other students in school since last Christmas?

For each item there were five response options: 'no, never', 'once or twice', 'sometimes', 'about once a week', or 'several times a week'. Pupils were classified as 'indirect victims', 'direct victims', and/or 'bullies/perpetrators', if they responded to the relevant question that this had happened to them at least sometimes (up to several times a week). The following two levels of response were distinguished for analysis:

(1) *low-level* definition (sometimes up to several times a week)
(2) *high-level* definition (once a week up to several times a week)

Pupils had to refer to the specific period from last Christmas half-term until the date of investigation. This time period 'from Christmas until now' was also applied by Olweus (1991). While for Olweus this corresponded to five months, in the present investigation this corresponded to six months (with data collection in June). However, this slight difference between the periods of time should not be of great concern and should not affect the comparability of the different investigations for two reasons: first, Olweus (1993) is of the opinion that bullying is an ongoing problem, and therefore the minor differences in the time periods are of negligible importance; and second, this definition of a time period in relation to an important time-marker such as Christmas is more understandable than using a phrase like 'for the last three months' or 'for the last 12 weeks'.

Administration of pupil questionnaires

The administration of the questionnaires was carried out at the same time at each school by the class teacher. To conduct the whole procedure no more than two lessons were required. The teacher received detailed written instructions beforehand regarding the procedure of the data collection. In the first lesson teachers were asked to explain to pupils the reason for the survey. Further, they were asked to explain the meaning of bullying to pupils in an age-appropriate manner. During the second lesson pupils were asked to fill in the questionnaire. For classes in primary schools a slightly modified version of the questionnaire was adapted in order to make it easier for pupils to understand the questions. In those classes the whole questionnaire was read aloud by the teacher, including the possible answers. Before pupils were asked to fill in the questionnaire they were told that it was not obligatory to put their names on the questionnaire and that nobody would know who had filled it in. After completion, the questionnaires were placed in an envelope in front of the pupils and sealed. It was important to inform pupils about this procedure prior to filling in the paper, in order to stress the anonymity of the investigation. On the envelope the date of data collection, the name of the school and class, as well as the number of boys and girls taking part and the number of absentees were recorded.

This procedure was repeated at the same time of year (June), two years later. In order to examine the effects of the program, χ^2 – tests were carried out on numbers of pupils. The data assessment was not a repeated measurement carried out as a pre-post-measurement analysing the effects in the same pupils. In the first measurement all participating pupils from grade 3 to 12 grade were assessed. The same procedure was done in the final measurement. Therefore, pupils being in the same grades at the two data assessments are compared (e.g. 5-graders and 5-graders).

School context assessment by headteachers

To determine co-relations among the changes of the victim/bully problems and different variables, the following 13 context variables were rated by the headteachers: size of the school; size of the schoolyard; quality of the schoolyard (assessed through school marks ranging from 1 = very good to 6 = very bad); proportion of male and female teachers; proportion of male and female pupils; ethnic mix of the pupils; average size of the class; average age of teaching staff; number of inhabitants in the geographical area; and size of the catchment's area; 'engagement of the staff in the beginning and during the implementation of the project' (measured via a percentage of engagement that had to be indicated); and 'external support' (measured via yes/no). The variables were co-related to the outcome variables of the pupils' questionnaire direct and indirect victimisation, and bullying, in the schools.

Evaluation data from teachers

At the end of the programme, teachers and headteacher received a questionnaire, assessing the measures that were carried out in their schools as well as degree of co-operation with parents and the occurrence of problems. The purpose of these data was to find out about possible factors for a successful implementation or any barriers that occurred during implementation of the programme.

What actually happened; achievements and difficulties in implementing the intervention

The project was carried out between 1994 and 1996. Participating schools were provided with the German adaptation of the anti-bullying manual developed by Olweus (1993). During the implementation, three central one-day-project meetings were conducted involving all schools participating in the programme.

Preparation for the programme

Before the implementation of the programme schools were asked to carry out three central measures:
(1) A questionnaire survey assessing indirect and direct bullying: Pupils filled in the questionnaire before the start of the programme, in order to get baseline data on the extent of the bullying problem in their own school. A second assessment after the programme implementation served to evaluate changes in the bullying behaviour in school. This enabled the schools to receive a direct feedback on their activities. All participating schools conducted the first survey.
(2) Pedagogic day: The meeting served to interpret the results of the baseline data assessment and the preparation of anti-bullying-measures in the school. The pedagogic day was conducted by the school psychologist and project staff. There was only one school that did not carry out a pedagogic day on the subject of prevention of bullying.
(3) School conference day: Schools were asked to carry out a school conference after the pedagogic day, to adapt the anti-bullying-programme in their own school. This procedure served to enhance commitment of the teachers and inform pupils and parents about the programme. In Germany, school conferences are held about four times a school year. Teachers and a delegation of pupils and parents meet in order to discuss school-relevant issues, such as the adaptation

of an anti-bullying programme. In all, 23 of the schools (62.2%) carried out a school conference. The other schools informed parents and pupils about the results of the pre-test survey.

Co-ordination groups in the schools

In 19 of the schools, teachers and the headteacher formed a co-ordination group; in 10 schools teachers formed a group without the headteacher's support; and in 5 schools only the headteacher was responsible for the programme implementation. Moreover, most of the schools involved parents actively in the programme. In only 1 of the participating schools did the responsibility change during the implementation phase. From 2 of the schools no information on the organisation was available.

External support

Schools were offered the opportunity to involve external experts, such as social workers in school internal-teacher-training days. They had the possibility to contact the project team if they faced problems or if they had questions regarding the implementation of the programme; 54% of the schools used the offer of external support and advice very often, often, or sometimes. There were only 3 schools (8.1%) that did not contact external professionals during the implementation phase. The main tasks of the external professionals were to help the schools with the data analyses and interpretation of the first survey; the organisation of workshops and teachers' training; and general supervision. The teachers' training and supervision during the project phase involved courses on communication skills, conflict moderation, working with rules and sanctions, as well as how to implement concrete measures in the schools. In all, 33 single days of teacher training were carried out in different schools.

Difficulties during implementation

It was planned that the programme would be implemented for 1 year in the participating schools. During the implementation, it became very clear that schools that reported internal problems, such as low motivation or conflicts among the staff, lack of sufficient co-operation, or organisational problems, also reported difficulties with the implementation of the programme. Therefore, the 1-year timetable was only possible in 2 schools. In 5 schools the programme was carried out over a period of 1.5 years and in 30 schools over 2 years.

From the majority of the 10 schools that dropped out from the intervention study, it is known that they were not able to implement the programme properly due to lack of support from the colleagues and/or the headteacher.

Main activities during the implementation

According to the headteachers, the main activities in the schools during the programme were (in order): restructuring of the school yard; class rules against bullying; teacher training courses; communications between victims and bullies; regular classroom discussions on the subject; better supervision during recess; talks with parents of involved students; co-operative learning; common class activities; and co-operation among teachers and parents. Olweus considers the *development of class rules* against bullying as the main part of the programme. The list of activities shows that this activity was an important part of the programme in the school; however it was not the most common activity in the schools.

Results of the evaluation

Effects of the programme on bullying and victimisation at the pupil level

Table 5.2 illustrates the main results for the three variables assessing direct and indirect victimisation as well as bullying, separately for the low-level and the high-level definition of bullying, for pupils differentiated by grades. For the analyses differences in reported victimisation and bullying were calculated and tested for significance via χ^2-tests.

The results show that low levels of direct victimisation could be reduced in grades 3–10 to varying extents, significant at grades 3, 5, 6, and 7. Only the grades 11 and higher could not benefit from the programme, and, indeed, levels of direct victimisation increased at grade 12.

The results are in line with the assumption that older pupils are less likely to be bullied since in school they come upon situations less often in which they are physically weaker than their opponent. This, however, is more likely for younger students. Consequently, it seems that if younger pupils are at the same school, older pupils bully the younger ones, since the older ones are physically stronger in comparison to the younger ones.

With regard to indirect victimisation, no effect of the intervention could be shown in reducing it; at grade 4 an increase was found (it could be possible that this is a chance finding). Indirect victimisation is perhaps

Table 5.2. *Prevalence rates for indirect victimisation, direct victimisation, and bullying, by grade. Analyses by chi-square tests*

	School grade									
	3	4	5	6	7	8	9	10	11	12
Direct victim										
Low level										
Pre- (%)	29.1	25.0	27.0	25.1	22.5	19.2	15.2	11.8	9.6	6.8
Post- (%)	24.8	22.5	21.7	21.1	18.9	17.6	13.4	8.4	9.2	13.4
% change	−14.8	−10.0	−19.7	−16.0	−16.0	−8.4	−11.8	−28.8	−4.2	+97.0
p <	0.05	n.s.	0.001	0.01	0.05	n.s.	n.s.	n.s.	n.s.	0.05
High level										
Pre- (%)	14.9	10.8	13.0	11.7	9.5	7.6	5.0	3.9	2.7	1.0
Post- (%)	12.7	9.5	10.2	9.9	9.0	7.9	5.9	3.5	6.9	7.1
% change	−14.8	−12.1	−11.6	−15.4	−5.3	+3.9	+18.0	−10.3	+155.5	+710.0
p <	n.s.	n.s.	0.05	n.s.	n.s.	n.s.	n.s.	n.s.	0.05	0.001
Indirect victim										
Low level										
Pre- (%)	19.1	13.6	14.0	12.5	10.7	9.7	8.8	6.7	5.9	9.6
Post- (%)	20.4	16.9	12.6	14.7	10.7	9.1	6.5	8.4	8.3	8.9
% change	+6.8	+24.2	−10.0	+17.6	0.0	−6.2	−26.2	+25.3	+40.6	−7.3
p <	n.s.	0.05	n.s.	n.s.	n.s.	n.s.	n.s.	n.s.	n.s.	n.s.

High level										
Pre- (%)	8.9	6.7	6.8	5.0	4.6	3.6	2.8	2.7	1.7	2.4
Post- (%)	9.9	8.1	6.0	6.4	5.3	3.5	2.9	3.5	5.0	3.8
% change	+11.2	+20.8	−11.8	+28.0	+15.2	−2.8	+3.5	+29.6	+94.1	+58.3
p <	n.s.	n.s.	n.s.	n.s.	n.s.	n.s.	n.s.	n.s.	0.05	n.s.
Bullying										
Low level										
Pre- (%)	10.8	16.7	16.8	21.7	27.8	28.0	28.1	25.9	18.3	12.8
Post- (%)	11.7	13.1	13.5	18.9	22.5	29.9	26.0	24.4	23.3	25.7
% change	+8.3	−21.6	−19.7	−13.0	−19.1	+6.7	−7.5	−5.8	+27.3	+100.7
p <	n.s.	0.05	0.05	n.s.	0.001	n.s.	n.s.	n.s.	n.s.	0.001
High level										
Pre- (%)	3.7	6.3	5.9	8.8	10.9	11.6	12.4	11.0	6.9	4.9
Post- (%)	5.2	4.8	4.8	7.8	11.2	13.0	12.8	12.7	11.3	12.2
% change	+40.5	−13.9	−8.7	−12.5	+2.7	+4.8	+3.2	+15.4	+63.7	+148.9
p <	n.s.	n.s.	n.s.	n.s.	n.s.	n.s.	n.s.	n.s.	n.s.	0.01

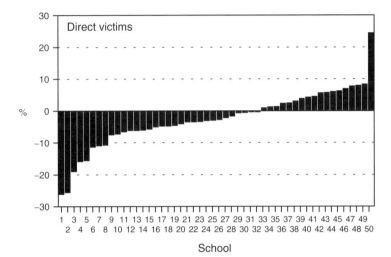

Fig. 5.1 Changes in low-level direct victimisation, for individual schools, from pre-test to post-test.

more difficult to influence, because it is not an expressive behaviour, and is not always so visible to teachers or others who might intervene.

Regarding bullying, there are significant reductions in grades 4, 5, and 7. Again, it is obvious that the older age groups especially – grades 11 and 12 – did not seem to benefit from the programme, with some increase at grade 12.

High levels of direct and indirect victimisation as well as bullying were not so significantly affected by the programme. There is a reduction in direct victimisation at grade 5, but an increase at grades 11 and 12; an increase in indirect victimisation at grade 11; and an increase in bullying at grade 12.

Effects of the programme at the school level

Figures 5.1, 5.2, and 5.3 illustrate the results of the programme as found at the different schools in the project, for low levels of direct and indirect victimisation, and bullying. Due to the co-relation of bullying and pupils' age, 13 combined schools that consisted of a primary as well as a secondary part, were analysed separately. This is sensible, since the pupils in the different school parts (primary or secondary) also have different teachers. Therefore, the analysis is not based on 37, but on 50 schools. As can be seen from fig. 5.1, there are clear differences among

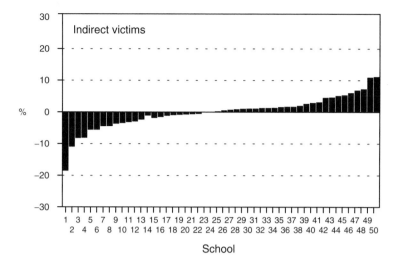

Fig. 5.2 Changes in indirect victimisation, for individual schools, from pre-test to post-test.

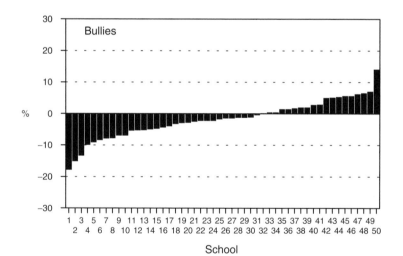

Fig. 5.3 Changes in taking part in bullying of other students, for individual schools, from pre-test to post-test.

the schools. In 18 of the schools, direct victimisation was reported to have even increased, while in 32 schools, direct victimisation decreased over time. In 8 of the schools the decrease in direct victimisation is more than 10% with regard to the total number of pupils in the schools. Regarding increases of direct victimisation in schools, only 1 school reported an increase of more than 10%. When examining the corresponding figures for indirect victimisation (fig. 5.2) and for bullying (fig. 5.3), there were also very clear differences among the different schools; however, the range of difference is smaller than that seen for direct victimisation.

Correlates of context variables and victim/bully problems

Correlations of the context variables were done over the 50 schools. There were no significant correlations ($p < 0.05$) between the changes in indirect and direct bullying and any of the context variables.

Discussion: the experiences of the schools with the Olweus programme

When reading Olweus' anti-bullying manual, one might get the impression that the suggested measures are easy to implement in schools. However, schools reported that the implementation of the programme in schools is not that easy. Schools that had problems, e.g. low motivation or conflicts in the staff, lack of sufficient co-operation, could only implement the programme partially. From our experiences, we suggest that the following prerequisites are necessary in order to enable schools to implement the programme successfully:
• the head of the school should be motivated and also able to encourage the staff;
• the staff should have a consensus about what they want to change;
• a co-ordination group should be established;
• concrete and for the whole school *visible* measures (e.g. teachers on duty during the breaks).
Teachers' workshops on communication skills, conflict moderation, working with rules and sanctions proved especially helpful for the teachers.

The effects of the programme at the pupil level

The main outcome variables were the occurrence of indirect and direct victimisation and the participation in bullying. With regard to the high levels of indirect victimisation, direct victimisation, and bullying, there are hardly any significant differences. Regarding low level of direct victimisation, in grades 3, 5, 6, and 7 significant differences could be found, while for indirect victimisation, there is only in grade 4 a significant difference that goes unexpectedly in the direction that pupils reported more indirect victimisation. With regard to low-level bullying, significant differences could be found for grades 4, 5, and 7. Some unexpected effects were found at higher grades (grades 11 and 12, especially), but the smaller sample numbers at these grades need to be borne in mind (table 5.1).

The effects of the programme at different schools

A detailed analysis at the school level showed clear differences among the schools. While the majority of schools could reduce the number of direct and indirect victims as well as bullies, in a few of the schools, there was even an increase of direct and indirect victims as well as bullies. One possible explanation could be that during the implementation of the programme, pupils developed an over-sensitive perception of bullying and over-estimated the prevalence of bullying, when they were assessed for the second time. In addition, it is known from some of the schools that a very persistent group of bullies constantly worked against the programme – with some success, as it seems.

In general, the effects go in the same direction as the results from the evaluation study Olweus carried out in Bergen, at least so far as younger pupils are concerned, but was much less successful. In the Olweus study, the prevalence of indirect as well as direct bullying could be reduced to a much larger scale than in the German study. In none of the grades was there any significant reduction in high-level bulling. In fact in 4 out of 7 years there was a percentage increase. One reason for the overall more positive results in Bergen could be the age of the pupils: in Olweus' study, the pupils were 11–14 years old, while in the German study, the children were aged 9–18. In both of the studies, the effects were most visible in younger grades.

This study has some methodological limitations. The sample is not representative of all schools, since the participating schools were not drawn randomly from the pool of all schools in the Land Schleswig-Holstein, Germany, but consisted of schools that had applied for participation in the project for the prevention of violence and aggression in schools. This is important with regard to the generalisation of the reported results to the whole population of pupils. Since in this investigation one can find a self-selected process that can be interpreted differently, one interpretation could be that schools with a pronounced bullying problem particularly chose to participate in the project and are therefore highly motivated in preventing those problems. Hence, one might surmise, a representative sample would show less improvement.

With regard to the validity of the pupil's self-reports, it should be reiterated that all participating pupils were reassured the investigation would be anonymous, in order to encourage truthful responses. For example, the administration of the questionnaires was carried out without asking any personal data of the pupils. Moreover, the teachers did not have the opportunity to view pupils' answers on the questionnaires; therefore in the self-assessment of pupils it is not assumed that they had response tendencies. With regard to the internal validity of the programme, it has to be pointed out that schools had great flexibility in carrying out the intervention. Therefore, the implementation of the programme in the schools varied, which makes it difficult to say to which elements the success or failure of the programme can be put down to.

Overall, the results indicate that the programme might be a suitable measure to prevent school-based bullying, especially when taking into account that not all participating schools placed the main emphasis on the core elements of the programme, the creation of rules against bullying in class, but concentrated mainly on elements of secondary interest, such as the restructuring of the school yard (e.g. planting trees).

Longer term effects or evaluation of the programme

In Germany the book written by Olweus is very successful and the third edition has already been published. Despite the wide interest in the study and the need for suitable measures for anti-bullying programmes in Germany, the project has not had any impact on school-related anti-bullying politics and even in Schleswig-Holstein the Ministry of Education did not carry on with the programme.

Dissemination and impact beyond the programme schools

The implementation of the programme received a high level of interest from the media, and a number of newspapers reported regularly on the results of the project. In fact, even nowadays, we receive requests across Germany from journalists when cases of bullying in schools are reported in the media. There is still a great demand for the questionnaire that was used in the programme. Even though this study was carried out eight years ago, it remains the study with the highest participation rate in Germany; some smaller studies were conducted, e.g. in Bremen, only applying the questionnaire, but not implementing the programme (Jugert, Scheithauer, Notz, and Petermann, 2000).

Despite awareness of the fact that German schools need suitable measures to deal with bullying in schools, the programme had neither local nor national impact; it did not influence national policy on anti-bullying measures. The programme has been adapted by single schools that decided to deal with bullying problems, however from our experience the feeling of not receiving help from politicians is frustrating and demotivating for schools and leaves them with the feeling of being a 'lonely fighter'. The consequence is that schools try out various single measures that have not been evaluated and which they get offered from institutions, such as at in-service courses given by institutes for teachers. What they need is a programme which is based on theory and evaluated, as well as explicit support from policy-makers, in order to convince parents and colleagues at school to co-operate and so as to integrate useful and effective prevention measures in their own school systems.

Acknowledgements

This research was supported by the Ministry of Education of the Land Schleswig-Holstein, Germany. I thank Reimer Knaack for his support with the data collection and implementation of the programme, and Gudrun Wiborg for her excellent support in various aspects.

References

Holtappels, H. G. (1987). Schülerprobleme und abweichendes Schülerverhalten aus der Schülerperspektive. *Zeitschrift für Sozialforschung*, 5, 291–323.

Jugert, G., Scheithauer, H., Notz, P., and Petermann, F. (2000). Geschlechtsunterschiede im Bullying: Indirekt-/relational- und offen-aggressives Verhalten unter Jugendlichen. *Kindheit und Entwicklung*, 9, 231–40.

Niebel, G., Hanewinkel, R. and Ferstl, R. (1993). Gewalt und Aggression in schleswig-holsteinischen Schulen. *Zeitschrift für Pädagogik*, 39, 775–98.

Olweus, D. (1991). Bully/victim problems among schoolchildren: Basic facts and effects of a school-based intervention program. In D. J. Pepler, and K. H. Rubin (eds.), *The development and treatment of childhood aggression*. Hillsdale, NJ: Erlbaum, pp. 411–48.

(1993). *Bullying at school: What we know and what we can do*. Oxford: Blackwell.

Smith, P. K., Morita, Y., Junger-Tas, J., Olweus, D., Catalano, R., and Slee, P. (1999). *The nature of school bullying: A cross-national perspective*. London: Routledge.

Tillmann, K. J. (1994). Gewalt in der Schule: Was sagt die erziehungswissenschaftliche Forschung dazu? *Recht der Jugend und des Bildungswesens*, 42, 163–74.

Todt, E. and Busch, L. (1994). Aggression und Gewalt an Schulen. *Recht der Jugend und des Bildungswesens*, 42, 174–86.

6   England: the Sheffield project

Peter K. Smith, Sonia Sharp, Mike Eslea, and David Thompson

Impetus for the intervention, early stages of planning, and funding

During 1989–90 school bullying started to become a topic of media attention and focused public concern in the UK. News was filtering through of the success of the Bergen evaluation in Norway. Several books on bullying appeared. The human rights issues involved in school bullying began to get a sympathetic hearing. The Gulbenkian Foundation (UK) started a 10-year period of making the topic of school bullying a priority area for funding and supported many important initiatives.

One project supported by Gulbenkian funds was the development of a 'survey service' for schools, at the University of Sheffield (Ahmad, Whitney, and Smith, 1991). This was based on a form of the Olweus questionnaire, modified for use in English schools. We piloted this questionnaire in several schools (Boulton and Underwood, 1992; Yates and Smith, 1989) and then carried out a survey of 24 schools in the Sheffield area, to give the first figures, based on a large-scale survey, of the extent of school bullying in English schools (Whitney and Smith, 1993).

At this time the Department for Education (DFE, as it then was: now, DfES or Department for Education and Skills) was not taking specific action on bullying. It had not been regarded as a major issue. The 1989 Elton Report on Discipline had raised it as one issue for schools to be concerned with, but the DFE had not acted specifically on this section of the report. However, one of our early studies, a survey in two secondary schools, attracted unusual publicity. Our findings (Yates and Smith, 1989) suggested that rates of being bullied were considerable; in these two schools they were about twice the rate reported in Norway (Olweus, 1991). A press release (for the book in which this study was to be a chapter) pointed this out, and asked 'Is Britain the bullying capital of Europe?' This was picked up by the media, and the phrase 'Britain is the bullying capital of Europe' appeared in newspapers and on television programmes! The statement was totally unjustified based on the very

99

limited evidence at that time, but it was helpful in the sense of rousing public opinion. Questions were asked in Parliament, and the DFE was responsive to suggestions for an intervention campaign to tackle bullying. This led to the 'Sheffield Project' – the first and still the most substantive, monitored, intervention project in the UK (Smith and Sharp, 1994). The project approved for funding was to take the 1990 survey as a pre-test of levels of bullying, carry out interventions in these schools, do a post-test, evaluate the success of interventions, and produce a pack for schools as a result of the lessons learned.

Selection of schools

The 24 schools that had taken part in the 1990 survey were contacted early in 1991 with details of the project and an invitation to take part further. Only 1 primary school from this original survey did not wish to continue with interventions. This left 7 secondary schools and 16 primary schools taking part; they agreed to implement interventions, allow them to be monitored by the research team, and take a post-test survey after four terms (two years after the initial survey).

The one school that declined to take part was willing to act as a 'control school', just taking the second 'post-test' survey. In fact, the idea of a pure 'control' school is difficult, if not impossible, in this domain. Schools not in the project were still affected by what was happening nationally (for example, they would have received a national circulation of anti-bullying materials in 1993) and might have taken various actions against bullying. Indeed, even the fact of having participated in a first survey and received a portfolio describing the findings in their school, was itself likely to produce some action. Nevertheless, it seemed desirable to have a few comparison schools that were not in the project. Besides the 1 junior school, we were able to use results from 3 'comparison' secondary schools which had taken part in the earlier surveys and which were willing to be surveyed again two years later.

Characteristics of schools and students

All the schools were publicly funded. While the majority of pupils were White, all schools had some ethnic minority pupils, sometimes very sizeable minorities, mainly Asian (Indian, Pakistani, Bangladeshi) and African-Caribbean in origin. Brief details of all project and comparison schools are given in table 6.1. A total of 7,043 pupils took part in the surveys in the project schools (2,389 primary, 4,654 secondary); together with 1,841 taking part in the comparison school surveys, a total of 8,884

Table 6.1. *Details of schools in the project (P = primary, S = secondary), and comparison (COM) schools*

School	Pupils in school	Pupils in surveys	WS	CV	CD	CL	CQ	AT	PM	PC	PT	PE
P1	240	192	X								X	X
P2	420	178	X	own interventions								
P3	230	86	X	X							X	X
P4	581	235	X	X	X						X	
P5	150	100	X								X	
P6	420	162	X	X							X	
P7	394	142	X		X			X			X	X
P8	240	53	X				X					X
P9	230	166	X	X	X			X			X	
P10	350	146	X	X	X	X		X			X	
P11	304	159	X	X		X	X				X	
P12	406	212	X			X	X	X			X	
P13	174	64	X									X
P14	430	276	X	X	X						X	
P15	255	107	X								X	X
P16	316	111	X					X			X	
S1	400	250	X	X						X		
S2	483	287	X								X	
S3	1,447	953	X	X	X			X	X		X	
S4	1,000	794	X	X	X			X		X		
S5	781	611	X	X	X				X		X	
S6	1,000	839	X						X			
S7	1,118	920	X	X	X							
COM P1	198	99	(X)									
COM S1	729	333	(X)									
COM S2	1,179	623	(X)									
COM S3	1,000	786	(X)									

WS = whole school policy; CV = video; CD = drama; CL = literature; CQ = quality circles; AT = assertiveness training; PM = Pikas method; PC = peer counselling; PT = playground supervisor training; PE = playground environment

pupils provided data for analysis. Ages of pupils ranged from 8 to 16 years. All schools were in the Sheffield area, except for the comparison secondary schools (1 in Yorkshire, 2 in the London area).

Components of the intervention programme

An orientation day in February 1991 launched the project. An overview of the project aims and the interventions available was provided. School representatives were provided with details of support available for the interventions, in the summer term, via staff training days, in-service training days, and provision of resource materials. This orientation day was the first of a series of termly meetings, which provided a forum for schools to share ideas with each other.

All schools participating were asked to agree to a Core Intervention comprising a basic 'whole school policy' on bullying. Previous work, including that by Foster, Arora, and Thompson (1990); and Thompson and Arora (1991), indicated that having a whole school policy was likely to be an essential framework within which other interventions could operate successfully and maintain continuity. In addition, some Optional Interventions would be supported by project resources. We selected interventions that were available at the time, targeted to bullying, and suitable in a UK context. These fell into three categories: curriculum-based strategies; direct work with pupils; and making changes to playgrounds and lunch breaks.

Whole school policy development (all 23 project schools)

At the time of the onset of the project (1991), hardly any schools had policies on bullying, although a few had policies on broader issues of discipline or positive behaviour. Both the DFE and the project team saw the development of an anti-bullying policy (either on its own, or at least explicitly mentioned within a broader policy) as essential as a guiding framework for action in the school. The project produced a leaflet outlining major stages in policy development: awareness raising about the issue; consultation through the school; developing the policy content; disseminating the policy widely; implementation of the policy; and evaluation of the effectiveness of the policy.

Curriculum-based strategies (15 schools)

These were materials and activities that could be used within the curriculum, to raise awareness of bullying, enhance awareness of the feeling of victims, and encourage pupils to feel able to talk about bullying and what should be done about it.

Video: 'Sticks and Stones' (5 schools)   This videofilm from Central Television featured interviews with pupils, simulated examples of bullying, and clips from the operation of a bully court. We prepared a package to accompany the video, containing ideas for discussion, drama, and creative writing activities for teachers to use. For schools particularly concerned with racial harassment another video available was 'White

Lies'. It covered many racist issues and was intended to stimulate discussion amongst young White people. Both videos were used only at secondary level.

Drama: 'Only Playing, Miss' by Neti Neti Theatre Company (11 schools) This play about bullying was available on video. The theatre company ran a half-day workshop to explore how drama techniques could be harnessed to develop anti-bullying work with pupils. This intervention was supplemented in the spring term by a visit from the Armadillo Theatre Company, who ran a workshop and worked with secondary- and primary- age pupils in some project schools.

Literature: 'The Heartstone Odyssey' (4 schools) This is a story for primary pupils that tackles issues of racial harassment and bullying. A training day helped teachers to develop ways of using the materials through 'story circles', dance, and mime.

Quality Circles (4 schools) The concept of the Quality Circle comes from industry but has been adapted for use in education (Cowie and Sharp, 1992). A group of pupils meets together regularly to identify common problems, evolve solutions, and present these solutions to the class teacher or senior management team. The participants are introduced to useful skills and strategies for problem solving and effecting change: skills for generating ideas, observation and data collection, developing strategies or solutions, and communication both within the circle and when presenting to management.

Direct work with pupils (12 schools)

The aim of these approaches is to work directly with pupils involved in bully/victim problems.

Assertiveness training for victims (7 schools) These techniques encourage the pupils to interact with others in an assertive rather than aggressive or submissive way. They also encourage the development of conflict resolution skills, ways of improving self esteem and enhancing social skills in joining in games and making friends. The training sessions for teachers covered basic assertiveness techniques that might be helpful in coping with or preventing bullying, as well as guidelines on how to run groups for children.

Working directly with bullies (5 schools) Anatol Pikas, a Swedish psychologist, trained project members and teachers in his method of working directly with bullies, 'The Method of Shared Concern'. This employs a carefully structured script to guide discussion with each pupil involved in a bullying incident (Pikas, 1989). It aims to stop the bullying behaviour and encourage tolerance.

School tribunals or 'Bully courts' (0 schools)   This approach was, at the time, advocated by Kidscape as part of a whole school approach to bullying (Elliott, 1991). Pupils are elected to sit on a 'court' with one or more members of staff. When an incident of bullying is reported the 'court' listens to all parties concerned and then makes a decision as to what action should be taken in response to the incident. Although 2 schools in the project showed initial interest in this intervention, no school actually set up a bully court.

Peer counselling (2 schools)   In 2 schools, pupils established a 'listening line' for other pupils. This involved pupils from across the age range undertaking some training in basic counselling skills. The pupils worked in small teams, comprising 2 or 3 'counsellors' and 1 'receptionist'. Each team was on duty one lunchtime per week and the pupils also attended their own support and supervision meeting on another lunchtime. The supervision was provided by a specific member of staff and there was also always a teacher 'on call' for the duty team each day. The pupils did not intervene in bullying situations themselves – they were purely a listening service; if appropriate they might suggest going to talk to a teacher.

Making changes to playgrounds and lunch breaks (18 schools)

The aim here was to improve the quality of children's break time and playtime experiences, bearing in mind the large proportion of bullying which had been found to occur in playgrounds.

Working with lunchtime supervisors (16 schools)   Schools were offered a range of activities, including: raising the status of lunchtime supervisors; training lunchtime supervisors; encouraging positive behaviour in the playground; improving the quality of play; building relationships between supervisors and pupils; building relationships between supervisors and teachers; responding to aggressive behaviour in the playground; and improving provision for wet playtimes. Within each activity domain, there were a number of practical strategies that schools chose to implement.

Redesigning the playground environment (6 schools)   For schools with uninteresting outside areas, a radical possibility was to redesign and improve the playground environment. An all-day session on the playground environment was led for interested schools, in collaboration with colleagues from the Department of Landscape Architecture. This work was extended by means of a grant from the Calouste Gulbenkian Foundation to support work on playground design.

Evaluation framework and procedures

Standardising interventions

From a research perspective, we wished to be able to identify the mechanisms for change within the school. However, there was no way that the team could control events to produce standard interventions in all the schools. All schools were coping with staff changes, the impact of resource reduction from current educational funding policies, varying school numbers, school mergers, meeting the national curriculum demands, and the demands of the new assessment procedures. They had differing mixes of pupils, both in terms of ethnic origins, mother-tongue languages, and social class.

Our solution to the problem was to provide a common framework for the interventions, in terms of training procedures and materials. All schools began with a common baseline upon which they imposed their own interpretation and adapted the intervention to fit the needs of their own institution. From the adaptations made by schools, we were able to understand possible flaws in the interventions themselves and how they could be overcome.

A key principle was that the outcomes should be replicable by other schools throughout the country. Other schools would not have access to an energetic research team, keen to see the project succeed. A decision was taken that support by the project team would be minimal, and would be based upon requests from the schools and at a level that might easily be replicated by a Local Education Authority (LEA). The project team could offer training, information, and advice, but would only do so if asked. In this way, the project was similar to the usual support services available to schools, such as educational psychology services and behaviour support services.

Monitoring the actual process of change

Quantitative and qualitative data were collected via staff and pupil interviews as well as a parent questionnaire, all of which helped to explain why and how any change occurred. Each half term, the project co-ordinator in each school was interviewed to track developments. Each of the interventions had its own monitoring procedures. These involved a set of specifically designed pupil questionnaires and/or interviews intended to identify whether or not the interventions were perceived to be appropriate; whether or not they led to any perceived change in behaviour and/or attitude (both personally and in peers). Staff were also interviewed to discover how they felt about the intervention; how they had implemented the intervention; and whether or not they felt any change in pupil behaviour or attitude had resulted from its implementation.

In 18 of the schools, pupils in certain year groups were involved in monitoring for 5 consecutive days in each half term. During these periods, each pupil in the class completed a short questionnaire on return from lunchtime that asked 'Have these things happened to you today?' followed by a list of 8 bullying behaviours (answers being on 3-point scales). These helped to identify changes over time in rates of bullying, seasonal variations in bullying behaviour, and which children in particular were being persistently bullied.

The major source of outcome effectiveness was the second survey of levels of bullying in all the project schools. This survey took place in November–December 1992, exactly two years after the first survey. For 3 comparison secondary schools (see table 6.1), the surveys were done in March 1990/92 in COM S1; in May 1990/92 in COM S2, and in March 1991/93 in COM S3. Thus, in all cases time-of-year effects were constant between the two surveys. Results for particular schools could be compared before, and after, the monitored interventions.

The comparisons we planned were for whole schools, comparing children of equivalent ages at two time points, as in the Bergen study analyses (Olweus, 1991). These comparisons were often complicated by organisational changes. In addition, some amalgamations and catchment area changes in several schools resulted in changes in the number of classes in a year group. To ensure comparability, it was necessary to have equivalent numbers of classes and, hence, approximately, pupils in each year group, at the two survey points. In order to achieve this, certain class and year groups who did the survey were omitted from our calculations; the actual pupil numbers contributing to the data analyses are shown in table 6.1.

The questionnaires were administered as they had been for the first survey. Teachers other than the pupils' usual teacher supervised the completion of questionnaires. Confidentiality was stressed. The questionnaires included two extra questions asking whether pupils thought the school had done much to try and stop bullying over the last year or so, and whether they thought that bullying in the school had generally got better or worse over the last year or so.

What actually happened; achievements and difficulties in implementing the intervention

Sheffield schools had undergone a major review during 1991–92, with the abolition of the middle-school system. The financial situation within the LEA also led to rationalisation in most schools and many lost staff in the spring or summer term, 1992. This reduction had an effect on staff morale. Within the project, 3 middle schools changed to being junior schools, with year 7s (11-year-olds) transferring to secondary school a year earlier than previously; and 3 junior schools were amalgamated with adjacent infant schools. Five project schools had a change of headteacher during the process of the project, and in four of these, the headteacher had been the original motivating force for involvement in the project. Fortunately, the new headteachers were generally supportive of the project continuing, although this meant a shift in priorities and a reduction in momentum within the schools. Despite professional uncertainty about the future, most schools still made the bullying project a priority. These changes did, however, delay the progress of the project.

The format of providing support to schools only when requested was helpful and clear for both schools and the project team most of the time. Problems arose when there was a communication difficulty within the school, such as following a change in project co-ordinator, and this information was not passed on directly, or when one person in the school knew that support was available but had not informed other colleagues. For the project team, it was hard to resist more overt direction in inactive schools or schools which were introducing approaches which were at odds with the philosophy of the project. In fact, some more direct action was taken by the project team on whole-school policy development after the first year.

Results of the evaluation

In looking at the changes in the schools over the two-year period, we examined three main aspects of our data.
(1) What had the schools done? We devised a number of measures of each school's 'INPUT' into the project, in terms of time and effort invested in anti-bullying interventions.
(2) What had the schools achieved? We similarly devised a number of measures of each school's 'OUTPUT', in terms of improvements or not in indicators of bullying.

(3) Why had schools varied? Here we looked at relations between input and output measures, that is whether schools which did more achieved more; and at differences between primary and secondary schools, as well as particular factors affecting individual schools.

What had the schools done?

'*Whole-school policy*' *development*: A grading system was devised that recorded whether schools had achieved particular aspects of the development process, and the degree of effort invested. Each school could score up to 65 marks for the development process, plus an additional 8 marks for the amount of time the policy had been completed (2 points per term). Inter-marker reliability was established at 0.78. All 27 schools could be scored as having made some steps towards producing a whole-school policy over the two years – including the 4 comparison schools, which had been affected by national initiatives during the period. Details of the total policy scores for each school are given in table 6.2.

Staff involvement: As part of the evaluation of whole-school policy development, interviews with teaching staff were carried out in each school. In primary schools, these interviews took place with two-thirds of staff, randomly selected; in secondary schools, with one-third of teachers. Teachers were asked to describe exactly how they had been involved in the process of policy development. This information was coded on a 4-point scale. Scores were summed and divided by the number of people interviewed in that school to derive a 'staff involvement' score for each school. This measure correlated only weakly (not significantly) with the total policy score: 0.32 for primary schools; and 0.27 for secondary schools. It was therefore analysed separately; scores are given in table 6.2.

Scoring of optional interventions: These were grouped under three general headings; *curriculum*, *direct work with pupils*, and *playground*. *Curriculum* reflected work done in the classroom through videos, drama, literature, and quality circles. *Direct work with pupils* included assertiveness training, the Pikas Method of Shared Concern, and peer counselling. Schools received a score for *playground* interventions if lunchtime supervisors had participated in training sessions or if they had taken some action to enhance the environment of the schoolyard. Based on our records and interviews, schools were graded on a 5-point scale according to the amount of effort they put into the implementation of each of these broad fields of intervention, during each of the 4 intervention terms. Inter-rater reliability averaged 0.67. The Options total is the sum of these, ranging from 1 to 31 (and 0 in the Comparison schools); scores are given in table 6.2. (Comparison schools had not used these optional interventions and were assigned a score of 0).

Total input scores Scores for the Policy total and Options total correlated highly (0.78 for primary schools; 0.67 for secondary schools). Thus, we added them to make a TOTAL INPUT measure, see table 6.2.

What had the schools achieved?

Using the comparable, age-equivalent samples from the first and second surveys, we selected certain items or composite measures which could be taken as indicators of success in tackling bullying:

Being bullied
- *the likelihood of being bullied* oneself during the term; we combined *all* the responses 'I haven't been bullied at school this term' in the questionnaire (7 items; 2-point scale on each) and calculated the mean number of responses as a percentage.
- *the frequency of being bullied* oneself during the term (1 item, 5-point scale)
- *the number of children* in the class who had been bullied (1 item, 7-point scale).

Bullying others
- *the likelihood of bullying others* during the term; we combined *all* the responses 'I haven't taken part in bullying others at school this term' in the questionnaire (3 items, 2-point scale on each) and calculated the mean number of responses as a percentage
- *the frequency of bullying others* oneself during the term (1 item, 5-point scale)
- *the number of children* in the class who had bullied others (1 item, 7-point scale).

Breaktime experiences
- frequency of being alone at playtime (1 item, 5-point scale)

Bystander behaviour
- how likely were they to not join in bullying others (1 item, 5-point scale)

Perceived role of adults
- how often teachers were seen as stopping bullying (1 item, 5-point scale)
- how likely a bullied child was to tell anyone; teacher or someone at home (2 items, 2-point scale on each)
- how likely a bullied child was to tell a teacher (1 item, 2-point scale)

Table 6.2. *Scores for each school on main Input variables, and percentage change scores on and Output variables (mean scores for Perceived action and Perceived change)*

School	Staff involvement	Policy total	Options total	Input total	Been bullied	Bullied others	Not join in	Tell teacher	Perceived action	Perceived change
P1	2.125	24	7	31	-15.4	-13.2	6.7	49.7	0.54	0.50
P2	3.750	15	1	16	-15.0	-15.1	-5.3	4.9	0.76	0.17
P3	2.600	50	23	73	-36.0	-63.5	18.9	15.3	1.73	1.18
P4	3.100	34	13	47	-12.0	-8.1	12.9	8.4	1.03	0.49
P5	3.000	16	5	21	-54.2	-43.8	5.3	-13.3	1.21	0.85
P6	2.500	24	13	37	-17.9	-41.8	13.8	-5.1	1.16	0.91
P7	2.080	22	22	44	17.0	16.0	-10.8	-2.0	1.01	0.47
P8	2.870	22	6	28	-24.7	-5.6	-6.6	-11.6	1.21	0.88
P9	3.076	41	22	63	-23.2	30.8	-4.9	10.5	0.90	0.73
P10	2.330	43	16	59	-1.0	22.5	-4.2	54.8	1.40	0.97
P11	3.077	61	30	91	-8.4	12.2	-10.6	-16.5	1.45	1.04
P12	2.000	18	14	32	2.8	-20.7	9.9	65.5	1.10	0.63
P13	3.500	32	4	36	-29.4	-37.2	14.9	0.3	1.16	0.44
P14	1.500	26	15	41	19.0	31.0	-6.7	-18.9	1.04	0.41
P15	2.580	38	22	60	-13.5	-32.7	18.1	-23.4	1.47	0.94
P16	2.800	36	13	49	-14.9	-17.2	-3.3	-15.0	1.59	0.84
S1	1.500	21	9	30	-7.8	12.8	-1.3	-6.3	1.02	1.82
S2	0	50	10	60	11.1	-21.2	22.0	13.9	1.12	0.85
S3	1.909	40	31	71	-7.7	-10.0	0.6	25.9	0.58	0.53
S4	2.660	57	22	79	4.4	-2.6	7.2	79.1	1.13	0.81
S5	3.125	42	22	64	-20.5	-7.4	0	60.8	1.39	0.85
S6	2.710	14	6	20	-22.7	-37.2	20.8	31.4	0.62	0.63
S7	1.100	23	6	29	-4.4	-16.7	13.9	22.5	0.89	0.64
COM P1	0	14	0	14	11.5	44.8	-13.3	11.8	0.96	0.38
COM S1	0	26	0	26	-13.4	-38.0	8.2	29.9	0.03	-0.09
COM S2	0	10	0	10	13.7	10.4	-10.8	-1.6	0.31	0.24
COM S3	0	30	0	30	-19.6	-21.2	1.8	-1.4	1.00	0.92

P = Primary; S = Secondary; COM = Comparison

- what proportion of children who had taken part in bullying others, had been talked to by a teacher about it (1 item, 2-point scale).

Perceived action and change
- whether the school had done much to try and stop bullying (1 item, 5-point scale)
- whether bullying in school had generally got better or worse (1 item, 5-point scale)

Differences between the first and second surveys, for the output indicators We calculated change scores for the above variables, comparing first and second surveys. For the first 12 of these output measures, we calculated percentage change over baseline. The last two measures had no prior baseline, so we report the mean scores at the second survey, which ranged from -2 to $+2$. Table 6.2 shows scores on these indicators, for each school.

Table 6.3 shows mean raw scores on the same variables, at T1 (first survey) and T2 (second survey), for our project sample ($N = 23$); and the t-value and probability level for the percentage difference scores between T1 and T2 on one-sample t-tests. These significance tests take schools as a unit. A lack of significance on some of these measures implies that the schools generally did not improve on this measure; it might still be the case that some individual schools showed appreciable improvement, but we did not attempt calculations of significance of change for individual schools.

Being bullied. Project schools showed a significant increase in pupils who had not been bullied, and a significant decrease in the frequency with which pupils were bullied. This change is appreciable in the project primary schools, averaging around 15%, and ranging up to 80%. In the secondary schools, however, there was not much change; although 5 of the 7 project secondary schools showed an increase in pupils who had not been bullied, the average becomes a decrease due to a large decrease in one school, S2. There was no significant change in the number of classmates who were reported to be bullied.

Bullying others. Most schools showed positive changes on all three indicators – an increase in pupils who had not bullied others; and a decrease in the frequency of bullying others and in the number of classmates thought to bully others. Only the result for frequency of bullying others was significant across schools, however; here, the change averaged about 12% for both primary and secondary schools.

Breaktime experiences. Surprisingly, in most schools (especially primary) more pupils reported spending breaktime alone at the second survey.

Table 6.3. *Change in mean raw scores in Output variables, from Time 1 to Time 2*

Output measure	Time 1	Time 2	Significance (t, p)
Haven't been bullied	50.6	53.9	2.12*
Frequency been bullied	0.9	0.7	3.40**
Number bullied	3.9	3.8	0.02 ns
Haven't bullied others	65.9	68.3	1.65 ns
Frequency bullied others	0.5	0.4	2.26*
Number bullied others	3.5	3.4	1.09 ns
Alone at breaktime	3.1	3.2	2.76*
Not join in bullying	1.9	2.0	2.20*
Teacher stops bullying	1.5	1.5	0.12 ns
Telling someone	69.3	72.3	1.84(*)
Telling teachers	47.0	50.5	2.32*
Someone talked to you	32.8	35.4	2.22*
School action	Assumed zero	1.1	17.06***
School change	Assumed zero	0.8	11.04***

(*) = .10; * = .05; ** = .01; *** = .001

(This may reflect the experiences of re-organisation that many schools went through.)

Bystander behaviour. Project schools showed a significant increase in pupils reporting that they wouldn't join in bullying others at the second survey. This was more marked in secondary schools, where the increase averaged 9%.

Perceived role of adults. There were no significant changes in perceptions of teachers stopping bullying. However, project schools showed increases in pupils telling someone, and especially teachers, if they were being bullied, and in reporting that someone had talked to them if they had bullied anyone. These increases were modest in primary schools, but very substantial, around 30%, in secondary schools.

Perceived action and change. All the mean scores for each school were positive (above midpoint). In the project schools, the Action scores ranged from 0.54 to 1.59, and the Change scores from 0.17 to 1.82. In all but 2 schools, however, Change scores were lower than Action scores.

Why had schools varied?

Project schools and comparison schools: We only had one primary comparison school, COM P1. It had done less whole-school policy work than any project school (table 6.2). It had relatively low perceived Action, and the lowest perceived Change score, from pupils. It also had the worst or near-worst scores on all the change measures of being bullied, and bullying others (table 6.2). On these main measures, it appeared to have done less than most project schools, was perceived to have done less by pupils, and had considerably less impact on bullying; in fact, bullying had generally got worse in this school (though there was an increase in the likelihood of bullied pupils telling someone, or bullied pupils being spoken to). In general, this pattern of findings supports the implication that the results in the project schools are due to the interventions.

In the secondary schools the picture was more complicated. Two schools, COM S1 and COM S3, had done some work on whole-school policy, within the range of project schools (table 6.2). COM S3 had high scores on Action and Change too, though COM S1 had very low values. These schools had as good or better results as project schools on indicators of being bullied and bullying others, and in addition COM S1 showed many more bullied pupils telling teachers, while COM S3 had many more bullying pupils being talked to. In most respects, these schools were like project schools in terms of Input and Output. School COM S2 was more like a traditional control school, with the least work on whole-school policy (table 6.2), and low Action and Change scores. It also had among the worst results on the indicators for being bullied and bullying others. As with the results for school COM P1, this supports the general finding relating intervention to positive outcomes.

Relationships between input and output measures: To what extent does the amount of effort put in by a school (Input) predict results obtained (Output)? We calculated a correlation matrix between Input and Output measures. To limit the number of correlations, we used for Input measures: (1) Input Total (the sum of Whole-school policy total plus Option total), (2) Staff involvement, and (3) Perceived action. We used as Output measures: (1) Been bullied, (2) Bullied others, (3) Not joining in (bullying), (4) Tell teacher (if you are bullied), and (5) Perceived change.

There were four significant correlations (those above $r = 0.48$) for the primary schools. The Input Total, and the Perceived Action, correlated to Perceived change (0.64, $p < .01$ and 0.79, $p < .001$, respectively). Schools which did more as judged by our ratings, or by pupil ratings, were thought by pupils to show more improvement in bullying generally. These inputs did not predict to the other Output measures. However the Input measure of Staff involvement did correlate significantly with the Output measures of changes in Been bullied (0.62, $p < .01$) and Bullied others (0.61, $p < .01$).

There were three significant correlations (those above r = 0.63) for the secondary schools. Both the Staff involvement measure and the Input total related to increases in pupils Telling teacher (0.70, p < .05 and 0.82, p < .01 respectively). Perceived action by pupils predicted to Perceived change by pupils (0.72, p < .05). None of the Input measures predicted significantly to the Output measures of Been bullied, Bullied others, and Not join in.

Interim monitoring

Analysis of results from playground monitoring – short questionnaires given daily for a week, each half-term, to certain year groups – provided another source of information on change. The results for the 10 days in each term were accumulated, to give composite scores over each of the four terms. Analyses of variance examined changes over time for each type of bullying. There were appreciable reductions in all types of bullying, averaging 46% between the first monitoring period in November 1991 and the final period in November 1992. Reductions were statistically significant for 4 of the 8 types of bullying assessed: direct physical violence (p < .01); threats or extortion (p < .001); being teased repeatedly (p < .0014); and having nasty rumours spread (p < .011). For all forms of bullying, the biggest reductions occurred between the latter part of the spring term and the first half of the summer term, coinciding with the most active period in whole school policy development and intervention work in the schools.

Summary

The results strongly suggest that the interventions had a positive impact, though the nature of the impact varied between primary and secondary schools. In general, schools improved on most measures of bullying – relating to reports of being bullied, bullying others, not joining in, telling someone if you were bullied, having someone talk to you if you bullied others. However, the main impact on the likelihood and frequency of being bullied was in primary schools, with some schools getting quite substantial reductions. These effects were smaller in secondary schools, which did, however, register substantial increases in the proportion of bullied pupils who would seek help, for example by telling a teacher.

Were these changes due to the interventions? The changes were better in the project schools than in comparison schools, which did not do much work on bullying (we count schools COM S1 and COM S3 as being more like project schools, in that they did quite a lot of work on bullying policies after they had received their first survey results). This suggests that the improvements in project schools are not just due to historical effects – indeed, if anything, COM P1 and COM S2 showed the problem getting worse in schools that were doing little about the problem. However, having only two comparison schools of this type obviously limits this conclusion.

The correlational analyses showed some significant Input–Output relationships; that is, those schools which made more effort with interventions achieved more reductions in bullying. School Input total (based on teacher reports and our own records) correlated significantly with Perceived action (the pupils' perception of how much the school had done); correlations were 0.53 (p < .05) in primary schools, and 0.63 (p < .05) in secondary schools. These are quite independent sources of information, and their agreement supports the validity of both measures.

In primary schools, *both* these Input measures also predict the amount of change generally perceived by pupils (Perceived change); while in secondary schools, the Input total measure predicts strongly to increases in bullied pupils telling teachers (Tell teacher), which is where the main improvements in secondary schools are found.

As compared to the *general* measure of school bullying assessed by Perceived change, the measures Been bullied and Bullied others are indicators of *personal* experiences of bullying, and of perceptions of bullying in one's class. These do not correlate significantly with the Input measures, with the exception of Staff involvement in primary schools. That the other correlations are not significant is surprising, but there is one plausible explanation: that schools which have taken a lot of action against bullying may have brought about heightened awareness of what bullying is among their pupils, and led more pupils to recognise that they were experiencing some form of bullying which they might previously have discounted.

The suggestion that some of these survey results under-estimate actual change would also be consistent with the finding that our other assessments produced generally larger indications of change. This is true of our interim monitoring in the playground; this had its own problems, being longitudinal, and thus liable to be confounded by age. However, after allowing for an average reduction of 15% for age effects over this time period (based on Whitney and Smith, 1993), this still leaves an estimated 'real' reduction of 31%, appreciably larger than the survey average of around 15%.

In summary, there is considerable evidence of success in the actions of schools against bullying, though this varies greatly between schools and takes a somewhat different form in primary and secondary schools.

If primary schools put effort into policy development and anti-bullying work, this will be perceived by pupils. Pupils will soon perceive a change in general bullying, and self-report levels will fall, especially when all staff are involved in the work. In secondary schools, staff involvement and general effort will first have an impact on the willingness of bullied pupils to seek help from a teacher. Also, school action will be noticed by pupils, and they will consider that general levels of bullying are falling.

Longer term effects or evaluation of the programme

The development of school anti-bullying policies often took a long time: up to two years in schools that maximised consultation and community involvement. In some cases the 1992 follow-up study was completed only a few months into the operation of the new procedures. We were, therefore, interested in how successfully these schools might reduce bullying in the longer term. We also wanted to know whether schools would maintain their anti-bullying activities once the project support was withdrawn. Follow-up studies were conducted in 1993, both in primary and secondary schools.

Follow-up in the primary schools (see Eslea and Smith, 1998)

Interviews: Interviews were conducted with headteachers and/or anti-bullying co-ordinators in 11 of the 16 project primary schools, approximately one year after the end of the interventions. Nine schools had successfully produced a document: 6 had developed dedicated anti-bullying policies, taking between one year (P3 and P15) and three years (P6) to complete the process; two schools (P7 and COM P1) had incorporated anti-bullying measures into a wider Positive Behaviour programme and P8 had addressed bullying through a more general Code of Conduct. The remaining two (P1 and P14) had produced only vague anti-bullying statements (for example: Always treat others how you would like to be treated). Of the 9 schools that had developed policies, all except P7 and P12 had circulated their document widely, and all except P12 had successfully implemented their chosen procedures. All 9 felt that their efforts had had a positive impact on reducing bullying.

All schools had made some improvements to the playground environment except P1, which blamed lack of money, and P5, which was under threat of closure. Many of the others, notably P3, P7, and P15, had made a major effort in this area. Extra supervision had also been provided in many cases. Classroom and curriculum resources (used extensively during the DFE-supported intervention) had been used more sporadically in

Table 6.4. *Percentage of pupils reporting (a) being bullied, and (b) bullying others, at least 'sometimes' in each school in each survey*

	School P3			School P6			School P7			School P10		
	All %	Girls %	Boys %	All %	Girls %	Boys %	All %	Girls %	Boys %	All %	Girls %	Boys %
(a) being bullied												
1990	23.2	25.5	20.6	27.3	25.1	29.6	23.4	19.4	27.9	26.9	23.3	31.1
1992	15.4	4.8	24.5	22.5	14.8	30.1	25.6	30.1	23.1	25.3	24.6	26.6
1993	30.5	42.2	19.5	20.1	20.4	19.9	27.7	36.1	24.1	17.1	22.4	12.5
(b) bullying others												
1990	12.8	8.4	18.4	11.8	8.9	14.7	10.8	4.5	17.8	8.3	8.4	8.2
1992	2.4	0	4.8	8.9	6.3	11.7	12.1	6.4	16.9	9.1	7.8	10.3
1993	5.5	0	11.1	10.1	11.4	9.0	12.5	6.5	18.9	6.1	5.2	7.0

1992–93, often where individual teachers had taken a particular interest rather than being applied at a whole-school level. The various strategies for dealing with bullies and victims were not widely used; most schools preferred to tackle subjects like assertiveness through their PSE curriculum and in assemblies. A few other interventions took place here and there. P6 conducted a video survey of playground behaviour, while P12 did a questionnaire survey of parents. P10 and P14 had provided assorted play equipment, but without long-term success. P5 used a positive rewards 'points' system in addition to their bullying policy.

Questionnaire surveys: 4 of the 11 schools (P3, P6, P7, and P10) volunteered to administer the modified Olweus questionnaire for a third time. In total, 657 children completed the questionnaires, following the same procedure as earlier, but one year after the post-test survey.

Results for each school were compared to the two previous surveys in the same schools. Table 6.4 shows how the percentage reporting being bullied 'sometimes' or more had changed since the start of the project. Two schools (P6 and P10) experienced a consistent decline in reports of being bullied; in P7 it had risen consistently; and P3 had initially reduced bullying but had since seen a rise. A clear sex difference is evident. Between 1992 and 1993, the number of boys being bullied in P6, P3, and P10 had fallen considerably; and while P7 had seen a slight rise the incidence there was still lower than their original 1990 results. For girls, however, the frequency of being bullied had risen in P6, P7, and particularly P3. Only P10 had seen a fall in the number of girls being bullied, smaller than was found for the boys.

Although most victims said they had told somebody about being bullied, they were more likely to have told someone at home than someone at school, and a sizeable minority had told nobody. This was as true in 1993 as it had been in 1990: even after three years of anti-bullying work, the proportion of victims who told school staff about being bullied had remained almost exactly the same. Nevertheless, the vast majority of children did recognise the efforts that their schools had made, and 68% felt that there had been an improvement since the previous year.

Conclusions: primary schools follow-up: Three main issues are suggested by the findings. First, schools need to be aware of the importance of maintaining the momentum of anti-bullying work. The two schools with thorough and continuing policy development and implementation had continued to reduce bullying; the two schools with older policies and less active had not done so. It is important to ensure that a school policy on bullying remains alive and active after the initial impetus has receded.

Second, there may need to be more focused efforts on girls' experiences of being bullied. All the schools in this study successfully reduced bullying among boys, but were less able to succeed with girls. Efforts must be made to ensure that anti-bullying work is not skewed by a male stereotype of bullying behaviour, and that it properly reflects and addresses the problems experienced by girls.

Third is the issue of reporting bullying when it happens. None of the four schools had managed to increase the proportion of self-reported victims who had told a member of staff about being bullied. However, this may not be the indictment it at first seems: if the staff are more vigilant and the children more assertive, then perhaps the need to report bullying is reduced by anti-bullying work.

Follow-up in the secondary schools (see Thompson, 1995)

Five of the 7 project secondary schools agreed to take part in a follow-up survey, two years after the post-test survey of the project. The same questionnaire was used, plus one further question about the length of time the bullying had been going on for those children reporting bullying taking place. At the same time, an interview study was carried out of selected teachers in each of the 5 schools: a member of the senior management team who had been present during the anti-bullying project, a teacher closely involved in implementing the project, a main-grade teacher who had been working in the school during the project but who had not been specifically involved in the project implementation, and a new member of staff who had joined after the end of the project. The focus of the study was to describe and reflect on the experiences of school staff

Table 6.5. *Changes in percentage of secondary school pupils reporting being bullied this term, after two and four year follow-up from time of the start of the intervention project; comparison between 'effective policy maintenance' school and average of 4 'ineffective policy maintenance' schools*

| | Effective policy maintenanceschool (N = 1) | | Ineffective policy maintenance schools (N = 4) | |
	T + 2yrs	T + 4 yrs	T + 2yrs	T + 4yrs
Not bullied	70	78	68	62 (all decreased)
Mild bullying(once–twice a term)	19	14	23	27
Moderate–severe bullying(once per two weeks to several times a week)	11	7	9	11

and children in the two years since the formal end of the intervention project.

Quantitative findings: The finding of most interest was the relative success of the schools in continuing to reduce the level of bullying, as reported by the students. The 5 schools split into two sets: 4 schools where the incidence of bullying had increased over the follow-up period in spite of the efforts of the schools; and 1 school where the incidence had continued to go down over the follow-up period. The comparative percentages of students responding are presented in table 6.5.

In the school that succeeded in continuing to reduce bullying, the proportion of students reporting they were not bullied rose from 70% to 78%; and in the schools that had experienced an increase in bullying in the follow-up period the average proportion of students reporting they were not bullied fell from 68% to 62%. The difference between the two sets of schools at the end of the follow-up period was significant at the $p < 0.01$ level (t-test).

Another interesting finding was that, in all the schools, there was an increase in the proportion of students reporting that they would be prepared to tell a teacher if they were aware of bullying taking place, and an increase in the proportion of students reporting that they would trust the staff to take effective action. This was true of the 4 schools where bullying had increased as well as the school where it had reduced. The continued efforts of the schools had clearly had some effect on the dynamics of the anti-bullying process, although further research will be necessary to understand the full complexity of the process.

Qualitative findings: The views of staff gathered by interviews and the views of the students gathered in the questionnaire gave some additional information that added to our understanding of the process. Virtually all the staff interviewed in the 'ineffective maintenance' set of schools judged that their schools were paying less attention to the anti-bullying work than in previous years. They regretted the change, and most could easily find various attributions as to why this was so, ranging from staff changes to needing to respond to new central government initiatives. The student questionnaire results indicated that the students also judged that less anti-bullying work was taking place. All the leaders of the original project groups in the school had moved on, and all the staff interviewed who had known the original project group regretted the changes. However, in none of them had the school management appointed anyone else to fulfil the role. There was no evidence of schools collecting continuing data or other evidence of the levels of bullying going on in the school, and no review or reporting back procedures appeared to be operating. There was no evidence of any induction process for the staff that had joined the schools after the end of the original project, which gave them any idea of the anti-bullying policy.

These data were collected in 1994–95, and at that time there was less nationally disseminated concern to establish and maintain anti-bullying policies in the UK than at the present time. It is likely that staff moving into these secondary schools in the period after the project would have had very little appreciation of anti-bullying work, and senior staff moving in would have been very likely to have come with their own priorities for school development, which would have been unlikely to include anti-bullying work.

In the 'effective policy maintenance' school the picture given by the staff interviews was very different. The staff all agreed that no decrease had occurred in the amount of anti-bullying work (again supported by the questionnaire data from the students) and the staff knew of the anti-bullying policy and how it worked. In particular, the new member of staff was well aware of the policy, and described an effective induction policy for new members of staff. In this school also the leader of the original anti-bullying project team had left the post, but had remained in the school and was currently the headteacher. The priorities for the school in the pastoral care area had been maintained, and the school was still actively supporting the policy. From the qualitative data gathered at the time it could be said that there were clear differences between the two sets of schools in terms of the knowledge of the policy and activities of the school in supporting the anti-bullying work identified in the policy.

Conclusions: secondary schools follow-up: One of the major questions concerning the continued success of anti-bullying work is the organisational priority given to it by the school and its senior management. There is a host of variables influencing schools and their effectiveness in various areas, and these 5 schools will undoubtedly have other differences and similarities between them apart from the extent of anti-bullying work. However, it certainly was the case that the 'effective policy maintenance' school was not different from the others in the general social class of its intake, or the resources it had available. The general management of whole-school anti-bullying policies is discussed in greater detail elsewhere (Thompson and Sharp, 1994, Thompson, Arora, and Sharp, 2002). More research into the policy-maintenance aspects of anti-bullying work is needed to clarify further ways effectively to maintain policies, and to ascertain how low bullying rates can be reduced, given consistent work over time. At present all we know is that bullying can continue to decline in schools committed to the programme after a period of 4 years. For the time being, however, a greater focus on organisational priority of such work in schools generally would be very welcome. Until this happens, as table 6.5 shows for this sample of schools, many students will continue to experience bullying, even in schools where effective anti-bullying work has taken place in the past.

Dissemination and impact beyond the programme schools

The initial Sheffield-based anti-bullying project had far-reaching effects across the UK. One main outcome of the project was a guidance pack, made available free of charge to all state-funded schools in England and Wales in October 1994. This described to schools the kinds of actions that could be taken to tackle bullying, including illustrative case studies. It was updated and re-issued by the DfES in December 2000. Additionally, other publications, including a practical handbook for school teachers, were published and have sold worldwide. All members of the project team have been active in providing training and consultancy to Local Authorities and schools. The National Association for Pastoral Care in Education has set up a library of materials and publications relating to bullying behaviour.

It is now typical for most Education Authorities in the UK to have an anti-bullying policy or statement, supported by locally relevant guidance materials and training and support for schools. Some authorities, for example Derbyshire and Birmingham, have published a set of standards that schools can use to self-evaluate their anti-bullying practice. Leicestershire have appointed an anti-bullying manager to ensure that there is continued impetus to challenge bullying behaviour.

In the early 1990s, when the anti-bullying project was initiated, there was often a reluctance to admit that bullying occurred in schools. Ten years on, all schools have anti-bullying policies that are examined during the school inspection process and there is recognition of the widespread nature of bullying along with a general willingness to take it seriously and intervene. The national government has specified in both legislation and guidance to schools that it is the headteacher's responsibility to ensure effective action against bullying behaviour. This does not mean, however, that all schools and Local Authorities are successful in tackling bullying. There are still too many reports of children and young people suffering significant physical and/or psychological duress at the hands of their peers.

References

Ahmad, Y., Whitney, I., and Smith, P. K. (1991). A survey service for schools on bully/victim problems. In P. K. Smith and D. A. Thompson (eds.), *Practical approaches to bullying*. London: David Fulton, pp. 103–11.

Boulton, M. J. and Underwood, K. (1992). Bully/victim problems among middle school children. *British Journal of Educational Psychology*, 62, 73–87.

Cowie, H. and Sharp, S. (1992). Students themselves tackle the problem of bullying. *Pastoral Care in Education*, 10, 31–7.

Elliott, M. (ed.) (1991). *Bullying: A practical guide to coping for schools*. Harlow: Longman.

Eslea, M. and Smith, P. K. (1998). The long-term effectiveness of anti-bullying work in primary schools. *Educational Research*, 40, 203–18.

Foster, P., Arora, C. M. J., and Thompson, D. A. (1990). A whole school approach to bullying. *Pastoral Care in Education*, 8, 13–17.

Olweus, D. (1991). Bully/victim problems among school children: Basic facts and effects of a school based intervention program. In D. Pepler and K. Rubin (eds.), *The development and treatment of childhood aggression*. Hillsdale, NJ: Erlbaum, 411–48.

Pikas, A. (1989). A pure concept of mobbing gives the best results for treatment. *School Psychology International*, 10, 95–104.

Smith, P. K. and Sharp, S. (eds.) (1994). *School bullying: Insights and perspectives*. London: Routledge.

Thompson, D. A. (1995). Two years on – problems in monitoring anti-bullying policies in school and their effects on the incidence of bullying. Paper presented at the BERA/EERA European Conference of Educational Research, University of Bath, UK.

Thompson, D. A. and Sharp, S. (1994). *Improving schools – establishing and integrating whole school behaviour policies*. London: David Fulton.

Thompson, D. and Arora, T. (1991). Why do children bully? An evaluation of the long-term effectiveness of a whole-school policy to minimise bullying. *Pastoral Care in Education*, 9, 8–12.

Thompson, D. A., Arora, T., and Sharp, S. (2002). *Bullying – effective strategies for long term improvement*. London: Routledge/Falmer.

Whitney, I. and Smith, P. K. (1993). A survey of the nature and extent of bully/victim problems in junior/middle and secondary schools. *Educational Research*, 35, 3–25.

Yates, C. and Smith, P. K. (1989). Bullying in two English comprehensive schools. In E. Roland and E. Munthe (eds.), *Bullying: An international perspective*. London: David Fulton, pp. 22–34.

7   Making a difference in bullying: evaluation of a systemic school-based programme in Canada

Debra J. Pepler, Wendy M. Craig, Paul O'Connell, Rona Atlas, and Alice Charach

Impetus for the intervention study, early stages of planning, and funding

Over the past decade, Canadians have become increasingly aware of the extent and consequences of bullying problems. Recently, there have been several high-profile cases of Canadian children who have suffered from prolonged victimisation, with severe consequences of suicide, revenge attacks, or death at the hands of peers. These cases have highlighted the need for empirically based prevention and intervention programmes. We will describe a school-based intervention programme developed prior to the recent surge in interest in the problem of bullying in Canada.

This anti-bullying initiative emerged from a survey conducted in the early 1990s by the Toronto Board of Education in collaboration with researchers from York University. The questionnaire used for the survey was modelled after the Olweus self-report questionnaire (Olweus, 1989), with some adaptations for the Canadian context. The survey indicated that bullying and victimisation were pervasive problems. During the past two months, 24% of the grade 3–8 students reported that they had bullied other students at least once or twice, and 15% more than once or twice. Half of the students (49%) indicated that they had been victims of bullying at least once, 20% more than once or twice, and 8% reported being victimised weekly or more often during the past two months (Charach, Pepler, and Ziegler, 1995).

We worked collaboratively with the Board of Education on developing a framework for school-based interventions within Toronto schools, fashioned closely after the Norwegian intervention as developed by Olweus in Bergen, which had demonstrated effectiveness in reducing the prevalence of bullying and victimisation (Olweus, 1991, 1993). The anti-bullying programme was piloted in 4 schools within the Toronto Board, then a full-scale evaluation was conducted in 3 elementary schools (kindergarten to grade 6) within the city. The programme implementation was funded by the Board of Education, and the evaluation component of the programme was funded through a research grant from the Ontario Mental Health Foundation.

Selection of schools

The design for the evaluation programme was quasi-experimental. In the first year of the programme, one school (School A) started the programme, with a second school (School B) serving as a waiting-list control. In the second year, School A continued the programme, School B formally initiated the programme, and a third school (School C) served as a waiting-list control. In the third year, Schools A and B continued with the intervention, and School C began its formal involvement in the anti-bullying programme. The schools were identified for inclusion in the programme because of the principals' and teachers' willingness to participate. We believed that without the commitment of the leadership and staff, the programme would not get off the ground.

Characteristics of schools and students

The schools were drawn from diverse areas of the city, which is the largest metropolitan centre in Canada and richly multi-cultural. All 3 schools had children from kindergarten to grade 6 (ages 5–11). School A was located in a disadvantaged area of the inner city and had an enrolment of approximately 800 students. The school was multi-culturally diverse, with about 70% of the students having a first language other than English. A large proportion of the students came from immigrant families, with approximately 30% of the children having immigrated within the past 5 years. The students were from primarily working-class families. School B was located in the centre of the city and had approximately 500 students. For approximately 40% of the children, English was not their first language; 10% of the students had immigrated within the past 5 years. Children in this school came from a range of working class through to professional families. School C was also located in the city and was similar to School B in the socio-economic levels of the families. It had an enrolment of approximately 400 students. Approximately 15% of the students had a first language other than English and about 2% had immigrated within the past 5 years.

Components of the intervention programme

The Canadian anti-bullying intervention was based on an understanding of bullying as a problem that extends far beyond the individual children involved as aggressors or victims. As we were developing the intervention, we were coding observations of bullying on the playground and in the classroom. Preliminary analyses of our observational and survey research informed the development of a whole-school intervention. Our observations on the playground and in the classroom indicated that bullying consistently unfolds within the context of a peer group (Atlas and Pepler, 1998; Craig and Pepler, 1997). Addressing the children's understanding of bullying and their responses to it was a central feature of the interventions.

The administrators and teachers also influence the nature of bullying within the school setting. They set the standards for behaviour and are responsible for supporting children who are having difficulties. Our observational research indicated that teachers seldom intervened in bullying: we observed teacher intervention in only 4% and 18% of the episodes on the playground and in the classroom, respectively (Atlas and Pepler, 1998; Craig and Pepler, 1997). The anti-bullying initiatives included many activities to raise the awareness and responsiveness of the school staff to bullying problems.

Finally, parents are implicated in addressing the problems of bullying. In our surveys, more students indicated that they had talked to parents than to teachers about problems relating to bullying and victimisation (Charach et al., 1995). Parents' communication with the school is, therefore, essential in establishing support for students who are involved in bullying, either as perpetrators or victims.

The interventions within the Toronto programme varied somewhat across the 3 schools; however, all schools introduced 3 critical elements: staff training; codes of behaviour; and improved playground supervision. There were specific interventions implemented at the school level, parent level, classroom level, and with individual children experiencing problems with bullying and/or victimisation (for a fuller description, see Pepler, Craig, Ziegler, and Charach, 1994).

The focus at the school level was on developing a code of behaviour, engaging teachers, and promoting positive playground interactions. At the parent level, information nights were held and communications were sent home related to the programme and its objectives. At the classroom level, children were involved in developing class rules, as in the Bergen intervention (Olweus, 1993). In addition, activities were introduced to change students' attitudes and to promote communication and support of peers. At the individual child level, those children who were experiencing problems of bullying and/or victimisation received specific interventions. Concerns about bullying were communicated to the children, their parents were contacted, and follow-up was implemented to ensure that bullying did not continue. Schools were encouraged to develop a system to document and track the children involved in bullying and the steps taken to correct the problems. In School B, a behaviour-management programme was implemented for a small group of children who had persistent problems with bullying.

Evaluation framework and procedures

The evaluation framework for the Toronto intervention reflected the systemic model of interventions required at many levels of the school system. There were evaluations at various levels of the programme implementation: with teachers, with students, with identified children, and with parents. For this evaluation, we relied on questionnaires (at all 3 schools) and observational data (at schools A and B only). As indicated above, the intervention implementation was lagged across three years to provide a waiting-list control comparison. The study started in fall 1992 and ended in 1995. Data collection for Schools A and B was conducted in the fall and spring of each of the three years; data collection for School C was conducted in the fall and spring of years two and three. Comparisons were of age-matched cohorts.

Participants

Because the data collection was intense, with playground and classroom observations, we did not have the capacity to include all of the children in the schools. Therefore, we randomly selected two classes from each of grades 1–6 (12 classes in all) from each school to participate in the evaluation research. Parental consent was obtained for participation in both elements of the evaluation: questionnaires and observations. Approximately 80% of the children in the chosen classes had consent to participate in the evaluation. In the first year of data collection, this comprised 319 children from School A and 300 children from School B. As children left the school and other children entered over the following two years, we recruited additional grade 1 and 2 classrooms into the evaluation. In the second year, there were 325 children in School A, 240 children in School B, and 303 children in School C, which became part of the evaluation.

In the final year, there were 306 children in School A, 163 students in School B, and 289 students in School C.

For the observations, we included children who were identified by two of three respondents (self, peer, and teacher) either as bullies, victims, bully-victims, or comparison children. Children from the comparison group were matched on grade and gender with the children in the bully, victim, and bully-victim groups. On average across the three years, there were 13 bullies, 25 victims, 15 bully/victims, and 65 comparison children observed. In total, 125 hours of video and remote audio recordings of playground behaviour were collected at Schools A and B. To maximise the numbers of children in the observational component of the study, we continued to observe all children who were in the earlier phases and replaced those children who had left the school (each year, the grade 6 class moved on to a junior high school).

Measures

The self-report questionnaire used in the original Toronto survey and adapted from Olweus' questionnaire (1989) was used to assess children's experiences of bullying, victimisation, intervention, teacher responses, and communication with teachers and parents. Observations on the school playgrounds at schools A and B were conducted for the sub-samples of children identified as described above. Cameras were set up on the school playground in the fall and the spring, shortly after the question-naire administration (for fuller details on the observational methods, see O'Connell, Pepler, and Craig, 1999; Hawkins, Pepler, and Craig, 2002).

What actually happened; achievements and difficulties in implementing the intervention

There were many challenges in our implementation of the anti-bullying programme and its evaluation. First, our waiting-list control design was ineffective. We learned that it is difficult to use one school as a control for another because schools differ dramatically in terms of their lead-ership, culture, and student population. Given that the implementation of an anti-bullying programme is prolonged and complex, School A was still developing the programme when School B started to implement their programme at the beginning of year two. Another challenge that we faced was that School B and School C teachers, students, and parents became sensitised to the issues of bullying with the initial data collection at the beginning of years 1 and 2, respectively. Even though no official interven-tions were implemented, the process of change appears to have started in School B and School C during the assessment-only phase. Therefore, our data analyses were conducted within school rather than between the intervention and control schools. A strength of our intervention evaluation was the inclusion of observations on the playground and in the classroom at Schools A and B.

The implementation of the interventions varied significantly across schools, largely dependent on the leadership of the school principals. At School A, a committee was established to guide the implementation, and the research team was invited in several times per year for staff training. There was a significant challenge in involving parents at School A because a large proportion of the parents were recent immigrants with little understanding of English and the school system. At School B, however, parents were actively involved in the development of the whole-school policy, which incorporated a focus on bullying. There were regular parent nights at School B at which parents were educated about the problems of bullying and about the programme that the school was implementing. School B also held regular sessions for teachers to engage them in the anti-bullying interventions. School C had the least amount of time to mount the programme. During the first year, there was an information night for the parents at School C and a staff-training session. All schools were supported in their anti-bullying efforts by the educational consultants and school social workers with the Board of Education. The drama consultant was particularly active in supporting the teachers and students in role-playing activities related to peer involvement in bullying. The school social workers were involved with some of the individual children who were experiencing difficulties with bullying and/or victimisation.

Results of the evaluation

In reporting the results of the evaluation, we will focus on different levels of the systemic intervention, starting with changes in individual children's involvement in bullying and victimisation, moving to teacher intervention, and finally peer intervention to stop bullying. The figures provide data from all 6 waves of data collection to reveal changes over the entire evaluation. The analyses, however, are conservatively conducted from the time that the intervention was formally initiated through the following 30 months for School A; 18 months for School B; and 6 months for School C.

Addressing the prevalence of bullies and victims

Our questionnaire data include two questions on the prevalence of bullying and victimisation: 'Have you bullied others (or been victimised) in the

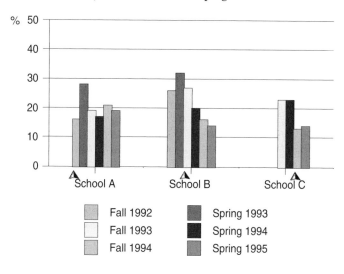

Note: Beginning of intervention marked by ▲

   For School A, intervention began in Fall of 1992.

   For School B, intervention began in Fall of 1993.

   For School C, intervention began in Fall of 1994.

Fig. 7.1 Percentage of children reporting bullying others at least once in past 2 months.

past 5 days?' and 'Have you bullied others (or been victimised) in the past two months?' Taking the latter criterion, the patterns for reports of bullying others are shown in fig. 7.1, and they differ somewhat from those of victimisation (being bullied), shown in fig. 7.2. In addition, observational data from the playground and classroom contribute to our understanding of the effectiveness of the anti-bullying intervention (table 7.1).

Bullying At School A, there was no decrease in the reports of bullying over the past 2 months, from the onset of the programme to the 30-month data collection point (fall 1992–spring 1995). At the outset, only 16% of children reported bullying others, which increased to 28% at the 6-month point, and returned to levels between these two rates for the subsequent 24-month period. The students' reports of bullying in the past 5 days reflected a similar stability in reports of bullying. At School B, the rates of bullying during the past 2 months showed a steady decline from the initiation of the programme (fall 1993: 27%) through the 18-month evaluation (spring 1995) and were significantly lower at the 12- and 18-month data collection points. The reports of bullying over the past 5 days

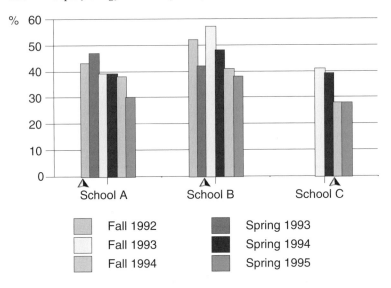

Note: Beginning of intervention marked by ▲

For School A, intervention began in Fall of 1992.

For School B, intervention began in Fall of 1993.

For School C, intervention began in Fall of 1994.

Fig. 7.2 Percentage of children reporting being bullied at least once in past 2 months.

also decreased significantly from the outset to the 18-month evaluation. The percentage decrease in the proportion of children reporting bullying at School B was similar to the 50% decrease reported by Olweus in the Bergen intervention. At School C, the rates of bullying were lower than at the other schools and did not show any decline over the first 6 months of programme implementation.

Victimisation   At School A, there was a decline in the number of children reporting being victimised in the past 2 months, with a significant difference between the reports at the beginning of and after 30 months of the anti-bullying programme (fall 1992 to spring 1995). There was also a steady decline in the numbers of children reporting victimisation over the past week, with significant differences between the initial reports and reports at 18, 24, and 30 months. In the pre-intervention testing at School B (fall 1993), over half of the students reported being bullied at least once during the past 2 months, with a significant decrease after 12 (fall 1994)

Table 7.1. *Observations of bullying on the playground and in the classroom*

Observed Behaviour	Fall 1992	Spring 1993	Fall 1993	Spring 1994	Fall 1994	Spring 1995
Rate of bullying on playground per hr						
School A	2.76	1.42	1.61	1.44	2.18	0.84
School B	5.83	1.98	2.64	1.65	1.88	2.04
Rate of bullying in classroom per hr						
School A	2.77	1.66	0.99	2.41	2.28	2.09
School B	2.43	3.42	5.06	3.10	3.67	1.62
Teacher intervention on playground %						
School A	16	13	4	10	7	1
School B	6	22	7	11	14	5
Teacher intervention in classroom %						
School A	12	16	20	14	18	19
School B	9	7	21	25	23	8
Peer intervention on playground %						
School A	29	13	21	10	22	40
School B	18	22	28	26	29	16
Peer intervention in classroom %						
School A	5	5	0	6	3	2
School B	6	7	0	5	3	5

and 18 months (spring 1995) of the anti-bullying programme. There was a similar significant decrease in the percentage of students reporting victimisation in the past five days from the outset to 6, 12, and 18 months of the programme. The percentage decrease in the reports of victimisation at Schools A and B were between 30% and 37%, which is slightly lower than the 50% decrease reported in the Bergen study (Olweus, 1991). At School C, the rates of victimisation were stable over the first six months of the programme.

Observations of bullying on the playground and in the classroom
   The observational data (table 7.1) provide another perspective on bullying and victimisation in addition to the students' reports. The rates of bullying observed on the playground and in the classroom showed a general decrease over the implementation of the anti-bullying programme. For example, at School A, the rate of bullying on the playground declined by 48% from the initiation (fall 1992) to the 18-month period (spring 1994) and by 70% from initiation to the 30-month period (spring 1995) The rate of bullying observed in the classroom declined by 13% and 24% from initiation to 18-month and 30-month

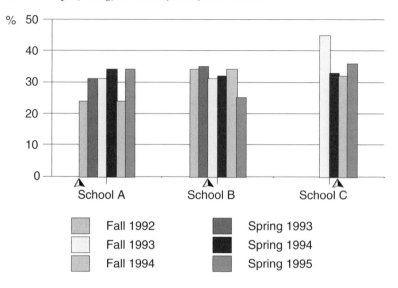

Note: Beginning of intervention marked by ▲

For School A, intervention began in Fall of 1992.

For School B, intervention began in Fall of 1993.

For School C, intervention began in Fall of 1994.

Fig. 7.3 Percentage of students indicating that teachers almost always intervene to stop bullying.

periods, respectively. At School B, the rates of bullying observed on the playground and in the classroom declined by 23% and 68%, respectively over the first 18 months of the programme (fall 1993–spring 1995).

A systemic intervention: the roles of teachers and peers

As with most interventions to address bullying problems, the Canadian intervention focused not only on the children who were bullying others and being victimised but also on the role of teachers and peers in intervening to stop bullying. From a systemic perspective, we expected that changes for the children involved in bullying and victimisation would depend on a concurrent change in the awareness and responsiveness of the school staff and of the peers who are always present during bullying episodes.

Teacher intervention   Data from the children's reports of teachers' responses to bullying are shown in fig. 7.3. At School A, there was a significant increase from the outset (fall 1992) to the 18-month (spring

1994) and 30-month (spring 1995) evaluations in the number of children reporting that teachers almost always intervened to stop bullying. At School B, however, the number of students reporting that teachers almost always intervened dropped slightly from the beginning (fall 1993) to 18 months (spring 1995) into the anti-bullying intervention. At School C, there was no significant change in the reports of teacher intervention over the first 6 months of the programme.

Our observations of teacher intervention indicated a marked decrease at School A in the proportion of episodes in which teachers intervened on the playground; however, there was a 50% increase in proportion of episodes in which teachers intervened in the classroom (table 7.1). At School B, the rate of teacher intervention on the playground did not change significantly; the rate of intervention in the classroom, however, decreased from the onset of the intervention (fall 1993) to 18 months into the programme (spring 1995). The two contexts provide a somewhat different picture of teacher responses to bullying consistent with our previous observations (Craig, Pepler, and Atlas, 2000): teachers are more likely to intervene in bullying that unfolds in the classroom compared to the playground context. Presumably, teachers can more readily observe the aggressive interactions in the constrained classroom context than on a large school playground.

Peer intervention   A major element of the Canadian anti-bullying programme was to raise awareness of, and responsiveness to, bullying by peers. Nevertheless, there were no significant increments in students' reports of peers almost always intervening at any of the schools and, in fact, the rates decreased in each school. At School A, 14% of students reported that children almost always intervened at the outset (fall 1992) and the rate was 11% after 30 months of the programme (spring 1995). At School B, the rates were 16% and 12% for the outset and 18-month evaluations, respectively. At School C, the initial rate was 20% and dropped to 14% over the 6-months of programme implementation. According to the students' reports, the focus on the roles of peers was an aspect of the programme that did not live up to the expectations for mobilising children to be concerned for victimised children and come to their defence.

Our observations of the rates of peer intervention on the playground indicate considerable variability over the 6 waves of observation (table 7.1). At School A, the percentage of episodes in which peers intervened at the start of the programme (fall 1992) was high at 29% and was lowest at the 18-month wave (spring 1994), but rose again to the highest observed rate of 40% at the final observation 30 months after the programme began (spring 1995). At School B, the rates of peer intervention from the start of the intervention (fall 1993) to 12-months follow-up were relatively stable, ranging from 26% to 29%, then dropping to 16% at the end of the evaluation (spring 1995). The rates of peer intervention in the context of the anti-bullying programme were generally higher than the 12% rate found in our initial observational study of bullying (Craig and Pepler, 1997).

In the classroom, the percentages of episodes in which peers intervened were considerably lower than those on the playground, and showed little improvement with the programme (table 7.1). At School A, peer intervention was observed in 5% of the episodes in the initial phase (fall 1992) and ranged between 0% and 6% for the subsequent 5 observation phases. At School B, the percentages were relatively stable, ranging from 0% to 7% until the 18-month wave (spring 1995), when there was intervention in 25% of the observed episodes. The difference between the initial and final rates was significantly different, but should be considered cautiously, because the final rate was anomalous with the rates at other times. The rates of peer intervention that we observed within the context of an anti-bullying programme were consistent with the 10% rate that we observed in the classroom in our initial study (Atlas and Pepler, 1998).

Longer term effects or evaluation of the programme

The evaluations of the anti-bullying interventions in Canada lasted 30 months, 18 months, and 6 months at Schools A, B, and C, respectively. The data indicate that it takes more than 6 months to effect change in bullying problems in elementary schools. There was little evidence of change in the first phase of the programme implementation and some indicators suggested that the problems may have worsened during the initial months. For example, at School A, the percentage of children reporting bullying and victimisation over the past 2 months increased from 16% to 28% and from 43% to 47%, respectively. The increases in students' reports of bullying may relate, in part, to their increased awareness of the problem and their ability to identify circumstances of bullying. Teachers frequently complained that the very act of completing the questionnaires had increased the prevalence of bullying among the students because more students were reporting bullying problems. Our observational data suggest that over the first 6 months, the actual incidence of bullying on the playground and in the classroom at School A had decreased by 49% and 40%, respectively, rather than increased. It is advantageous, therefore, to gather data from multiple informants and through multiple methods to determine the effectiveness of an anti-bullying intervention. Although observational data, such as those we collected, are both expensive and labour intensive, less-elaborate methods, such as asking the children to make a brief report of bullying following regular lunchtime or recess periods, can be used as an alternative assessment.

The long-term data on programme implementation suggest that significant improvements in bullying problems can be identified over 18- to 30-month periods. The challenge is to ensure that the concerns for, and responses to, bullying are kept alive among the school and that teachers do not become complacent about having addressed the problem once and for all. In fact, the evaluation data on peer intervention indicate little or no improvement, even after 2.5 years of programming at School A. If school is a place where all children are to feel safe and included, considerably more work needs to be done on establishing the peer culture and skills to promote interventions to stop bullying. Our analyses of the interventions in the present study indicate that peers are effective in stopping bullying: when a peer intervened, bullying stopped within 10 seconds in 57% of the episodes (Hawkins, Pepler, and Craig, 2001).

The opportunity to implement and evaluate a systemic school-based anti-bullying programme has provided an unprecedented learning experience. We have started to understand the central challenges and essential elements of a programme to reduce bullying. First, adults are essential in addressing bullying problems. From a systemic perspective, we recognise all adults involved in children's lives as important, including teachers, parents, as well as community leaders such as sports coaches, recreation leaders, and the police. Adults are responsible for leadership in the anti-bullying programme and for creating interest and support for maintaining the programme. Adults are also responsible for being role models. When adults take a concern for the problem and respond to address bullying, they validate children's experiences and model solutions. Teachers and parents are needed to intervene and support both children who bully and those who are victimised. There was considerable variability among schools in the extent and success of the intervention implementation. This variability may relate to the different demographic characteristics of the schools and the extent to which teachers and parents became actively involved. Evaluations of the process of intervention, such as those conducted by Olweus and Alsaker (chapters in this volume), provide guidance to critical elements in the implementation of anti-bullying interventions.

Secondly, because peers form the audience for bullying, they are essential to addressing bullying problems within a school context. Students can contribute in many important ways. They serve as role models for other students, especially when they intervene to stop bullying among children. Students can also serve as leaders in the anti-bullying initiatives, serving as essential members of safe-school committees and collaborating with teachers and parents in supporting and maintaining the initiative.

Finally, our evaluation highlighted the importance of different methods of assessment in examining change associated with anti-bullying programmes. A comprehensive evaluation of a bullying-prevention programme needs to include assessments of change at different levels of the system: with the students who bully and/or are victimised, with the peer observers, with the teachers, and with the parents. It is likely that change in one element of the system depends on change within another element. The longitudinal data indicate that evaluation of a bullying initiative is an ongoing process. The variability in various perceptions of bullying problems over time and among respondents and methods highlights the domains in which additional efforts need to focus. As the longitudinal data indicate, mounting an effective anti-bullying programme is an ongoing, rather than a one-time-only, process.

Dissemination and impact beyond the programme schools

In the past decade, there has been a marked increase in concern about violence within Canadian schools. The concerns for bullying have emerged particularly for elementary and junior high schools, and programmes have been implemented as a potential means of preventing the serious incidents of violence in high school. Educational policy is a provincial mandate in Canada and there has been a wide variety of responses to concerns of bullying in the different jurisdictions across the country. In one way or another, there has been attention to the problems of bullying within all of the provinces; however, much of the movement on this front has emerged at a local level, with specific programmes being developed to address the problems in a wide variety of ways (e.g. Bully Beware: www.bullybeware.com; League of Peaceful Schools: www.leagueofpeacefulschools.ns.ca, Focus on Bullying – A Resource for Elementary Schools, Government of British Columbia). Most programmes are based on an understanding of bullying as a problem that unfolds in the context of the peer group and that requires attention and responses from the adults in children's lives.

There is a groundswell of interest in bullying and a movement towards building a national awareness of the problem. Several of our diverse national organisations, such as the Family Services Association, the Canadian Parks and Recreation Association, the Canadian Association of Public Health, and the Canadian Safety Council, have identified bullying as a significant concern for children, and have developed materials to raise awareness about the issue. The federal government's National Crime Prevention Centre (NCPC) has encouraged the development of local community-based programmes to respond to bullying and prevent juvenile crime. Our concern is that few of these programmes appear to be evidence-based and rigorously evaluated. In 2002, the NCPC provided funds for a national strategy to raise awareness and to provide appropriate assessment tools and empirically based intervention strategies to address these problems across this vast country. Canada lags behind many European countries on addressing problems of bullying; however, some highly publicised cases of bullying are serving as a catalyst for renewed interest and activity.

Acknowledgements

The research reported in this chapter was supported by the Ontario Mental Health Foundation. An earlier version of this chapter was presented at the American Society of Criminology conference, Toronto, 1999. We are indebted to the Toronto Board of Education administrators, anti-bullying team leaders, teachers, school staff, and the children and their parents from the three schools where the anti-bullying intervention was implemented. Their efforts and commitment to making schools safe and equitable are reflected throughout this chapter.

References

Atlas, R., Pepler, D. J., and Craig, W. (1998). Observations of bullying in the classroom. *American Journal of Educational Research*, 92, 86–99.

Charach, A., Pepler, D., and Ziegler, S. (1995). Bullying at school: A Canadian perspective. *Education Canada*, 35, 12–18.

Craig, W. and Pepler, D. (1997). Observations of bullying and victimization in the schoolyard. *Canadian Journal of School Psychology*, 2, 41–60.

Craig, W. M., Pepler, D. J., and Atlas, R. (2000). Observations of bullying on the playground and in the classroom. *International Journal of School Psychology*, 21, 22–36.

Hawkins, D. L., Pepler, D., and Craig, W. (2001). Peer interventions in playground bullying. *Social Development*, 10, 512–27.

O'Connell, P., Pepler, D., and Craig, W. (1999). Peer involvement in bullying: Issues and challenges for intervention. *Journal of Adolescence*, 22, 437–52.

Olweus, D. (1989). Questionnaire for students (junior and senior versions). Unpublished manuscript.

    (1991). Bully/victim problems among school children: Basic facts and effects of a school-based intervention program. In D. Pepler and K. Rubin (eds.), *The development and treatment of childhood aggression*. Hillsdale, NJ: Erlbaum, pp. 411–448.

    (1993). *Bullying at school: What we know and what we can do*. Oxford: Blackwell.

Pepler, D. J., Craig, W., Ziegler, S., and Charach, A. (1994). An evaluation of an anti-bullying intervention in Toronto schools. *Canadian Journal of Community Mental Health*, 13, 95–110.

8 Interventions against bullying in Flemish schools: programme development and evaluation

Veerle Stevens, Paulette Van Oost, and Ilse De Bourdeaudhuij

Impetus for the intervention, early stages of planning, and funding

The development and evaluation of the Flemish anti-bullying intervention programme was based on the results of a prevalence study among primary and secondary school students on the extent of bullying and victimisation at school, as well as on previous research on bully/victim problems. Especially, the work done by Olweus (1994) and the information drawn from the DFE Sheffield anti-bullying project (Smith and Sharp, 1994) were a trigger for programme development and further evaluation. Two successive projects were carried out. Funding was obtained from the Department of Social Affairs and from Ghent University, respectively. The first project developed an anti-bullying intervention programme adapted to the Flemish educational context. The second project aimed at implementing and evaluating the programme outcomes of the Flemish anti-bullying intervention. Following a description of these projects, we will give an overview of some critical issues related to the programme outcomes observed.

The first project: Programme development

The development of the Flemish anti-bullying intervention programme was founded on the principles of health education research (Green and Kreuter, 1991; Damoiseaux et al., 1993; Bartholomew et al., 1998) and included four successive steps for programme development. The first step consisted of a prevalence study to analyse the seriousness and characteristics of bully/victim problems in Flemish schools. The second step aimed at identifying the behavioural determinants of bully/victim problems. Conducting prevention and/or intervention programmes to improve child and adolescent well-being assumes that such programmes are based on a clear insight into the causal relationship between the problem behaviour and relevant risk or protective factors involved, and that they provide evidence about how they are supposed to improve the health conditions towards which the intervention is directed (Kazdin, 1996; Valente and Dodge, 1997). The third step focuses on the production of the intervention. Activities include discussion with programme users and pre-testing of the intervention as well as the final production of the programme materials. Finally, the programme has to be evaluated to see whether programme outcomes are linked with programme objectives. This evaluation included the measurement of programme impact and an examination of the implementation process.

A prevalence study on bully/victim problems in Flemish schools

Bully/victim problems in Flanders were measured in a representative sample of 9,983 children aged 10–16 at 84 Flemish schools, using Olweus' self-report Bullying questionnaire (Stevens and Van Oost, 1994). Based on this survey, 23% of 10–12-year-olds and 15% of 13–16-year-olds reported being bullied 'sometimes or more frequently'. Indirect victimisation (social isolation and exclusion from a group) had a prevalence of 3%. In primary and secondary schools, 16% and 12%, respectively, reported that they had bullied others 'sometimes or more frequently'. Bullying and peer victimisation in Flemish schools was clearly a significant problem. Its prevalence was in line with rates of bullying and victimisation observed in other countries (Smith et al., 1999). Frequencies of bullying varied from 3.5% to as much as 23% in primary schools, and from 4% to 19% in secondary schools. Levels of victimisation ranged from 8.5% to 46% in primary schools, and from 5% to 29% in secondary schools. These findings revealed a need for specific interventions in schools that would deal effectively with problems of bullying and victimisation.

Determinants of bullying and victimisation

Different factors may explain the occurrence of bully/victim problems at school. Individual characteristics of bullies and victimised children contribute to the emergence and maintenance of the problem. In particular, bullies' social cognitions about the use of aggression and their positive evaluation and outcome beliefs regarding aggressive strategies (Olweus, 1994; Slee and Rigby, 1993; Smith et al., 1993; Boulton and Underwood, 1992, Coie et al., 1991), along with the poor social skills and more anxious or dependent attention-seeking behaviour of victims (Van Lieshout et al., 1992; Smith et al., 1993; Olweus, 1994), have been identified as salient predictors of peer aggression. Next to personal characteristics, relationships are crucial factors. Peer-group characteristics such as attitudes towards peer aggression, perception of a student's social position, willingness to provide help, and their actual intervention skills are important (Rigby and Slee, 1991; Boulton and Underwood, 1992; Whitney and Smith, 1993; Stevens and Van Oost, 1994; Pepler et al., 1998). Moreover, group characteristics, particularly negative interactions among students, low cohesion, and high levels of competitive play, affect bully/victim problems (Olweus, 1984, 1994; Smith et al., 1993; Scholte et al., 1997; Haselager, 1997). A third and fourth group of predictors external to the individual are the school and home environments. Peer aggression is positively associated with methods that adults use to handle aggression and group processes, teaching strategies, and supervision during playtime (Mooij, 1998; Baker, 1998; Olweus, 1984). Parental monitoring and support emerge as important determinants in the home (Rican et al., 1993; Bowers et al., 1994; Rigby, 1994; Olweus, 1984, 1994; Oliver et al., 1994).

Individual characteristics of children involved in bully/victim problems are the most salient risk factors for being involved in bullying conflicts (Olweus, 1978, 1984; Haselager, 1997; Mooij, 1998). However, the peer, home, and school environments contribute in their own way to, and increase, the risk of peer aggression and victimisation at school. Taken together, the underlying mechanisms of bully/victim problems can be understood as follows. Bullying behaviour is considered to be a form of proactive aggression, the goal of which is to gain social outcomes, in this case dominance or status among peers. When peers join in bullying acts, form an audience, or refuse to help victims of peer abuse, they consistently reinforce the bully's behaviour (Olweus, 1984, 1994; Schwartz et al., 1993). Moreover, bullying behaviour intensifies when bullies experience no, or few, negative consequences from parents or teachers following their aggressive act.

As a consequence, anti-bullying intervention programmes should restructure the social environment by implementing clear rules against bullying behaviour, so that the positive consequences of bullying are reduced, while the negative behavioural outcomes increase (Olweus, 1994). An awareness of peer conflicts and their damaging outcomes and an active involvement of adults in constructive peer interactions are prerequisites for a supportive school environment. According to Olweus, the intervention should be founded upon 'an authoritative adult–child interaction' (Olweus, 1992: 116) that aims at instilling a warm and positive climate as well as introducing clear rules against unacceptable peer interactions.

Initially, efforts in the educational context to prevent emotional and behavioural problems in children and adolescents mainly focused upon the individual determinants of children's psychosocial problems (Felner and Felner, 1989), thus ignoring the impact of factors external to the individual. Research on programme effectiveness revealed that prevention efforts turned out to be more effective when they took into account the social environment (Bond and Compas, 1989; Weissberg et al., 1991; Kazdin, 1993).

Programme development, pre-testing, and final production

From the 1980s on, several countries started interventions to deal with bullying problems at school, with the anti-bullying intervention in Norway, in particular the work done around Bergen by Dan Olweus (1978, 1984, 1994), forming a trigger for this. Olweus observed a reduction of up to 50% in bullying and in being bullied after 2 years of intervention. There was no displacement from bullying at school to bullying on the way to and from school. Moreover, the results revealed more positive social relationships and a significant drop in rates of vandalism, theft, and truancy, thereby strongly confirming the extra benefits of involving the school environment in the overall equation. Because of its positive outcomes on bullying and victimisation, the Norwegian anti-bullying intervention programme was considered to be a good model for other countries to develop anti-bullying interventions within schools. However, model programmes cannot merely be copied as they may affect other educational settings in a different way (Price et al., 1993; Roberts and Hinton-Nelson, 1996; Elias, 1997), which implies the need to adapt the intervention to the new setting. Although programme adaptation is encouraged, it includes the risk of changing the core features of the intervention. As a consequence, adapting model programmes involves a process of solving the dilemma of remaining true to the model programme while at the same time thoroughly changing the intervention in order to fit the new setting.

In Flanders, the development of the intervention programme (Stevens and Van Oost, 1994) was inspired by the Norwegian model programme and the DFE Sheffield Anti-Bullying Project. To face the problem of programme adaptation, the intervention was additionally based on contacts with programme developers in the Netherlands and the experiences of Flemish schools and school psychological services. Moreover, interviews with 100 children and focus-group discussions within 10 classes provided information about how children perceived bully/victim problems. Based on these experiences, a video was produced for children and adults (*How was your day?*), to increase awareness of peer-victimisation problems. A draft of the programme was developed that describes the intervention objectives and strategies designed to involve parents, peers, teachers, non-teaching staff members, bullies, and victims. This draft was pre-tested during a pilot phase. In all, 18 schools (7 primary schools and 11 secondary schools) participated in the pilot phase. A linkage system with all programme users provided opportunities for programme adaptation and re-invention. During the process of programme implementation, schools could adapt programme components to their own situation. The research team monitored the process of programme development and implementation intensively, making sure that essential parts of the programme were incorporated in an appropriate way. After 6 months of implementation, the project co-ordinator, the school principal, and another teacher of each school were interviewed about programme feasibility, barriers to implementation, and training needs. Results (Van Oost and Stevens, 1995) revealed a need for training in active teaching methods, like problem-solving techniques and role play, and in communication skills in order to manage individual talks with bullies and victims. Based on this information, a final version of the programme was drawn up. Additional training sessions were then provided for another group of schools for the second project, in which the intervention programme would be implemented and evaluated.

Selection of schools

The second project aimed at examining the behavioural outcomes of the Flemish anti-bullying intervention and their relationships with process variables: 24 schools – 13 primary and 11 secondary – were recruited for this evaluation study. These schools were drawn randomly from a pool of 50 schools willing to participate in the research. Of these, a subset of 18 schools was used for some analyses.

Characteristics of schools and students

All schools were part of the regular educational system. The secondary schools provide general as well as vocational education. The main research sample of 24 schools had 719 primary and 1,013 secondary school students, aged 10–16 years. The sample of 18 schools used in the main analyses of bully and victim prevalence rates had 392 primary- and 712 secondary-school students (total 1,104): respectively 151 and 284 (total 435) in 6 schools in a Treatment with Support group; 149 and 277 (total 426) in 6 schools in a Treatment without Support group; and 92 and 151 (total 243) in 6 schools in a Control group.

Components of the intervention programme

Like the Norwegian programme, the Flemish anti-bullying intervention programme consists of three modules that focus on the social system (adults and peers) as well as on students directly involved in bully/victim problems. A manual was provided that describes the intervention objectives and strategies for each module. In addition, the video '*How was your day?*' shows one day in the school-life of two students (one girl, one boy) who are victims of bullying.

Intervention in the school environment

The first module deals with intervention in the school environment. Its main objective is the development of a whole-school anti-bullying policy. School staff are recommended to develop clear rules against bullying behaviour, including a clear description of bully/victim problems, while making it clear to all students that bullying will not be tolerated. This is the core intervention activity (Olweus, 1984; Smith and Sharp, 1994). The programme additionally aims at increasing adults' and students' awareness of bully/victim problems and enhancing active involvement in solving bullying incidents.

The development and implementation of a whole-school policy towards bullying involves three successive phases. The first phase focuses on increasing awareness of bully/victim problems among students, parents, teaching and non-teaching staff, consultation of the entire school community on the content of the policy, and completion of a final draft. The phase that follows aims at informing the school community about the final policy; the last phase provides specific training sessions for all target groups, which are intended to enhance the social skills needed to respond to bully/victim incidents.

Intervention within the peer group

The second module describes the curriculum-based activities for the peer group. The intervention within the peer group aims at enhancing positive attitudes towards children who are bullied and encouraging peer involvement in reducing bully/victim problems. The programme consists of four group sessions directed at students who are not actively involved in problems with bullying, based on a social cognitive orientation and using cognitive perspective-taking, problem-solving strategies, and social skills training.

The first session starts with the video '*How was your day?*' (Stevens and Van Oost, 1994). The aim of this session is to increase students' involvement in problems with bullying and to introduce rules against bullying behaviour. To reach these goals, attention is given to the role peers can play in reinforcing bullying behaviour. The positive and negative effects for the bully, the victim, and for themselves are progressively discussed within the group. Afterwards, clear class rules are formulated, indicating that bullying will not be tolerated.

The second session deals with inventing adaptive ways of reacting to bully/victim incidents. Peers themselves are encouraged to tackle bully/victim problems. As most peers are not used to taking any action against bullying (Stevens and Van Oost, 1994), alternative solutions are generated, including reactions against bullies, support for victims, and seeking help from teachers. The advantages and disadvantages of possible peer intervention are discussed among students.

The third session deals with specific training to help peers to find their own solutions to bully/victim incidents, using modelling techniques and role play.

Session four aims at implementing these solutions by means of intensive feedback and additional training. Each session takes about 100 minutes, thus resulting in a training course of about 8 teaching periods. Additionally, booster sessions are encouraged throughout the school year.

Support for bullies and victims

The third module focuses on the students directly involved in peer aggression, either as bullies or as victims. This module is based on social learning theory and primarily aims at changing a bully's behaviour by using repair procedures and behavioural contracting. An extensive procedure is provided to manage bully/victim problems in the playground. When bullying is observed, teaching and non-teaching staff are prepared to react immediately in order to stop bully/victim incidents. Teachers then discuss the bullying incident separately with bully and victim. When the class rules on bullying have been violated, students are encouraged to understand other children's feelings and to make up for the consequences of their aggressive behaviour by doing something for the victim or the class group. Contracting is used between bully and teacher to formulate the agreement and as a basis for follow-up. If helpful, self-control sessions or problem-solving training are organised for aggressive children.

Furthermore, the module focuses on intensive support for the victims of bullying. When bully/victim incidents are observed, the teacher also discusses the incident with the victim him/herself. Victims are supported intensively by means of emotional help and discussion about strategies for handling bullying incidents more effectively. The intervention also aims at enhancing social skills, like group entry and assertive behaviour in peer conflict situations.

Evaluation framework and procedures

The second anti-bullying project that aimed at implementing and evaluating the programme outcomes of the Flemish intervention lasted for 2.5 years. Pre-test assessment was carried out in September 1995. Students participated at post-test measurements at the end of the school year (June 1996: post-test1) and one year afterwards (June 1997: post-test2). This longitudinal procedure has the same pupils in pre-test and post-test (for a full description of dropout analyses see Stevens et al., 2000). Main effects of 'Time' are thus partly age-related changes; but the use of control schools permits an evaluation of what are intervention, rather than age, effects, through examining Condition × Time interactions.

The evaluation study had three main aims. First was to assess changes in rates of bullying and victimisation (being bullied). Second was to assess changes in the peer group (making non-involved students more aware of bully/victim problems and enhancing students' support to intervening in bullying incidents). Third was to assess the process of programme implementation; impaired programme implementation is often defined as a major threat to programme success (Resnicow et al., 1996; Valente and Dodge, 1997; Black et al., 1998).

Besides examining whether bullies and victims would benefit from an anti-bullying intervention that includes the social environment (Stevens et al., 2000), we additionally evaluated the impact of external support on programme effectiveness. Training and support for schools during programme implementation have been suggested to be essential in obtaining positive programme outcomes (Smith and Sharp, 1994). Therefore, it was hypothesised that the Flemish anti-bullying intervention programme would be effective in reducing levels of bullying and victimisation in schools *and* that schools obtaining additional help from the research group would obtain larger reductions in bullying and victimisation due to the intervention.

To examine these research hypotheses, a quasi-experimental pre-test/post-test comparison was used, including a control group (Windsor et al., 1984; Parry and Watt, 1989). The experimental conditions included two treatment conditions. The first treatment condition involved students from schools that implemented a school-based anti-bullying intervention with additional support from the research group. Schools within this condition participated in an extensive training programme and could rely on the research group for additional help during the implementation of the anti-bullying intervention. The second treatment condition also involved students from schools that implemented a school-based anti-bullying programme. However, this group of schools could not appeal to the research group for additional help nor did they receive specific training sessions on the anti-bullying programme. The third condition involved students from schools that did not implement the anti-bullying programme; these served as a Control condition. Of the 24 schools participating, 12 schools were randomly assigned to the Treatment with Support condition, 6 schools to the Treatment without Support condition, and 6 schools to the Control condition.

Measures: effects on bullying and victimisation

The instrument for assessing this consisted of three scales, based on the self-report Bullying Inventory (Olweus, 1989; Liebrand et al., 1991) and the Life in School Checklist (Arora, 1994). They measure levels of bullying (8 items, Cronbach alpha .82), victimisation (8 items, Cronbach alpha .81), and positive interactions among students (6 items, Cronbach alpha .68).

We found that the unequal number of students in each of the conditions strongly affected the homogeneity of variances in the ANOVAs used for analyses of this data. Therefore, 6 schools in the Treatment with Support group (3 primary and 3 secondary schools) were randomly excluded. As a consequence, only 18 schools were included in the analyses of these measures. Condition × Time interactions from the ANOVAs were crucial for the hypothesis testing.

Measures: effects on the peer group

In addition, the intervention programme focused on changing the peer environment. Only non-involved students were selected for these analyses. The students were selected by means of the Bullying Inventory (Olweus, 1989). Students who reported 'not or rarely being bullied' or 'not or rarely having bullied others' at pre-test, post-test1, and post-test2 were identified as non-involved students. This sample consisted of 374 primary-school students and 548 secondary-school students from all 24 schools.

Five scales were constructed based on the available literature (Olweus, 1991, Rigby and Slee, 1991; Boulton and Underwood, 1992) and on the programme objectives, to measure student attitudes towards bullies' behaviour (9 items, Cronbach alpha .69), their attitudes towards victims of bullying (7 items, Cronbach alpha .62), their self-efficacy in intervening in bully/victim problems (3 items, Cronbach alpha .54), their intention to intervene (3 items, Cronbach alpha .62), and their actual level of intervention, including reactions against bullying, support for victims, and seeking teachers' help (3 items, Cronbach alpha .65). Repeated measures analysis of variance was used to investigate this research hypothesis. Again, Condition × Time interactions from the ANOVAs were crucial for the hypothesis testing.

Measures: issues of programme implementation

In the first place, the intention was to describe the process of programme implementation. For this a qualitative description was used by means of a cross-case analysis. Semi-structured interviews with project leaders from schools within the Treatment with Support condition ($N = 12$) were conducted at the end of the first year and at the end of the second year. Secondly, the study also intended to examine the relationship between programme implementation and programme effectiveness. The interviews were coded using a descriptive analysis system based upon the coding schedule developed by Smith and Sharp (1994). A total implementation score for each school (minimum = 0, maximum = 36) was computed by simply aggregating all parts of the programme that were successfully implemented. Inter-rater reliability from two independent raters was $r = .95$. Levels of implementation were related to rates of effect sizes (eta-squared). It was hypothesised that successful programme implementation would be related to better outcomes.

What actually happened; achievements and difficulties in implementing the intervention

The cross-case analysis that was carried out to describe variations between schools in the process of implementing the anti-bullying programme resulted in a summary of the parts that schools succeeded in (for a detailed overview, see Stevens et al., 2001). Regarding the core intervention, the results of the cross-case analysis revealed that schools (primary and secondary) succeeded in developing a policy against bullying for their school. They all informed students, teaching staff, non-teaching staff, and parents about this anti-bullying document and made it known that it would be applied. The policies clearly indicated that bullying behaviour would not be tolerated. At primary-school level, most schools provided extensive information for teaching staff on how they could react to bullying incidents. For the secondary-school level, the analysis revealed that the policies primarily provided information about students' actions against bullying behaviour. Few schools indicated responses for non-teaching staff and parents. One may conclude that most difficulties in implementing the anti-bullying programme are related to these parts of the programme.

Results of the evaluation

Effects on bullying and victimisation

Effects on bullying and victimisation in primary schools   The findings for rates of bullying and victimisation revealed a mixed pattern of positive results and no change (Stevens et al., 2000). Significant differences were found between the primary- and secondary-school level. At the primary-school level, significant effects of the programme were observed in bullying behaviour (table 8.1), with no change over time or a slight decrease in both treatment conditions (Treatment with Support, and Treatment without Support), while mean scores of the Control group increased over time. For victimisation, mean scores slightly decreased in all conditions.

Effects on bullying and victimisation in secondary schools   In secondary schools, the data revealed significant differences between conditions over time for bullying and for victimisation (table 8.1); but with a more complex pattern of outcomes. After 1 year of intervention, a slight increase emerged on bullying in the Treatment with Support condition and the Control condition. For victimisation, a slight increase was observed within the Treatment with Support condition only. One year afterwards, at post-test2, mean scores on the bully scale differed in all conditions. A slight increase was observed within the Treatment with Support condition while a slight decrease emerged in the Treatment without Support condition. Mean scores on victimisation showed a slight decrease in the Treatment without Support condition and the Control condition. Series of planned contrasts analyses between pairs of conditions revealed significant differences between the Treatment with Support condition and the Treatment without Support condition. However, both treatment conditions did not differ significantly from the Control group.

One can conclude that in primary schools the intervention was successful in reducing levels of bullying behaviour and that external help from the research group did not result in more positive outcomes. The impact on victimisation was affected by a strong main effect of time, which is

Table 8.1. *F-ratios, mean scores, and standard deviations of primary- and secondary-school students on bullying and victimisation*

	Treatment with Support condition Mean (sd)	Treatment without Support condition Mean (sd)	Control condition Mean (sd)	Condition × Educational Level × Time F-ratio	Condition × Time F-ratio	Time F-ratio
Bullying						
Primary schools				3.44**	3.97**	3.46*
pre	1.02 (.11)	1.12 (.14)	1.05 (.12)			
post1	1.02 (.11)	1.12 (.13)	1.07 (.12)			
post2	1.02 (.10)	1.10 (.14)	1.10 (.15)			
Secondary schools						
pre	0.99 (.09)	1.02 (.11)	1.02 (.12)			
post1	1.02 (.11)	1.02 (.10)	1.03 (.13)			
post2	1.00 (.10)	1.01 (.12)	1.02 (.12)			
Being bullied						
Primary schools				2.84*	0.94	15.68***
pre	1.09 (.13)	1.16 (.15)	1.14 (.15)			
post1	1.08 (.15)	1.16 (.14)	1.14 (.13)			
post2	1.06 (.13)	1.10 (.15)	1.11 (.15)			
Secondary schools						
pre	1.02 (.11)	1.04 (.12)	1.03 (.12)			
post1	1.05 (.14)	1.03 (.11)	1.04 (.13)			
post2	1.02 (.12)	1.03 (.13)	1.02 (.13)			

*p < .05, **p < .01, ***p < .001

Reproduced with permission from the *British Journal of Educational Psychology*, © The British Psychological Society in line with the findings relative to the prevalence of victimisation by age (Olweus, 1984; Rigby and Slee, 1991; Hoover et al., 1992; Whitney and Smith, 1993; Stevens and Van Oost, 1994). In secondary schools, the programme did not succeed in achieving the expected outcomes on bullying or on victimisation. External help was not able to increase the impact on the behavioural outcomes.

Effects on the peer group

Effects on the peer group in primary schools   Comparing the Treatment classes (combining with and without Support) and Control classes, the Condition × Time interaction did not reach significance for the attitudes to bully scale, the attitudes-to-victim scale, the self-efficacy scale, or the intention-to-intervene scale. Mean differences on the actual level of intervention scale were not significant after 1 year of intervention; however, after 2 years a slight trend emerged, indicating a smaller decrease in rates of intervening for pupils within the Treatment classes as compared to students within the Non-Treatment classes.

Additional analyses on students' strategies for solving bully/victim problems showed higher rates after 2 years of intervention for students of the Treatment classes with regard to supporting victims and seeking teachers' help, but not on reacting against bullies themselves.

Effects on the peer group in secondary schools   After 1 year of intervention, there were significant Condition × Time interactions for the attitudes to bully, attitudes to victim, self-efficacy, and actual level of intervention scales. There was also a trend for significance regarding intention to intervene. Compared to students in the Control classes, students in the Treatment classes had more negative attitudes towards bullies, more positive attitudes towards victims, higher rates of self-efficacy, and actually intervened to a larger degree.

However, after 2 years of intervention the results indicated no significant Condition × Time interactions for the attitudes to bully, attitudes to victim, self-efficacy, intention to intervene, or extent of intervening scales. For both Treatment and Control groups, mean scores on all dependent variables did not differ significantly from each other after two years of intervention.

Additional analyses on pupils' strategies in solving bully/victim problems, showed higher rates for students within the Treatment classes on reacting against bullies and seeking teachers' help, and a slight tendency to support the victim more.

The results of these analyses suggest that programmes that focus on the peer environment in tackling bully/victim problems can successfully change the attitudes and behaviour of non-involved children, in the short term, and especially at secondary-school level.

Programme implementation and outcome measures

Finally, the study related levels of implementation with programme effectiveness. In line with our hypothesis, we found a positive dosage–response relationship between programme implementation and outcome measurements at primary-school level. The more actively and intensively students, parents, teaching and non-teaching staff were involved in the anti-bullying activities in primary schools, the larger the behavioural outcomes. Given the empirical findings, the consultation phase was identified as the most critical part of the programme.

At secondary-school level, no positive programme outcomes on bullying and victimisation were observed and effect levels equalled zero. However, in comparison to primary schools, no significant differences were found, related to level of implementation ($t = 0.50$, $p > .05$). At the primary-school level, implementation scores ranged from 14 to 30. For secondary schools, a variation of 8–20 was found. Secondary schools did not obtain positive programme outcomes in spite of the same amount of intervention efforts.

Additional analyses revealed less consultation activities but more multi-disciplinary anti-bullying working groups in secondary schools. These analyses confirm that the consultation phase is an essential part for programme success. Moreover, they indicate that secondary schools might fall into the trap of representativeness of multi-disciplinary working groups, indicating that discussion among working-group members could become a 'replacement' for thorough consultation within the whole-school community.

Discussion of the programme outcomes

The central question underlying our study is whether anti-bullying interventions at school are able to reduce levels of bullying and victimisation. Positive programme outcomes were expected in this study; however, in contrast with the very positive outcomes observed in the Norwegian study, other evaluations of the adapted interventions have yielded moderate (Smith and Sharp, 1994) to small, zero, or even inconsistent results (Munthe and Roland, 1989; Pepler et al., 1994).

Our findings illustrated that the adapted anti-bullying interventions were not as effective in reducing peer aggression and victimisation as the model programme. Other evaluations of anti-bullying activities that differ from the Norwegian model programme in goals, methods, or timing, and in their evaluation instrument or design, also revealed less-positive outcomes compared to the Norwegian programme (Smith et al., 1999). In general, health interventions yield moderate programme outcomes, which nevertheless have to be considered as quite substantial from a health-promotion perspective (Kok et al., 1997). The amount of change that was observed by Smith and Sharp (1994) as well as in our study at the primary-school level (varying from small through moderate to large programme outcomes) indicates that these results are in line with what can be expected from health-promotion interventions.

However, given these mixed findings, further consideration deserves to be given as to why the beneficial outcomes of the anti-bullying campaign in Bergen (Olweus, 1984, 1992) were not replicated elsewhere. We suggest that the variance found in programme outcomes may be explained by several factors, including: (1) aspects of programme adaptation; (2) characteristics of children directly involved in bully/victim problems; (3) characteristics of the peer group; (4) problems related to the implementation process; and (5) limitations of the methodological designs selected.

Aspects of programme adaptation

In order to discuss the impact of programme adaptation on the outcomes of the interventions, we have compared the adapted anti-bullying intervention programmes to the Norwegian model programme (Stevens et al., 2001). Extensive analyses of the programmes revealed that the adapted interventions largely succeeded in incorporating the core components of the Norwegian programme. We concluded that poor programme adaptation was not the main explanation for the differences observed in programme outcomes.

However, it is possible that the weaker outcome results in the adapted interventions (Pepler et al., 1994; Smith and Sharp, 1994; Stevens et al., 2001) were caused by cultural influences in the programmes. As Olweus reported, his research was part of a nationwide campaign on bully/victim problems. The suicide of three children who had been bullied at school caused a storm of indignation, and problems with bullying became a matter of great public concern. As a result, the intervention was encouraged by this nationwide attention, and the convincingly positive outcomes of the Bergen project may be confounded by the so-called 'Hawthorn effect'. If so, the work of Olweus in the Bergen area combined with the nation-wide attention may explain why Roland (Munthe and Roland, 1989) at the same time did not succeed in confirming positive results after 3 years of intervention, and also why the other countries, where bullying had not become a nationwide concern, failed to replicate the strong effects.

Characteristics of children directly involved in bully/victim problems

The findings of different studies support the idea that anti-bullying inter-ventions at school affect younger and older students in different ways. More than one moderator can be found that helps us to understand the more-positive outcomes on primary-school students and the zero-outcomes at the secondary-school level. To explain this finding, the results are primarily considered from a developmental perspective.

During childhood, children tend to conform to the rules of figures of authority such as their teachers or parents (Durkin, 1995). Adults' rein-forcement or disapproval of students' (non)compliance with these rules is of great importance in sustaining or limiting their behaviour. In the case of anti-bullying interventions, clear rules against bullying acts are imple-mented. Students develop their own anti-bullying rules together with their classroom teacher, who can consistently observe their interactions. When the class rules are violated, the teacher's disapproval is considered to be a substantial negative consequence. All these factors taken together may have diminished the probability of continued bullying and can clar-ify why the intervention programme was successful in reducing problems with bullying in primary schools.

In contrast, adolescents consider the rules of such figures of author-ity as changeable agreements between people, and conflicts can possi-bly arise when an incongruence is observed between their own needs and those of adults (Durkin, 1995). The implementation of clear rules against bullying behaviour in secondary schools may cause an imbalance between teachers' and bullies' needs, as the school staff aims to reduce problems with bullying, whereas most bullying behaviour is proactive and is intended to gain social rewards from peers (Olweus, 1984, 1991; Dodge, 1991; Schwartz et al., 1993). During adolescence, the peer group becomes more important and plays a central role. If bullies change their behaviour, this implies a drop in social rewards. The implementation of an anti-bullying policy in secondary schools may create an adverse sit-uation for bullies in which the disadvantages of losing peer rewards are of considerable importance and definitely of more importance than in primary school.

Moreover, the implementation of an anti-bullying policy in secondary schools may be confounded by organisational characteristics. Secondary schools are usually characterised by having a more complex timetable compared to primary schools. It is reasonable to assume that secondary-school teachers find it more difficult to react with contingent negative consequences. This results in less impact on a bully's behaviour.

Next to explanations based on principles of operant learning, social cognitive deficits among the adolescents concerned may also have affected the results. The implementation of clear rules against bullying behaviour in secondary schools assumes that students have the social cognitive skills to take into account other students' well-being when reflecting on, and accepting, these rules. This assumption is not confirmed in anti-bullying studies; little perspective-taking and understanding of victims' suffering have been reported among bullies (Boulton and Underwood, 1992; Olweus, 1994). Accordingly, interventions against bullying behaviour at school should focus more intensively on a bully's perspective-taking skills, especially at the secondary-school level.

These factors, the risk of losing peer rewards combined with less-contingent reinforcement, and less commitment to the rules of figures of authority along with less understanding of the reasons for these rules, may explain why the data did not reveal the same amount of change in secondary schools when compared to the primary-school level.

Characteristics of the peer group

The results of our study confirm that programmes that focus on the peer environment in tackling bully/victim problems can successfully change the attitudes and behaviour of non-involved children, in particular in secondary-school children, although only for a limited period of time. These short-time effects among secondary-school students were observed on intervening in bully/victim incidents and on reacting against the aggressor in particular. The results also revealed a small effect on encouraging primary-school children to seek teachers' help and in heightening their support for victims, though no changes were observed with regard to reacting against bullies.

More detailed research on bystanders' responses to peer victimisation (Tisak and Tisak, 1996) has revealed a difference in younger and older students' reactions to bully/victim incidents. Younger students (10-year-olds) feel more comfortable with involving an adult when witnessing peer victimisation, whereas older students (14-year-olds) prefer to react against the aggressors themselves. These findings are in line with the results of our own study, and indicate that primary-school students do not feel competent enough to react against the aggressor in bully/victim incidents. Maybe it is unrealistic to think intervention programmes can change this at such a young age.

Finally, the observation that non-involved peers' behaviour in bully/victim incidents has been successfully changed while bullying behaviour did not decrease among the same age group (as indicated by secondary-school students' self-reports) deserves further consideration. Two explanations may help us to understand the findings. The results may be affected by the mechanism of intermittent reinforcement. In response to the loss of a positive reinforcer, some behaviour temporarily increases because the actor still hopes to get the desired outcome. The results indicate that, especially in secondary schools, peer reward has decreased and bullies may have attempted to receive the desired outcomes by over-reaction. Another explanation could be related to the characteristics of aggressive behaviour in general. It is known that the overt aggressive pathway, including bullying behaviour (Loeber and Hay, 1997; Olweus, 1984) is rather stable, indicating that obtaining behavioural changes in adolescents are more difficult than with younger children and probably need a more-intensive intervention strategy.

Problems related to the implementation process

Another explanation for the lack of overall positive programme outcomes involves the inadequate implementation of the intervention programme, the so-called type III error (Resnicow et al., 1996; Elias, 1997; Black et al., 1998). The cross-case analyses in our evaluation study revealed qualitative differences in implementation between primary and secondary schools. This finding can be explained in different ways. Firstly, programme implementation in secondary schools is usually found to be more difficult (Weissberg et al., 1989). Secondary schools have more complex timetables, more complicated organisational structures, larger organisational sizes, and more people to get involved (Weissberg et al., 1989). Moreover, extensive multi-year intervention programmes are hard to integrate into the curriculum (Weissberg et al., 1991).

Secondly, the quality of the implementation process is affected by teachers' training and technical assistance (Kazdin, 1993; Gottfredson et al., 1997). In our study we did not find better programme outcomes due to additional training sessions. We did indicate that the training was unable to bring about the expected outcomes and that other or additional aspects need to be included. However, empirical findings show that *training on its own* is not enough to explain the variation in programme implementation and related outcomes, and that other factors, like organisational characteristics, may influence the quality of the implementation process (Gottfredson et al., 1997). In line with this finding, it can be argued that the training sessions in the Flemish anti-bullying programme did not take into account the organisational characteristics of each school.

However, another explanation may account for the findings, as schools that received help from the research group did not 'own' the intervention as was intended, and this might affect the implementation process. Finally, although training needs were derived from a previous study among teachers implementing the Flemish anti-bullying programme during the pilot phase (Stevens and Van Oost, 1994), one may argue that schools received the wrong sort of help.

Limitations of the methodological designs selected

The statistical analyses deserve further consideration as multi-level analyses can be recommended. Typically, in educational research data are characterised by the dependency of the observational units (Bryk and Raudenbush 1992; Paterson and Goldstein, 1992; Uhl, 1999), with multiple measurements within individual students, who are nested within classes, which are nested within schools. Hierarchical linear models have the advantage that they explain the variation of a dependent variable by a set of independent variables that are analysed at different levels, thus providing information about the effects of personal characteristics as well as about how these are influenced by class or school characteristics.

It is of particular importance to analyse the influence of class characteristics, like group cohesion, degree of conflict, and amount of competitive play, and of changes in these characteristics reflected in the programme outcomes (Olweus, 1978, 1984; DeRosier et al., 1994). The same reasoning is valid for school characteristics, including aspects of concentration of power at school, teachers' and students' observance of rules, the organisational atmosphere, leadership variables, and the mission of the school (Rogers, 1983; Gottfredson et al., 1997).

Longer term effects or evaluation of the programme

The second anti-bullying project had its focus on an extensive assessment of the intervention outcomes. This evaluation phase lasted 2.5 years and resulted in the findings described above. At the end of that project, research activities on programme outcomes were finished and no further measurements on behavioural changes were carried out. No follow-up measurements were made.

Dissemination and impact beyond the programme schools

The Flemish anti-bullying programme has been widely implemented at the primary- and secondary-school level. Teachers clearly observed a need to tackle bully/victim problems. For that reason we planned a proactive implementation strategy in which primary- and secondary-school teachers were informed about the strategy and methods used in the intervention. In addition to these information sessions, members of school service centres were intensively trained in using the anti-bullying programme and giving support to schools that asked for it. As the programme became well known and was more and more disseminated, it encouraged other organisations to develop additional anti-bullying materials for schools, like books for children, an anti-bullying exposition, and drama. Most of these materials had a focus on awareness-raising activities. Currently the issue of bullying and victimisation has become part of a wider concern on students' well-being at school.

Implications for school-based anti-bullying interventions

Anti-bullying evaluation studies have shown that involving the social environment, *including the implementation of an anti-bullying policy*, seems to be a potentially powerful means of arriving at the desired outcomes. However, because both positive and zero-outcomes were observed in this study, as well as in the other adapted interventions, we have provided several explanations that help us to understand the complex pattern of findings. Based on this information, some recommendations have been made to further the programme content and outline of the Flemish anti-bullying intervention.

First, we observed differences in the reactions of bullies from primary and secondary schools to the core components of the intervention. It was concluded that behaviour modification in secondary schools is more complicated and needs more time. Accordingly, more attention to bullies' perspective-taking skills would encourage beneficial programme outcomes, especially in secondary schools. Additionally, in the light of effective health promotion, aspects of positive reinforcement were considered. Schools are not used to reinforcing students who try to change their behaviour in a positive way. However, when children try to alter their behaviour, they need to be given full support and positive encouragement by their teachers.

Second, the data revealed a difference in attitudes and rates of intervention in bully/victim problems between non-involved children from primary and from secondary schools. The behavioural changes observed were affected by students' age-related competence to intervene in problems of peer aggression. *Given these findings, the benefits of a rule-focused approach for younger students has been confirmed.* Moreover, one may suggest the importance of adapting anti-bullying interventions to children's developmental phases. It seems that younger children may benefit from training programmes that focus on active listening skills and on giving support to victims of bullying, whereas an older student may benefit more from acquiring competence in assertiveness towards aggressors.

Finally, the findings have uncovered some barriers to programme implementation. In particular, a risk for effective implementation was detected when consultation of staff, students, and parents about the anti-bullying rules was limited. To increase the impact of the anti-bullying intervention, the programme has to stress the importance of the consultation phase, by labelling it as the most critical part for programme success.

References

Arora, C. M. J. (1994). *Measuring bullying with the 'life in school' checklist*. Sheffield: Education Division, Sheffield University.

Baker, J. A. (1998). Are we missing the forest for the trees? Considering the social context of school violence. *Journal of School Psychology*, 36, 29–44.

Bartholomew, L. K., Parcel, G. S., and Kok, G. (1998). Intervention mapping: A process for developing theory- and evidence-based health education programs. *Health Education and Behaviour*, 25, 545–63.

Black, D. R., Tobler, N. S., and Sciacca, J. P. (1998). Peer helping involvement: An efficacious way to meet the challenge of reducing alcohol, tobacco, and other drug use among youth? *Journal of School Health*, 68, 87–93.

Bond, L. A. and Compas, B. E. (eds.) (1989), *Primary prevention of psychopathology, Vol. X11: Primary prevention and promotion in the schools*. London: Sage.

Boulton, M. J. and Underwood, K. (1992). Bully/victim problems among middle school children. *British Journal of Educational Psychology*, 62, 73–87.

Bowers, L., Smith, P. K., and Binney, V. (1994). Perceived family relationships of bullies, victims and bully/victims in middle childhood. *Journal of Social and Personal Relationships*, 11, 215–32.

Bryk, A. S. and Raudenbush, S. W. (1992). *Advanced quantitative techniques in the social sciences series 1. Hierarchical linear models*. London: Sage.

Coie, J. D., Dodge, K. A., Terry, R., and Wright, V. (1991). The role of aggression in peer relations: An analysis of aggression episodes in boys' play groups. *Child Development*, 62, 812–26.

Damoiseaux, V., van der Molen, H. T., and Kok, G. J. (1993). *Gezondheidsvoorlichting en verandering*. Assen: Van Gorcum.

DeRosier, M. E., Cillessen, A. H. N., Coie, J. D., and Dodge, K. A. (1994). Group social context and children's aggressive behavior. *Child Development*, 65, 1068–79.

Dodge, K. A. (1991). The structure and function of reactive and proactive aggression. In D. J. Pepler and K. H. Rubin (eds.), *The development and treatment of childhood aggression*. Hillsdale, NJ: Erlbaum, pp. 201–18.

Durkin, K. (1995). *Developmental social psychology: From infancy to old age*. Oxford: Blackwell.

Elias, M. J. (1997). Reinterpreting dissemination of prevention programs as widespread implementation with effectiveness and fidelity. In R. P. Weissberg, T. P. Gullotta, R. L. Hampton, B. A. Ryan, and G. R. Adams (eds.), *Issues in children's and families' lives, Vol. 9: Establishing preventive services*. London: Sage, pp. 253–89.

Felner, R. D. and Felner, T. Y. (1989). Primary prevention programs in the educational context: A transactional-ecological framework and analysis. In L. A. Bond and B. E. Compas (eds.), *Primary prevention of psychopathology, Vol. 12: Primary prevention and promotion in the schools*. London: Sage, pp. 13–49.

Gottfredson, D. C., Fink, C. M., Skroban, S., and Gottfredson, G. D. (1997). Making prevention work. In R. P. Weissberg, T. P. Gullotta, R. L. Hampton, B. A. Ryan, and G. R. Adams (eds.), *Issues in children's and families' lives, Vol. 9: Establishing preventive services*. London: Sage, pp. 219–52.

Green, L. W. and Kreuter, M. W. (1991). *Health promotion planning: An educational and environmental approach*. Palo Alto: Mayfield.

Haselager, G. J. T. (1997). *Classmates: Studies on the development of their relationships and personality in middle childhood*. Ph.D. diss. University of Nijmegen: Mediagroep KUN/AZN.

Hoover, J. H., Oliver, R., and Hazler, R. J. (1992). Bullying: Perceptions of adolescent victims in the midwestern USA. *School Psychology International*, 3, 5–16.

Kazdin, A. E. (1993). Adolescent mental health: prevention and treatment programs. *American Psychologist*, 48, 127–41.

   (1996). Conduct disorders in childhood and adolescence. 2nd edn. *Developmental Clinical Psychology and Psychiatry*, 9, London: Sage.

Kok, G., van den Borne, B., and Mullen, P. D. (1997). Effectiveness of health education and health promotion: Meta-analyses of effect studies and determinants of effectiveness. *Patient Education and Counseling*, 30, 19–27.

Liebrand, J., Van Ijzendoorn, H., and Van Lieshout, C. F. M. (1991). *Klasgenoten Relatie Vragenlijst*. Nijmegen: Vakgroep Ontwikkelingspsychologie, Katholieke Universiteit Nijmegen.

Loeber, R. and Hay, D. (1997). Key issues in the development of aggression and violence from childhood to early adulthood. *Annual Review of Psychology*, 48, 371–410.

Mooij, T. (1998). Pupil-class determinants of aggressive and victim behaviour in pupils. *British Journal of Educational Psychology*, 68, 373–85.

Munthe, E. and Roland, E. (eds.) (1989). *Bullying: An international perspective*. London: David Fulton.

Oliver, R., Hoover, J. H., and Hazler, R. (1994). The perceived roles of bullying in small-town midwestern schools. *Journal of Counseling and Development*, 72, 416–20.

Olweus, D. (1978). *Aggression in the schools: Bullies and whipping boys.* Washington, DC: Hemisphere.

(1984). Aggressors and their victims: Bullying at school. In N. Frude and H. Gault (eds.), *Disruptive behavior in schools.* New York: Wiley, pp. 57–76.

(1991). Bully/victim problems among schoolchildren: Basic facts and effects of a school based intervention program. In D. J. Pepler and K. H. Rubin (eds.), *The development and treatment of childhood aggression.* Hillsdale, NJ: Erlbaum, pp. 411–48.

(1992). Bullying among schoolchildren: Intervention and prevention. In R. V. Peters, R. J. McMahon, and V. L. Quinsey (eds.), *Aggression and violence throughout the life span.* Newbury Park: Sage, pp. 100–25.

(1994). Annotation: Bullying at school: Basic facts and effects of a school-based intervention program. *Journal of Child Psychology and Psychiatry*, 35, 1171–90.

Parry, G. and Watts, F. N. (1989). *Behavioural and mental health research: A handbook of skills and methods.* East Sussex: Erlbaum.

Paterson, L. and Goldstein, H. (1992). New statistical methods for analysing social structures: An introduction to multilevel models. *British Educational Research Journal*, 17, 387–93.

Pepler, D. J., Craig, W. M., Ziegler, S., and Charach, A. (1994). An evaluation of an anti-bullying intervention in Toronto schools. *Canadian Journal of Community Mental Health*, 13, 95–110.

Pepler, D. J., Craig, W. M., and Roberts, W. L. (1998). Observations of aggressive and non-aggressive children on the school playground. *Merrill-Palmer Quarterly*, 44, 55–76.

Price, R. H., Cowen, E. L., Lorion, R. P., and Ramos-Mckay, J. R. (1993). *Fourteen ounces of prevention: A casebook for practitioners.* Washington, DC: American Psychological Association.

Resnicow, K., Robinson, T. N., and Frank, E. (1996). Advances and future directions for school-based health promotion research: Commentary on the CATCH intervention trial. *Preventive Medicine*, 25, 378–83.

Rican, P., Klicperova, M., and Koucka, T. (1993). Families of bullies and their victims: A children's view. *Studia Psychologica*, 35, 261–66.

Rigby, K. (1994). Psychosocial functioning in families of Australian adolescent schoolchildren involved in bully–victim problems. *Journal of Family Therapy*, 16, 173–87.

Rigby, K. and Slee, P. T. (1991). Bullying among Australian school children: reported behavior and attitudes toward victims. *Journal of Social Psychology*, 131, 615–27.

Roberts, M. C. and Hinton-Nelson, M. (1996). Models for service delivery in child and family mental health. In M. C. Roberts (ed.), *Model programs in child and family mental health.* NJ: Erlbaum, pp. 1–21.

Rogers, E. M. (1983). *Diffusion of innovations.* New York: Free Press.

Schwartz, D., Dodge, K. A., and Coie, J. D. (1993). The emergence of chronic peer victimization in boys' play groups. *Child Development*, 64, 1755–72.

Scholte, R. H. J., Van Aken, M. A. G., and Van Lieshout, C. F. M. (1997). Adolescent personality factors in self-ratings and peer nominations and their prediction of peer acceptance and peer rejection. *Journal of Personality Assessment*, 69, 534–54.

Slee, P. T. and Rigby, K. (1993). The relationship of Eysenck's personality factors and self-esteem to bully–victim behaviour in Australian schoolboys. *Personality and Individual Differences*, 14, 371–73.

Smith, P. K., Bowers, L., Binney, V., and Cowie, H. (1993). Relationships of children involved in bully/victim problems at school. In S. Duck (ed.), *Understanding relationship processes, Vol. 2: Learning about relationships*. London: Sage, pp. 184–212.

Smith, P. K. and Sharp, S. (eds.) (1994). *School bullying: Insights and perspectives*. London: Routledge.

Smith, P. K., Morita, Y., Junger-Tas, J., Olweus, D., Catalano, R., and Slee, P. (eds.) (1999). *The nature of school bullying: A cross-national perspective*. London: Routledge.

Stevens, V. and Van Oost, P. (1994). *Pesten op School: Een actieprogramma*. Kessel-Lo: Garant Uitgevers.

Stevens, V., De Bourdeaudhuij, I., and Van Oost, P. (2000). Bullying in Flemish schools: An evaluation of anti-bullying intervention in primary and secondary schools. *British Journal of Educational Psychology*, 70, 195–210.

Stevens, V., Van Oost, P., and De Bourdeaudhuij, I. (2000). The effects of an anti-bullying intervention programme on peers' attitudes and behaviour. *Journal of Adolescence*, 23, 21–34.

Stevens, V., De Bourdeaudhuij, I., and Van Oost, P. (2001). Anti-bullying interventions at school: Aspects of programme adaptation and critical issues for further programme development. *Health Promotion International*, 16, 155–67.

Stevens, V., Van Oost, P., and De Bourdeaudhuij, I. (2001). Implementation process of the Flemish anti-bullying intervention and relation with program effectiveness. *Journal of School Psychology*, 39, 303–17.

Tisak, M. S. and Tisak, J. (1996). Expectations and judgements regarding bystanders' and victims' responses to peer aggression among early adolescents. *Journal of Adolescence*, 19, 383–92.

Valente, E. and Dodge, K. A. (1997). Evaluation of prevention programs for children. In R. P. Weissberg, T. P. Gullotta, R. L. Hampton, B. A. Ryan, and G. R. Adams (eds.), *Issues in children's and families' lives, Vol. 9: Establishing preventive services*. London: Sage, pp. 183–218.

Van Lieshout, C. F. M., Haselager, G. J. T., and Cillessen, A. H. N. (1992). *Achtergronden en vroege risico indicatoren van pesten en gepest worden*. Studiedag Pesten op school aangepakt, Amersfoort, 13 October.

Van Oost, P. and Stevens, V. (1995). *Helping schools to tackle bullying. The effect of support for primary and secondary schools on the way they implement bullying intervention programmes*. Book of abstracts. International conference on conflict and development in adolescence, Ghent, Belgium 21–24, November.

Uhl, A. (1999). Research and evaluation in the field of primary prevention: a problem area? *International Journal of Mental Health Promotion*, 1, 33–44.

Weissberg, R. P., Caplan, M. Z., and Sivo, P. J. (1989). A new conceptual framework for establishing school-based social competence promotion programs. In L. A. Bond and B. E. Compas (eds.), *Primary prevention of Psychopathology, Vol. 12: Primary prevention and promotion in the schools*. London: Sage, pp. 255–96.

Weissberg, R. P., Caplan, M., and Harwood, R. L. (1991). Promoting competent young people in competence-enhancing environments: A systems-based perspective on primary prevention. *Journal of Consulting and Clinical Psychology*, 59, 830–41.

Whitney, I. and Smith, P. K. (1993). A survey of the nature and extent of bullying in junior/middle and secondary schools. *Educational Research*, 35, 3–25.

Windsor, R. A., Baranowski, T., Clark, N., and Cutter, G. (1984). *Evaluation of health promotion and education*. Palo Alto, Calif.: Mayfield.

9   SAVE model: an anti-bullying intervention in Spain

Rosario Ortega, Rosario Del Rey, and Joaquín A. Mora-Merchán

Impetus for the intervention, early stages of planning, and funding

The first thing we should say about educational programmes against bullying in Spain is that, in the beginning, they ran up against the absence of information about the nature of bullying in our culture. Spanish schools, which are mainly public, have developed a very academic educational tradition that has left the aspects of social and emotional development to one side. They have taken little account of interpersonal relationships and the problems that arise within them (including bullying). Teachers were trained to focus their work on the teaching of basic disciplines, such as languages, sciences, or mathematics, within the compulsory education period from 6 to 14 years. As a result, neither our teachers nor our society had been sensitive to the interpersonal problems that we now recognise in our schools. In fact, the word *bullying* still does not have an accepted translation in our language. This has been one of the most serious problems that we have encountered: the need to explain to teachers and students what constitutes this type of violence, which some students can exercise over others. However, in recent years we have been attempting to develop a global education where socio-emotional aspects and concern for the world of interpersonal relationships have a place, even though this process is still unfinished.

This growing preoccupation has been reflected in the number of investigations carried out on the topic of bullying in our country in the last decade (Vieira, Fernández, and Quevedo, 1989; Ortega, 1992, 1994a,b; Cerezo, 1997; Ortega and Mora-Merchán, 1997, 1999, 2000; Defensor del Pueblo, 2000; Ortega, Del Rey, and Mora-Merchán, 2001). However, none of these studies made any systematic attempts at intervention except for the SAVE project (Ortega, 1997; Ortega and Lera, 2000; Del Rey and Ortega, 2001).

SAVE stands for Sevilla Anti-Violencia Escolar (Seville Anti-Violence in School). It was the first project to come up with a global process of intervention linked to research work. This link between intervention and research is the defining factor of the SAVE project. In this intervention model, funded by the national government and applied in primary and secondary schools, we aim to involve staff in the slow process of making decisions about the problem, to help teachers distinguish and pay attention to bullying phenomena, to incorporate violence prevention in their educational objectives, to be conscious that we cannot tolerate violence, and that we cannot consider it as an individual problem (bully or victim) but as a problem for the whole educational community. In this chapter, we analyse the principal trends in the SAVE project, and its most relevant outcomes.

Selection of schools

In collaboration with the local education administration we selected, in the 1995–96 academic year, some primary and secondary schools from Seville and its province of Andalucia which were situated in areas of special need because of their socio-cultural characteristics: low earnings, high unemployment, and high social conflict. To establish contact we held a seminar about bullying to which we invited the headteachers, at least three other teachers from the staff of each school, and the school counsellors. Following this meeting, 23 schools agreed to participate in the first stage of the project, which aimed to collect information about bullying through a questionnaire (Ortega, Mora-Merchán, and Mora, 1995). Three more schools joined the project, because they were interested in knowing about bullying in their schools. In the end we gave the questionnaire to 4,914 students between 8 and 18 years old, in 26 schools. Of these, only 10 schools became involved in the intervention model, because they had to comply with two requirements: that there would be the involvement of a minimum of four teachers; and that this project would have to be approved of, and included in, the school policy by the whole staff, even if they were not going to be involved in it. And, of these, only 5 schools completed both pre-test and post-test questionnaires; another 4 schools took part as post-test only controls. All were from deprived areas.

Characteristics of schools and students

Of the 5 schools doing both pre-test and post-test, 3 were primary (8–12 years) and 2 were secondary (12–16 years). There were 731 pupils in intervention schools at pre-test (36.5% primary and 63.5% secondary) and 901 at post-test (25.4% primary and 74.6% secondary). The 4 control schools comprised two primary and two secondary, with 440

Table 9.1. *Sample distribution (numbers of boys and girls) for intervention schools (pre-test–post-test) and for control schools*

| | Intervention schools | | | | | Control schools | | |
| | Pre-test | | Post-test | | | Post-test only | | |
	Boys	Girls	Boys	Girls			Boys	Girls
School A (secondary)	62	57	102	100	School CA (primary)		58	49
School B (primary)	96	85	62	52	School CB (primary)		47	51
School C (primary)	82	64	61	54	School CC (secondary)		40	30
School D (secondary)	66	64	164	161	School CD (secondary)		84	81
School E (primary)	78	77	73	72				

* Missing sex data are not included.

pupils (45.1% primary and 54.9% secondary). See table 9.1 for details by school. No significant differences were found between pre-test and post-test groups, or between intervention and control groups, in terms of age or sex composition.

Components of the intervention programme

In the SAVE project, we have proposed an educational intervention model, starting with ecological analysis, which goes further than the personal perspective, attempting to uncover the system of rules, values, feelings, and behaviours which lie behind violence in all its forms.

The model proposes, as a starting-point, the design of an educational project about interpersonal relationships in two dimensions: the dimension of *convivencia*; and the dimension of activity. The Spanish term *convivencia* can be translated as *coexistence*, but it is used to signify not merely sharing time and space nor merely tolerance of others (though that obviously is part of the concept), rather, *convivencia* has to do with a spirit of solidarity, fraternity, co-operation, harmony, a desire for mutual understanding, the desire to get on well with others, and the resolution of conflict through dialogue or other non-violent means.

These two linked dimensions give us a vision of the social, psychological, and academic reality of the schools as real communities of *convivencia* where we learn not only what is planned through the curriculum but also that which is not planned and yet which becomes a hidden or implicit curriculum (Ortega, 1997). We have used the community model, imported from other scientific and professional areas, such as anthropology and health sciences, for our proposal of educational and research work. From this intervention perspective, every school is presented as a unit of *convivencia*, where, for better or worse, the different people who participate in the school (teachers, students, and families) are linked together.

Programmes and tools of the SAVE model

Students go to school to learn and teachers to instruct. Teachers have certain curriculum objectives, contents, and evaluations that they have to achieve as part of their role within the educational system. Notwithstanding, both students and teachers should also attempt to construct *convivencia*. Clearly, teaching and learning can be done in many different ways. In the Spanish education system, teachers have some freedom to choose the contents and evaluation methods they use. In addition, teachers can decide how to manage the social rules, the communication channels, and the degree to which power is shared by pupils within both the classroom and the school. They have to carry out specific objectives, but can reach these in different ways.

The insertion of instructive activity within the development of the curriculum gives rise to a process that allows differentiation between school communities (i.e. teachers, pupils, and families). This process, like the previous one, emerges from the consideration of the wider school environment that has to be borne in mind when we analyse the *convivencia* of a school with the intention of improving it.

In this respect, we find three processes that, in our view, become relevant when we want to design an anti-bullying project. These are:
1. management of the social environment, and the ways in which children interact, within the classroom;
2. the specific method of instructive action: teaching and learning; and
3. activities geared towards feelings and values education.

Democratic management of interpersonal relationships   To be conscious that the activity in the classroom can be managed in different ways, either democratic or authoritarian, is the first step towards developing a classroom that is more, or less, participatory. Thus, the first thing is to realise that life within the classroom requires management and that it can, indeed should, be democratic, as without this teachers risk losing their moral authority.

Attending to the democratic management of both the class and the school includes the analysis of all the events related to daily *convivencia*. This is necessary for students and teachers to progress towards co-operative and democratic participation together.

To create a progressive way for teachers and pupils to approach one another, there has to be a task that is common for all since *convivencia* comes from the group and not from a specific person. With this in mind, there should be an elaboration of clear and explicit rules, including the setting up of an easy and transparent model of discipline. Equally important is agreement from everyone regarding rules about what is acceptable and unacceptable behaviour, and a positive emphasis on liberty, solidarity, and equality among everybody in the school.

The description and comprehension of the management of social life in each classroom permits us to establish a profile of what usually happens. This, in turn, allows prediction of what is possible in the future in terms of the relationships among all those participating: among pupils and teachers, but also, and more importantly, among the peer microsystem.

The analysis of management systems of *convivencia* has become a necessary conceptual tool to tackle the problems that can appear in school. We have to consider the management of *convivencia* as this is an important factor in understanding life within the school. Some proposals inside this programme are: assemblies, establishment of rules by consensus, debates, conflict resolution, suggestion boxes, design of specific materials by teachers, and the encouragement of participation in school life.

Co-operative group work   To work in co-operative groups includes acceptance that some subjects could be learned better if work is carried out not only in the company of others but also with their co-operation. To approach classroom activity through the co-operative model involves consideration of the overall communicative process, including both the teaching and the learning process, and in this way it becomes a common task that can improve all those involved.

Co-operation has been identified as one of the most successful ways of covering all the teaching objectives (Ortega and Fernández, 2000), not only for those who are helped by others but also for more able students who help the less-able pupils. Co-operation is sharing ideas, activities, criticisms, and evaluations in a joint task.

The ways in which people work and interact in school are impregnated with values regardless of whether or not this is intentional. Work aiming to prevent school violence demands that the ways of teaching and learning be changed towards a co-operative model that encourages communication and negotiation. Only in this way will students have experiences that improve the affective climate, the attitudes, and the positive values that guide their behaviour towards each other.

Education of feelings, attitudes, and values   All teaching and learning activity is based on motivations and interests, which teachers and students alike develop, and these motivations basically depend on their emotional and attitudinal states. Everything that happens in the classroom, as with all that is human, has emotional connotations that could be pleasant or unpleasant. These feelings may provoke in us a positive or enthusiastic attitude, or a negative, rejected, or unpleasant attitude, if not one of fear or anger.

Although our curriculum proposes an education of attitudes and values in a transverse way that may be unspecific, it is of greater interest, from our point of view, to develop a concrete work programme whose contents refer to emotions, feelings, attitudes, and values. It tries to work directly with interpersonal and psychological knowledge; to explore more about one's self and others in all their dimensions, but especially with those whose emotions and feelings affect social relations; to recognise that we can damage others if we do not understand them and respect them; and also to learn to appreciate our own feelings and values to avoid injuring our personal rights.

Some examples of techniques from our proposal are: the use of play, stories, role playing, analysis of communication media, case studies, design of specific materials by the teachers about solidarity, respect, self-esteem, and self-concept.

Direct intervention with students at risk or involved in bullying
Although the SAVE project highlights prevention, it does not mean that we forget that there are children who, because of their personal, family, and social conditions, are at risk of involving themselves in bullying, or are already involved. So, our educational centres must implement direct intervention systems. In this sense the SAVE project offers them specific lines of intervention directed towards helping these students through programmes that, necessarily, are outside the developed curriculum, although they can, and must, be implemented with a view to establishing coherence between the two.

For those children we propose, among others, 6 programmes: quality circles (Sharp, Cowie, and Smith, 1994), conflict mediation (Fernández, 1998), peer support (Cowie and Wallace, 1998), Pikas Method (Pikas, 1989), assertiveness training (Ortega, 1998), and empathy training (Ortega, 1998).

The shared aim of the first three programmes is to offer the children social support, in the majority of the cases from their peers, to solve situations where before they felt insecure. In this sense, experience has taught us that peers can carry out an important task, assisting the social development of these children, because they share conventions, values, and a moral reciprocity with their peers that is not possible for adults.

The last three programmes are characterised by very specific objectives and are very systematic. We see the objective of the Pikas Method as the destructuralisation of the social networks that support the bullying situation, and their replacement with help systems. Also with victims we need a direct intervention, focused on the development of their lost assertiveness and damaged self-esteem. Finally, a lot of bullies need a special process to re-educate their capacity to be sensitive towards others' feelings. Programmes of empathy training are designed for them.

Evaluation framework and procedures

The evaluation of the SAVE model has been made from two different perspectives. We used a pre-test / post-test model to evaluate changes in the number of students involved in bully or victim roles, as well as possible changes in attitudes and other related aspects. For this we used an anonymous questionnaire about bullying (*Cuestionario sobre intimidación y maltrato entre iguales*; Ortega, Mora-Merchán, and Mora, 1995). This instrument was given twice in classrooms without the presence of teachers: once before starting the intervention (1995–96) and again four years later (1999–2000), in 5 schools; classes were of equivalent age. It was also given, during the post-test period, to 4 control schools; see table 9.1.

We also explored the effectiveness of the programmes developed within the SAVE model. To do this, we used a short questionnaire asking students what the teachers have done to improve relations between peers; how long they have been doing it; and (for each intervention component) what effects these interventions have had.

What actually happened; achievements and difficulties in implementing the intervention

The first phase, to raise awareness and to involve people, was carried out through a series of seminars, where we presented the project and the bullying issue to Local Education Authorities. The aim of these meetings was not only to get permission from the administration to contact the schools but also to raise awareness among the people who affect educational policy about the importance of bullying as an issue. In a model to raise awareness which tries to involve different people in a common project, it is necessary to give to each group a role in the process. We tried not only to inform but also to ask people for their thoughts on the project, and to ask which schools were most appropriate for the project.

Approaching the schools

The second group whose help we needed to raise awareness was the teachers. We achieved this using the same procedure. Selected schools were sent a letter describing the project and were invited to a seminar, in which we talked about the bullying problem with representatives from each school (the headteacher, some teachers, and the counsellor).

The seminars, held over a 3-week period, took a total of 20 hours, and finished with the decision, in the majority of the cases to participate in the first stage of the project: giving questionnaires at the pre-test phase. After collecting data, the staff from each school had to decide about their participation in the intervention, while we analysed the information. During this time, we maintained contact with the educational psychologists who worked with the schools involved, and also with the teacher teams if they asked us. In any case, to continue their participation in the project they needed to tell us, or to accept an invitation to a new meeting when the reports from each school were made.

The second phase: working together

When the SAVE project entered its second phase, there was also at that time large-scale reform in the Spanish education system which included two more years of compulsory schooling. During this period there was a great deal of change in the way in which schools were organised. The majority of the SAVE schools were affected by this change, and some of their teachers were transferred to other schools. However, despite this, 10 schools still asked to be involved in the second phase of the project.

Starting was a difficult task, as teachers needed to design their own anti-bullying projects, in an autonomous way, yet according to our intervention model. Furthermore, the social characteristics of the students, who lived in marginalised areas with a variety of social problems, meant this aim had to be achieved within a stressful academic environment. During the 1996–97 academic year, our team had to visit each school several times to establish the intervention programmes. We also held some formative seminars, in some of which we had the presence and participation of colleagues from the Sheffield Project (Smith and Sharp, 1994), who gave us the benefit of their experiences. Finally, we received official recognition regarding the SAVE project.

In June 1997, at the end of an intensive period of work, we held a large meeting, at which 75 teachers shared their impressions, thoughts, and opinions about the development of the SAVE project in their schools. The main conclusion arrived at was the importance of continuing what was perceived to be a valuable programme of work.

There were groups of teachers within schools who had progressed quickly in their own projects; others worked more slowly. But even the slowest had met to discuss the project at least every 2 weeks, for 2 hours. These meetings provided the opportunity to share worries, initiatives, and encouragement, and improved the group cohesion and the motivation to continue together. All groups started to realise two things: first, that SAVE was a long-term project, which implied a slow change in their ideas and attitudes towards the bullying problem; second, that we needed to improve the social climate and the management of the interpersonal relationships in the school through more co-operative and more democratic curricular work where we attended not only to 'teaching' but also to the students' feelings and values. This reflection process made the majority of teachers think about their own behaviours which, although not intentionally promoting interpersonal violence, may have appeared to condone such behaviours via intolerant or ambiguous attitudes.

We finished the meeting with the decision to continue the work during the next academic year, though only if the restructuring of the educational system allowed the creation of groups with at least 4 or 5 teachers in the same school. This was indeed the case and, despite changes in some teams, the work was able to continue. The groups of teachers established new challenges for their work, which caused, in some cases, a change in the intervention proposals of the school.

The project has maintained the same dynamic up to the present time: each group meets once every 2 weeks, and the chairs of these school-working groups meet with our team once every 2 months. At the end of each academic session, all the staff involved in the SAVE project meet to assess the progress and design the next year.

During the implementation of the SAVE project, it has experienced some changes, above all due to the movement of teachers. This movement has created two separate dynamics of change: first, the groups which were working are often split up and so need to recruit new members to continue; and second, members moving to new schools want to continue the work and so organise new groups. In table 9.2, we show the intervention programmes developed in each of the 10 SAVE schools during these 4 years of work (the 5 schools taking both the pre-test and post-test

Table 9.2. *Programmes of intervention developed by each of the 10 SAVE schools (schools A–E, in bold, are those in the pre-test/post-test assessments)*

Schools	Programmes of Intervention						
	Democratic management of social relationships	Education of feelings and values	Working in co-operative groups	Direct intervention with bullies, victims	Working with families	Teacher training	Others
B (primary)	X	X		X		X	
C (primary)	X	X	X	X		X	
E (primary)		X			X	X	'Comprehending and transforming'
F (primary)	X	X					
G (primary)	X	X	X				
H (primary +secondary)	X	X	X				
I (primary +secondary)	X	X			X	X	Social abilities training
A (secondary)	X		X	X			
D (secondary)	X				X	X	
J (secondary)	X	X				X	

assessments are schools A–E). These interventions were not necessarily simultaneous, since teacher groups could tailor their objectives to respond better to their needs and interests.

Results of the evaluation

We have structured the assessment of the SAVE model's impact around three different indicators which, although in some ways independent, are clearly related and allow us to examine the effects of the intervention. The first is an exploration of the number of students involved and their distribution into the different roles that they can assume (bullies, victims, bully/victims, and bystanders). The second is related to the different aspects assessed in the questionnaire used (risky places, types of bullying, etc.). Both of these indicators were planned to evaluate the differences between pre-test and post-test. The third measurement, from a retrospective approach, aimed to assess the students' perceptions of the intervention programmes developed in their schools.

Chi-squared tests were used in all the analyses reported in this chapter. In every case, we tested all the responses included in each question, although only the most relevant results are pointed out in the text.

Numbers of students involved

This indicator is the most important for gauging the success of the intervention with regards to the bullying problem. We asked students: 'How often have you been bullied by other students?' and 'How often have you bullied other students?' In both cases, the questions referred to the last term.

After analysing the pre-test data in the experimental schools, and comparing these with the answers collected 4 years later, we found that the participation of the students has significantly changed. The number of pupils involved as victims (who respond that they have been a victim more than a few times and aggressor less than a few times), bullies (who respond that they have been an aggressor more than a few times and victim less than a few times), and bully/victims (who respond that they have been aggressor, and victim, each more than a few times) decreased, see fig. 9.1. The number of victims more than halved, from 9.1% (N = 83) to 3.9% (N = 35), and the same is true for the bully/victim group, which decreased from 0.7% (N = 6) to 0.3% (N = 3). There was a less dramatic decline for bullies, from 4.5% (N = 41) to 3.8% (N = 34). Correspondingly, the bystander or non-involved group (who respond that they have been aggressor, and victim, each less than a few times) increased from

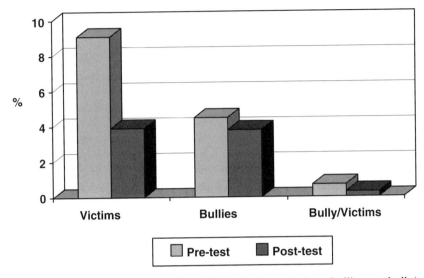

Fig. 9.1 Percentages of pupils involved as victims, bullies, or bully/victims, at pre-test and post-test.

85.7% (N = 780) to 92.1% (N = 838). The differences in the number of students involved in bullying problems are significant at chi-squared (p < 0.001) between pre-test and post-test.

The post-test results from the 5 intervention schools were compared with the 4 control schools in the same or similar areas, in which we did not apply the SAVE project. The intervention schools had a lower incidence of bully/victim problems than control schools (p < 0.01 over all 4 roles), see fig. 9.2. Again, this is especially marked for victims and bully/victims, less so for bullies. Of course, the control schools were assessed only at the post-test period, so we do not know what changes they had experienced over the period.

Aspects of bullying from the questionnaire

We organised the information of these indicators into aspects that help us to understand the effects that the intervention had produced: first, relationships between pupils in the school and the level of satisfaction that they have; second, information about the victimisation experience (duration and help looked for); third, analysis of differences in attitudes towards bullying; finally, an analysis of changes relating to types, places, and causes of bullying.

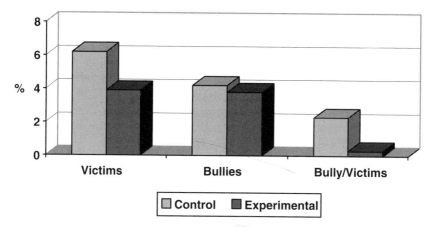

Fig. 9.2 Percentages of pupils involved as victims, bullies, or bully/victims, at pre-test and post-test, in intervention and control schools.

The quality of interpersonal relationships is an effective protector in the social life of an individual. It is, therefore, an important topic and of special interest to us. Pupils were asked: 'How do you get along with the majority of your schoolmates?' The results were encouraging; after the intervention, pupils showed more satisfaction with relationships with peers ($p < 0.001$); the positive response increased from 66.4% at pre-test to 77.2% at post-test, while the negative response decreased from 2.2% to 1.8%. When asked: 'How is it going in your school?', there was an increased satisfaction with school life in general ($p < 0.01$); the positive response increased from 61.8% at pre-test to 66.6% at post-test; while the negative response decreased from 4.8% to 4.1%. The number of students stating that they felt alone or isolated during breaktime a lot of the time decreased from 6.6% to 3.5%, and those who said that they felt that way occasionally, from 31.5% to 15.2%; these differences are significant ($p < 0.001$).

The intervention was also found to affect the experience of victimisation, in two main respects. Regarding duration, there was a reduction of the number of long-term victims (options 'from the beginning of the year' or 'forever') from 25.4% at pre-test to 15% at post-test ($p < 0.001$). These data are complemented by the changes in active looking for help from victims. The number of pupils who decided not to say anything about their victimisation decreased ($p < 0.01$) from 12.4% to 9.3%. The most chosen option is to tell peers (19.1%), the next family or relatives (17.8%), and the last teachers (13.5%); this did not change appreciably between pre-test and post-test.

Table 9.3. *Changes from pre-test to post-test in types of bullying (percentages)*

	Pre-test %	Post-test %
Verbal	51.8	51.6
Physical	27.0	30.6
Steal property	4.3	5.9
Threaten	21.8	27.8
Social exclusion	12.1	17.8
Other types	1.7	0.8

Regarding attitudes towards bullying, we also found significant differences between pre-test and post-test ($p < 0.001$). The number of students who judge bullies in a negative way (I do not like people who bully others) increased from 6.7% to 7.9%. On the other hand, the number of pupils who justified or approved of bullying events (I think bullying others is a normal thing or I think people who bully others have reasons to do it) decreased from 13% to 8.8%. There was also a significant change among the students when asked if they would ever bully others ($p < 0.001$); the number of students that said they would never bully others increased from 43.4% to 52.2%, and the number of pupils who recognised that they might bully others decreased from 35.8% to 27.3%.

Concerning types, places, and causes of bullying, we asked three different questions: 'In your opinion, which are the two ways most used to bully others?'; 'In which places does bullying happen more often?'; and 'Why do you think some students bully others?' Regarding types of bullying (see table 9.3), we found that direct forms of aggression (physical and verbal) maintained the same levels as in the pre-test, but indirect or social aggression increased significantly ($p = 0.015$). These data might seem to contradict the results that bullying declined. From our point of view, this transformation reflects a greater awareness of the less-visible forms of bullying, perhaps because pupils identify as bullying some events that before the intervention they did not recognise as such.

When pupils were asked about the main places of risk, we found that after the intervention the classroom became a safer place ($p < 0.001$): from 37.8% at pre-test to 27.6% at post-test. There were also changes in relation to the perceived causes ($p < 0.001$). The number of answers that indicated previous provocation (38.9% to 30.4%) or desire to make a joke (28% to 22.5%) decreased, whereas responses related to the bullies' intention to gain social status increased (1.2% to 15.5%). Possibly, these variations are due to improved accuracy on the part of students at distinguishing reasons for bullying events.

Perceived effectiveness of interventions

To evaluate further the effectiveness of the interventions carried out in their schools against bullying, we asked students: 'What have your teachers done to improve the relationships among pupils?' All aspects of the SAVE project (as shown in table 9.4) were evaluated, by those pupils who had some direct knowledge through it having been carried out in their schools. For each aspect of intervention, students could respond in three main ways: 'it didn't help', 'the problem has got better' (with three possibilities: 'bullying decreased', 'peer relations got better', and/or there were 'unspecified improvements') and 'the problem has got worse' (with three possibilities: 'bullying increased', 'peer relations got worse', and/or there were 'unspecified deteriorations', although this last category was actually never used).

In examining these data, we did not find significant differences between the bullies, victims, and bystanders, so in the results we do not distinguish among roles (see table 9.4). The row totals amount to more than 100% because a pupil could respond with more than one positive, or negative, effect.

All aspects of the project were assessed positively by students, although not always in the same way. Most aspects scored highly on improving relations within the peer group. The democratic management of social relationships intervention was given the best evaluation, and direct intervention with victims got the highest rating for reducing bullying. Education in feelings and values was also evaluated very positively, although a considerable number of students thought that it had no effect. The least-effective strategies were seen as direct intervention with bullies, and work on co-operative groups; however, both of these still had positive overall ratings.

We examined gender differences in responses; the only appreciable differences were more positive evaluations by girls of education in feelings and values (60.5% girls, 39.5% boys; p < 0.01) and of direct interventions with bullies (52.5% girls, 47.5% boys; p < 0.01).

Conclusions

In relation to the aim of reducing bullying, the data permit us to be optimistic. Certainly, the problem has not disappeared, but it has significantly decreased, particularly with respect to the number of victims. We

Table 9.4. *Effectiveness of the interventions as perceived by pupils (percentage of pupils responding to each category)*

	Positive effects			No effect	Negative effects	
	Decrease in bullying %	Improved relationships %	Unspecified improvements %	It didn't help %	Increase in bullying %	Worse relationships %
Democratic management of social relationships	21.3	83.6	19.7	2.2	0	1.6
Education of feelings and values	22.2	73.2	22.2	16.2	1.0	0
Working in co-operative groups	13.6	63.6	22.7	31.8	0	0
Direct intervention with bullies	16.9	64.9	16.3	22.4	0.6	0.6
Direct intervention with victims	28.8	70.4	19.0	9.7	1.6	0
Intervention during conflicts	16.0	72.0	9.3	5.9	0	0
Working with families	11.9	71.4	21.4	6.5	1.2	1.2
Other interventions	13.8	73.2	18.8	14.6	0	0

think that the work designed to improve interpersonal relationships in the schools functioned as a protective factor, and the students seemed to agree. This was possible, we feel, because of the nature of the teachers' autonomous position which, as proposed in the SAVE model, involved their active participation in solving the problem. Indeed, the project proposes programmes and the resources to develop them, but teachers have the right to decide to adapt them in the way they consider best.

Equally, the evaluation of the SAVE model gives us valuable information about the elements which should be promoted when we design intervention programmes in the future. Perhaps the best example is the 'democratic management of social relationships', as this was perceived by students as the most effective way to improve relationships among them. However, there needs to be more work carried out to determine with more certainty the influence of each programme on bully/victim problems. One of the difficulties we had in comparing the relative merits of each intervention, and perhaps this is a part of our success, was the freedom that teacher groups had in deciding which combination of programmes to use. This is a problem which future intervention evaluation work will have to address.

Longer term effects or evaluation of the programme

At the time of writing, we are planning a new assessment of the SAVE programme to establish the maintenance of intervention effects 5 years after the first post-test. Some indicators in our contacts with the schools where SAVE was applied, although not yet systematically explored, suggest that they are continuing preventive work against bullying and other problems that affect school climate. In the new study, we will focus our attention on teachers' memories regarding the original programmes that they implemented in their schools and how these memories affect their educational activities now.

Dissemination and impact beyond the programme schools

Our objectives of making society, and in particular the educational community, more aware of the need for research and intervention in bully/victim problems, has had some success. In fact, there are now demands made of our team from many different groups: schools who want to begin SAVE programmes ask for our support; centres dealing in continuous teacher training and development ask us to help them to design courses relating to tackling bullying; and the public administration has asked for help setting up broader programmes which will also include these processes and more.

An additional indication of our success is the agreement between the Andalucian Public Administration and the University of Seville to explore the extent of the bullying problem in our region of Andalucia; to design a teacher and counsellor training programme; to make Andalucian people more aware of the problem; and to develop existing and future programmes of intervention (as part of this objective we have started a telephone helpline).

The SAVE project clearly indicates that we need to go forward in two distinct directions: intervention and research. However, we also feel that the ways in which we can continue action against bullying are a little clearer than before, although there is much work still to be done.

References

Cerezo Ramirez, F. (ed.) (1997). *Conductas agresivas en la edad escolar.* Madrid: Pirámide.

Cowie, H. and Wallace, H. (1998). *Peer support: A teacher manual.* London: The Prince's Trust.

Defensor Del Pueblo (2000). *Violencia escolar: El maltrato entre iguales en la Enseñanza Secundaria Obligatoria.* Madrid: Publicaciones del Defensor del Pueblo.

Del Rey, R. and Ortega, R. (2001). La formación del profesorado como respuesta a la violencia escolar. La propuesta del modelo de Sevilla Antiviolencia Escolar (SAVE). *Revista interuniversitaria de formación del profesorado, 41,* 59–71.

Fernández, I. (1998). *Prevención de la violencia escolar y resolución de conflictos: El clima escolar como factor de calidad.* Madrid: Narcea.

Ortega, R. (1992). *Violence in schools. Bully-victims problems in Spain.* Fifth European Conference on Developmental Psychology. Seville, p. 27.

(1994a). Violencia interpersonal en los centros educativos de enseñanza secundaria. Un estudio descriptivo sobre el maltrato y la intimidación entre compañeros. *Revista de Educación, 303,* 253–80.

(1994b). Las malas relaciones interpersonales en la escuela. Estudio sobre la violencia y el maltrato entre compañeros de Segunda Etapa de EGB. *Infancia y Sociedad, 27–28,* 191–216.

(1997). El proyecto Sevilla Antiviolencia Escolar. Un modelo de intervención preventiva contra los malos tratos entre iguales. *Revista de Educación, 313,* 143–60.

(1998). Trabajo con víctimas, agresores y espectadores de la violencia. In R. Ortega et al., *La convivencia escolar: Qué es y cómo abordarla.* Seville: Consejería de Educación y Ciencia de la Junta de Andalucía.

Ortega, R. and Fernández, V. (2000). Un proyecto educativo para prevenir la violencia. In R. Ortega (ed.), *Educar la convivencia para prevenir la violencia.* Madrid: Antonio Machado Libros.

Ortega, R. and Lera, M. J. (2000). Seville anti-bullying school project. *Aggressive Behavior*, 26, 113–23.

Ortega, R. and Mora-Merchán, J. A. (1997). El Proyecto Sevilla Anti-Violencia Escolar. Un modelo ecológico de intervención educativa contra el maltrato entre iguales. In F. Cerezo (ed.), *Conductas agresivas en la edad escolar*. Madrid: Pirámide.

(1999). Spain. In P. K. Smith, Y. Morita, J. Junger-Tas, D. Olweus, R. Catalano, and P. Slee (eds.) *The nature of school bullying: A cross-national perspective*. London: Routledge.

(2000). *Violencia Escolar. Mito o realidad*. Seville: Mergablum.

Ortega, R., Del Rey, R., and Mora-Merchán, J. A. (2001). Violencia entre escolares. Conceptos y etiquetas que definen el fenómeno del maltrato entre escolares. *Revista interuniversitaria de Formación del Profesorado*, 41, 95–113.

Ortega, R., Mora-Merchán, J. A., and Mora, J. (1995). *Cuestionario sobre intimidación y maltrato entre iguales*. Universidad de Sevilla.

Pikas, A. (1989). The Common Concern Method for the treatment of mobbing. In E. Munthe and E. Roland (eds.), *Bullying: An international perspective*. London: David Fulton.

Sharp, S., Cowie, H., and Smith, P. K. (1994). Working directly with pupils involved in bullying situations. In P. K. Smith and S. Sharp (eds.), *School bullying: Insights and perspectives*. London: Routledge.

Smith, P. K. and Sharp, S. (eds.) (1994). *School bullying*. London: Routledge.

Vieira, M., Fernández, I., and Quevedo, G. (1989). Violence, bullying and counselling in the Iberian Peninsula. In E. Roland and E. Munthe (eds.), *Bullying: An international perspective*. London: David Fulton.

10 Australia: the Friendly Schools project

Donna Cross, Margaret Hall, Greg Hamilton,
Yolanda Pintabona, and Erin Erceg

Impetus for the *Friendly Schools* intervention study

In Australia, approximately 1 in 6 school students reports being bullied at least once a week, and 1 in 20 reports bullying others in the past 6 months (Rigby, 1997; Zubrick et al., 1997). Slee and Rigby (1993; Slee, 1995) found that while most of these episodes of bullying last for a day or two, 17% last for 6 months or more. Australian primary-school children of both genders report being bullied more often than secondary-school students, with more boys than girls bullying others and being bullied (Rigby and Slee, 1991; Rigby, 1997; Rigby and Slee, 1998).

Despite Australian schools' increasing need systematically to address bullying, prior to 1999 no system-level, evidence-based recommendations or state curriculum materials to help to reduce bullying were available. Many school staff reported that they were unsure of the effectiveness of the strategies they utilised, and often did not know what actions could be taken at a whole-school level to reduce, or prevent, the harm from student bullying.

In response to this situation, in 1999, the Curtin University, Western Australian Centre for Health Promotion Research, applied for and received funding extensively to review and synthesise international published empirical and theoretical evidence of successful school-based strategies to reduce the harm experienced by children from being bullied or bullying others. This systematic review provided a set of 'successful' practice principles and exemplar case studies to develop a whole-school approach to reduce bullying. The findings from this review were used in 2000 to conceptualise and design a 3-year randomised control trial of these 'successful practices' in Western Australian schools. This programme was called the *Friendly Schools* project.

Early stages of planning and funding

In 1999 a year-long formative research project used a meta-evaluation of published empirical literature and a systematic validation of these findings using international experts and practitioner case studies to provide guidelines, legitimacy, and a focus for whole-school actions to reduce bullying. The findings from this formative research provided a set of *Principles of Successful Practice to Reduce Bullying in Schools* that included recommendations for school policy and practice; classroom management and curriculum; school ethos; school–home and community links; student services and the physical environment.

The Friendly Schools project

In 2000, a 3-year randomised control trial, called the *Friendly Schools* project, was funded by the Western Australian Health Promotion Foundation. This project used the *Principles of Successful Practice for Bullying Reduction in Schools* to design, implement, and assess a multi-level and multi-component whole-school bullying reduction intervention. While the ultimate goal of the project was to reduce bullying in primary schools, this intervention also aimed to build both the school's capacities to respond to bullying and to empower teachers, parents, and students to cope more effectively with these situations. This universal intervention provided a variety of whole-school strategies linked to each component of the Health Promoting School model (World Health Organization, 1996).

Grade 4 students (8–9 years), their teachers, and parents formed the project's primary cohort. Primary-school students were previously found to be more amenable to bullying behaviour change, as they are often more supportive of a student who has been bullied than are older children (Smith, 1991; Slee and Rigby, 1992; Slee, 1994; Zubrick et al., 1997). Primary-school students also tend to be more prosocial and are more likely to want bullying to stop (Slee and Rigby, 1992). Further, social skills-based interventions to ameliorate the effects of, or to reduce, bullying in schools have been found to be more successful with this age group (Smith, 1991; Slee and Rigby, 1992; Olweus, 1994). The secondary target group comprised all other school staff, students, and parents.

Selection of schools

Government primary schools in the Perth, Western Australia, metropolitan area (population 1.3 million) were stratified according to size (based on the number of grade 4 students enrolled) and socio-economic status (SES). Individual schools with a grade 4 enrolment of 50 or more students were classified into tertiles of socio-economic disadvantage. The tertiles were named 'low socio-economic status' (most disadvantaged), 'middle socio-economic status', and 'high socio-economic status'

Table 10.1. *Stratified random sampling procedure for study schools*

| | Intervention N = 15 | | Control N = 14 | | |
| | Size[a] | | Size[a] | | Total number of schools |
	50–65	>65	50–65	>65	
Low SES	2	3	2	3	10
Middle SES	2	3	2	2	9
High SES	2	3	2	3	10
Total	6	9	6	8	29

[a] Number of students enrolled in grade 4 at the school
SES = socio-economic status

(least disadvantaged). Schools were randomly selected from each socio-economic and size stratum for participation and randomly assigned to either the intervention or control group (table 10.1): 29 intervention and control primary schools were randomly selected to participate.

The number of schools selected was based on power calculations using the primary outcome variable; the proportion of children who report being bullied at least once a week. In Western Australia, parents and teachers report that approximately 14% of schoolchildren are bullied at least once a week (Zubrick et al., 1997). Using this estimate, with simple random sampling, comparisons between samples of 350 children in each group had 80% power, at a (two-sided) significance level of 0.05 to detect a difference of 8% in the proportion of children who report being bullied (Murray and Hannan, 1990). Since the unit of analysis was the student and the unit of assignment the school, the sample size calculations were inflated to account for the clustering of student responses within schools. The sample was adjusted using a conservative intracluster correlation of 0.02 (Murray, 1998), and a 20% projected attrition over the two years. The project needed to recruit 1,396 grade 4 students (698 to each of the intervention and control conditions) to yield the requisite number of students to detect the projected effects.

The principal of each randomly selected intervention and control school was sent a letter outlining the project and inviting him/her to participate. As an incentive for participation, control schools were offered, free of charge, road-safety education materials and teacher training. Every school approached agreed to participate. Within each school the grade 4 students, their teachers, and parents, and a 'whole-school committee' of 4–6 interested teachers and parents were recruited using passive consent procedures.

Characteristics of schools and students

Of the 29 schools, 15 were intervention and 14 control. At baseline, 91 grade 4 teachers (50 intervention, 41 control), 2,068 grade 4 students and their parents (1,087 intervention, 981 control) and 174 whole-school committee members (90 intervention, 84 control) were recruited for the 2-year study.

Of the student respondents 50% were female, with the majority (44%) residing in middle SES suburbs. Mean age was 8.6 years. Although schools were stratified by socio-economic status prior to their random selection, significantly more control students were found to reside in higher SES suburbs than intervention students ($p < 0.001$).

At baseline significant differences were found between the intervention- and control-group students for only 3 variables: 'number of friends'; 'feeling safe at school'; and 'telling if they were bullied'. For each of these variables the control group was significantly more likely to feel safer at school ($p = 0.02$), have more good friends ($p = 0.02$), and was significantly more likely to tell if they were bullied ($p = 0.033$). No significant differences were found at baseline between the intervention and control students for the bullying-related outcome variables.

Student response rates

Of the 2,068 students available, 1,968 (95.2%) (1,046 intervention, 922 control) completed the baseline questionnaire. At post-test1, 94% (N = 1847; 983 intervention, 864 control) completed the questionnaire, and by post-test2, 82% (N = 1609; 847 intervention, 762 control) had completed both follow-up questionnaires and comprise the longitudinal student cohort. Of those students lost to follow-up, 8% moved to other non-study schools and the remaining 10% whose names were still on class lists, were sick or did not complete the questionnaire during its administration and follow-up.

The representation of the longitudinal student cohort was assessed both within and between intervention groups to determine selective and differential attrition. Selective attrition was assessed by comparing the demographic and outcome data for the longitudinal student cohort (N = 1,609) with data for the lost to follow-up students (students who did not complete the two follow-up questionnaires, N = 359). The cohort and lost to follow-up students differed on three characteristics: how frequently they were bullied last term; some of the ways they were bullied; and the number of good friends they had. The lost to follow-up group reported significantly fewer good friends ($p = 0.001$), were more likely to report being bullied frequently (p = 0.031), and were more likely to report they were called names, had things taken, and had nasty stories told about them than did the longitudinal student cohort.

Differential attrition was examined by comparing the demographic and outcome data for the intervention- and control-group students lost to follow-up. The intervention (N = 199) and control (N = 160) group students who were lost to follow-up were similar for all characteristics except their willingness to tell someone if they were bullied. The control group students lost to follow-up were significantly more likely to tell someone (p = 0.044) than were the lost to follow-up intervention students.

This longitudinal procedure has the same pupils in the pre-test and post-test groups. This evaluation procedure differs from that used in some other evaluation studies, for example in Bergen (chapter 2) or Sheffield (chapter 6), where different children from age-matched cohorts were compared. However, the comparison of randomly selected intervention and control students permits an evaluation of what are intervention, rather than age, effects.

Components of the intervention programme

The Friendly Schools intervention was provided for the first 2 years of this 3-year study, when the student cohort were in grades 4 and 5. The intervention was based on contemporary educational and behavioural research as well as several theoretical models of how young children learn and how learning influences their health behaviour.

Social Cognitive Theory (Bandura, 1977), the Health Belief Model (Janz and Becker, 1984), and Problem Behaviour Theory (Jessor, 1987) were used to develop cognitive-based teaching and learning activities addressing social support, reinforcement, and outcome expectancies. Also derived from these theories, classroom strategies addressed empathy building for individuals being bullied and self-efficacy related to psychosocial and cognitive skills outcomes (e.g. co-operation skills, friendship-building skills, conflict-resolution skills, self-esteem building, decision-making, assertiveness training, and encouraging and supporting the reporting of bullying). The *Friendly Schools* programme incorporated educational techniques derived from these theories, including drama activities, stories, role modelling, skills training, and observational learning.

To reduce bullying and to enhance students' social skills, the *Friendly Schools* intervention programme targeted three levels:
• the whole-school community as part of building their commitment (through policy) and capacity to address bullying;

- students' families through awareness raising and skills-based self-efficacy activities; and
- grades 4–5 students and their teachers through the provision of teacher training and comprehensive teaching and learning support materials.

Whole-of-school intervention component

The whole-of-school intervention component centred on a *Friendly Schools* committee comprising key staff (selected by the school) who co-ordinated and facilitated their response to bullying. These committees typically included the school health education co-ordinator, a representative from administration, a parent representative, allied health staff such as the school nurse and school psychologist, and other teaching staff.

The committees were provided with a 4-hour training designed to build the committees' commitment and capacity to address bullying more comprehensively within their schools. Also, with the aid of detailed planning and strategy manuals plus trainer support, the committee members used the training to identify, plan, and prepare for the whole-school strategies they decided to implement within each of the 6 domains of the Health Promoting School Model (World Health Organization, 1996). The *Whole-school planning and strategy manual* provided a step-by-step guide to help the committees to review, disseminate, actively implement, and monitor school activity to reduce bullying. The manual also included:

- case-study examples from the *Principles of successful practice for bullying reduction in Schools* document;
- sample school-bullying reduction policies;
- whole-of-school strategies to mobilise peer-group pressure effectively to discourage school bullies;
- ideas to enhance the quality of playtimes and lunch breaks;
- strategies for peer support and social problem-solving;
- example responses to bullying incidents, including the Pikas 'Method of Shared Concern'(Pikas, 1989), and the 'No Blame' approach; and
- suggestions for case management.

Schools were also provided with data reports that summarised their school's grade 4 (2000) and grade 5 (2001) students' and their parents' knowledge and attitudes to bullying behaviour as well as students' self-report of behaviours associated with bullying.

Family intervention component

The *Friendly Schools* intervention for families included home activities linked to each classroom-learning activity. These were used to reinforce and to help students to practise skills learned in the classroom.

Additionally, 16 skills-based newsletter items (8 for each year of the intervention) targeting all parents of children in the intervention schools were developed. Each newsletter item provided parents with a brief overview of research information with actions and tips to help them to deal more effectively with issues, such as what to do if their child is being bullied and/or bullying other children.

Grades 4 and 5 classroom curriculum

The grades 4 and 5 *Friendly Schools* curriculum comprised 9-learning activities (approximately 8 hours) per year, implemented with the cohort in each of the 2 years of the intervention (2000–2001). Trained classroom teachers taught the learning activities in 3 blocks of 3 60-minute lessons, over a 3-school-term period. The *Friendly Schools* learning activities were designed to promote:

* understanding of what behaviours constitute bullying and why bullying is an unacceptable behaviour;
* students' ability to talk about bullying with each other and adults;
* adaptive responses to being bullied, including reporting bullying, seeking support, and responding assertively;
* peer and adult support for students who are being bullied; and
* peer and adult discouragement of bullying behaviour.

The learning activities provided many opportunities for students to build empathy for individuals being bullied and to practise social and intrapersonal skills, including making friends, conflict resolution, self-efficacy to cope with bullying incidents, decision-making, and assertive communication. Other cognitive-based strategies addressed social support, reinforcement, and outcome expectancies.

The classroom teacher manuals were designed to be entirely self-contained to maximise the likelihood of teacher implementation. The manuals included background information, teachers' notes, cross-curricular learning activities, and key learning outcomes. Associated teacher-support materials such as game pieces, resource sheets, and videos were also provided. Students each received a booklet comprising resource sheets, review and reflection logs, and family activities to take home. These student booklets were also used as a criterion measure of teacher implementation of the classroom materials. In the second year of the study, 6 additional cross-age learning activities were developed to support the teaching of social skills and strategies to deal with bullying in grade levels other than 4 and 5.

In each year of the study the *Friendly Schools* project staff provided a 6-hour training for all intervention teachers. The teacher training incorporated information about the prevalence and effects of bullying, utility

Table 10.2. Friendly Schools *study design*

Study condition	Baseline grade 4 (Mar. 2000)	Intervention phase 1	Post-test1 grade 4 (Nov. 2000)	Intervention phase 2	Post-test2 grade 5 (Nov. 2001)
Intervention	O_1	X_1	O_2	X_2	O_3
Control	O_1	X_3	O_2	X_4	O_3

O = Observation
X = Intervention
$X_{1,2}$ = Whole-school bullying intervention
$X_{3,4}$ = Road-safety curriculum

information for children about bullying – e.g. identifying bullying situations, action planning, identifying their support group, plus teacher skill development for classroom teaching and strategies effectively to respond to bullying incidents. Interactive modelling was used to enhance teacher comfort with these skills.

Both the control and intervention schools received the standardised state health education curriculum, which included some activities related to mental health and skill development. Intervention teachers were asked to substitute the *Friendly Schools* learning activities for those related to mental health from the state curriculum.

Evaluation framework and procedures

Study design

Data were collected from all intervention and control grade 4 students, their teachers, and their parents. The study design and the timing of the intervention delivery and data collection are summarised in table 10.2. Four instruments (for teachers, students, parents, and whole-school committee members) were developed for this study. The student instruments were administered by trained project staff at baseline (March 2000), post-test1 (November 2000) and post-test2 (November 2001).

Instrumentation

The student questionnaire items were based on other bullying questionnaires developed for use in primary schools (Olweus, 1996; Rigby, 1998; Rigby and Slee, 1998). All items were designed to enable comparison with other studies of bullying behaviour. The items were divided into 3 sections measuring bullying-related behaviours, perceptions/attitudes, and outcome expectancies if they bullied others.

Bullying-related behaviours   These included the frequency of being bullied and bullying others, the types of bullying experienced, and the reporting of bullying if bullied or a bystander. Items were based on The Peer Relations Questionnaire (Rigby, 1998; Rigby and Slee, 1998), a measure developed for use with Australian primary- and secondary-school students, and the bullying measure designed by Olweus (Olweus, 1996) that has been used extensively in international research.

Perceptions of social support/attitudes towards victims   Student attitudes towards the victims of bullying were examined using a 9-item Likert scale, based on the pro-victim scale developed by Rigby and Slee (1991). Factor analyses yielded two factors: dislike of bullying behaviour; and dislike of children who are bullied.

A loneliness scale was included to measure students' satisfaction with their peer relationships. This 7-item Likert scale was adapted from the Loneliness and Social Dissatisfaction Questionnaire designed by Asher and Wheeler (Asher and Wheeler, 1985). Factor analyses revealed one principal factor on which all loneliness items load.

The perceptions of peer-support scale were modified from the Ladd, Kochenderfer, and Coleman (1996) Friendship Features Interview for Young Children. This 17-item Likert scale aimed to measure children's perceptions of the quality of their classroom friendships. Factor analysis resulted in one factor.

The Students' Social Competence with Peers Pupil Questionnaire developed by Spence (1995) was used to measure the consequences of social behaviour. The 10 items formed one factor. To measure how many good friends students have in their school, 4 items from the Peer Relations Questionnaire (Rigby and Slee, 1998) were adapted. One other 4-item Likert scale was developed by the project to measure to what extent students like school.

Outcome expectancies if bullied others   An outcome-expectancy scale was based on a similar questionnaire developed by Rigby (Rigby, 1997) to measure students' perceptions of what might happen to someone if they bullied another child. Factor analyses revealed two factors: one related to the perceived positive outcomes for the person bullying; and the other indicating negative outcomes for the person bullying.

Other questionnaires   Parent, teacher, and whole-school committee questionnaires were also developed to assess knowledge, attitudes,
and skills in these groups, along with process measures of programme
satisfaction and implementation. Results from these questionnaires will
be published elsewhere. Validity measures included the assessment of
face and content validity, using expert and target group review (Windsor
et al., 1994).

Procedure

All questionnaires were pilot tested, in 3 primary schools, with groups
similar to the study cohort. The pilot schools were randomly selected from
schools that were not part of the study cohort, and represented each of the
three socio-economic status strata. The pilot test with the target groups
and the expert review resulted in changes to the length, organisation, and
wording of items. In particular, the definition of bullying was identified
as being too difficult for the majority of students (and some parents)
to understand. To address this, illustrations were used to enhance the
understandability of the definition and different types of bullying.

The test–retest procedure was used to determine the reliability of the
student questionnaire. Students completed the questionnaires on 2 occasions, separated by 2 weeks. The intra-class correlation coefficient (ICC)
was used as an approximation of a weighted kappa statistic (Peat, 2001)
to determine the reliability of the questionnaire. Similar to other primary
school-based research, the reliability analysis was lower than would be
expected in older children or adults (Rivara et al., 1991; Parcel et al.,
1995; Cross et al., 2000). The coefficients for the student questionnaire
ranged from 0.1 to 0.97, with a mean of 0.49. Limited variability in student responses increased the percentage of agreement by chance, which
led to a lower-than-desirable ICC for some items. Individual items found
to be unreliable were excluded from the analyses.

Trained research staff administered the questionnaire to all students
in each group at baseline and at both post-tests in November 2000 and
2001. Because of the students' age (9 years) and associated reading level,
the administrators read all items on the questionnaire slowly and aloud to
students. Staff who administered the questionnaire received an administration guide and attended a 2-hour prior training. To maintain student
attentiveness, the questionnaire was divided into two parts (each taking
30–40 minutes) and administered either side of a recess break.

Prior to the questionnaire administration, all grade 4 students in the
study schools received an information letter and a passive consent form

to take home to their parents. Those students whose parents indicated no consent were excluded from the data collection. Parents and teachers were asked to sign a consent form that formed part of their questionnaires.

To secure high response rates, teachers were trained to administer follow-up questionnaires to students who were absent on the day of the initial administration. Research staff collected these late questionnaires from the schools. The administration procedure for the parent question-naire involved the students. They were asked to write a letter to the parent who talked to them the most about bullying, asking them to complete the questionnaire the students carried home in an unsealed envelope. A cover letter asked parents to return the questionnaire, either completed or blank (to indicate they received it but have chosen not to participate) by sealing it in the envelope in which it came and returning it to class. To enhance response rates parents were given a small incentive (a chance to win one of three $50 shopping vouchers) and teachers were provided with reminder letters and asked to give these to students who did not return a parent questionnaire.

The grades 4–5 teacher questionnaires and the whole-school commit-tee questionnaires were distributed to the school staff involved in the project when the student questionnaires were being administered. Staff were asked to complete these and return them with late student ques-tionnaires or in reply-paid envelopes.

Data analysis

As the response variables were ordinal and continuous, ordinal logis-tic regression, multi-nomial logistic regression models, and Analyses of Covariance (ANCOVA) were used. Normality tests were performed using the Kolmogorov–Smirnov test of normality. All data were significantly different to the normal curve.

Logistic regression models and ANCOVA models were used to deter-mine if differences between groups existed at the final post-test while controlling for any baseline differences. These models incorporated the final post-test data as the response variable with the baseline data, sub-group (intervention or control), and sex as factors, the total number of students in the school, and the students' socio-economic status as covariates. Within the ordinal regression, a test of parallel lines was per-formed to determine if the parameters were equivalent across all levels of the response variable. If the parameters were not equivalent, then multi-nomial logistic regression was used to analyse the data. Future analysis of the student quantitative data will include multi-level modelling (MLwiN and Mplus) to address the nested structure of these data (Rowe and Hill, 1998).

What actually happened; achievements and difficulties in implementing the intervention

While it was not implemented as comprehensively as intended, preliminary analyses reveal the *Friendly Schools* programme was successful. Evaluation of teachers' and the whole-school committees' implementation of the project found that programme components were modified to suit student needs as well as time constraints and other demands of the schools. The following provides an overview of the barriers and enabling factors associated with the project's implementation:

Differential programme and implementation

The *Friendly Schools* intervention components were based on considerable evidence that comprehensive/multi-component programmes are more effective than those that address only classroom curriculum (Puska et al., 1982; Vartiainen et al., 1986; Flay, 2000). However, intervention schools were able to provide a higher 'dose' of the classroom programme than the other whole-school activities. According to process data collected from members of the whole-school committees, the majority of intervention schools, by the end of the 2 years, had completed less than 30% of the recommended whole-school programme. In contrast, the mean proportion of classroom activities implemented over the 2 years of the project was 67%. A lack of time and, in some cases, a lack of capacity (e.g. skills, structures, resources, and commitment) appears to have contributed to the under-implementation of the whole-school (and some parts of the classroom-curriculum) intervention.

Involving parents in whole-school strategies

Whole-school strategies to engage parents were described by intervention schools as the most difficult to implement. Similar to other school-based parent research (Hahn et al., 1996), several barriers appeared to discourage the intervention schools from involving parents. These included a lack of resources (especially for parents for whom English was not their first language), time to build a rapport with parents to make them feel welcome to engage in whole-school activities, poor appreciation by both teachers and parents of the potential benefits, and perceptions that parents were not motivated to be involved or interested in school programmes.

Loss of trained staff

Although a 3-hour training was provided for the whole-school committees for each year of the *Friendly Schools* project, the transfer of trained staff and administrators (principals and deputy principals) to other schools challenged the momentum, commitment, and effectiveness of the whole-school committee. This was especially true with the changing of principals in intervention schools. As would be expected, the principal's involvement was pivotal to the success of the project's implementation, particularly the whole-school activities. The most promising gains in policy implementation initiatives were made in intervention schools where the principals attended the training and were actively involved in their whole-school committee.

Increase in reported bullying of students and staff

A heightened awareness of bullying, as a result of the introduction of a school-based initiative to address it, has contributed in some cases to initial increases in reported bullying by students (Eslea and Smith, 1998; Naylor and Cowie, 1999). Intervention schools were informed of this potential phenomenon at the pre-intervention training, and later reported that this did occur and that they felt prepared to respond appropriately. An unanticipated programme effect, however, was the request by some teachers for support to deal with bullying by other teachers or their school's administration. Schools reported being unable to provide adequate support to deal with these situations, although several staff reported that they found the strategies suggested to students useful.

Time required to teach learning activities

Many teachers reported that while the classroom programme was excellent, the learning activities took more class time than they had planned. Whereas these activities were designed to take approximately 40–60 minutes to implement, most teachers indicated that some took nearly double that time. The interactive nature and the amount of interest shown by students in the learning activities (especially those addressing co-operation and bystander problem-solving) were among the most common reasons provided by teachers for needing extra time. Teachers who integrated their teaching of this programme across a variety of curriculum areas, versus treating it as a categorical component of their health-education programme, were able to complete more of the learning activities.

Schools wanted the materials for other age groups

While grade 4 students were selected for the 2-year study cohort, nearly all intervention schools requested additional support materials for teachers in other grade levels. In response to this demand, in the second year of the study, five cross-age learning activities (called the Teachers' Starter Pack) that addressed the nature of bullying, protective responses, and social-skill development were developed for use by grades 1–3 and 6–7 intervention teachers.

Home activities

The whole-school committees and teachers at the training welcomed the self-help Friendly Schools home activities designed to reinforce classroom learning. However, teachers found that the majority of these activities were completed and returned by less than one-third of parents. Some teachers commented that the time and energy taken to follow up with parents to complete the home activities discouraged them from sending further copies home. To overcome problems of parental completion in the second year of the study, 6 additional inserts for the popular parent newsletter items were developed.

Demand from non-study schools

Information about the *Friendly Schools* project disseminated by the funding organisation to its clients and the local media generated much interest in the intervention materials from non-study schools. This increasing interest threatened to 'contaminate' the results of this study, as these schools (including some control schools) tried to obtain copies of the intervention from study schools and project staff. Non-study schools were asked to wait until the intervention study had completed, when copies were made available to them. This demand may have encouraged the study schools to value the *Friendly Schools* resources more highly than might otherwise have been the situation.

Results of the evaluation

The following summary of the results from the longitudinal student cohort describes the extent to which the *Friendly Schools* intervention reduced bullying behaviour and perceptions of social support and competence among a cohort of grade 4–5 students.

Behaviours

From baseline to post-test2, in both the intervention and control groups, there was a slight increase in the percentage of students who reported they were bullied (table 10.3). For those intervention and control students who reported they bullied others at least once or twice last term, an increase of 28% and 30%, respectively, was evident from baseline to post-test2 (baseline–13%, 15%, post1–16%, 15%, and post2–41%, 45% for intervention and control students, respectively). While a larger proportion of students in the control group reported being bullied at post-test2 (50%) compared to the intervention group (47%), this difference was not significant. Of those who reported being bullied at post-test2, 32% of intervention and 36% of control students reported being bullied only once or twice. Also at post-test2, 9% of intervention and control students reported being bullied about once a week/every few weeks, with 6% of intervention and control students reporting being bullied almost every day.

A figure of 59% of intervention students and 55% of control students reported at post-test2 that they did not bully another student during the previous term (table 10.3), however, this difference was not significant. After controlling for baseline differences, socio-economic status, size of school, and gender, logistic regression analyses at post-test2 revealed no difference between intervention and control groups for being bullied or bullying others (table 10.4).

The majority of children in both the intervention and control groups reported being teased or called hurtful names more often than any other type of bullying (table 10.5). For all types of bullying at post-test2, except having things taken and being made afraid that they would get hurt, control students were significantly more likely to report being bullied sometimes, than intervention students. Table 10.4 shows that intervention students had significantly diminished odds, compared with the control group, of reporting being bullied at post-test2, for most types of bullying behaviour.

At post-test2 the majority of intervention and control students reported they would tell someone if they saw another student being bullied at

Table 10.3. *Proportion of reported bullying behaviour in the longitudinal student cohort from baseline to post-test2 (percentage unless otherwise stated with number in parentheses)*

	How often last term did another student or group of students bully you?				How often last term did you on your own or in a group bully another student?			
	Almost every day	Once every 1–2 weeks	Once or twice	Not at all	Almost every day	Once every 1–2 weeks	Once or twice	Not at all
Intervention								
Baseline	7.8 (77)	8.4 (82)	25.3 (248)	58.6 (575)	1.3 (13)	1.3 (14)	10.4 (108)	87.0 (903)
Post1	5.2 (52)	7.9 (79)	29.1 (288)	57.7 (571)	1.9 (19)	2.1 (21)	12.4 (123)	83.6 (829)
Post2	6.0 (52)	8.7 (76)	31.9 (277)	53.4 (464)	2.3 (18)	3.1 (24)	35.4 (277)	59.3 (464)
Control								
Baseline	6.6 (57)	9.1 (78)	24.5 (211)	59.8 (514)	1.3 (12)	1.7 (16)	12.1 (111)	84.9 (780)
Post1	5.5 (48)	8.4 (74)	35.1 (309)	51.0 (449)	0.8 (7)	2.1 (19)	12.2 (107)	84.8 (742)
Post2	5.6 (44)	9.1 (72)	35.5 (281)	49.9 (395)	2.6 (19)	3.2 (23)	39.1 (281)	55.0 (395)
Total								
Baseline	7.2 (134)	8.8 (160)	25.0 (459)	59.2 (1,089)	1.3 (25)	1.5 (30)	11.2 (219)	86.0 (1,683)
Post1	5.4 (100)	8.1 (153)	31.9 (597)	54.5 (1,020)	1.3 (26)	2.2 (40)	12.3 (203)	84.1 (1,571)
Post2	5.8 (96)	8.9 (148)	33.7 (558)	51.6 (859)	1.0 (16)	1.5 (23)	10.9 (173)	86.6 (1,372)

Table 10.4. *Summary of regression analysis results adjusted for baseline differences, socio-economic status, size of school, and gender*

	Intervention group		
	Odds ratio	95% confidence interval	p value

Frequency of Bullying

How often did another group of students bully you? (N = 835; control group 758)

| Bullied at some stage | 1.1 | 1.0–1.4 | 0.194 |

This term, how often did you, on your own or in a group, bully another student? (N = 825; control group 759)

| Bullied at some stage | 1.0 | 0.8–1.3 | 0.754 |

Types of Bullying

I was made fun of and teased in a hurtful way (N = 804; control group 736)

| Lots of times | 1.3 | 0.7–2.4 | 0.414 |
| Sometimes | 0.7 | 0.6–1.0 | 0.041* |

I was called mean and hurtful names (N = 802; control group 730)

| Lots of times | 0.4 | 0.2–0.7 | 0.001* |
| Sometimes | 0.6 | 0.4–0.8 | 0.001* |

Kids ignored me, didn't let me join in, or left me out of things on purpose (N = 803; control group 727)

| Lots of times | 0.3 | 0.1–0.5 | <0.001* |
| Sometimes | 0.4 | 0.3–0.6 | <0.001* |

Bullied by being hit, kicked, or pushed around (N = 807; control group 728)

| Lots of times | 0.3 | 0.2–0.6 | <0.001* |
| Sometimes | 0.5 | 0.3–0.7 | <0.001* |

Kids told lies or spread nasty stories about me and tried to make other kids not like me (N = 797; control group 722)

| Lots of times | 0.3 | 0.2–0.5 | <0.001* |
| Sometimes | 0.6 | 0.4–0.8 | 0.005* |

I had money or other things taken away from me or broken (N = 799; control group 723)

| Lots of times | 0.2 | 0.1–0.6 | <0.001* |
| Sometimes | 0.6 | 0.3–1.2 | 0.333 |

I was made afraid that I would get hurt (N = 790; control group 725)

| Lots of times | 1.2 | 0.9–1.7 | 0.175 |
| Sometimes | 1.2 | 0.9–1.7 | 0.175 |

Reporting

If you saw another student being bullied at school would you tell someone? (N = 828; control group 753)

| I would tell someone | 3.5 | 1.5–8.2 | 0.005* |
| I might tell someone | 3.7 | 1.3–10.7 | 0.015* |

Last term did you tell anyone that you were being bullied? (N = 828; control group 758)

| Wasn't bullied | 1.1 | 0.9–1.4 | 0.455 |
| Told no one | 0.9 | 0.6–1.2 | 0.412 |

* Significant at p < 0.05

Table 10.5. *Proportion (%) of types of reported bullying behaviour in the longitudinal student cohort from baseline to post-test2*

	Intervention			Control		
	Baseline (N = 1,046)	Post1 (N = 997)	Post2 (N = 876)	Baseline (N = 922)	Post1 (N = 883)	Post2 (N = 793)
Hurtful teasing						
Lots	5.0	4.8	6.0	6.2	5.1	5.4
Sometimes	24.4	24.1	25.2	22.4	27.8	29.8
Never	70.6	71.1	68.8	71.4	67.1	64.8
Hurtful names						
Lots	6.9	6.4	7.1	6.8	6.2	5.7
Sometimes	25.6	23.2	26.1	25.6	25.3	30.4
Never	67.5	70.4	66.8	67.6	68.5	63.9
Ignored, left out						
Lots	8.0	5.1	4.4	6.9	5.0	3.2
Sometimes	23.2	16.4	14.7	20.5	19.1	17.9
Never	68.8	78.5	80.9	72.6	75.9	78.9
Pushed, hit, kicked						
Lots	5.4	4.9	3.4	5.7	3.5	4.4
Sometimes	19.0	16.8	16.2	17.7	19.7	15.8
Never	75.6	78.3	80.4	76.6	76.8	79.8
Nasty stories						
Lots	8.5	6.3	4.6	8.0	6.6	4.5
Sometimes	19.7	16.5	18.2	16.4	17.3	20.5
Never	71.8	77.1	77.2	75.5	76.2	74.9
Things taken						
Lots	4.0	2.8	1.9	3.3	2.4	2.1
Sometimes	10.8	9.0	7.8	9.2	11.5	7.8
Never	85.2	88.1	90.3	87.4	86.1	90.1
Made afraid						
Lots	4.7	2.6	3.1	5.4	3.3	2.9
Sometimes	16.7	14.5	10.8	15.4	15.6	13.1
Never	78.6	82.9	86.1	79.1	81.0	84.0
Another way						
Lots	3.2	2.0	2.7	2.1	2.1	2.0
Sometimes	5.3	6.5	4.5	6.2	6.6	9.0
Never	91.4	91.4	92.8	91.8	91.3	88.9

Table 10.6. *Summary of ANCOVA regression analysis results, adjusted for baseline differences, socio-economic status, size of school, how often student was bullied, and how often student bullied others and gender*

Intervention group (N = 847)	Unstandardised coefficients				95% confidence interval for B	
	B	Std error	T	p value	Lower bound	Upper bound
Loneliness scale	−0.017	0.046	−0.383	0.702	−0.11	0.07
Friendship scale	0.059	0.046	−1.272	0.204	−0.15	0.03
Peer support scale	−0.114	0.048	−2.370	0.018*	−0.21	−0.02
Pro-victim scale (attitude to bully)	−0.062	0.052	−1.188	0.235	−0.16	0.04
Pro-victim scale (attitude to victim)	0.020	0.049	0.409	0.683	−0.08	0.12
Social competence scale	−0.053	0.048	−1.105	0.269	−0.15	0.04
Liking of school scale	−0.099	0.045	2.193	0.028*	0.01	0.19
Negative outcome expectancies if bully scale	0.115	0.049	2.332	0.020*	0.02	0.21
Positive outcome expectancies if bully scale	0.042	0.053	0.795	0.427	−0.06	0.15

Reference: control group (N = 762)
* Significant at $p < 0.05$

school (72%). Of those students who were bullied, 70% reported they told someone when they were bullied. As shown in Table 10.4, students in the intervention group had significantly increased odds from baseline to post-test2 of telling someone if they saw another student being bullied.

Perceptions of social support/attitudes towards victims

For all perceptions and attitudes scales except liking of school and peer support, no significant differences were detected between the intervention and control students from baseline to post-test2 (table 10.6). Intervention students were only significantly more likely to report they found school to be a nice place and liked coming to school than control group students. Control students, however, were significantly more likely to report greater peer support than the intervention groups from baseline to post-test2.

Outcome expectancies if bully others

From baseline to post-test2 students were asked to indicate what they think might happen if they were to bully another student. This outcome-expectancies scale was divided into two factors: positive outcomes from bullying others; and negative outcomes from bullying others. For positive outcome expectancies such as 'other kids would like me and think I was tough', there were no significant differences between intervention- and control-group students (table 10.6). However, intervention students were significantly more likely than control students to indicate they would expect negative consequences such as 'I would get into trouble' and 'I would feel bad about myself', if they were to bully other students.

Longer term effects or evaluation of the programme

Given the *Friendly Schools* project concluded its third-year follow-up data collection in October 2002, a longer term evaluation of the programme is not yet available. This follow-up will be used to determine to what extent the whole-of-school activity to address bullying has been continued and to what extent the behavioural effects observed in intervention students in 2001 have sustained or decayed.

A new research project called the *Friendly Schools Friendly Families* project was funded and began in 2002 to build on the intervention and outcomes of the *Friendly Schools* project. This project is also a 3-year randomised control trial designed to address two particular weaknesses of the *Friendly Schools* project: the intervention schools' capacity to manage whole-school change to address bullying; and more-expansive strategies involving parents. The target audience is again the whole primary-school community, a representative committee, grades 2, 4, and 6 students, and their teachers and parents. The study schools were randomly selected from all those schools that were not involved in the *Friendly Schools* project.

The *Friendly Schools Friendly Families* project has a cohort of 4,000 grades 2, 4, and 6 students, and their parents and teachers from 20 randomly selected schools in the Perth metropolitan area. This cohort is to be tracked from April 2002 until November 2003. Schools were randomly assigned to 1 of 3 intervention conditions, to test the effect of differing levels of a comprehensive whole-school programme on staff, student, and parent responses to bullying. The high-intervention schools have received a whole-school programme manual (revised and improved from the *Friendly Schools* project), incorporating intensive parent involvement through the use of home activity sheets, newsletter items, and other activities designed to enhance students' social skills and to reduce bullying.

Schools in the moderate-intervention condition also received a whole-school programme similar to the high intervention, but without the expanded parent component. The whole-school programme for both high- and moderate-intervention schools encourages the review and refinement of schools' current bullying or behaviour management policy and procedures, and provides strategies and activities for schools to implement this policy actively to engage staff, students, and parents to help reduce bullying. In both intervention conditions teachers from pre-primary grades to grade 7 receive a set of introductory learning activities about bullying and social-skill development for use in their classrooms.

The two intervention groups are also receiving innovative capacity-building strategies for staff and parents to enhance the likelihood of implementation success (9 hours in each of the 2 intervention years).

The low-intervention condition received only a framework with information about strategies that they could utilise to address bullying, based on the *Principles of successful practice for the reduction of bullying*. These schools received a brief (15-minute) meeting with project staff who talked about the framework and associated information. No other training or support was provided.

Dissemination and impact beyond the programme schools

A potential confounding factor during the *Friendly Schools* intervention trial was the interest in, and demand from, non-study schools to obtain copies of the project's intervention materials. Schools were assured that at the conclusion of the study in 2002, if the results were promising, the intervention materials would be available nationally for purchase. Due to this ongoing demand, in April 2002 the materials were released for sale to government and non-government schools throughout Western Australia. Following the official launch of the project's results in September 2002, information about the project and the intervention materials are to be disseminated for sale to schools throughout Australia.

Rarely, prior to the release of educational materials for schools are educators given empirical evidence of the materials' effectiveness. Resoundingly educators, who have seen or used the materials, have commented on the value of the extensive formative work to construct the *Principles of successful practice for bullying reduction in schools* and the extent to which these match and are easily integrated with schools' experiences and practices. The release of the formative research process and findings has largely contributed to the current demand for the *Friendly Schools* materials.

The timing of this bullying-related research has been fortuitous for the dissemination of the *Friendly Schools* project intervention materials. Since the late 1990s in Australia, there has been a greater commitment by government and non-government agencies to enhance the mental and emotional health of children, and a desire for evidence-based programmes for this to be achieved.

Acknowledgements

The authors acknowledge the valuable contribution of Dr Clare Roberts, Leanne Lester, Therese Shaw, and the Western Australian Centre for Health Promotion Research staff, Curtin University, health promotion and psychology students, the *Friendly Schools* project teachers, principals, school students, and their parents and the Project Advisory Committee. The Western Australian Health Promotion Foundation (Healthway) funded the *Friendly Schools* project.

References

Asher, S. R. and Wheeler, V. A. (1985). Children's loneliness: A comparison of rejected and neglected peer status. *Journal of Consulting and Clinical Psychology*, 53, 500–05.

Bandura, A. (1977). *A social learning theory*. Englewood Cliffs, NJ: Prentice Hall.

Cross, D., Stevenson, M., Hall, M., Burns, S., Laughlin, D., Officer, J., and Howat, P. (2000). Child pedestrian injury prevention project: Student results. *Preventive Medicine*, 30, 179–87.

Eslea, M. and Smith, P. K. (1998). The long-term effectiveness of anti-bullying work in primary schools. *Educational Research*, 40, 203–18.

Flay, B. R. (2000). Approaches to substance use prevention utilising school curriculum plus social environment change. *Addictive Behaviors*, 25, 861–85.

Hahn, E. J., Simpson, M. R., and Kidd, P. (1996). Cues to parent involvement in drug prevention and school activities. *Journal of School Health*, 66, 165–70.

Janz, N. K. and Becker, M. H. (1984). The health belief model: A decade later. *Health Education Quarterly*, 11, 1–47.

Jessor, R. (1987). Problem-behaviour theory, psychosocial development, and adolescent problem drinking. *British Journal of Addiction*, 82, 331–42.

Ladd, G. W., Kochenderfer, B. J., and Coleman, C. C. (1996). Friendship quality as a predictor of young children's early school adjustment. *Child Development*, 67, 1103–18.

Murray, D. M. (1998). *Design and analysis of group randomised trials*. New York: Oxford University Press.

Murray, D. M. and Hannan, P. J. (1990). Planning for the appropriate analysis in school-based drug-use prevention studies. *Journal of Consulting and Clinical Psychology*, 58, 458–68.

Naylor, P. & Cowie, H. (1999). The effectiveness of peer support systems in challenging school bullying: The perspective and experiences of teachers and pupils. *Journal of Adolescence*, 22, 467–79.

Olweus, D. (1994). Bullying at school: Basic facts and effects of a school based intervention program. *Journal of Child Psychology and Psychiatry*, 35, 1171–90.

(1996). *The revised Olweus bully/victim questionnaire*. Mimeo. Bergen, Norway: Research Center for Health Promotion, University of Bergen.

Parcel, G. S., Edmunson, E., Perry, C. L., Feldman, H. A., O'Hara-Tompkins, N., Nader, P. R., Johnson, C. E., and Stone, E. J. (1995). Measurement of self-efficacy for diet-related behaviors among elementary school children. *Journal of School Health*, 65, 23–27.

Peat, J. (2001). *Health science research: A handbook of quantitative methods*. Crows Nest, NSW: Allen & Unwin.

Pikas, A. (1989). A pure concept of mobbing gives the best results for treatment. *School Psychology International*, 10, 95–104.

Puska, P., Vartaianen, E., Pallonen, U., Salonen, J., Pohyhia, P., Koskela, K., and McAlister, A. (1982). The North Karelia Youth Project: Evaluation of two years of intervention on health behaviour and CVD risk factors among 13–15-year old children. *Preventive Medicine*, 11, 550–70.

Rigby, K. (1997). Attitudes and beliefs about bullying among Australian school children. *The Irish Journal of Psychology*, 18, 202–20.

(1998). *The Peer Relations Questionnaire technical manual*. Point Lonsdale, Vic.: The Professional Reading Guide.

Rigby, K. and Slee, P. T. (1991). Bullying among Australian school children: Reported behaviour and attitudes towards victims. *Journal of Social Psychology*, 131, 615–27.

(1998). *The Peer Relations Questionnaire (PRQ)*. Point Lonsdale, Vic.: The Professional Reading Guide.

Rivara, F. P., Booth, C. L., Bergman, A. B., Rogers, L. W., and Weiss, J. (1991). Prevention of pedestrian injuries to children: Effectiveness of a school training program. *Pediatrics*, 88, 770–75.

Rowe, K. J. and Hill, P. W. (1998). Modelling educational effectiveness in classrooms: The use of multilevel structural equations to model students' progress. *Educational Research and Evaluation*, 4, 307–47.

Slee, P. T. (1994). Situational and interpersonal correlates of anxiety associated with peer victimisation. *Child Psychiatry and Human Development*, 25, 97–107.

(1995). Peer victimisation and its relationship to depression among Australian primary school students. *Personality and Individual Differences*, 18, 57–62.

(1993). Australian school children's self appraisal of interpersonal relations: The bullying experience. *Child Psychiatry and Human Development*, 23, 272–83.

Smith, P. K. (1991). The silent nightmare: Bullying and victimisation in school peer groups. *The Psychologist: Bulletin of the British Psychological Society*, 4, 243–48.

Spence, S. H. (1995). *Social Competence with Peers Questionnaire – Pupil. Social skills training: Enhancing social competence with children and adolescents.* Berkshire: NFER-NELSON.

Vartiainen, E., Pallonen, U., McAlister, A., Koskela, K., and Puska, P. (1986). Four year follow-up results of the smoking prevention program in the North Karelia Youth Project. *Preventive Medicine,* 15, 692–98.

Windsor, R., Baranowski, T., Clark, N., and Cutter, G. (1994). *Evaluation of health promotion, health education, and disease prevention programs.* Mountain View, Calif.: Mayfield.

World Health Organization (1996). *School health promotion – Series 5: Regional guidelines: Development of health promoting schools: A framework for action.* Manila: WHO.

Zubrick, S. R., Silburn, S. R., Gurrin, L., Teo, H., Shephard, C., Carlton, J., and Lawrence, D. (1997). *Western Australian Child Health Survey: Education, health and competence.* Perth, WA: Australian Bureau of Statistics.

11   The Expect Respect project: preventing bullying and sexual harassment in US elementary schools

Barri Rosenbluth, Daniel J. Whitaker, Ellen Sanchez, and Linda Anne Valle

Impetus for the intervention, early stages of planning, and funding

The Expect Respect project was developed by SafePlace, the sole provider of comprehensive sexual and domestic violence prevention and intervention services in Austin, Texas. Since 1989, SafePlace has been providing school-based counselling and support groups for students who have experienced dating, sexual, or domestic violence, and educational programmes in schools for students, parents, and school staff. These services began in response to requests from school counsellors who were aware of young women in physically abusive dating relationships. SafePlace counsellors initiated weekly support groups at several local high schools and middle schools to help abused girls to increase their personal safety, social support, and skills for healthy relationships. Over the years, additional counselling and support-group services were added to respond to the needs of boys and girls in grades K-12 who had experienced dating, sexual, or domestic violence. In an effort to reduce the incidence of dating violence SafePlace began in 1995 to investigate strategies for promoting safe and respectful relationships among younger children, with the intent of raising their expectations and skills for respectful behaviour in future dating relationships.

Discussions with elementary school teachers and counsellors revealed that children as young as 11 years were already engaging in dating behaviours, and that frequently these relationships involved behaviours that could be described as bullying and sexual harassment, including hitting, pushing, unwanted touching, name-calling, and put-downs. A review of the research on bullying and sexual harassment revealed similarities with the dynamics seen in abusive dating relationships. The terms bullying, sexual harassment, and dating violence all refer to aggressive acts that are intended to hurt or control another person, are often repeated over time, and occur in the context of a relationship in which the bully/harasser/abuser has more physical or social power than the target/victim. The effects of these hurtful and intimidating behaviours impact not only the targeted individual but also contribute to a hostile school environment, one that teaches all students that abusive behaviour is acceptable in peer relationships. It has been asserted that

Indeed, if school authorities sanction the students who sexually harass by not intervening, the schools may be encouraging a continued pattern of violence in relationships. This encouragement goes beyond those directly involved; it also conveys a message to those who observe these incidents that to engage in such behavior is acceptable. Other bystanders may receive the message that they may be the next to be harassed, and no one will do anything to prevent it. (Stein, 1995: 148)

With these theoretical linkages in mind, SafePlace, in partnership with the Austin Independent School District (AISD) and researchers from the University of Texas (UT), received funding from the Centers for Disease Control and Prevention in 1997 to develop, implement, and evaluate a programme for the primary prevention of intimate partner violence. The previous decade of collaboration between SafePlace and AISD provided a strong foundation for an effective partnership for conducting the project: 12 AISD schools participated.

The Expect Respect project targeted the involvement of all members of the school community in recognising and responding to bullying and sexual harassment among students. The project's design was based upon the previous research of Olweus and his colleagues (Olweus, Limber, and Mihalic, 1999), who demonstrated significant reductions in bullying and improvements in school climate following a multi-level intervention programme. To achieve reductions in bullying and sexual harassment behaviours and improvement in campus climate, the Expect Respect project utilised 5 programme components, including classroom curriculum; staff training; policy development; parent education; and support services. The intervention was delivered for 2 consecutive years.

Selection of schools

Elementary schools were selected because they were believed to provide greater opportunity for changing social norms among young children and the adults in their lives. Only fifth-grade students were selected for the curriculum component because staff resources were not sufficient to provide curriculum to all grade levels. Fifth-grade students were selected for the curriculum component because they were the oldest students in the school and thus might provide role models for younger children on campus. Project staff also believed fifth-graders would benefit most from the project because they would soon be exposed to more serious forms of bullying and sexual harassment in middle school and, for many, new roles as boyfriend or girlfriend. With the support of the AISD Director of Guidance and Counseling, 6 pairs of schools representing a cross-section of the AISD were selected.

Characteristics of schools and students

The pairs of schools were located in 4 distinct geographic areas of Austin that served ethnically and economically distinct communities. The school pairs were matched and similar on variables including ethnicity, limited-English proficiency, and the socio-economic status of students, the school's passing rates on the statewide academic skills test (TAAS), total school population, and fifth-grade population. Through random assignment, 1 school in each pair was placed in the intervention group and 1 school was placed in the comparison group.

At the beginning of the intervention, there were 929 and 834 students in the intervention and comparison schools, respectively, aged 10–11 years. The sample was evenly split between boys (50.3%) and girls (48.3%); 55% self-identified as White, 27.6% as Hispanic, and 15.4% as African American. Ethnic distributions were nearly identical across the intervention (54.9% White, 27.1% Hispanic, 15.9% African American) and comparison schools (55.1% White, 28.0% Hispanic, 15.0% African American).

Components of the intervention programme

Classroom curriculum

Twelve weekly sessions, adapted from *Bullyproof: a teachers' guide on teasing and bullying for use with fourth and fifth grade students* (Stein and Sjostrom, 1996), were provided to all fifth-grade students in the intervention schools. The *Bullyproof* curriculum was selected because it focused on increasing the ability and willingness of bystanders to intervene, and thus might reduce the social acceptance of bullying and sexual harassment. In addition, *Bullyproof*, a joint publication of the Wellesley College Center for Research on Women and the National Education Association Professional Library, had been developed and piloted in classrooms by teachers, and was designed to be taught in conjunction with literature typically read by students in the fifth grade. Because *Bullyproof* best fit the project's goals and was designed to integrate easily into existing classroom lessons, it was selected by project staff despite the absence of a completed programme evaluation.

In 3 of the 6 intervention schools, the intervention was conducted in the fall semester, and in the other 3 intervention schools, it was conducted in the spring semester. The *Bullyproof* lessons were designed to help students to distinguish playful teasing and joking around from hurtful teasing and bullying, enhance students' knowledge about bullying and sexual harassment, and develop students' skills for responding as a target or bystander of bullying or harassment. Students were encouraged to become 'courageous bystanders' by speaking up or getting help from an adult when they witnessed someone being mistreated. The lessons included writing assignments, role plays of how to intervene upon witnessing bullying, and class discussions.

Staff training

At the beginning of the project, the author of *Bullyproof* provided a 6-hour training to administrators, counsellors, and fifth-grade teachers. In addition, 3-hour training sessions were provided once per semester at each campus for all personnel, including bus drivers, cafeteria workers, hall monitors, and office staff. A combination of lecture, discussion, and experiential activities from the curriculum was used. Training was designed to raise awareness of bullying and sexual harassment and to prepare school personnel to respond effectively to witnessed or reported incidents. The training presentation included research on bullying and sexual harassment; strategies for building a consistent response at the individual, classroom, and school-wide levels; strategies to enhance mutual respect among students; practice in using lessons from the curriculum; and methods for integrating the lessons into other subject areas including social studies, language arts, and health.

Policy development

The project staff encouraged administrators to develop a campus policy to ensure consistent responses by all staff members to incidents and reports of bullying and sexual harassment. To facilitate this process, project staff developed a policy template that was provided to campus administrators. The template included a statement of philosophy, working definitions of bullying and sexual harassment, expectations for actions in response to incidents and reports, and a statement of commitment to maintaining the confidentiality of targets, witnesses who report incidents, and students accused of bullying or harassing others. Principals were urged to solicit input from school staff and create a policy document that would be approved by the Campus Advisory Council (consisting of staff and parent representatives) at each school. Principals were expected to present the policy to school staff, students, and parents, and to provide training as needed for implementation. The extent to which this happened varied between schools.

Parent education

Project staff attempted to build support for the project and its objectives among parents through educational presentations and newsletters. Educational presentations were offered twice each year in the evening at each school, with parent attendance varying by site. The presentations provided information about the project, the vocabulary being used to discuss bullying and sexual harassment at school, strategies for helping children who are bullied, bully others, and witness bullying, tips for responding to and preventing bullying among siblings, and school and community resources for children and families experiencing bullying, sexual harassment, and dating, sexual, or domestic violence. Each semester, parent newsletters were sent home with students in participating schools. The newsletters contained updates on the project activities, students' *Bullyproof* class work, strategies for helping children with bullying problems and for responding to bullying behaviour among siblings, summer reading lists of children's books dealing with the subject of bullying, and information about relevant school and community resources.

Support services

SafePlace counsellors were available to assist school counsellors by providing school-based counselling and advocacy for victims of sexual and domestic violence. A specialised session was also provided to school counsellors to help them to respond effectively to students who repeatedly are targets or perpetrators of bullying or harassment. This exposure provided information on concrete strategies that reduced victim vulnerability (e.g. alternatives to conflict resolution and miscommunication approaches), as well as legal issues. At the beginning of the project, all school counsellors received a comprehensive resource manual containing reading and resource materials for bullying, sexual harassment, and dating, sexual, and domestic violence. The manual was intended to help school counsellors in their efforts to link children and families with community resources. The extent to which counsellors used the manual was not formally assessed, albeit anecdotal evidence obtained through requests to

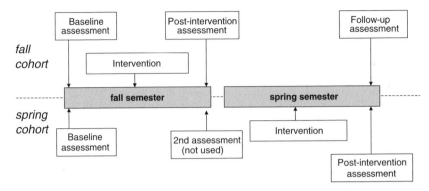

Fig. 11.1 Intervention and assessment schedule for the fall and spring cohorts.

SafePlace for additional training and support suggests that some counsellors used the materials.

Evaluation framework and procedures

This chapter reports the results of a student survey that was administered in all participating schools at the beginning of the fall semester, at the end of the fall semester, and at the end of the spring semester. This longitudinal evaluation procedure differs from the age-matched cohort procedure found in some other evaluation studies, such as in Bergen (chapter 2) or Sheffield (chapter 6). However, the comparison of randomly selected intervention and control schools permits an evaluation of what are intervention, rather than age, effects.

The first survey administration (at the beginning of the fall semester) was considered the baseline datum-point for all students. The post-intervention datum-point differed, however, according to when the intervention was delivered. At schools in which the intervention was delivered in the fall semester and the corresponding comparison schools, the post-intervention datum-point was the second survey administration (i.e. end of the fall semester). At schools in which the intervention was delivered in the spring semester, the post-intervention datum-point was the third survey administration (i.e. the end of the spring semester); see fig. 11.1. Students at fall-intervention schools thus completed the baseline assessment approximately 3 weeks before the intervention began, whereas students at spring-intervention schools completed the baseline assessment about 5 months before the intervention began. Semester of intervention delivery was statistically controlled in analyses involving post-intervention survey results. Only students from schools in which the intervention was delivered in the fall and their corresponding comparison schools were considered to have completed the follow-up survey. For these students, the follow-up assessment was completed approximately 5 months after the end of the intervention. A total of 1,763 students completed the baseline survey, 1,406 completed the post-intervention survey, and 700 completed the follow-up survey.

Several variables were measured at each assessment point. Analyses were focused on variables congruent with the goals of the curriculum, including reports of bullying behaviours and students' reactions to different bullying behaviours, students' intentions to act in specific ways upon witnessing bullying behaviours (name-calling and physical violence), students' perceptions of the actions of adults who witness bullying behaviours, and students' awareness of bullying and sexual harassment behaviours. Indices were constructed via factor analyses of baseline data whenever possible and the students' scores on the various factors were analysed.

Bullying behaviour and student responses

At baseline students were asked if they had ever been bullied, and at post-intervention and follow-up students were asked if they had been bullied in the past 3 months. Students who indicated they had experienced bullying were asked what the bully did (i.e. name calling, threatening, hit/kick/shove) and what they did when it happened. Two categories of bullying behaviours were created: physical bullying (i.e. hit/kick/shove) and verbal bullying (i.e. name-calling, threats). Students' responses to being bullied were factor analysed and 3 factors were derived: told an adult (2 items: told a parent; told an adult at school); made a verbal response (3 items: told the bully to stop; asked friends for help; said something to make the bully stop); and ignored the bullying (2 items: ignored the behaviour or hit, kicked, or shoved the bully (reverse scored)). Finally, students reported how often they had witnessed bullying in the past week (never, once or twice, almost every day), and this measure was dichotomised into witnessed or did not witness bullying.

Student intentions to act upon witnessing bullying behaviour

Students were asked to select specific actions they intended to take if they witnessed a student beating up on another student or calling another student names. Two factors were derived: telling someone (2 items: telling a parent; telling an adult at school); and directly intervening (2 items: telling the bully to stop; helping the student to get away).

Student perception of adult action

Students reported the actions they believed adults at their school would take if they witnessed a student beating up on another student. Two factors were derived: intervention (5 items: calling the parent; sending the bully to the office; punishing the bully; telling the bully to stop; sending the bully to an alternative school); and, no intervention (3 items). Students also reported the actions they believed adults at their school would take if they heard name-calling. The 3 derived factors were mild intervention (3 items: telling the bully to stop; punishing the bully; telling the victim to ignore the bully); strong intervention (3 items: calling the parents; sending the bully to the office; sending the bully to an alternative school); and, no intervention (2 items).

Bullying and sexual harassment awareness

For each of 14 behaviours, students indicated if they believed the behaviour constituted bullying - 9 items consisted of bullying behaviours (e.g. pushing, taking things, threatening); and 5 items did not (e.g. telling someone to leave you alone, not sharing). The measure of bullying awareness was the number of behaviours students correctly identified as a bullying or non-bullying item (range 0–14). Similarly, students indicated if they believed each of 9 behaviours constituted sexual harassment - 6 items consisted of sexual harassment behaviours (e.g. pressuring someone for sex), and 3 did not (e.g. telling someone you like him or her). The measure of sexual-harassment awareness was the number of behaviours students correctly identified (range 0–9).

Attitudes

Students responded to 21 attitude items using a 3-point agree–disagree scale. (Students in year 2 used a 5-point scale, but responses were recoded to a 3-point scale to combine the data.) Items were factor analysed and fell into five factors: (1) positive attitudes about bullies (6 items: e.g. I would be friends with someone who bullies others; A boy is weak if he doesn't fight a bully); (2) feeling safe at school (3 items: I feel safe at school, The adults at my school do a good job of stopping bullying); (3) bullying is OK in relationships (6 items: e.g. It's okay for a boyfriend to hit his girlfriend if she calls him mean names; Someone who hits his or her girlfriend or boyfriend is a bully); (4) beliefs that sexual harassment happens only to adults and girls (2 items); (5) attitude about asking for help if bullied (3 items: A boy is brave if he asks an adult for help with a bully).

Hypotheses

Based on the goals of the project, we hypothesised that students in the intervention schools, compared to students in the comparison schools, would demonstrate greater increases in their levels of awareness of behaviours that constitute bullying and behaviours that constitute sexual harassment. We also hypothesised that, compared to students in the comparison schools, students in the intervention schools would report a greater increase in the appropriate actions they would take upon being bullied or witnessing another student being bullied, and would perceive adults as taking a more active role upon witnessing bullying behaviours, and would change their attitudes to be less tolerant of bullies.

No hypotheses were generated about the impact of the intervention on students' reports of bullying or harassment behaviours (witnessing, being a victim, or being a perpetrator of bullying). Because the intervention was designed to increase students' awareness, identification, and willingness to report bullying and sexual harassment, the intervention conceivably could be associated with an increase in reported bullying behaviour. In contrast, the intervention emphasised that bullying was not acceptable and conceivably could be associated with a decrease in the frequency of reported bullying behaviour. It was thus unclear how to interpret changes in reported bullying behaviour, and analyses were exploratory.

What actually happened; achievements and difficulties in implementing the intervention

To complete the project, staff had to be flexible and able to adapt activities and schedules to meet the unique needs of each school, resulting in some modifications to the original design and materials. The modifications are described below.

Participating schools

Of the 6 intervention schools, 2 declined to participate in the project during the second year. One of the schools became the focus of the

state education agency's response to serious educational and management problems that precluded continuation in the project. At the other
school, the principal felt the first year of intervention was sufficient to
reduce bullying and chose to use staff time for other priorities. The two
corresponding comparison schools also were removed from the study in
the second year.

Classroom curriculum

All classes in the intervention schools received the same lessons and
utilised the same materials. Project educators facilitated the lessons with
varying involvement of school staff. Although teachers and school counsellors were expected to co-facilitate the lessons, many preferred to have
the lessons facilitated solely by the project's educators.

At the beginning of the project, staff selected lessons from *Bullyproof*
to include in a 12-session facilitator's guide to ensure all students in the
project received the same lessons. Project staff created one additional
lesson to address the influence of gender roles on boys and girls, and
their expectations for dating relationships. Based on focus-group data
at the end of the first year, project staff replaced one of the *Bullyproof*
lessons with a new lesson on healthy relationships. In addition, one of
the *Bullyproof* lessons was modified at the beginning of the second year
at the request of several parents who objected to the content of a scenario included in the lesson about sexual harassment. The parents were
concerned that the scenario, based on a real-life peer sexual harassment
case, might frighten fifth-graders. To maintain consistency across schools,
project staff used the revised version in all classes during the second year.

Monolingual Spanish-speaking students presented additional challenges. Although materials were translated into Spanish, there is no
Spanish term that is equivalent to the English word 'bully' or 'bullying',
and neither the term nor the concept translates accurately. Although some
project staff spoke Spanish (e.g. project co-ordinator, SafePlace counsellors), the project educators did not, and depended on the classroom
teacher to facilitate the lessons. These limitations raise concerns about the
consistency with which the programme was implemented for Spanish-
speaking students, and their data were excluded from the evaluation.
In addition to language, there were concerns regarding cultural differences in gender role expectations and definitions of healthy relationships.
Thus, the cultural sensitivity and cultural relevance of the programme
for Spanish-speaking students have not been established, indicating the
need for additional modifications and evaluation before implementing
the programme with monolingual Spanish-speaking groups.

Staff training

Year 1 trainings were conducted as previously described. During the second year, however, training time was limited due to increased emphasis district-wide on raising standardised test scores. In some schools, the project's staff training was divided into two parts and presented after school hours at regularly scheduled faculty meetings. Teachers were often tired at the end of the day, and some may have been resentful at having to stay late for the training. In some schools, non-teaching staff and staff not regularly on duty during training hours did not receive the training.

Policy development

The development and implementation of school-wide policies and procedures varied with the commitment of the principal on each campus. Principals who were supportive of the project arranged for adequate training time and involved their faculty in policy development. During the second year, 2 of the 4 principals involved faculty members in writing policies and procedures. The other principals adopted the template provided to them by project staff without significant discussion or involvement of their staff.

Results of the evaluation

Dependent variables were analysed using hierarchical modelling using the SAS Proc Mixed for normally distributed dependent variables and the SAS macro GLIMMIX for dependent variables lacking a normal distribution. Two sets of analyses were done for each variable. The first tested changes from baseline to post intervention, and the second tested changes from baseline to follow-up. For each variable, the statistical model crossed Group (intervention vs. comparison), Time (baseline vs. post or baseline vs. follow-up), and Gender (male vs. female). Year (1 vs. 2) and Semester of intervention (fall vs. spring) were included as control variables. (Note: semester was controlled only in post-intervention analyses. Analyses indicated Year and Semester did not moderate interactions between Group, Time, and Gender for most dependent variables.) The primary effect of interest was the Group × Time interaction, so the discussion focuses on variables for which this was significant.

Table 11.1 shows the means (standard deviations in parentheses) or percentages for the relevant dependent variables by Group (intervention vs. comparison) and Time (baseline, post intervention, follow-up). The

Table 11.1. *Baseline, post-intervention, and follow-up means (standard deviations) or percentages for intervention and comparison groups*

	Intervention			Comparison			Significant effects	
Variable	Baseline	Post	Follow-up	Baseline	Post	Follow-up	Baseline to post	Baseline to follow-up
Behaviours								
Victim of any bullying	40.8%	36.7%	30.1%	47.5%	34.7%	28.7%	T, G×T	T
Victim of physical bullying	15.2%	11.1%	7.8%	19.5%	13.4%	7.9%	G, T	T, S
Victim of verbal bullying	31.2%	29.8%	19.0%	36.8%	26.8%	17.0%	T, G×T	T, S
Response to physical bullying:	0.77 (.82)	0.87 (.71)	074 (.85)	0.83 (.80)	0.55 (.79)	0.62 (.82)	G×T	S×G×T
Told an adult								
Boys	0.70 (.70)	0.96 (.86)	0.84 (.90)	0.73 (.81)	(0.44 (.73))	0.44 (.78)	—	G×T
Girls	0.85 (.72)	0.73 (0.75)	0.58 (.79)	0.97 (.77)	0.69 (.86)	1.16 (.75)	—	T
Response to physical bullying:	0.84 (.87)	1.04 (.80)	0.93 (.77)	0.90 (.83)	0.77 (.79)	0.71 (.81)	S×G×T	None
Verbal response								
Boys	0.87 (.93)	1.04 (.86)	0.95 (.78)	0.90 (.84)	0.54 (.65)	0.61 (.70)	G×T	—
Girls	0.81 (.81)	1.03 (.72)	0.92 (.67)	0.90 (.82)	1.08 (.87)	1.00 (1.09)	None	—
Response to physical bullying:	1.06 (.61)	1.14 (.60)	1.00 (.68)	0.93 (.65)	1.00 (.74)	1.17 (.76)	S×G×T	None
Ignored								
Boys	1.01 (.59)	1.06 (.62)	1.00 (.67)	0.83 (.67)	1.10 (.79)	1.22 (.81)	T	—
Girls	1.11 (.63)	1.26 (.57)	1.00 (.74)	1.07 (.60)	0.86 (.64)	1.00 (.63)	G×T	—
Reaction to verbal bullying:	0.59 (.69)	0.44 (.66)	0.50 (.69)	0.64 (.75)	0.48 (.72)	0.61 (.77)	S, T	T, S
Told an adult								
Reaction to verbal bullying:	0.59 (.76)	0.60 (.68)	0.63 (.69)	0.70 (.75)	0.58 (.72)	0.75 (.59)	S	S
Verbal response								
Reaction to verbal bullying:	1.34 (.60)	1.33 (.59)	1.28 (.59)	1.34 (.59)	1.39 (.64)	1.36 (.59)	none	none
Ignored								

Witnessed bullying in past week	38.4%	60.6%	53.8%	47.3%	53.0%	42.4%	T, G×T	T, G×T, S×G×T
Boys	35.7%	58.4%	47.6%	45.7%	49.6%	47.0%	—	T, G×T
Girls	40.2%	63.2%	60.5%	49.1%	55.8%	38.7%	—	T, G×T
Bullied another student in the past week	10.6%	17.0%	20.8%	11.2%	17.8%	13.7%	T, G	S, G×T
Intended self-action if witnessed physical (beating up on) or verbal (name calling) bullying								
Physical bullying: Tell an adult	1.06 (.75)	1.21 (.78)	1.22 (.77)	1.02 (.75)	1.14 (.80)	1.19 (.81)	T, S	T, S
Physical bullying: Directly intervening	0.90 (.81)	1.26 (.81)	1.23 (.81)	0.94 (.81)	1.06 (.83)	1.02 (.83)	T, G×T	T, G×T
Verbal bullying: Tell an adult	0.85 (.78)	0.88 (.86)	0.89 (.84)	0.80 (.78)	0.88 (.83)	0.90 (.84)	T, S×T×G, G×T	None
Boys	0.70 (.76)	0.67 (.83)	0.77 (.85)	0.67 (.76)	0.79 (.82)	0.78 (.84)	T	—
Girls	1.00 (.76)	1.09 (.84)	1.00 (.84)	0.93 (.78)	0.96 (.83)	1.01 (.81)	T, G×T	S, T, S×G×T
Verbal bullying: Directly intervening	0.86 (.75)	1.08 (.76)	1.06 (.77)	0.93 (.76)	0.92 (.80)	0.93 (.75)		
Boys	0.79 (.73)	0.99 (.77)	0.89 (.74)	0.86 (.73)	0.80 (.78)	0.83 (.76)	—	None
Girls	0.92 (.77)	1.17 (.74)	1.23 (.77)	1.00 (.78)	1.03 (.80)	1.02 (.74)	—	T, G×T
Students' perceptions of adults' likely reactions to witnessing physical (beating up on) or verbal (name calling) bullying								
Physical bullying: Intervention	2.50 (1.46)	2.91 (1.51)	2.87 (1.47)	2.59 (1.49)	2.88 (1.53)	2.94 (1.47)	T	T
Physical bullying: No intervention	0.19 (.44)	0.26 (.49)	0.22 (.45)	0.17 (.41)	0.20 (.44)	0.20 (.43)	G, T	T
Verbal bullying: Strong intervention	0.94 (1.00)	0.85 (1.04)	0.89 (1.02)	0.97 (1.02)	0.97 (1.06)	1.00 (1.07)	None	None
Verbal bullying: Mild intervention	0.95 (.74)	1.20 (.75)	1.25 (.75)	1.04 (.78)	1.17 (.78)	1.24 (.77)	T, G×T	T

(cont.)

Table 11.1. (*cont.*)

Variable	Intervention			Comparison			Significant effects	
	Baseline	Post	Follow-up	Baseline	Post	Follow-up	Baseline to post	Baseline to follow-up
Verbal bullying: No intervention	0.11 (.34)	0.14 (.37)	0.12 (.33)	0.07 (.27)	0.13 (.35)	0.10 (.30)	G, T	None
Awareness								
Bullying awareness score	11.16 (2.77)	11.66 (2.27)	11.83 (2.30)	11.19 (2.74)	11.46 (2.45)	11.40 (2.52)	T	T
Sexual harassment awareness score	7.11 (1.53)	8.09 (1.18)	8.09 (1.17)	7.13 (1.52)	7.85 (1.30)	7.68 (1.43)	T, G×T	T, G×T
Attitudes								
Pro-bully attitude	2.97 (2.12)	3.23 (2.36)	3.26 (2.30)	3.05 (2.17)	3.50 (2.47)	3.32 (2.34)	T, S, S×G×T	T, S
Boys	3.27 (2.32)	3.80 (2.71)	3.66 (2.58)	3.34 (2.36)	3.75 (2.68)	3.77 (2.60)	none	—
Girls	2.63 (1.79)	2.63 (1.76)	2.80 (1.80)	2.72 (1.95)	3.19 (2.26)	2.82 (2.00)	T, T×G	—
Feeling safe at school	5.64 (1.43)	5.26 (1.83)	5.42 (1.74)	5.82 (1.41)	5.49 (1.66)	5.56 (1.61)	T	S×G×T
Boys	5.75 (1.39)	5.33 (1.86)	5.61 (1.67)	5.93 (1.33)	5.51 (1.67)	5.56 (1.71)	—	T
Girls	5.57 (1.46)	5.20 (1.80)	5.22 (1.81)	5.73 (1.46)	5.50 (1.65)	5.59 (1.55)	—	T
OK to bully in relationship	11.09 (1.91)	11.28 (1.74)	11.50 (1.53)	11.27 (1.88)	11.36 (1.76)	11.56 (1.81)	T, S	T, S
Only girls/adults sexually harassed	2.49 (1.43)	1.82 (1.04)	1.85 (1.07)	2.28 (1.32)	1.89 (1.12)	1.88 (1.08)	T, S, T×G	T, S
OK to ask for help if bullied	5.30 (0.45)	4.99 (0.43)	4.99 (0.46)	5.28 (0.46)	5.01 (0.46)	4.85 (0.47)	T, S	T, S

Effects: T = Time (baseline vs. post), G = Group (intervention vs. comparison), S = Gender (male vs. female).
Only Time and Group effects that are significant at p < .05 are shown. All analyses included Gender as a factor in the model and controlled for year and semester of intervention.

final two columns list the significant effects for Group (G), Time (T), and Gender (S). Where Gender moderated the Group × Time interaction, analyses were conducted separately for boys and girls.

Bullying behaviour

For the percentage of students reporting having been bullied in any way, there was a Group × Time interaction. Students in the intervention schools reported equal amounts of bullying at baseline and post intervention (p = .10), whereas students in the comparison schools reported having been bullied less at post intervention than at baseline (p < .001). There was a significant Group × Time interaction for verbal bullying, but not for physical bullying, suggesting that the decrease in bullying from baseline to post intervention in comparison schools was primarily due to the decrease in verbal bullying. Students in intervention schools reported no differences in being verbally bullied from baseline to post intervention (p = .60), whereas students in comparison schools reported a decrease (p < .001). The Group × Time interaction from baseline to follow-up was not significant for any type of bullying behaviour.

Because reactions to physical and verbal bullying were expected to differ, students' responses to being bullied (i.e. told an adult, verbal response, ignored the bullying) were analysed separately for students who were physically bullied and students who were verbally bullied. The Group × Time interaction for telling an adult was significant for responses to physical bullying (p < .001), with students in intervention schools indicating a similar likelihood of telling an adult at baseline and post intervention (p = .49), and students in comparison schools reporting a decrease in telling an adult (p = .01). At follow-up, this significant decrease was present only for boys. There was a significant Gender × Group × Time interaction for students' verbal responses to physical bullying. Analyses by gender indicated the effect was limited to boys. In intervention schools, boys' verbal responses to being physically bullied did not change from baseline to post intervention (p = .11), whereas boys in comparison schools reported a decrease in verbal responses (p = .009). Analyses of baseline to follow-up differences were not significant. There was a Gender × Group × Time interaction for ignoring physical bullying (p = .02). Follow-up analyses indicated that Group effects were limited to girls. In intervention schools, girls' reports of ignoring physical bullying did not change from baseline to post intervention (p = .42), whereas girls in comparison schools reported a decrease in ignoring bullying (p = .04); the baseline to follow-up comparison was not significant. None of the students' responses to verbal bullying (i.e. told an adult, made a verbal response, ignored) demonstrated a significant Group × Time interaction at post intervention or at follow-up.

There was a significant Group × Time interaction for the frequency of witnessing bullying. Students in intervention schools reported an increase in witnessing bullying (p < .001), whereas students in comparison schools did not (p = .06). The interaction was significant at follow-up, but was moderated by Gender. Follow-up analyses indicated the difference was larger for girls than it was for boys. In analyses of bullying other students, the Group × Time interaction was non-significant at post intervention, but significant at follow-up. Students in intervention schools reported an increase in bullying others at follow-up (p < .001), whereas students in comparison schools did not change (p = .73).

Students' intended responses to witnessing bullying

Analyses of students' intentions to tell an adult if they witnessed a student beating up on another student resulted in only Gender and Time main effects at post intervention and follow-up. Analyses of responses that students intended to directly intervene revealed a Group × Time interaction. Students in both intervention (p < .001) and comparison schools (p = .003) reported greater intentions to directly intervene at post intervention than at baseline, but the mean difference was larger for students in intervention schools than in comparison schools. The Group × Time interaction was significant at follow-up, but only for students in intervention schools (p < .001) and not for students in comparison schools (p = .28). Analyses of students' intentions to tell an adult or directly intervene upon witnessing name calling revealed a Gender × Group × Time interaction for telling an adult. Data were analysed separately for boys and girls, with no significant results for girls. For boys, there was a Group × Time interaction. In intervention schools, boys' intentions to tell someone did not change from baseline to post intervention (p = .71), whereas in comparison schools, boys' intentions to tell someone increased (p = .006). The results of analyses of baseline to follow-up analyses were not significant. Students' intentions to intervene directly upon witnessing name-calling revealed a Group × Time interaction with increases from baseline to post intervention observed for students in intervention schools (p < .001), but not in comparison schools (p = .60). At follow-up, this Group × Time interaction was moderated by Gender, and subsequent analyses indicated significant effects only for girls in the intervention group.

Perceptions of adults' actions upon witnessing bullying

Of the 5 dependent variables assessing students' beliefs about what adults would do upon witnessing a student beating up on another student or overhearing name-calling, the only Group × Time interaction that was significant was adults' mild intervention for name-calling. Although both the intervention and comparison groups were more likely to believe adults would respond with a mild intervention (ps < .001), the change from baseline to post intervention was greater for students in intervention schools than in comparison schools.

Bullying and sexual-harassment awareness

The Group × Time interaction for bullying awareness was not significant. There was a significant Group × Time interaction for sexual-harassment awareness from baseline to post intervention and from baseline to follow-up. Students in both intervention and comparison schools reported increases in sexual-harassment awareness (ps < .001), but the increase was greater for students in intervention schools than in comparison schools.

Attitudes

For the 5 attitudes measures, only two Group × Time interactions were significant from baseline to post intervention, and one Group × Time interaction was significant from baseline to follow-up. For pro-bully attitudes, there was a Gender × Group × Time interaction from baseline to post intervention. Separate analyses for males and females showed that a Group × Time interaction was found for females only. Attitudes of girls in intervention schools did not change baseline to post (p = .95), whereas attitudes of girls in control schools became more pro-bully (p < .001). The second baseline to post effect was for beliefs about who is bullied, which revealed a significant Group × Time interaction. Both groups showed a decrease in beliefs that only girls get bullied from baseline to post (both p < .001), but the decrease was larger for students in intervention schools. Last, the baseline to follow-up analyses of feeling safe at school showed a Gender × Group × Time interaction. Follow-up analyses showed a similar pattern for boy's and girl's data. For both boys and girls, there was only a main effect of Time with both feeling less safe over time, and no significant Group × Time interaction (both p > .19).

Discussion

The Expect Respect project was designed to promote awareness of bullying and sexual harassment behaviours and to increase students' ability and willingness to intervene on behalf of targets by speaking up themselves or getting help from an adult. The overarching goal of the programme was to create a positive school climate in which bullying and sexual harassment are not tolerated, and school staff respond consistently to incidents and reports.

Although no significant differences in students' bullying awareness were observed, students who participated in the intervention, relative to students in the comparison schools, showed a greater increase from baseline to post intervention in their awareness and accurate identification of behaviours constituting sexual-harassment. However, both groups of students increased their sexual-harassment awareness over time. The absence of significant results in bullying awareness may be associated, in part, with the design of the student survey. The survey asked students to identify behaviours that constituted bullying and sexual harassment from a simple listing of behaviours, whereas the curriculum focused on discriminating bullying and sexual-harassment behaviours within specific contexts that were absent in the survey. The mismatch between the curriculum content and the survey questions may obscure the potential impact of the curriculum.

With respect to appropriate responses to hypothetical bullying scenarios, students in the intervention schools also were more likely to report intending to intervene directly when witnessing another student being physically or verbally bullied. In contrast, boys in the comparison schools were more likely to report intending to tell an adult if they witnessed verbal bullying. The intervention students, relative to the comparison students, were also less likely to demonstrate a decrease over time in appropriate responses to being bullied. Students in intervention schools, relative to comparison students, were more likely to show an increase in their beliefs that adults in their school would intervene upon witnessing verbal bullying. The programme appeared to impact girls' attitudes towards bullies, as girls at intervention schools did not change their attitudes over time, while girls at control schools became more pro-bully. The programme did not appear to impact perceptions of safety, with all students feeling less safe at school over time.

The impact of the intervention on reported bullying behaviours (being a victim, witnessing bullying, bullying others) are difficult to interpret. At baseline the survey asked about lifetime victimisation, whereas at post intervention and follow-up the survey asked about victimisation over the

past 3 months. A decrease is therefore expected, with no readily inter-
pretable explanation for the greater decrease in reports of being bullied
over time that was reported in the comparison schools. There was an
increase in reported bullying in the intervention schools relative to the
comparison schools for witnessing bullying (girls in particular) and perpetrating bullying (at follow-up). As already noted, it is difficult to know
whether the increase was due to actual increases in bullying behaviours or
greater vigilance and willingness to report bullying behaviours on the part
of students in the intervention schools. One evaluation strategy that can
provide help here is the use of in-depth debriefings following the implementation of a curriculum. Asking open-ended questions to students
who receive such a curriculum can allow a researcher to understand students' reactions to that curriculum that quantitative surveys may miss.
Although focus groups and interviews were conducted with fifth-graders
at participating schools, the results of those sessions are not included in
this chapter.

The difficulty in interpreting the results is increased by the fact that
no independent criteria for assessing bullying or sexual harassment
behaviours (e.g. school disciplinary reports, direct observation) were
included. All results reported here are based on students' self-reports,
which may be subject to demand characteristics, particularly in the intervention schools. This represents a major flaw in the evaluation, particularly if the ultimate goal of the programme is to decrease tolerance for,
and incidents of, bullying and sexual harassment. The lack of behavioural
data limits the conclusions that may be drawn regarding the efficacy of
the programme. Similarly, the measures used in the evaluation did not
permit adequate assessment of the programme goals of improving school
climate and staff consistency in responding to incidents, albeit students'
perceptions of the safety of their schools, as assessed by the questionnaire
used in the study, did not change.

Several additional limitations should be noted that suggest caution in
interpreting the evaluation results. Although statistical analyses focused
on theoretically based hypotheses, there was no correction for multiple
analyses, and some of the observed group differences may have been due
to chance. Many analyses were conducted with few significant effects,
particularly at follow-up. Finally, the mean differences, standard deviations, and percentages presented in table 11.1 suggest relatively small
changes and substantial overlap among the intervention and comparison
students' responses at pre-test and post-test. Students' responses in the
intervention and comparison schools appeared to change similarly over
time. In spite of statistically significant differences on some variables, the
practical significance of the observed changes appears to be limited.

Longer term effects or evaluation of the programme

In 2003 the Austin Independent School District in collaboration with SafePlace developed and adapted district-wide policies and procedures concerning the intervention and prevention of bullying, sexual harassment, and dating violence. However, these have not yet been further evaluated.

Dissemination and impact beyond the programme schools

Media coverage

During the two years of implementation (1998–2000), local media covered project activities on 6 occasions (3 television, 1 radio, 2 print), and 6 state and national pieces were produced (1 television, 4 satellite broadcasts, 1 print). Media coverage typically included information about the incidence of bullying and sexual harassment in schools, and the relationship of these behaviours to other forms of school violence. The television and satellite broadcasts included footage of project activities including staff training and classroom sessions. In some pieces, students, teachers, principals, and project staff were interviewed about their role in the project and the impact of the project's activities. SafePlace utilised copies of these videotapes and articles to illustrate project activities to funding sources, for training, and to increase awareness and support for SafePlace programmes.

Presentations and training

By the end of the first year of implementation (1999), 10 non-participating schools had requested staff and parent training and classroom presentations for students. In response, project staff provided an abbreviated version of the services consisting of 1 staff training session, 1 parent session, and 2 classroom presentations per fifth-grade class. By the end of the second year of implementation (2000), project staff had presented at 17 local, state, and national conferences. These presentations typically addressed the research on bullying and sexual harassment, intervention and prevention strategies, and the project's results. In Austin, training also was provided for all school bus drivers, and school guidance counsellors, and numerous Parent Teacher Associations.

In June 2001, SafePlace hosted 2 consecutive trainings serving a total of 80 school and agency personnel from across the USA. Entitled '*From bullying to battering: School-based programs for preventing bullying, sexual harassment, and gender violence*' each 2-day session was conducted by the author of *Bullyproof*, the director of school-based services at SafePlace, and featured a panel of local-school personnel. Participants learned a variety of school-based intervention and prevention strategies, including how to implement selected curriculum, provide school staff training, create disciplinary responses, and conduct counselling and support groups. This training was conducted again in June 2002, serving 50 participants from throughout the USA.

During the 2001–02 school year, SafePlace worked closely with the Austin Council of Parent Teacher Associations (ACPTA) to provide a series of trainings on stopping bullying and sexual harassment for parents throughout AISD. These sessions were attended by parents of children in K-12 schools as well as school administrators, counsellors, and school-board members. In January 2003 the ACPTA, in conjunction with a local foundation, will host a 3-part series on bullying prevention for the Austin community.

Summer Teen Leadership programme

The Summer Teen Leadership programme (STLP) was developed by project staff to build teenagers' leadership skills for confronting the problems of bullying, sexual harassment, and dating violence in their lives, among peers, and in their communities. Each summer since the project ended, SafePlace has provided an average of 13 teenagers with intensive leadership training and work experience. Teenagers are recruited from local schools and paid by the City of Austin's Summer Youth Employment programme, with additional funds provided by SafePlace. Serving as role models and educators for younger children, the Teen Leaders facilitate bullying- and harassment-prevention programmes for children at SafePlace and at summer recreation sites throughout Austin.

The National Resource Center on Domestic Violence

The Expect Respect programme (referring to all of SafePlace's school-based services) was selected in 2002 as a 'Promising Practice' by the National Resource Center on Domestic Violence. A document entitled '*Expect respect: A school-based programme promoting safe and healthy relationships for youth*' describing the programme's development, implementation, evaluation, and replication guidelines can be obtained by contacting the National Resource Center on Domestic Violence at (800) 537–2238 or on the website. (www.vawnet.org)

Recent and future activities

Although the original Expect Respect Elementary School project ended in 2000, the lessons learned have been helpful in further developing a school-based model for intervening and preventing bullying and sexual harassment. The collaborative relationship between AISD and SafePlace continues to grow, benefiting students and families experiencing abuse, and increasing access to specialised training for school staff on these issues. In 2002 SafePlace was awarded a grant from the Criminal Justice Division of the Governor's Office under the Safe and Drug-Free Schools and Communities Act Fund to establish school-wide bullying prevention programmes in 4 Austin elementary schools. This project and its evaluation plan have been designed to build on the lessons learned from the original project and to overcome some of the limitations identified. Safe-Place continues to work with additional local schools with the financial support of individuals, schools, and community groups.

Conclusions

The substantial interest in, and implementation of, the Expect Respect project demonstrates the broad recognition of bullying and sexual harassment as a problem requiring intervention early in childhood. School officials chose to participate in this project despite the absence of a published programme evaluation. This demonstrates the clear need both for the development of programmes that address bullying and sexual harassment for young children, and the careful evaluation of those programmes. Although this project positively impacted children's awareness of sexual harassment and intentions to intercede upon witnessing bullying, observed changes were often small and appeared to diminish over time, and the impact of the project on other outcomes, such as school climate, staff responses to bullying and sexual harassment, and actual incidence rates of bullying and sexual harassment could not be determined with the existing data. Finally, the cultural relevancy of the programme has not yet been demonstrated.

The current evaluation provides lessons in conducting future evaluations of school-based and other prevention programmes; it most notably speaks to the importance of selecting well-designed and valid assessment tools that adequately measure programme goals and objectives, and of obtaining independent assessments of behaviours targeted for change. Follow-up assessments need to be conducted across time to determine the long-term efficacy of interventions. In addition, attention to elements of process evaluation (e.g. training-programme implementers to predetermined performance criteria, adherence to intervention protocols, collection and interpretation of qualitative data) is essential in interpreting the outcomes of evaluations.

References

Olweus, D., Limber, S., and Mihalic, S. F. (1999). *Blueprints for violence prevention: Book nine, Bullying Prevention Program.* Boulder, Colo.: Center for the Study and Prevention of Violence.

Stein, N. (1995). Sexual harassment in school: The public performance of gendered violence. *Harvard Educational Review*, 65, 145–62.

Stein, N. and Sjostrom, L. (1996). *Bullyproof: A teachers' guide on teasing and bullying for use with fourth and fifth grade students.* Wellesley, Mass.: Wellesley College Center for Research on Women and the National Education Association Professional Library.

12 A follow-up survey of anti-bullying interventions in the comprehensive schools of Kempele in 1990–98

Maila Koivisto

Impetus for the intervention study, early stages of planning, and funding

In Finland, the increase of violent behaviour and the more and more brutal forms of violence by children and adolescents were widely discussed in the 1980s. The tone of the discussion was often accusing. At times, it was the parents who were held responsible for causing this undesirable development, at other times the blame was put on schools and teachers, or it was felt that society in general was at fault by neglecting children and adolescents. To counteract this negative development, two national Finnish civic organisations, the Mannerheim League for Child Welfare (briefly Mannerheim League) and the Finnish Red Cross, launched a nationwide campaign against violence, the Non-Violent Campaign. Preparations for the campaign began in 1989, and the campaign itself was conducted in 1990. The campaign was aimed at the whole population of Finland, but the work done by Mannerheim League involved children and adolescents. One of the goals of the campaign was to raise awareness of the violence and bullying that takes place at schools, and to find ways to reduce and prevent violence. The campaign was based on a solution-oriented model, which does not so much aim to find causes and guilty parties, but rather concentrates on solving problems through constructive discussions (Pikas, 1987).

Inspired by the Non-Violent Campaign, the local Kempele association of Mannerheim League, together with the Mannerheim League district organisation, decided to carry out a survey of the prevalence and patterns of school bullying in the Kempele comprehensive schools in 1990. The representatives of the Kempele schools and the local school authorities had a very positive attitude towards the suggested project. As president of the local Kempele Mannerheim League association, the present author undertook to conduct this survey on this topic, which she found very interesting, partly through her work at the paediatric clinic of Oulu University Hospital. The 1990 survey set out to provide a basis for discussion and anti-bullying action in the Kempele comprehensive schools, and the initial project was later extended to include a follow-up process. The following report will discuss the effects of the 1990 survey and the resulting school policies and strategies on the occurrence of bullying in the Kempele comprehensive schools during the 8-year follow-up period.

No special funding was provided for the survey. The Mannerheim League and its district organisation trained and employed a full-time project manager for the 1-year campaign (1990) and a part-time manager for the following 2 years to organise the work in Northern Finland, which has a population of about 500,000. After the follow-up survey, a report was published in Finnish. The costs of printing and distribution were paid by the Research Foundation of the Mannerheim League for Child Welfare, the Kempele local government, and the district organisation of Mannerheim League.

Selection of schools

The Finnish comprehensive-school system provides children of all abilities a 9-year education, and school is started at the age of 7. The co-educational comprehensive school is divided into a 6-year Lower stage (elementary grades 1–6) and a 3-year Upper stage (junior high grades 7–9). School legislation has been amended recently, and the division between the Lower and Upper stages will be eliminated in the future. In the Lower stage, the instruction in each grade is mainly given by a class teacher. The change from the Lower to the Upper stage is usually of major significance in the pupils' lives, as in most cases they move from the familiar neighbourhood school to a big central school. The teaching system is also different, as instruction in the Upper stage is given by subject teachers. All the comprehensive schools in Kempele municipality were chosen to participate in this survey.

Characteristics of schools and students

At the time of the initial survey in 1990, the northern Finnish town of Kempele, situated near the city of Oulu (population 120,000), had a population of 10,000. By the end of the follow-up period in 1998, the population had increased by 10%, mainly due to immigration. At the time of the survey, there were 4 Lower-stage schools and 1 Upper-stage school in Kempele. In 1990, two Lower-stage schools provided education for all elementary grades 1–6, and two schools only for the first four grades 1–4. Since 1992 3 schools, and since 1996 all the 4 Lower-stage schools

Table 12.1. *Number of the pupils participating in the survey*

	Year and grade	Girls	Boys	Total
1990	4th	82	90	172
	6th	85	93	178
	7th	65	70	135
1992	4th	81	95	176
	6th	79	88	167
	7th	74	107	181
1994	4th	99	95	194
	6th	78	98	176
	7th	94	98	192
1996	4th	93	93	186
	6th	97	88	185
	7th	86	93	179
1998	4th	110	114	224
	6th	92	93	185
	7th	104	95	199
Total		1,319	1,410	2,729

in Kempele have provided education for all elementary grades 1–6. In 1998, the smallest Lower-stage school had about 100 pupils, whereas the biggest Lower-stage and the Upper-stage school had about 600 pupils each.

All the participants in this survey were pupils in the Kempele comprehensive schools. The first survey was carried out in 1990 and the follow-up evaluations in 1992, 1994, 1996, and 1998. All the fourth-, sixth-, and seventh-graders present on the appointed day in each survey year took part in the study by completing the questionnaire. There were some key considerations that affected the choice of pupils to be surveyed. Fourth-graders (aged 10–11) were thought to be mature enough to understand the topics and questions the survey was about. Sixth-graders (aged 12–13) are the oldest pupils in the Lower stage, and this position was considered a possible factor in becoming a school bully. It was also believed that the position of seventh-graders (aged 13–14) as the youngest age group in the Upper stage could make them more liable to bullying. The number of pupils completing the questionnaire each year grew slightly during the follow-up period, as the population of Kempele increased. During the 8-year follow-up period, 2,729 pupils aged 10–14 completed the questionnaire. The distribution of pupils according to the survey year, grade, and sex is presented in table 12.1.

Baseline survey

The pupils filled in a 23-item questionnaire anonymously under the supervision of their teacher. The questionnaire was completed during one lesson in April in each survey year. The questionnaire was based on a Finnish version of the questionnaires used in Scandinavian surveys, and the version was further modified to suit the purposes of this survey. No consistent verbal information on how to interpret the terms was given, as the present writer was not able to administer the questionnaires personally, but written examples were provided to clarify some questions (Olweus, 1973, 1978, 1991).

The questionnaire asked, for instance, how pupils spent their break time ('in a big group', 'in a small group', 'alone'). The pupils were asked to give peer evaluation about the occurrence of bullying during breaks, during lessons, and on the way to or from school ('never', 'seldom', 'sometimes', 'fairly often', 'very often'). They were also asked to judge whether they had been victims of bullying themselves or had bullied others during the previous 3 months ('never', 'sometimes', 'fairly often', 'almost every day', 'every day').

The pupils who had been victims of bullying were asked about where and by whom they had been bullied, and what the bullying had been like ('physical', 'psychological', or 'both'). The bullies were asked the same questions as the victims. At the end of the questionnaire, the pupils were invited to assess some suggested solutions to the bullying problem and to indicate what they would do to reduce bullying.

In the analysis of the questionnaire, bullying was considered prevalent if the pupil had chosen 'very often' or 'fairly often' in the peer evaluation section. The pupils who had chosen the alternatives 'fairly often', 'almost every day', or 'every day' in the self-evaluation section were classified as victims or bullies.

Components of the intervention programme

The results of the initial 1990 survey gave a realistic starting-point for developing strategies that could be used against bullying and for making these strategies more effective. The results of the initial survey were discussed by the school staff and in parent–teacher (PTA) meetings. Even though the ways in which the school community reacts to bullying varied slightly from school to school and changed over the years, the basic principle remained unchanged in all the participating schools: bullying is not tolerated. The school staff intervene in all incidents of bullying without delay.

In co-operation with the parents, the school communities tried to make the school climate more open, more respectful of others, and more encouraging by arranging parent–teacher meetings, various campaigns and action days, and by distributing information in leaflets and face-to-face meetings. The pupils, too, were involved in improving the school climate. They participated in the process by working out a set of school rules together, which helped them to learn good manners as well. The schools paid attention to how and where the pupils spent their break time, to have the younger and older pupils in the Lower-stage schools spend their time in different parts of the playground. The largest Lower-stage school increased the number of teachers responsible for supervising the children during breaks.

To make the transition from the Lower to the Upper stage easier, it was agreed that sixth-graders should familiarise themselves with the customs and rules of the new school while they were still attending the Lower stage. As seventh-graders, the pupils continued learning the rules mainly with the help of their own group teacher in the Upper stage. Even before this study and outside this project, the Upper-stage school community in Kempele had provided, and continues to provide, peer tutoring and counselling for pupils to create and foster a sense of belonging and solidarity. A number of peer-counsellor and tutor pupils are elected and trained each year to act as a peer-support group for all Upper-stage pupils. The Mannerheim League supports this type of work in Finnish schools.

To prevent bullying, the schools implemented curricular measures, and anti-bullying strategies were incorporated in the annual work plans of the schools as well as in the pupil-welfare system. Individual cases of bullying were discussed in mutual understanding and in a positive atmosphere with the people concerned. The pupil-welfare group, including the headteacher, a representative of the teaching staff, the school psychologist, the school welfare officer, the school doctor, and the school nurse, participated in solving the most difficult cases. Sometimes experts from outside the school were consulted. If the pupils who were victimised or who resorted to bullying behaviour failed to adapt to normal classroom teaching, it was possible to transfer them to a special small group unit parallel to the mainstream classes, in which they were able to continue their education.

Evaluation framework and procedures

In 1990 the Non-Violent Campaign prepared the ground for this project. In that year, the problem of school bullying was frequently discussed in the media, and several educational events on the topic were arranged for teachers. The Mannerheim League had collected information about ways to prevent bullying and to solve problems in line with a solution-oriented model. No detailed instructions were issued to schools, however.

Although the actual campaign only lasted for 1 year, the participating schools were followed up at 2-year intervals for 8 years. The results of the questionnaire surveys were reported to the schools after each follow-up year. The results were compared to the results of the corresponding age-graders over time, and there were no control schools for comparison. Because the sample size was quite small, only a few statistical significances were analysed, and this was done with the help of the Chi-squared test.

One weakness of the study is that no consistent verbal instructions were given to the classes on how to interpret the terms used before the questionnaires were first administered, and the questions concerning the frequency of bullying could also have been more specific. It is possible that, because of this, the significance of indirect bullying especially, which is more frequently used by girls than boys, was under-estimated. Since, however, the same method was used throughout the follow-up period, the comparison of findings was not distorted, though the overall prevalence of bullying may actually have been slightly too low.

What actually happened; achievements and difficulties in implementing the plan of intervention

The primary purpose of this study was to evaluate the prevalence of school bullying at a local level in the comprehensive schools of Kempele and, in co-operation with the schools and homes, to find ways to prevent bullying and to solve bully/victim problems. What, then, actually happened at the schools? Discussions with the heads of schools and individual teachers indicated that the baseline survey provided realistic information of bullying at each school and motivated a change in attitudes. The teachers became more solidly committed to anti-bullying action. They agreed that all bullying was unacceptable and required immediate intervention. The topic was discussed at different levels (school staff, children, and parents), and children, therefore, found it easier to tell their teachers and parents about bullying.

How effectively and how soon the changes came about at different schools could not be determined within this survey, except indirectly with the questionnaires presented to the pupils. External changes, which can be taken to reflect attitudinal changes took place gradually over the years. Here are a few examples. In 1990, a non-violence committee was set up in the municipality, and the chief education officer was appointed its chair. The committee continued its work for 2 years. School bullying (unacceptable, immediate intervention) began to be recorded in the annual curricula from 1994 onwards. At the largest Lower-stage school, the playgrounds were divided between the younger and older pupils in 1995, and the number of supervising teachers during breaks was simultaneously increased. At the same school, nearly all parents have signed a written co-operative agreement since 1997. The agreement identifies such situations as bullying, truancy, vandalism, etc., after which the parents involved will be contacted. By signing the agreement, parents undertake to consider such contact the teacher's right and obligation, not an accusation.

The school staff were extremely positive about the project and considered it important, which is why the implementation of the plan was unproblematic, but both the planning and the follow-up of the project could have been better organised.

Results of the evaluation

Peer evaluation of the occurrence of bullying at school

According to peer evaluation, bullying was most common during breaks. In 1990, 20–25% of the pupils surveyed said that they had witnessed bullying 'fairly often' or 'very often' at breaks (and almost everybody had witnessed bullying during breaks at least occasionally). Bullying during lessons has been witnessed by 10–14% of pupils surveyed and on the way to or from school by 3–7%. The questionnaire in 1992 established that the occurrence of bullying had decreased during breaks, during lessons, and on the way to or from school. The difference between the years 1990 and 1992 was statistically significant concerning bullying during breaks ($p < 0.001$), during lessons ($p < 0.01$), and on the way to or from school ($p < 0.05$), when all the studied grades were analysed together. Bullying remained at the 1992 level, or continued to decrease throughout the follow-up period (fig. 12.1). The follow-up survey revealed no significant differences between the answers of boys and girls, with one notable exception. In 1994, the girls in the fourth grade had witnessed bullying equally as often as the pupils questioned in the initial survey in 1990, and twice or three times as often as the boys. Peer evaluation did not reveal significant differences between the answers of pupils in different grades.

Self-reports of being a victim of bullying

According to the self-reports, being a victim of bullying was on the decrease during the follow-up period among both boys and girls in all

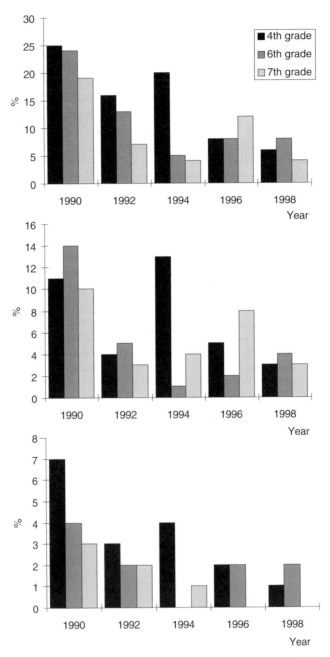

Fig. 12.1 Peer evaluation of the occurrence of bullying 'fairly often' or 'very often' during breaks (top), during lessons (middle), and on the way to and from school (bottom) (boys and girls combined).

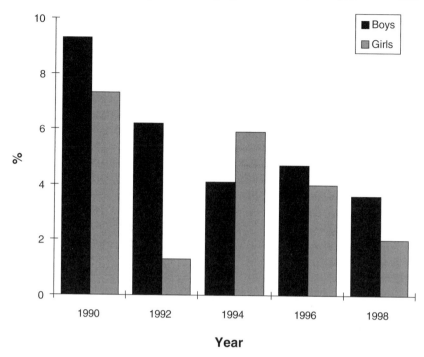

Fig. 12.2 Self-report of being a victim of bullying 'fairly often' or 'very often' during the last 3 months, among boys and girls (all studied grades combined).

grades surveyed, except among the fourth-grade children in the year 1994. In 1990, 9.3% of the boys and 7.3% of the girls who responded had been victims of bullying 'fairly often' or 'very often' during the previous 3 months. In 1992, the corresponding percentages were 6.2 (ns) and 1.3 (p < 0.01); and at the end of the survey in 1998, they were 3.6 and 2.0 (p < 0.01 in both) (fig. 12.2). No significant differences emerged between the answers of pupils in different grades (with the exception of the year 1994, see fig. 12.3), although there appeared to be a slight overall decrease in the number of victims in the upper grades. When the number of victims in all the studied grades combined in 1990 was compared to that in 1992 and with the numbers of victims in the following years, the differences were statistically significant (p < 0.025 – 0.001).

Analogously with the results of peer evaluation, the victim self-report data showed that being a victim was most often reported during breaks in the playground, where about 85% of the victimised boys and about

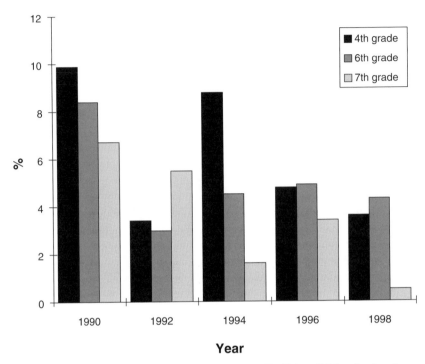

Fig. 12.3 Self-report of being a victim of bullying 'fairly often' or 'very often' during the last 3 months, by grade (boys and girls combined).

75% of the victimised girls had been bullied. Even though being a victim showed a decreasing trend during the follow-up period, the percentages of the most common locations remained the same. Being bullied on the way to or from school was not common, and became even less common among the older pupils. Only a few pupils (3–7% in the fourth, 1–5% in the sixth, and 0–4% in the seventh grade) spent their break time mainly alone without peer support, but such pupils fell victims of bullying about 10 times more often than those spending the break time in groups. Over half of the victims, girls slightly more often than boys, said they had been bullied psychologically (verbally or indirectly). Being bullied in only a physical way was quite uncommon, and appeared to decrease even further in the seventh grade. When asked about the bully, the victims mainly reported that they had been bullied by a classmate or an older pupil. About 20% reported that they had been bullied by a group of pupils, and about 30% by always the same pupil, while the rest said that they had been bullied by different people at different stages.

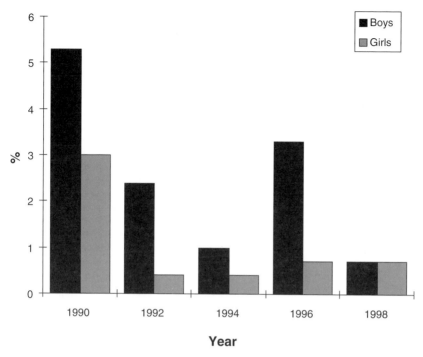

Fig. 12.4 Self-report of bullying others 'fairly often' or 'very often' during the last 3 months, among boys and girls (all studied grades combined).

Self-reports of bullying others

According to the self-reports, fewer pupils had been involved as bullies than ones who had been involved as victims. During the follow-up period, the number of pupils who admitted having bullied others decreased in all grades surveyed. At the beginning of the survey in 1990, 5.3% of the boys and 3.0% of the girls who responded said that they had bullied others 'fairly often' or 'very often' in the previous 3 months, and the corresponding percentages in 1992 were 2.4 (ns) and 0.4 ($p < 0.05$), while in 1998 they were 0.7 in both groups (among boys $p < 0.001$, girls $p < 0.05$) (fig. 12.4). There were no significant differences between the answers of pupils in different grades, even though there were fewer of those who admitted having bullied others among the fourth-graders than among the older pupils (fig. 12.5). When the total number of bullies in all the studied grades in the year 1990 was compared with that in 1992 and with those in the following years, the differences were statistically

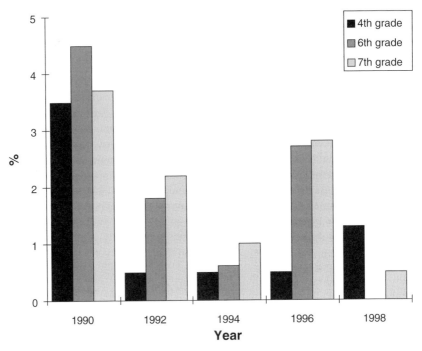

Fig. 12.5 Self-report of bullying others 'fairly often' or 'very often' during the last 3 months, by grade (boys and girls combined).

significant (p < 0.05 – 0.001). The bullies' self-report data concerning the locations and types of bullying were analogous to that of the victims.

Ways to reduce bullying suggested by pupils

When the pupils were asked to suggest ways to reduce bullying, one alternative was clearly more popular than the others. At the beginning of the follow-up in 1990, about 65% of the pupils said that bullying could be reduced by discussions and/or by seeking solutions together. In 1992 and later, this alternative was proposed by about 80% of the pupils, slightly more often by girls than by boys. In addition to that, very many pupils suggested that bullying could be prevented or reduced by working together even outside school. They hoped for more action days and camps, for example. Heavier penalties were proposed by slightly less than 10% of girls and slightly more than 15% of boys, and these percentages remained roughly unchanged throughout the follow-up. The following other alternatives were mentioned: forget about it, respond by bullying yourself, do nothing, or drop out of school. The last two alternatives were no longer mentioned after 1994.

Longer term effects or evaluation of the programme

The nationwide Non-Violent Campaign in 1990 prompted the Kempele local association of the Mannerheim League to carry out this follow-up survey. The results of the initial questionnaire survey in 1990 raised awareness of the bullying problem in the comprehensive schools of Kempele. The results of the follow-up survey showed that the school can reduce and prevent new bullying cases by adopting firm anti-bullying attitudes and by co-operating with the parents. To counteract bullying, the school personnel have tried to create a positive, warm, school climate. The attitudes of the teachers as well as those of the whole peer group play a key role in tackling the bullying problem (Galloway, 1994; Olweus, 1994; Salmivalli, 1999).

According to the pupils' evaluation, the number of both victims and bullies decreased from 1990 to 1992 and remained more or less at the 1992 level throughout the 8-year follow-up period. The figures were of the same magnitude as in some other intervention studies (Olweus, 1994; Tikkanen, 1997). Although the campaign itself was short, the effect seemed to be long-lasting. Since 1998, no more pupil evaluations have been made, but according to a discussion with the chief education officer in 2002, the topic of bullying is discussed even when recruiting new teachers. According to feedback from headteachers of schools, strict anti-bullying principles have been permanently adopted by schools.

This study did not use a control group to gather reference information, but the surveys carried out in other parts of Finland at approximately the same time have established that bullying has not decreased in a similar fashion elsewhere (Kannas et al., 1995; Salmivalli et al., 1996; Tikkanen, 1997). Systematic intervention in bullying situations has been a clear signal that bullying is not tolerated. The open and encouraging school climate has made it easier to discuss the bullying problem as well as other important issues. Earlier studies have shown that victims keep quiet about bullying and avoid telling their teachers or parents about it (Olweus, 1994). Either they do not dare to tell (for fear of what the bullies will do to them if they tell) or they do not want to tell anybody, feeling that it will not help anyway or feeling ashamed of the situation (Boulton and Underwood, 1992; Whitney and Smith, 1993). Peer evaluation showed that fellow pupils and classmates were well aware of bullying, but parental or teacher awareness was not studied in this survey.

One of the shortcomings of this survey is that no consistent verbal instuctions were given to the classes on how to interpret the terms used before the questionnaires were first administered. It is possible that the significance of indirect bullying especially, which is a method utilised more frequently by girls than by boys, was under-estimated (Olweus, 1994; Salmivalli, 1998). An indication of this might be the fact that, in the self-report section, very few girls admitted to having bullied others compared with other Finnish studies (Salmivalli et al., 1996; Kaltiala-Heino et al., 1998). The research team realised this after analysing the results of the initial questionnaire, but decided to use the same method and questionnaire throughout the follow-up period to facilitate comparison of the results over time. Thus, the results concerning the prevalence of bullying obtained in this survey should be evaluated by keeping this deficiency in mind. The results of the follow-up survey were promising, however.

Dissemination and impact beyond the programme schools

The study has been published earlier only in Finnish in the *Finnish Medical Journal* (*Suomen lääkärilehti*). A more comprehensive report was printed in the University of Oulu in 1999 and distributed through the Mannerheim League of Child Welfare organisation throughout Finland. The Finnish National Board of Education has also expressed their interest in the study. Moreover, the author has presented and discussed the findings in different media. No evaluation of the significance of the project outside the participating schools has been made. It can be assumed, however, that it has, at least in the surrounding communities, encouraged open discussion about bullying and made school staff more convinced about the possibility of reducing bullying.

References

Boulton M. and Underwood, K. (1992). Bully/victim problems among middle school children. *British Journal of Educational Psychology*, 62, 73–87.

Galloway, D. (1994). Bullying: The importance of a whole-school approach. *Therapeutic Care Education*, 3, 19–26.

Kaltiala-Heino, R., Rimpelä, M., Rantanen, P., and Rimpelä, A. (1998). Koulukiusaaminen, masentuneisuus ja itsetuhoajatukset. *Suomen Lääkärilehti*, 53, 2799–805.

Kannas, L., Välimaa, R., Liinamo, A., and Tynjälä, J. (1995). Oppilaiden kokemuksia kouluviihtyvyydestä ja kuormittuneisuudesta sekä koulukiusaamisesta Euroopassa ja Kanadassa. In L. Kannas (ed.), *Koululaisten kokema terveys, hyvinvointi ja kouluviihtyvyys.* Opetushallitus, Helsinki: Hakapaino Oy, pp. 131–49.

Olweus, D. (1973). *Hackkycklingar och översittare. Forsning om skolmobbing.* Stockholm: Almqvist & Wecksell.

—— (1978). *Aggression in the schools. Bullies and whipping boys.* Washington, DC: Hemisphere.

—— (1991). Bully/victim problems among schoolchildren: Basic facts and effects of a school based intervention program. In D. Pepler and Rubin, K. (eds.), *The development and treatment of childhood aggression.* Hillsdale, NJ: Erlbaum, pp. 411–48.

—— (1994). Annotation: Bullying at school: Basic facts and effects of a school based intervention program. *Journal of Child Psychology and Psychiatry,* 35, 1171–90.

Pikas, A. (1987). *Irti kouluväkivallasta.* Espoo: Weilin & Göös.

Salmivalli, C., Lagerspetz, K. M. J., Björkvist, K., Österman, K., and Kaukiainen, A. (1996). Bullying as a group process: participant roles and their relations to social status within the group. *Aggressive Behavior,* 22, 1–15.

Salmivalli, C. (1998). Not only bullies and victims. Participation in harassment in school classes: some social and personality factors. Annales Universittatis Turkuensis.

Salmivalli, C. (1999). Participant role approach to school bullying: implications for interventions. *Journal of Adolescence,* 22, 453–59.

Tikkanen, T. (1997). *Kiusaaminen ja normi-ilmasto: intervention vaikutus Helsingin peruskouluissa.* Psykologian laitos Jyväskylän yliopisto.

Whitney, I. and Smith, P. K. (1993). A survey of the nature and extent of bullying in junior/middle and secondary schools. *Educational Research,* 35, 3–26.

13 Targeting the group as a whole: the Finnish anti-bullying intervention

Christina Salmivalli, Ari Kaukiainen, Marinus Voeten, and Mirva Sinisammal

Impetus for the intervention study, early stages of planning, and funding

Why is there bullying in schools? How should we try to reduce it? Our answers to the former question have implications for our ideas about the latter. The Finnish intervention project was inspired by the increasing literature, as well as our own studies, stressing the group nature of bullying.

It has recently been pointed out, and also empirically shown, that peer bystanders play an important role in encouraging and maintaining bullying, and, therefore, they should also be targeted by intervention programmes (Cowie and Sharp, 1994; O'Connell, Pepler, and Craig, 1999; Olweus, 2001; Sutton and Smith, 1999; Stevens, Van Oost, and de Bourdeaudhuij, 2000). In our research group, the different *participant roles* the bystanders or students who are neither bullies nor victims take in the bullying process have been in the focus for several years (Salmivalli, 2001a; Salmivalli, Huttunen, and Lagerspetz, 1997; Salmivalli, Lagerspetz, Björkqvist, Österman, and Kaukiainen, 1996; Salmivalli, Lappalainen, and Lagerspetz, 1998; Salmivalli and Voeten, 2004). Our own studies, as well as the literature at large, point to the direction of trying to affect the bystanders' reactions to bullying, and also to study such changes in a systematic way.

Besides the increasing literature on the group involvement on bullying, our intervention project was inspired by the previous large-scale interventions, especially the most famous ones at the time when the planning of our project started, i.e. studies carried out in Bergen (Olweus, 1991) and in Sheffield (Whitney, Rivers, Smith, and Sharp, 1994; Eslea and Smith, 1999).

The most notable funding for the project came from the Academy of Finland, in the form of a post-doctoral research fellowship to the first author (1999–2002). The Academy of Finland provided additional funding for some expenses of the project as well, which enabled us to have assistants for data collection and coding. Smaller research grants were

251

received from the Finnish Cultural Foundation, the Jenny and Antti Wihuri Foundation, and the Foundation of the University of Turku. Further financial support was received from the city of Helsinki.

Beyond the bully–victim dyad: The participant roles

The participant roles in bullying refer to students' ways of being involved in bullying, such as being a peer bystander. Besides *victims*, who are systematically attacked by others, and *bullies*, who have an active, initiative-taking 'ringleader' role in the process, *assistants of bullies* can be identified as those who eagerly join in the bullying when someone else has started it. *Reinforcers of bullies*, on the other hand, offer positive feedback to the bully by laughing, by encouraging gestures, or just by gathering around as an audience. *Outsiders* withdraw from bullying situations, without taking sides with anyone. The behaviour of *defenders* is clearly anti-bullying: they may comfort the victim, or actively try to make others stop bullying.

Although anti-bullying attitudes are common (Menesini et al., 1997; Rigby and Slee, 1991), few students actually express such attitudes to their peers or try to intervene in bullying (Pepler, Craig, Ziegler, and Charach, 1994). At least in pre-adolescence, as many as 35–40% of school-aged children and adolescents take on the roles of bully, assistant, or reinforcer, and the frequency of those who withdraw and silently witness the bullying is around 25–30% (Salmivalli, 2001a). Many students thus behave in ways that incite rather than discourage the bully. It was shown in a recent study (Salmivalli and Voeten, 2004) that, while individual students' attitudes are moderately associated with their participant role behaviours, group norms predict additional variance in these behaviours at the classroom level.

The participant-role approach provides educators with a new perspective for preventing and intervening in bullying: we should try to effect changes in the dynamics of the whole group. In addition to trying to make the bully behave differently, we should be able to affect the behaviour of peer bystanders. For instance, with this approach, we should encourage: reinforcers and assistants to stop what they are doing; outsiders to show that they actually do not approve of bullying; and more students to take on the role of defender. Changing attitudes might be a good starting-point, but perhaps an even more critical issue in prevention and intervention work is how to help students cope with the social pressure from the peer group and thus *convert the anti-bullying attitudes into behaviour in actual bullying situations*. This was the central focus in planning our intervention project.

Selection of schools

The first 16 schools (8 from Helsinki and 8 from the Turku area) that volunteered to participate on the basis of an announcement sent to the education bureau of each town were included in the programme. The intervention was based on teacher education, and the only precondition for inclusion was that, from each project school, 3 classes (1 from grade 4, 1 from grade 5, and 1 from grade 6), along with their class teachers, participated in the programme. The idea was that the 'team of 3' would provide not only support for each other but would also be a resource for the whole school in its anti-bullying work. Since 3 classes from each school participated, we ended up with 48 school classes and their homeroom class teachers involved in the intervention programme.

Characteristics of schools and students

As stated, of the participating schools, 8 were from Helsinki, the capital of Finland, and 8 were from 4 small to mid-sized towns in the area of Turku, on the west coast of Finland. According to the pre-test, 16.2% of students reported being systematically victimised by their peers at school, which suggests that, although volunteers, the project schools were not exceptionally 'good' ones with no bully–victim problems to begin with. When the project started, the total number of students in the 48 classes was 1,220 (600 girls, 620 boys). They were from grades 4, 5, and 6, corresponding to 9–10, 10–11, and 11–12 years of age. The class sizes varied from 19 to 33, mean class size being 25 students. In all classes, there were both boys and girls, but the proportions of each gender varied across classes. The teachers involved were the homeroom teachers of the participating classes: 31 were female; 17 were male. Most of them had been working as teachers for several years (on average, for 14 years; only 4 had just started, in autumn 1999).

Components of the intervention programme

Intervention training for teachers

Teachers are the natural group to intervene in bullying. Our intervention programme was based on teacher training for a number of reasons. First, much of the bullying going on remains unidentified, not only because it is well hidden within the peer group but because many teachers, as well as other adults, may have a working definition of bullying that involves only direct aggression or physical violence, or they may not distinguish systematic bullying from occasional conflicts and teasing (Hazler, Miller, Carney, and Green, 2001). Second, adults often perceive bullying as a problem of an individual child, or of the bully–victim dyad, not as a phenomenon involving the whole group. Consequently, the focus of interventions is on individual children, the aggressors. Third, although intervention methods have been developed to tackle bullying, they have not come to the full attention of the educators. Finally, teachers need support from their colleagues in their efforts to tackle bullying.

The 48 teachers involved in the project attended a 1-year training course. There were two separate training groups, one in Helsinki and the other in Turku, with 24 teachers in each. The training consisted of 4 meetings during the school year 1999–2000, 2 (whole) days in the autumn term, and 2 (1 whole day, 1 half-day) in the spring term. The training was carried out by the first and second authors.

During the training, the teachers were provided with:

(1) feedback about the situation in their own classes, based on the pre-intervention data collected in October 1999;

(2) facts about bullying: research findings on the phenomenon and its mechanisms;

(3) information about alternative methods of intervening in bullying at individual, class, and school level, with emphasis on class-level interventions;

(4) freedom to discuss and share experiences about effective ways of intervening, and to plan further interventions; and

(5) consultation on individual cases they found difficult to deal with.

Rather than having a clearly defined standard intervention to be accomplished in each classroom, our aim was to provide general information, research findings, and ideas about bullying and its effective prevention, as well as intervention strategies that the teachers would adapt and further develop to meet their own needs.

The intervention strategies presented during the teacher training covered, however, the three systemic levels that have been considered important in previous literature (Olweus, 1991; Mooij, 1999a,b): school, class, and individual-student level. The main emphasis was, however, on the group mechanisms of bullying and, therefore, on intervening at the class level.

Class-level interventions

The participant role approach provided a common framework for teachers to utilise in curriculum-based, class-level work. Three general principles to be adapted in such work in classrooms were stressed:

awareness-raising; self-reflection; and commitment to anti-bullying behaviour.

It has been previously suggested (Salmivalli, 1999, 2001b) that *raising awareness* about bullying in general, and the group mechanisms involved in it in particular, is a starting-point for effective curriculum-based intervention work. This approach involves discussing bullying with the whole class, starting with themes such as what bullying is (for instance, how it differs from occasional teasing or conflicts between students) and how it feels to be bullied, and moving on to the group mechanisms involved.

Second, students should be encouraged to *reflect on their own behaviour* in bullying situations. Introducing the different participant roles to students provides conceptual tools for such self-reflection. Most students have attitudes against bullying, yet in actual bullying situations they may behave in ways that encourage and maintain bullying in the class. Therefore, making students aware of the discrepancy between their attitudes and behaviour is important.

Third, fostering *commitment to anti-bullying behaviour* means helping the students find, and commit themselves to, alternative ways of behaving as individuals and as a group in order to put an end to bullying. For instance, it is possible and often beneficial to rehearse positive roles in drama and role play wherein students perform differently from how they might ordinarily (see Cowie and Sharp, 1994). Role-play exercises provide a safe context in which to rehearse anti-bullying behaviours that the students have not tried before, such as telling others to stop bullying, and to explore the feelings associated with these strategies.

As has been pointed out, developing *class rules against bullying*, together with students themselves, is one way to enhance commitment to anti-bullying behaviours (Olweus, 1991). In accordance with our view of bullying as a group phenomenon, it was emphasised in the training that the class rules should not be just about bullying behaviours (such as Don't bully others), but cover bystander behaviours as well (such as When you see bullying, show that you don't accept it or Try to help the bullied children).

Some concrete examples of working out the participant role theme with the class (by discussions, through role play and drama exercises, utilising literature, and so on) were introduced, and the teachers themselves developed these ideas further during the training. In Finland, some materials have been prepared to aid curriculum-based work on the participant roles in bullying. These include a package with overhead transparencies and suggestions for discussions prepared by the first author, as well as role-taking exercises developed by a group of drama pedagogues, Theatre in Education. These were introduced to the teachers, and they were utilised as auxiliary materials in their class-level work by some of them.

Individual-level interventions

Curriculum-based, class-level intervention work is important, but probably not sufficient to reach all children. Acute cases of bullying that come to the attention of the teacher require work with individual students, such as having serious discussions with the bully or offering support to the victim. Such interventive discussions can be found in the literature, but they are not widely known among teachers in Finland.

During the teacher training, we introduced individual discussion methods with pupils involved in bullying; the Pikas method (Pikas, 1975), the No Blame Approach by Maines and Robinson (see Sharp and Smith, 1994), and the Farsta method (Ljungström, 1990), all of which stem from a very similar understanding of the nature of bullying and follow a rather similar format. Regardless of the method used, the role of *systematic follow-ups* after the intervention discussions was very much emphasised.

School-level interventions

The role of whole-school policies in tackling bullying has been highlighted especially by Smith and colleagues in their intervention project in Sheffield (see Whitney et al., 1994; Sharp and Thompson, 1994). In our training course, the role of a *whole-school policy against bullying* was stressed, and guidelines were given for developing such a policy (based on Sharp and Thompson, 1994). The teachers were encouraged to 'take the message' to their schools and foster the process of developing a whole-school anti-bullying policy. As it turned out, 6 schools already had such a written policy; some of these schools started developing it further during the intervention programme.

Evaluation framework and procedures

Multiple quantitative measures were used to evaluate the outcome of the intervention, based on a set of questionnaires the students filled in at each time point. The analyses from the project that have been conducted so far (Salmivalli, Kaukiainen, and Voeten, in press), which we review here, were based on two measurement points: the pre-test measurement in October 1999; and the post-test measurement 12 months later, in October 2000. We have data collected in April 2000 as well (after 6 months of intervention) and we intend to conduct further analysis utilising the complete data set in order to examine the process of change in more detail.

The primary design utilised in evaluating the programme success was a cohort-longitudinal design with adjacent cohorts (Olweus and Alsaker, 1991), which we describe in more detail later (and see table 13.3). The data were also explored longitudinally, examining the pre-test/post-test differences in our measures. We give only a brief overview of the question-naire measures here; a more detailed description of the measures, along with their psychometric properties, can be found elsewhere (Salmivalli, Kaukiainen, and Voeten, in press).

Outcome measures

In the questionnaire, the students were first presented with the follow-ing definition of bullying: '(It is bullying when) . . . one child is repeat-edly exposed to harassment and attacks from one or several other chil-dren. Harassment and attacks may be, for example, shoving or hitting the other one, calling him/her names or making jokes about him/her, leaving him/her outside the group, taking his/her things, or any other behaviour meant to hurt the other one.' It was further pointed out that 'It is not bullying when two students with equal strength or equal power have a fight, or when someone is occasionally teased, but it is bullying when the feelings of one and the same student are hurt repeatedly and on purpose.'

Victimisation and bullying

The students were asked to give a forced-choice, i.e. yes/no response to the following questions: 'Have you been bullied in a way described in the definition (repeatedly) during this term?' and 'Have you bullied others during this term?' Students' answers to these questions served as dichoto-mous variables of *being victimised* and *bullying others*. The students were also asked: 'Who in your class gets bullied? Write the names of the bullied students here.' Based on students' answers, scores for *peer-reported victim-isation*, ranging from 0.00 to 1.00, were calculated by dividing the number of nominations received by each child by the number of evaluators, i.e. peers in the classroom.

Observed and experienced bullying

Students evaluated, on a scale ranging from 0 = never to 3 = almost every day, the extent to which they had (1) observed and (2) experienced (being targets of) 9 different types of bullying in their class during the ongoing term: hitting; shoving; kicking; name-calling; ridiculing, embarrassing, or making fun of; leaving out of the group; slandering; spreading nasty rumours; and taking, hiding, or breaking other's possessions.

Anti-bullying attitudes

Students' bullying-related attitudes were measured by asking them to evaluate on a 5-point scale (from $0 =$ strongly disagree to $4 =$ strongly agree) the extent to which they agreed or disagreed with 10 statements about bullying, such as: 'One should try to help the bullied victims', 'Bullying may be fun sometimes' (reverse coded) and 'Joining in bullying is a wrong thing to do'. A high score on the attitude scale (formed by averaging the students' scores on the items) indicated anti-bullying attitudes.

Efficacy beliefs

Students' efficacy beliefs (beliefs about their ability to do something about bullying) were measured as their mean score of 2 items: 'I can affect whether or not there is bullying in my class' and 'It is not my business to do anything about bullying' (reverse coded). Again, students evaluated their agreement with the items on a 5-point scale ($0 =$ strongly disagree, $4 =$ strongly agree) and the efficacy scale was the mean score of the items, high scores indicating higher efficacy beliefs.

Behaviour in bullying situations: The participant-role questionnaire

In the Participant Role Questionnaire (PRQ), the students were asked to think of situations in which someone in their class was bullied. They were presented with 15 items describing different ways to behave in such situations, and they indicated, on a 3-point scale (blank space = never, $1 =$ sometimes, $2 =$ often) how often each of their classmates, including themselves, behaved in ways described. The names of all students in the class were printed in the questionnaire beforehand. The items form 5 sub-scales reflecting different participant role behaviours associated with bullying. There are 3 items on each scale, such as 'Starts bullying' (bully scale), 'Joins in the bullying, when someone else has started it' (assistant scale), 'Comes round to see the situation', 'Laughs' (reinforcer scale), 'Tries to make the others stop bullying' (defender scale), and 'Stays outside the situation' (outsider scale).

In a class of 30 students, the PRQ procedure yields 29 peer-evaluations of each student, reflecting his or her behaviour with various peers in numerous situations, along with the self-reports of the corresponding behaviours. Each student's peer-reported item scores are divided by the number of evaluators (the number of classmates present), and averaged to yield continuous scores ranging from 0.00 to 2.00 for each student on each scale. Self-reported scores on each scale are the mean scores of the three self-report item scores, also ranging from 0.00 to 2.00.

What actually happened; achievements and difficulties in implementing the intervention

Four times during the school year, reports were collected from the teachers about the concrete actions they had taken in order to reduce bullying in their classes. What the teachers had actually done varied considerably from class to class and school to school. In some schools, it was obvious that the intervention strategies presented had not been fully accomplished, but the teachers had done something else, or they had done nothing at all. Other teachers described very general curriculum-based exercises to improve the class atmosphere, without really addressing bullying. In other schools, the teachers seemed to have fully utilised their 'anti-bullying team' of 3 and planned and carried out the interventions in co-operation.

The teacher reports were scored by two independent raters according to pre-established criteria. Based on all 4 reports from each teacher, a score was given for curriculum-based, class-level work (min. = 0, max. = 3) and for handling acute cases of bullying (min. = 0, max. = 3). In case of class-level work, the scores were based on whether there had been general discussions about bullying with the whole class, whether group mechanisms and participant roles involved in bullying had been addressed in such discussions, and whether these issues had really been worked out in the class by means of role play, or by developing class rules in which bystander behaviours were also addressed. The scores were given not only on the basis of *what* had been done, but also for *how* it seemed to be done, for instance, whether or not there was continuity in the actions taken. With respect to acute cases, the scores were based on whether the teachers had intervened in such cases, whether they had discussed with different parties, whether or not follow-up discussions had been organised, and whether there was co-operation with parents, school psychologists, etc.

As a result, each class had a total score from 0 to 6 reflecting the degree of implementation of the programme by the class teacher. These scores were aggregated to the school level, and an additional school-level implementation score (min. = 0, max. = 3), reflecting the degree of

Table 13.1. *Distribution of implementation scores across schools; numbers of schools with each score out of a total of 16 (8 in Helsinki, 8 in Turku)*

Implementation score	Helsinki	Turku	All
4	0	2	2
5	2	1	3
7	2	1	3
8	0	1	1
9	1	1	2
10	1	0	1
11	1	0	1
12	1	0	1
14	0	1	1
21	0	1	1

Table 13.2. *Numbers of classes (out of a total of 48), across different grade levels (16 classes in each), in which various core components of the programme were implemented*

	Grade 4	Grade 5	Grade 6	All
Class level:				
Class meetings with discussions	13	14	15	42
with participant roles addressed	9	10	8	27
Drama/role play	5	5	6	16
Class rules	3	3	2	8
Individual level:				
Individual discussions (e.g. Pikas method)	10	11	9	30
with follow-ups	3	3	1	7
Co-operation with parents	9	6	7	22

implementation of the programme at the school level, was given for each school. The schools received scores for starting the whole-school policy development, for further developing their policy if they already had one, for communicating their policy within the school and/or to the parents, and also for some other school-level action taken, such as discussing bullying problems in a whole-school meeting with all teachers and students present. The possible maximum score for a school (actually received by 1 school!), was thus $(3 \times 6) + 3 = 21$. The distribution of the total implementation scores is summarised in table 13.1.

To give a more concrete idea of what was actually behind the implementation scores, table 13.2 displays the frequencies of classes in which several core components of the programme were implemented.

Table 13.3. *Design of the intervention project; see text for details*

Cohort	October 1999	Intervention	October 2000
1	grade 4		grade 5
2	grade 5		grade 6
3	grade 6		not available

Results of the revaluation

Design

In order to analyse the effects of the intervention programme we applied a cohort-longitudinal design with adjacent cohorts (Olweus and Alsaker, 1991). This matches groups of students of equivalent age, who have, or have not, experienced the intervention. The basic structure of the design is displayed in table 13.3.

Two data sets were prepared for the analyses: the post-test data from cohort 1 (grade 5, October 2000) and the pre-test data from cohort 2 (grade 5, October 1999) were included in the first set. Similarly, the other file consisted of the post-test data of cohort 2 and the pre-test data of cohort 3. The first data file was used to evaluate the intervention in grade 4, after these students (from cohort 1) had been exposed to the intervention for 12 months. The pre-test scores from cohort 2 (grade 5) were used as a baseline. Similarly, the second data file was used to evaluate the intervention in grade 5, and now the pre-test scores from cohort 3 (grade 6) were used as a baseline. In this way, post-test data from students in 2 cohorts (1 and 2) were always compared with baseline data from same-aged students from the same schools, who had not yet been exposed to intervention. The students from cohort 2 were used twice in these comparisons, once as a baseline group and once as an intervention group; therefore, separate analyses were performed.

The implementation data were utilised in the analyses as well. The classes in both data files were categorised into 3 groups: first, the baseline group, always including the pre-test data (fifth-graders of cohort 2 in the first data file, sixth-graders of cohort 3 in the second). The second group consisted of intervention schools with a low degree of implementation (with total implementation scores of 0–9). In the third group, there were intervention schools with a high degree of implementation (implementation scores 10–21) – 11 schools were in the low-implementation group; only 5 in the high-implementation group.

Data analyses

For the estimation of intervention effects on the outcome variables, multi-level modelling was applied. This method is especially appropriate when analysing school-based data, which is hierarchical in nature (students are nested within classes, which are nested within schools). In studies of school bullying, however, the data are often treated as if they consist of independent observations, i.e. students. Multi-level modelling takes into account not only the variability between students but also the variability between classes – and this is important, if we take the 'group nature' of bullying seriously. Furthermore, in multi-level modelling we can introduce predictor variables that characterise the school or classroom context, such as the implementation variables in intervention studies. (For an introduction to multi-level modelling, see Lee, 2000; Snijders and Bosker, 1999.)

In specifying the models, predictor variables were introduced at 2 levels: the individual level; and the classroom level. The school was not introduced as a level in our analyses because there were only 16 schools, and only 2 classes from each school (1 baseline, 1 intervention class) in each data set. At the individual level, gender was included in the models because it is a strong predictor of bullying behaviour. In our models, gender was the only predictor variable that could explain individual variation. Next to average effects of gender on the outcome variables, we explored whether the gender difference within a classroom differs over classrooms. Such differences were found in Salmivalli and Voeten (2004) for the peer reports on participant role behaviours. In addition, the possibility of heterogeneous variances at the individual level, associated with gender, was taken into account. Furthermore, we wanted to assess whether the intervention had different effects for boys and girls. As control variables at the classroom level, we introduced city (Helsinki/Turku), proportion of boys in the classroom, and school's previous commitment to anti-bullying work: these variables could explain variation only at the class level.

The intervention effects were represented in the regression equations by 2 dummy variables: the first indicating whether or not the class belonged to the 'low-implementation' group; the other one indicating whether the class belonged to the 'high-implementation' group. The dummy variables were introduced at the classroom level, so they could explain variation only at the classroom level. Also, 2 dummy variables were used to test for gender by intervention interaction. In some cases the outcome variable was dichotomous; then multi-level logistic regression was used. The results will be summarised in the following section. A more detailed description of the multi-level modelling itself (models were constructed for the 2 age groups, and for each outcome variable separately) with regression coefficients and standard errors for each predictor variable can be found elsewhere (Salmivalli, Kaukiainen, and Voeten, in press).

Intervention effects

Intervention effects were explored while controlling for gender effects (at the individual level) and for city, proportion of boys in classroom, and previous commitment to anti-bullying work in the school (at the classroom level). Class-level control variables were removed from the analysis, when they showed no statistically significant relationship with an outcome variable. Statistically significant intervention effects were found for several outcome variables.

Anti-bullying attitudes were higher in the intervention as compared with the baseline classes. This finding was consistent across both age groups. The mean scores of the baseline-, low-implementation, and-high implementation groups are displayed in fig. 13.1 separately for the 2 grade levels. In grade 4, the intervention effect was statistically significant for the low level of implementation. The effect was larger, however, for classes from schools in which the intervention was better implemented, i.e. the high-implementation group. In grade 5 classes, there was a significant intervention effect only for classes from schools with high levels of implementation.

For *efficacy beliefs*, i.e. students' beliefs concerning their ability to do something about bullying, a similar pattern of findings emerged (fig. 13.1). In both age groups, efficacy beliefs were higher in the intervention as compared with the baseline classes, but significantly different only in the high-implementation group.

There were several outcome variables indicating the extent of bully–victim problems in classes. These were the dichotomous variables *self-reported bullying* and *self-reported victimisation*, as well as *peer-reported victimisation*, the latter being based on peer nominations. Significant intervention effects were found, but only for the 2 self-report variables, and only for grade 4. Again, the effects were larger for the high-implementation group, although they were significant for the low-implementation group for self-reports of bullying others. In grade 5 classes, similar trends could be detected but the effects were not statistically significant (fig. 13.2). For peer-reported victimisation, no intervention effects were found in either age group. The proportion of students being nominated as victims by their peers was equal in the baseline, 'low-implementation', 'as well as' 'high-implementation' groups.

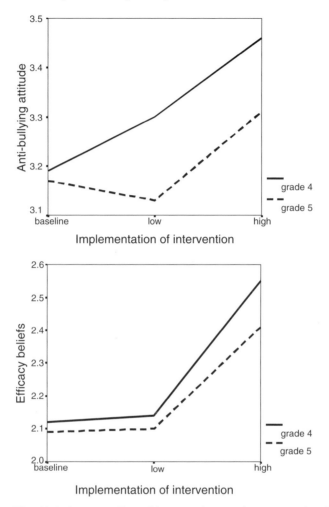

Fig. 13.1 Average effect of intervention on the means of anti-bullying attitude and of beliefs about one's efficacy to do something about the bullying.

For *observed bullying* and *experienced bullying* the pattern of findings was similar as for the above variables. However, the intervention effects reached the level of significance only for the high-implementation classes in grade 4.

When it comes to participant-role behaviours, which were of particular interest to us, only a few significant intervention effects were found. These effects emerged more often in the self-reports than in the peer-reports. In

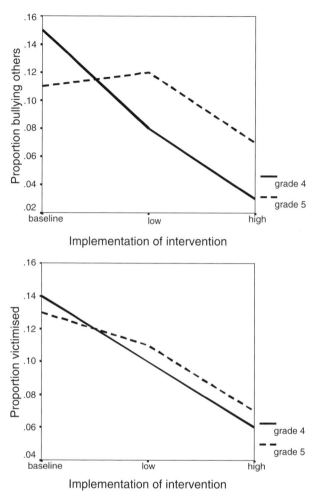

Fig. 13.2 Average effect of intervention on proportion of children bullying others and proportion of children being victimised.

grade 4, self-reported *reinforcing the bully* and *assisting the bully* were lower in the intervention, as compared with the baseline classes. For reinforcing, this effect was significant only in the high-implementation group. In grade 5, on the other hand, we found a significant positive intervention effect for self-reported *defending the victims* – again, the difference was significant only in the high-implementation classes.

In summary, most of the intervention effects were in the positive direction. There were, however, a few effects that were less welcome. In the low-implementation group in grade 5, peer-reported *bullying* was significantly higher than it was in the baseline – this was not true for the high-implementation group, however. For *withdrawing* from bullying situations (*outsider* on the PRQ), there were inconsistent effects across the different implementation groups and grade levels. In grade 5, peer-reported withdrawing from bullying situations was significantly lower in the low-implementation group, as compared with the baseline. The opposite was the case in grade 4, where there was more peer-reported withdrawing in both 'low'- and 'high'- intervention groups, than there was in the baseline classes.

Discussion

Taken together, the findings suggest that there were positive intervention effects for attitudes and efficacy beliefs, for the extent of bullying others and being victimised (at least in grade 4), and for some bystander behaviours (in grade 4, less assisting and reinforcing bully; in grade 5, more defending of the bullied victims after the intervention). Were these effects really caused by the intervention programme, or can they be accounted for by some other factors?

In our design, the baseline, or control, data must be considered only quasi-comparable with the post-intervention data. The fact that the baseline and intervention classes came from the same schools makes them more comparable. However, selection effects (having, just by chance, a cohort with exceptionally low or high degrees of bully–victim problems) or genuine cohort effects (historical effects) might still be responsible for finding 'intervention effects' in this kind of design (see also Olweus and Alsaker, 1991).

We have some evidence, however, supporting the plausibility of intervention effects rather than such alternative explanations. First, the effects were associated with the degree of implementation. In most cases, the intervention effects were larger for the 'high-implementation' group, and often they reached significance only in this group, i.e. when the intervention was well implemented. The link between improvement and the degree of implementation contributes evidence to the plausibility of intervention effects rather than alternative explanations such as cohort (historical) effects or sampling effects.

Second, one of the cohorts (cohort 2) served as a baseline group in one data set and as an intervention group in another. As pointed out by Olweus and Alsaker (1991), a sampling bias would operate in opposite directions in the two data sets. We found similar trends in both data sets for several outcome variables, and for some variables (anti-bullying

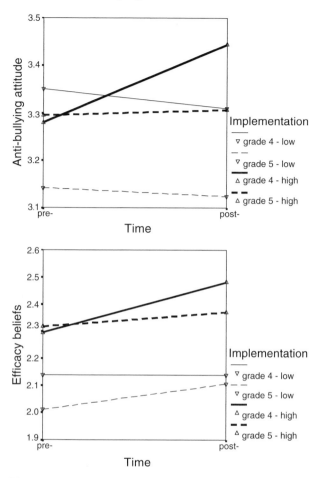

Fig. 13.3 Mean changes from pre-test to post-test in attitude and efficacy beliefs as a function of level of implementation of the interventions in grades 4 and 5.

attitudes, efficacy beliefs) the findings were completely parallel in both age groups. This means that cohort effects can hardly be responsible for our findings (although we cannot rule out the possibility that they have an effect in *some* cases).

Third, our preliminary explorations of the pre-test/post-test differences within the low- and high-implementation groups seem to support the findings from the cohort-longitudinal approach. Figures 13.3 and 13.4 display the pre-test and post-test mean scores for the bullying-related

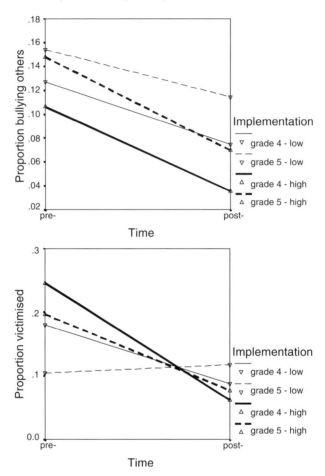

Fig. 13.4 Mean changes from pre-test to post-test in proportion bullying and proportion victimised as a function of level of implementation of the interventions in grades 4 and 5.

beliefs (anti-bullying attitudes and efficacy beliefs), and the self-reported degrees of bullying others and victimisation in the low- and high-implementation classes from different grade levels. As can be seen from fig. 13.3, there was a pre-test to post-test change in a positive direction, especially for the high-implementation classes, and especially in grade 4. Fig. 13.4 shows that bullying and victimisation went down more strongly for the high-implementation classes.

Another observation that can be gleaned from figs. 13.3 and 13.4 is that, for some outcome variables, the values of the high-implementation group were already more positive at the time of the pre-test. This may mean that the teachers in the high-implementation group had been doing more prevention/intervention work before participating in our programme and, therefore, were more inclined to implement the programme as well. Our findings regarding the intervention effects cannot be explained away by pre-test differences between the high- and low-implementation groups, however. First, as shown in figs. 13.3 and 13.4, the change was generally more marked in classes with high implementation of the programme. Second, there were also many outcome measures in which the pre-test situation was *worse* for the high-implementation group; however, it improved after the intervention. In the frequencies of students who reported being bullied by others, for instance, there was an overall reduction from 14.9% to 10.5% in the low-implementation group (percentage change of -29.5% overall, being -50% in grade 4 and $+5.5\%$ in grade 5 classes), while the corresponding frequencies were 21.7% and 6.7% in the high-implementation group (percentage change of -69% overall, -75% in grade 4 and -62% in grade 5 classes).

In grade 5, only a few intervention effects reached significance when multi-level models were utilised to assess such effects. Observations of pre-test–post-test differences also suggest that the impact of the intervention was more substantial in grade 4. It has been found by previous studies that bullying interventions tend to be more influential among younger students (Whitney et al., 1994; Stevens et al., 2000) at least when primary and secondary schools are being compared. In our case, however, all classes were from primary schools and there was only a one-year age difference between the younger and the older students. It is possible, however, that even such a small age difference affects the effectiveness of a bullying intervention. Anti-bullying attitudes and group norms are known to be more common among younger students (Menesini et al., 1997; Salmivalli and Voeten, 2004). It is possible that when the 'message' delivered is initially acceptable to students, it has more effect on their behaviour, or the effects take less time and can be detected after 12 months of intervention. Furthermore, younger students are more likely to respect the authority of adults, such as class teachers. Our fifth-graders, who were 10–11 years old when the project started and 11–12 years at time of the post-test measurement, were reaching adolescence and may have been less willing to conform to the rules of their teachers than the students in the younger age group.

The effects of anti-bullying interventions probably vary markedly not only in different age groups and from one class to another but also from one student to another. As part of our analyses, we tested for gender by intervention interaction effects, which were hardly ever found. Further analyses are needed to determine, *who* is really affected by interventions and in which ways. It is possible that students' attitudes, as well as their typical participant role behaviours *before* the intervention, help to predict the changes that will take place during the intervention. To be able to interpret some changes, it is important to know for which students these changes take place. For instance, the *meaning* of intervention effects for withdrawing from bullying situations (i.e. taking on the role of outsider) can only be understood by knowing which students are changing in this respect. If there is an increase in withdrawing among former assistants or reinforcers of bullies, it could be interpreted as a positive trend. If, on the other hand, it reflects a general increase in passivity with respect to bullying going on in the classes, it is certainly a negative finding.

The overall degree of implementation of the intervention by the schools was lower than we expected. If we look at our project from this point of view (i.e. implementation being part of the programme success), the results were rather disappointing. Only 5 of the 16 schools belonged to the 'high-implementation' group, and many schools had very low implementation scores (table 13.1). Introducing a more clearly structured intervention programme might have facilitated its implementation. Even though there was a clear theoretical background or 'framework' in our programme, adapting it to classroom work was very much the responsibility of the teachers. Some teachers did a lot of work tailoring the intervention components to their needs, planning and carrying out curriculum-based work and role-play exercises together with their 'team of three' participating in the programme – others were more passive (table 13.2). Perhaps more support could have been given to teachers in the form of visits to schools, or consultations between the meetings.

In addition, getting teachers really involved in an intervention programme probably demands better back-up from part of the school management. It is not clear to us how much support and resources the teachers received from their colleagues in general and the school principals especially. Even though the schools in our project volunteered to participate, this may not have guaranteed commitment to implementing the programme adequately. Educating teachers for anti-bullying work is not sufficient as such, if they lack either motivation to implement the programme, or resources to do so. Furthermore, it might be a drawback to our programme that there were only 3 classes from each school, instead of including whole schools; a whole-school approach might have had a more positive impact on both programme implementation and its effects.

Longer term effects or evaluation of the programme

Since the evaluation in fall 2000, no longer term evaluation of the effects has been either carried out or planned.

Dissemination and impact beyond the programme schools

It remains to be seen how much impact the intervention programme described in this chapter will have in Finnish schools at large. Both during and after the project, the first and second author have been lecturing quite extensively about intervening in bullying in various further education courses for teachers and school psychologists. A Finnish book, written by the first author, describing the intervention programme and its effects was recently published (Salmivalli, 2003).

In general, there is quite a lot of concern about bullying problems in Finland, and several national initiatives for promoting safety in schools have taken place during the past few years. It is stated in article 29 of the Finnish Basic Education Act, which came into force in 1999, that every student has the right to a safe school environment. Education providers have the responsibility of making sure that students do not experience acts of violence or bullying while at school. The legislation concerns all educational levels.

The laws amending the Finnish Comprehensive School Act (453/2001) and the Senior School Education Act (454/2001) introduced *health education* as an independent subject in comprehensive schools and senior secondary schools. One goal of health education is to 'foster physical, mental and social health and well-being and the students' acquisition of good manners. The students shall be educated for responsibility and co-operation and activities that pursue tolerance and trust among ethnic groups, peoples, and cultures. The education shall also promote growing up as responsible members of society and provide capabilities to function in a democratic and equal society as well as uphold sustainable growth . . .' (from section 2 of the latest decision on comprehensive schools education, issued in December 2001). There has been discussion about the potential of the new obligatory health education courses in preventing and dealing with bullying problems, too. This is a possibility that will, it is hoped, be taken by many Finnish teachers: class-level anti-bullying work now has its place in the curriculum!

References

Cowie, H. and Sharp, S. (1994). Tackling bullying through the curriculum. In P. K. Smith and S. Sharp (eds.) *School bullying: Insights and perspectives.* London: Routledge, pp. 84–107.

Eslea, M. and Smith, P. K. (1999). The long-term effectiveness of anti-bullying work in primary schools. *Educational Research*, 40, 203–18.

Hazler, R., Miller, D., Carney, J., and Green, S. (2001). Adult recognition of school bullying situations. *Educational Research*, 43, 133–46.

Lee, V. L. (2000). Using hierarchical linear modeling to study social contexts: The case of school effects. *Educational Psychologist*, 35, 125–41.

Ljungström, K. (1990). *Mobbning i skolan. Ett kompendium om mobbning samt on mobbningbehandling enligt Farstametoden.* Stockholm: Ordkällan/Pedaktiv.

Menesini, E., Eslea, M., Smith, P. K., Genta, M. L., Giannetti, E., Fonzi, A., and Costabile, A. (1997). Cross-national comparison of children's attitudes towards bully/victim problems in school. *Aggressive Behavior*, 23, 245–57.

Mooij, T. (1999a). Promoting prosocial pupil behaviour: 1-A multilevel theoretical model. *British Journal of Educational Psychology*, 69, 469–78.

(1999b). Promoting prosocial pupil behaviour: 2-Secondary school intervention and pupil effects. *British Journal of Educational Psychology*, 69, 479–504.

O'Connell, P., Pepler, D., and Craig, W. (1999). Peer involvement in bullying: Insights and challenges for intervention. *Journal of Adolescence*, 22, 437–52.

Olweus, D. (1991). Bully/victim problems among schoolchildren: Basic facts and effects of a school-based intervention program. In D. Pepler and K. Rubin (eds.), *The development and treatment of childhood aggression*. Hillsdale, NJ: Erlbaum, pp. 411–48.

(2001). Peer harassment: A critical analysis and some important issues. In J. Juvonen and S. Graham (eds.), *Peer harassment in school: The plight of the vulnerable and victimized*. New York: Guilford Press, pp. 3–20.

Olweus, D. and Alsaker, F. (1991). Assessing change in a cohort-longitudinal study with hierarchical data. In D. Magnusson, L. Bergman, G. Rudinger, and B. Törestad (eds.), *Problems and methods in longitudinal research: Stability and change*. Cambridge: Cambridge University Press, pp. 107–32.

Pepler, D., Craig, W., Ziegler, S., and Charach, A. (1994). An evaluation of an anti-bullying intervention in Toronto schools. *Canadian Journal of Community Mental Health* (Special Issue: *Prevention: Focus on children and youth*), 13, 95–110.

Pikas, A. (1975). Så stoppar vi mobbning. Stockholm: Prisma.

Rigby, K. and Slee, P. (1991). Bullying among Australian school children: Reported behaviour and attitudes towards victims. *Journal of Social Psychology*, 131, 615–27.

Salmivalli, C. (1999). Participant role approach to school bullying: implications for interventions. *Journal of Adolescence*, 22, 453–59.

(2001a). Group view on victimization – empirical findings and their implications. In J. Juvonen and S. Graham (eds.), *Peer harassment in school: The plight of the vulnerable and victimized*. New York: Guilford Press, pp. 398–419.

(2001b). Peer-led intervention campaign against school bullying: Who considered it useful, who benefited? *Educational Research*, 43, 263–278.

(2003). *Koulukiusaamiseen puuttuminen: Kohti tehokkaita toimintamalleja* [*School bullying: Towards effective interventions*]. Jyväskylä: PS-Kustannus.

Salmivalli, C., Huttunen, A., and Lagerspetz, K. M. J. (1997). Peer networks and bullying in schools. *Scandinavian Journal of Psychology*, 38, 305–12.

Salmivalli, C., Kaukiainen, A., and Voeten, M. (in press). Anti-bullying intervention: Implementation and outcome. *British Journal of Educational Psychology*.

Salmivalli, C., Lagerspetz, K., Björkqvist, K., Österman, K., and Kaukiainen, A. (1996). Bullying as a group process: Participant roles and their relations to social status within the group. *Aggressive Behavior*, 22, 1–15.

Salmivalli, C., Lappalainen, M., and Lagerspetz, K. (1998). Stability and change of behavior in connection with bullying in schools: A two-year follow-up. *Aggressive Behavior*, 24, 205–18.

Salmivalli, C. and Voeten, M. (2004). Connections between attitudes, group norms, and behavior in bullying situations. *International Journal of Behaviored Development*, 28, 246–258.

Sharp, S. and Smith, P. K. (1994). *Tackling bullying in your school: A practical handbook for teachers*. London: Routledge.

Sharp, S. and Thompson, D. (1994). The role of whole-school policies in tackling bullying behaviour in schools. In P. K. Smith and S. Sharp (eds.), *School bullying: Insights and perspectives*. London: Routledge, pp. 57–83.

Snijders, T. A. B. and Bosker, R. J. (1999). *Multilevel analysis: An introduction to basic and advanced multilevel modelling*. London: Sage.

Stevens, V., Van Oost, P., and de Bourdeaudhuij, I. (2000). The effects of an anti-bullying intervention programme on peers' attitudes and behaviour. *Journal of Adolescence*, 23, 21–34.

Sutton, J. and Smith, P. K. (1999). Bullying as a group process: An adaptation of the participant role approach. *Aggressive Behavior*, 25, 97–111.

Whitney, I., Rivers, I., Smith, P. K., and Sharp, S. (1994). The Sheffield project: Methodology and findings. In P. K. Smith and S. Sharp (eds.), *School Bullying: Insights and perspectives*. London: Routledge, pp. 20–56.

14 Ireland: The Donegal Primary Schools' anti-bullying project

Astrid Mona O'Moore and Stephen James Minton

Impetus for the intervention, early stages of planning, and funding

A nationwide study of bullying behaviour in Irish schools was undertaken in 1993–94. Covering 20,442 pupils (9,599 pupils aged 8–12 years, drawn from 320 primary schools, and 10,843 pupils aged 11–18 years, drawn from 211 second-level schools), the sample comprised 10% of the primary schools in each of the 26 counties, and 27% of all post-primary schools in the Republic of Ireland. It revealed that the problem of bullying was widespread throughout primary and post-primary schools in Ireland. Indeed, 31.3% of primary-school pupils and 15.6% of post-primary pupils reported having been victimised within the last term; 26.5% of primary-school pupils and 14.9% of post-primary pupils reported that they had bullied others within the last term (O'Moore, 2000; O'Moore, Kirkham, and Smith, 1997).

In light of these and similar findings in earlier, smaller scale Irish studies (Byrne, 1987; O'Moore and Hillery, 1989), the publication of the *Guidelines on preventing and countering bullying in primary and post-primary schools* (*Department of Education*, 1993), and research undertaken elsewhere in Europe, in particular Scandinavia (Olweus, 1978, 1993; Roland, 1989, 1993; Roland and Munthe, 1997) and the United Kingdom (Smith and Sharp, 1994), it was felt that Irish schools could benefit from a nationwide anti-bullying programme that incorporates the training of school management, teaching staff, parents, and pupils (O'Moore and Minton, 2001; O'Moore, Kirkham, and Smith, 1997). As co-ordinator of Trinity College Dublin's Anti-Bullying Research and Resource Centre (established January 1996), Dr O'Moore submitted proposals to the Department of Education and Science, and the Calouste Gulbenkian Foundation, stating an initial intention to conduct pilot work with a sample of the primary schools within the county of Donegal.

In studies that have preceded this in Europe, when a 'whole-school' approach has been applied to the issue of countering and preventing bullying in schools – in Norway (Olweus, 1993, and chapter 2; Roland, 2000; Roland and Munthe, 1997), England (Smith and Sharp, 1994, and chapter 6), and Andalucia (Ortega and Lera, 2000, and chapter 9) – varying levels of success have been observed. The proposed nationwide programme to prevent and counter bullying behaviour in Irish schools is based around such an approach – one that, quite naturally, was reflected in the work undertaken in Donegal primary schools.

Selection of schools

All 100 primary schools in Area 1 of the county of Donegal (for the purposes of administration, Donegal is split into two areas) were invited to participate in the study; in total, 42 schools were actually involved. Donegal is a predominantly rural county; just 4 of the schools served small towns (1,000–5,000 inhabitants), the rest being situated in villages (<1,000 inhabitants) or open country.

Characteristics of schools and students

The number of pupils in the 42 schools ranged from 21 to 410, the average being 108 per school. Most of the schools can be considered to be small: just 3 exceeded 200 pupils; 20 schools had less than 100 pupils enrolled, with 10 of these schools having less than 50 pupils. The average class size ranged between 4 and 30; the mean was 18.2 pupils per class; 8 of the schools had been designated as serving areas of disadvantage by the Department of Education.

At the time of analysis (see below), it was possible to match pre-test and post-test data from only 22 schools. It is those data that are reported in this chapter. The number of pupils in these 22 schools ranged from 21 to 280; the mean was 92. Most of these schools could be considered to be small, as just one exceeded 200 pupils; 15 schools had less than 100 pupils enrolled, with 9 of these schools having less than 50 pupils. In most of the schools, school grades 1–6 (ages 6–11 years) were represented by a single class, with 3 of the smallest schools combining grades within a single teaching class. The average teaching class size ranged between three and 28; the mean was 13.9 pupils per class. Just one of the schools served a small town (1,000–5,000 inhabitants), the rest being situated in villages (<1, 000 inhabitants) or open country. The socio-economic backgrounds of the pupils varied widely between, and indeed within, the schools.

Components of the intervention programme

The proposed Irish national schools programme is based on the second nationwide programme to prevent and manage bullying in Norwegian schools (Roland, 2000; Roland and Munthe, 1997; Roland and Vaaland, 1996; Roland, Bjørnsen, and Mandt, 2001). Four key elements appear in this 1996 Norwegian programme that are to be included in the Irish national programme; thus, these were applied in this study. These components are as follows:

Training of a network of professionals

Eleven teachers were trained, through a programme of workshops and seminars, to provide training and support for boards of management, staff, pupils, and parents in the prevention and countering of bullying in their school communities.

Teachers' resource pack

A pack containing information about bullying behaviour (drawing on the Department of Education Guidelines and the nationwide survey (O' Moore, Kirkham, and Smith, 1997) was given to each member of the trained network, for use in the provision of training and support for the network member's allocated schools. The material in the pack contained information provided to the network member during her or his own training, and had an overall emphasis on classroom management, the development of a positive atmosphere in class and school, staff leadership, and parent–teacher co-operation.

Parents' resource pack

An information leaflet, entitled 'Bullying: What parents need to know', was produced by the first author especially for this project. This leaflet was distributed to the parents of every pupil in the schools involved in this project; it provided information on the prevalence, types, causes, effects, and indicators of bullying behaviour, as well as how to deal with alleged or actual incidents of bullying.

Work with pupils

Schools were assisted, through the intervention of the trained teachers that formed the professional network, in creating a climate that does not accept bullying. As part of a general awareness-raising campaign, pupils had access to age-related handbooks, which included ideas for the prevention and countering of bullying in their class and school. Pupils were encouraged, through peer leadership, to support children whom they witnessed being bullied.

Evaluation framework and procedures

An evaluation of the effectiveness of the programme was made via the pupils' completion of pre-test/post-test modified Olweus Bully/Victim Questionnaires (Olweus, 1989; Whitney and Smith, 1993). The class teachers administered these questionnaires in normal school time; steps were taken by the schools' principals to ensure, as far as possible, that different classes within the school filled in the questionnaires simultaneously. Class tutors were instructed to ascertain that pupils understood that they could make their questionnaire responses anonymously and in confidence. Pupils were to be seated separately, in order that no conferring, talking, or copying could take place, and were to be asked to respond truthfully; pupils were to be instructed to 'treat it like you would a test'. After giving these instructions to the pupils, the class teachers were to ask the pupils to fill in the name of their school, class, and the date, and the teacher was to work through how they might answer the first few questions with them.

The overall effectiveness of the programme was ascertained by a comparison of the pre-test and post-test questionnaire responses from the 22 schools. The sampling was designed so that those pupils who had answered as third-class pupils in the pre-test questionnaire should answer the post-test questionnaire as fourth-class pupils the following year, and those who appeared as fourth-class pupils in the pre-programme sample should answer the post-programme questionnaire as fifth-class pupils. This procedure does have an advantage of having the same pupils in the pre-test and post-test groups; however, a disadvantage is a confound with age effects (as reports of victimisation, for example, generally decrease with age; see chapter 2). In this respect, the evaluation procedure differs from that used in many other evaluation studies, for example in Bergen (chapter 2) or Sheffield (chapter 6).

Pre-test: prior to the implementation of the programme, in the first two terms of the school year 1998–99 (when the training of the professional network was taking place), data were obtained from 527 third- and fourth-class pupils.

Post-test: 1 year after the implementation of the programme, in summer 2000, data were obtained from 520 fourth- and fifth-class pupils.

What actually happened; achievements and difficulties in implementing the intervention

The training of the professional network was of 12 full days' duration, and was undertaken at weekends at the local (Donegal) Centre of Education. Training input was provided upon definitions of bullying; profiles of children who bully, and children who are bullied; diagnostic criteria of victimisation and bullying; adverse effects of bullying; whole-school approaches to bullying; classroom and individual intervention strategies; dealing with parents of children who bully, and those of children who are bullied; and presentation skills.

These 11 trained teachers then took responsibility for 3–5 schools each. They held an in-service day for teachers (a total of 197 teachers participated in these in-service days) and an after-school meeting for parents in their respective schools. The members of the professional network also acted as an adviser/support to schools in relation to bullying problems thereafter. The awareness days organised by the members of the professional network included advice and assistance to the schools in developing an anti-bullying policy within the overall framework of the school code of behaviour and discipline.

The *difficulties* experienced in this project came in the evaluation process, and primarily sprang from the devolvement of the administration of evaluation materials to the schools themselves. Although all 42 schools were invited to participate in both the pre-test and post-test phases of the evaluation, due to differential responses to the pre-programme and post-programme questionnaires by the schools, and anomalies in the administration of the questionnaires by the schools to the correct class groupings, it was possible to match data from only 22 schools in terms of pupils who had responded to both the pre-test and post-test questionnaires according to the planned design.

Results of the evaluation

In tables 14.1–14.7, data are presented from the *pupils' responses* to the Olweus Bully/Victim Questionnaire, administered at pre-test (labelled 'before') and post-test (labelled 'after').

The extent of having been victimised

In terms of lowering the incidence of pupils' involvement in bullying behaviour, as evidenced by their own responses to the pre-programme and post-programme Olweus questionnaires, the programme would

Table 14.1. *Percentage of pupils who reported being bullied during the last school term*

How often	Before	After
Not at all	63.3	70.5
Occasionally (once or twice)	18.6	17.4
Moderately (sometimes)	10.7	8.5
Frequently (once a week or more)	7.3	3.6

Table 14.2. *Percentage of pupils who reported being bullied in the last 5 school days before the survey*

How often	Before	After
Not at all	77.9	87.4
Once	9.3	6.2
Twice	6.8	2.9
Three or four times	3.0	2.1
Five or more times	2.9	1.2

appear to have been successful (tables 14.1–14.2). There was a significant reduction of 19.6% in reports of being victimised in the last school term, from 36.7% of all pupils prior to the implementation of the programme to 29.5% after ($\chi^2 = 5.77$, 1 df, p < 0.02). There was also a statistically significant decrease of some 43.0% in the number of pupils reporting that they had been bullied within the last 5 school days, from 22.1% of all pupils prior to the programme to 12.6% after ($\chi^2 = 16.99$, 1 df, p < 0.001).

The extent of bullying others

Fewer pupils reported bullying at all within the last school term after the implementation of the programme than before, a reduction of 17.3%, from 27.1% to 22.4% (table 14.3); this was only of marginal statistical significance ($\chi^2 = 2.89$, 1 df, p < 0.10). However, there was a strongly significant reduction of 51.8% of reports of having taken part in bullying of others within the last 5 school days, from 13.7% to 6.6%, ($\chi^2 = 14.13$, 1 df, p < 0.001) (see table 14.4).

Table 14.3. *Percentage of pupils who reported taking part in bullying other pupils during the last school term*

How often	Before	After
Not at all	72.9	77.6
Occasionally (once or twice)	17.7	18.2
Moderately (sometimes)	6.7	3.3
Frequently (once a week or more)	2.7	0.8

Table 14.4. *Percentage of pupils who reported taking part in bullying other pupils during the last 5 school days before the survey*

How often	Before	After
Not at all	86.3	93.4
Once	7.2	4.3
Twice	4.0	1.4
Three or four times	1.9	0.4
Five or more times	0.6	0.6

Who is told about bullying?

Sadly, the implementation of the anti-bullying programme had no positive effect on the reporting of bullying behaviour by victims of it; in fact, there was a slight decrease in reporting apparent in the responses of pupils to the second questionnaire. This was the case whether those being 'told' were teachers (from 48.7% before the programme, to 52.0% after indicating 'no, I haven't told them') or people at home (from 31.2% before the programme, to 34.8% thereafter).

Who tries to prevent bullying?

Pupils' estimations of the frequencies of their teachers' attempts to put a stop to bullying (table 14.5) improved slightly with the implementation of the programme: 52.6% of pupils responded that their teachers 'sometimes' or 'almost always' did so before the programme, whereas 58.4% responded in such a way after. This finding was of only marginal statistical significance ($\chi^2 = 3.70$, 1 df, $p < 0.10$).

There was no significant change in pupils' estimations of the likelihood of their peers attempting to put a stop to bullying (table 14.6). Before the programme, 45.9% responded that other pupils 'sometimes' or almost

Table 14.5. *Percentages of pupils' perceptions as to how often teachers try to put a stop to it when a pupil is being bullied at school*

How often	Before	After
I don't know	39.4	34.6
Almost never	8.0	7.0
Sometimes	17.2	12.8
Almost always	35.4	45.6

Table 14.6. *Percentages of pupils' perceptions as to how often other pupils try to put a stop to it when a pupil is being bullied at school*

How often	Before	After
I don't know	40.3	40.3
Almost never	13.7	14.5
Sometimes	32.0	32.3
Almost always	13.9	12.8

Table 14.7. *Percentages for what pupils responded that they usually do when they see a pupil of their own age being bullied at school*

Response	Before	After
Nothing, it's none of my business	15.9	9.2
Nothing, but I think I ought to help	22.2	19.2
I try to help her or him in some way	61.8	71.4

always' tried to put a stop to bullying; in the post-programme sample, 45.1% did so.

In contrast, pupils were significantly more likely to report that if they saw a pupil of their own age being bullied that they would 'try and help her or him in some way' after (71.4%) than before (61.8%) the implementation of the anti-bullying programme ($\chi^2 = 10.72$, 1 df, $p < 0.01$). Just 9.2% of pupils reported that in such a situation they would do 'nothing, it's none of my business' after the programme, whereas prior to it, this figure had been 15.9%; this finding, too, reached statistical significance ($\chi^2 = 10.58$, 1 df, $p < 0.01$) (table 14.7).

Discussion of the pre-test and post-test changes

In terms of lowering the incidence of pupils' involvement in bullying behaviour in school, the programme would appear to have been successful. Similar studies that have preceded ours, conducted elsewhere in Europe, have found disparate levels of programme success (Olweus, 1997, 1999; Roland, 1989, 1993; Roland and Munthe, 1997). It should also be noted that Roland, among others (notably Eslea and Smith, 1998) has suggested that a heightened awareness of bullying and bullying behaviour among pupils might have led to an elevation in levels of reporting. In other words, the implementation of a programme may produce an over-vigilance concerning episodes which, rightly or wrongly, might not have been categorised as incidents of bullying beforehand.

In the Sheffield Anti-Bullying Project (Smith and Sharp, 1994; Smith, 1997; and chapter 6), reductions of 17% in reports of victimisation, and 7% in reports of bullying others were obtained at the primary level. The Donegal schools project evaluation findings – of a reduction of 19.6% in reports of being victimised in the last term (from 36.7% before the programme to 29.5% thereafter), and a reduction of 17.3% in reports of bullying others in the last term (from 27.1% before the programme to 22.4% thereafter) – are therefore, we believe, indicative of a reasonable level of success. In the admittedly rather less robust 'last 5 days' category, reduction rates indicate still greater success – here we see a reduction in reports of being victimised of 43.0% (from 22.1% before the programme to 12.6% thereafter) and of 51.8% in reports of bullying others (down from 13.7% to 6.6% thereafter).

However, in comparing these results with the Norwegian and English projects, the different evaluation procedures have to be borne in mind. These projects used age-equivalent groups for pre-test and post-test comparison, thus avoiding the age confounds that are likely given the natural age-related decrease in reports of being victimised found consistently in large-scale surveys (O' Moore, Kirkham, and Smith, 1997; Smith, Madsen, and Moody, 1999).

Nevertheless, age-related decreases in involvement in bullying behaviour did not appear in either our pre-programme or post-programme samples. Chi-squared analyses showed that differences between third- and fourth-class pupils' reports in the pre-programme sample of having been bullied within the last school term, having been frequently bullied within the last school term, having been bullied within the last 5 school days, having taken part in bullying others within the last school term, having frequently taken part in bullying others within the last school term, and having taken part in bullying others within the last 5 school days did not reach statistical significance ($\chi^2 = 1.47$, 0.05, 3.07, 0.27, 1.37, and 3.00, respectively; all below the critical value of $\chi^2 = 3.84$, p < 0.05, 1 df).

Similarly, in the post-programme sample, differences between fourth- and fifth-class pupils' reports of having been bullied within the last school term, having been frequently bullied within the last school term, having been bullied within the last 5 school days, having taken part in bullying others within the last school term, and having taken part in bullying others within the last 5 school days did not reach statistical significance ($\chi^2 = 0.81$, 0.08, 0.04, 0.38, and 0.06, respectively).

An area in which the Donegal schools programme met with rather less success was in the attempt to increase levels of reporting of bullying behaviour, by those who are victims of it, to teachers and parents. Eslea and Smith (1998: 217) suggest that the issue of anti-bullying programmes failing to increase the reporting rate of bullying 'is not the indictment it at first seems'. They argue that anti-bullying programmes foster both increased teacher vigilance (the pupils have less need to report incidents) and increased pupil assertion (as bullying is taken seriously in a school running an anti-bullying programme, the mere threat of 'telling' works).

Whether Eslea and Smith are over-optimistic in assuming the existence of these masking phenomena, though, remains to be seen – the data in their (and our) evaluation study pointing to stasis in reporting rates are firm, whereas the evidence for a increased consciousness of teacher vigilance and greater assertive qualities amongst pupils is rather less so. This being noted, however, in terms of pupils' perceptions of the efficacy and willingness of those who stop bullying, it seems from the results that, as Eslea and Smith (1998) suggested, pupils *are* aware of the teachers' commitment to the anti-bullying programme. This is evidenced by a slight increase in the proportion of pupils responding that they think that their teachers 'sometimes' or 'almost always' put a stop to incidents of bullying (table 14.5). Perhaps the non-resolution of this particular point is a further demonstration of the fact that the need for the further development and careful implementation of evaluation studies of anti-bullying interventions is absolutely imperative.

The rather more negative view of their peers' attempts or willingness to stop bullying, though (table 14.6), is less easy to interpret optimistically. It is possible that the programme prompts a certain mindfulness, or awareness, of *both* past successes and past shortcomings in stopping bullying among the pupils. Furthermore, it might be reasonable to speculate that successes will be 'claimed' by the individual pupil (hence the positive increases in table 14.7), whereas the shortcomings will be disavowed, and be subjectively experienced as more typical of their peers.

Longer term effects or evaluation of the programme

There have been no further evaluations of bullying behaviour in the Donegal primary schools since the post-programme evaluation in summer 2000. However, it should be possible to gather such data over the coming years, as a second nationwide survey of bullying behaviour in Irish schools (to include the pre-programme evaluation phase of the forthcoming nationwide intervention programme) is due to commence in summer 2004.

Dissemination and impact beyond the programme schools

Whilst the Donegal schools anti-bullying project has shown itself to be successful in reducing the incidence of pupils' involvement in bullying behaviour as both perpetrators and victims, there remain, with a view to the development and future implementation of the proposed nationwide programme to counter and prevent bullying in schools, some areas of concern.

It is evident that increasing levels of reporting of bullying behaviour among primary pupils is a tough nut to crack. However, it may well be the case that pupils might not report bullying because they do not feel confident in the school's ability to deal adequately with bullying. Pupils know that they *should* report bullying; they also need to believe that it will be *safe* for them to do so. If the school has a clear anti-bullying policy, with provisions made for detecting, reporting, and dealing with bullying, upon which all staff are agreed and act, then the pupils can feel confident in reporting the bullying behaviour that they witness and experience. For as long as this is not always the case, reporting may always seem to carry a risk.

Generally, in terms of programme success, Smith and Sharp (1994) feel that their research in England demonstrates that 'those [schools that] did the most, achieved the most'; in Norway, Roland and Munthe (1997) indicate 'continuity', and the integration of the anti-bullying programme's principles into the day-to-day school management are key factors. In the evaluation of their 1996 nationwide programme for Norwegian schools, Roland et al. (2001) stated that '. . . the broad profile of the programme and the material were well received by the schools, but the system of local assistance has to be improved' (Roland, Bjørnsen, and Mandt, 2001: 7). This in itself, and the fact that a substantial amount of the anti-bullying programme evaluation research to date has demonstrated the importance of the internal and external organisational support in underpinning anti-bullying intervention efforts and preventing bullying in schools, provides food for thought. In other words, it may well be possible to attend to such areas of concern via increased attention to the professional network aspect of our programme.

References

Byrne, B. (1987). A study of the incidence and nature of bullies and whipping boys (victims) in a Dublin city post-primary school. Unpublished Master's thesis, Trinity College, Dublin.

Department of Education and Science (1993). *Guidelines on countering and preventing bullying behaviour in primary and post-primary schools*. Dublin: The Stationery Office.

Eslea, M. and Smith, P. K. (1998). The long-term effectiveness of anti-bullying work in primary schools. *Educational Research*, 40, 203–18.

Olweus, D. (1978). *Aggression in the school: Bullies and whipping boys*. Washington, DC: Hemisphere.

(1989). *Bully/Victim questionnaire for students*. Department of Psychology, University of Bergen, Norway.

(1993). *Bullying at school: What we know and what we can do*. Oxford: Blackwell.

(1997). Bully/victim problems in school: Knowledge base and an effective intervention programme. *Irish Journal of Psychology*, 18, 170–90.

(1999). Norway. In P. K. Smith, Y. Morita, J. Junger-Tas, D. Olweus, R. Catalano, and P. Slee, P. (eds.), *The nature of school bullying: A cross-national perspective*. London: Routledge.

O'Moore, A. M. (2000). Critical issues for teacher training to counter bullying and victimisation in Ireland. *Aggressive Behavior*, 26, 99–111.

O'Moore, A. M. and Hillery, B. (1989). Bullying in Dublin schools. *Irish Journal of Psychology*, 10, 426–41.

O'Moore, A. M. and Kirkham, C. (2001). Self-esteem and its relationship to bullying behaviour. *Aggressive Behavior*, 27, 269–83.

O'Moore, A. M., Kirkham, C., and Smith, M. (1997). Bullying behaviour in Irish schools: A nationwide study. *Irish Journal of Psychology*, 18, 141–69.

O'Moore, A. M. and Minton, S. J. (2001). Tackling violence in schools: A report from Ireland. In P. K. Smith (ed.), *Violence in schools: The response in Europe*. London and New York: RoutledgeFalmer, pp. 282–97.

Ortega, R. and Lera, M. J. (2000). The Seville Anti-Bullying in School project. *Aggressive Behavior*, 26, 113–23.

Roland, E. (1989). Bullying: The Scandinavian research tradition. In D. P. Tattum and D. A. Lane (eds.), *Bullying in schools*. London: Trentham Books.

Roland, E. (1993). Bullying: A developing tradition of research and management. In D. P. Tattum (ed.), *Understanding and managing bullying*. Oxford: Heinemann Educational Books.

(2000). Bullying in school: Three national innovations in Norwegian schools in 15 years. *Aggressive Behavior*, 26, 135–43.

Roland, E. and Munthe, E. (1997). The 1996 Norwegian program for preventing and managing bullying in schools. *Irish Journal of Psychology*, 18, 233–47.

Roland, E. and Vaaland, G. S. (1996). *Mobbing i skolen: En lærerveiledning*. Oslo: Kirke-, utdannings- og forskningsdepartmentet.

Roland, E., Bjørnsen, G., and Mandt, G. (2001). 'Taking back adult control': A report from Norway. In P. K. Smith (ed.), *Violence in schools: The response in Europe*. London and New York: RoutledgeFalmer, pp. 200–15.

Smith, P. K. (1997). Bullying in schools: The UK experience and the Sheffield Anti-Bullying Project. *Irish Journal of Psychology*, 18, 191–201.

Smith P. K., Madsen, K. C., and Moody J. C. (1999). What causes the age decline in reports of being bullied at school? Towards a developmental analysis of risks of being bullied. *Educational Research*, 41, 267–85.

Smith, P. K. and Sharp, S. (eds.), (1994). *School bullying: Insights and perspectives*. London: Routledge.

Whitney, I. and Smith, P. K. (1993). A survey of the nature and extent of bullying in junior/middle and secondary schools. *Educational Research*, 35, 3–25.

15 Bernese programme against victimisation in kindergarten and elementary school

Françoise D. Alsaker

Impetus for the intervention, early stages of planning, and funding

Despite the growing interest in victimisation problems in school (see Smith et al., 1999), studies that have addressed this issue in the pre-school years are extremely rare. The existence of victimisation in pre-school children, however, had been systematically studied and demonstrated in earlier studies: in day-care centres in Norway (Alsaker, 1993a, 1993b); in the United States with kindergarten children (Kochenderfer and Ladd, 1996); and in kindergarten in Switzerland (Alsaker, 2003; Alsaker and Valkanover, 2001). All three studies showed that the extent to which victimisation occurs in the early childhood years is comparable with that in grade school and that it has an immensely stressful effect on young children.

Studies from Australia (Slee and Rigby, 1993), Finland (Lagerspetz, Björkqvist, Berts, and King, 1982), Ireland (Neary and Joseph, 1994), the United Kingdom (Boulton and Smith, 1994), Norway (Alsaker and Olweus, 2002; Olweus, 1993), Sweden (Olweus, 1978), and Switzerland (Alsaker, 2003) have all shown detrimental effects of victimisation on self-esteem. Repeated victimisation experiences may elicit intense emotional experiences, including feelings of helplessness, worthlessness, and shame. In addition, they may result in highly stable negative expectations for peer relationships and negative self-evaluations, even after the victimisation has stopped (Alsaker and Olweus, 2002; Olweus, 1991). Such negative perceptions of self and peers may, in turn, influence the child's behaviour in school, thus making him or her more vulnerable to victimisation. Therefore, it is important that prevention of victimisation starts in pre-school contexts. The conditions in kindergartens are ideal for the implementation of preventive programmes against victimisation, given the generally high adult to child ratio, flexibility as to scheduling and teaching, and last, but not least, the admiration of many children for their teachers.

With this understanding, I applied for funding within the framework of the 'National Programme on Daily Violence and Organised Crime' (financed by the Swiss National Science Foundation), a national research programme launched to respond to the increasing awareness of violence in Swiss daily life (including school). In addition to an in-depth study of victimisation in pre-school children (Alsaker, 2003; Alsaker and Valkanover, 2001), the project set out to develop, implement, and evaluate a prevention programme against victimisation in kindergarten.

The development of the Bernese programme against victimisation in kindergarten and elementary school was based on well-known principles used in school programmes against bully/victim problems (e.g. Olweus, 1993; Sharp and Smith, 1993) and in various programmes for social–cognitive skills. These programmes had, by and large, been designed for school settings with the associated challenges of implementation. Therefore, in recognition of the special context of kindergarten, we designed the Bernese prevention programme against victimisation in kindergarten and elementary school (Be-Prox). This programme was flexible and adaptable to the very different situations and needs encountered by teachers, and focused on enhancing and maintaining teachers' motivation to prevent victimisation (Alsaker, 2003).

Selection of schools

A pre-test/post-test design with a control group was used to evaluate the effects of the Be-Prox programme. The programme was implemented in 8 kindergarten classes. Another eight kindergarten classes comprised the control group; nothing was done in the control groups, except for teachers making notes of educational work with children, in logbooks. Each class was in a different school or institution. The project took place over 7 months, from November 1997 (pre-test) to June 1998 (post-test).

Because we wanted the study to reflect a real situation, we let teachers 'self-select', as would be the case if a counselling office or a teachers' educational institution offered special training in tackling bully/victim problems. All kindergarten teachers in Berne received information about the prevention project, except those who had participated in the in-depth study on victimisation and teachers from kindergartens within the immediate neighbourhood of the previously investigated kindergartens. We described the purpose of the programme, the kind of co-operation it would require, and our intention to implement the programme in some kindergartens immediately and to make the same offer one year later to the other kindergartens. Teachers were also informed about how much time supervision meetings and programme evaluation would 'cost' them. Of the 88 kindergarten teachers provided with information, and after several phone calls and an information meeting for all teachers who were interested in the endeavour, 18 teachers (from 16 kindergartens) indicated that they were interested. Teachers who wanted to participate immediately (10 teachers from 8 kindergartens) were selected as the intervention group. The other teachers (8 kindergartens) preferred to wait another year and were therefore selected as the control group.

The self-selection to the prevention and control groups introduced a (real-life) bias. The teachers who wanted to participate immediately were experiencing bullying problems in their classrooms to a greater extent than their control colleagues. In fact, 50% of the teachers in the intervention group indicated an 'urgent need' for implementing a prevention programme compared to only 25% of teachers in the control group.

Characteristics of kindergartens and students

In all, 319 parents allowed their children to participate in our evaluation study (99.4% of all children in the 16 kindergartens). There were 152 children (50% girls) in the prevention group and 167 children (50.9% girls) in the control group. The children's ages varied between 5 years and 7 years 11 months ($M = 6.2$, $SD = .59$), and 31% of the children were foreign citizens.

Components of the prevention programme

The basic principle of the prevention programme was to *enhance teachers' capability of handling bully/victim problems*. Kindergarten teachers in the intervention group were offered an intensive focused supervision for approximately 4 months. The design of the general procedure is illustrated in fig. 15.1.

In 8 meetings, issues central to the prevention of bullying were addressed. All meetings followed the same basic schedule: information about specific topics regarding victimisation and its prevention (step 1, 1a, etc. in fig. 15.1) and implications of the new information were discussed (step 2); then specific implementation tasks were introduced (step 3) and the teachers worked in groups on the preparation of the practical implementation (step 4). During the 2 or 3 weeks between meetings teachers were encouraged to implement some specific preventive elements (step 5). The next meeting then started with a discussion of teachers' experiences with the implementation of the task (step 6).

As noted earlier, one of the central characteristics of Be-Prox is *flexibility*. Teachers who take part in the prevention courses are assumed

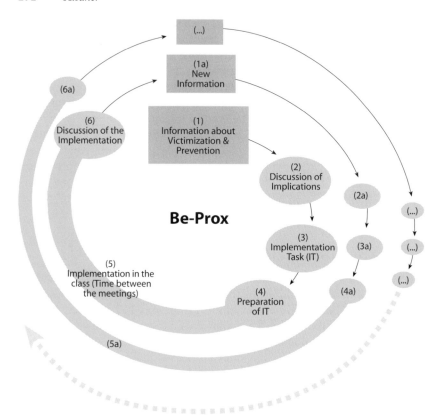

Fig. 15.1 Overview of the structure of the prevention programme Be-Prox.

to be motivated to prevent victimisation. Therefore, everything is done to maintain and even enhance their motivation. In my opinion, this can only be done when individual needs, resources, and limitations are taken into account. This, in turn, means that the prevention process should be allowed to follow different paths and to occur at different paces in the various classes.

Another central feature of Be-Prox is its emphasis on *co-operation*. The consultants and the teachers work together on the concretisation of the programme. The consultants are defined as experts regarding knowledge about victimisation and prevention; the teachers are experts regarding educational techniques and knowledge about the children in their classes and their own personality. Co-operation between teachers and parents is also emphasised.

Another feature of the programme regards expectations: expectations and goals have to be realistic. That is, teachers have to learn to define *intermediate goals*, to recognise that prevention of (or intervention against) victimisation is a long-term process characterised by small steps and to acknowledge success even when the achievements seem trivial.

Finally, we emphasise the usefulness of *group discussions and mutual support*. Following these principles, 8 meetings were planned. An outline of the factual contents of these meetings is given below.

What actually happened; achievements and difficulties in implementing the intervention

First meeting: sensitisation

The main purpose of the first meeting was sensitisation. Specific aspects of victimisation were presented and the kindergarten teachers were asked to give an account of the situation in their kindergarten regarding aggressive behaviour in general and victimisation in particular. An emphasis was put on early diagnosis of victimisation patterns and the differentiation between conflicts and victimisation.

Also, the main principles of the programme were presented and discussed including expectations both of teachers and consultants, and the importance of contact between kindergarten and parents.

At the end of the meeting, the teachers were assigned an observation task. Different approaches were discussed, but they were free to choose a method they felt comfortable with. They were also invited to start preparing a meeting with parents. The purpose of this meeting was threefold: first, to sensitise them to bully/victim problems; second, to inform them about the major elements of the programme in order to increase their co-operation; and third, to improve communication patterns between teachers and parents when difficult situations arise.

Second meeting: sensitisation of the children and behaviour code

The second meeting started with teachers' reports from their observations (step 6 in fig. 15.1). The teachers talked about their own reactions during these episodes, and alternative reactions were discussed.

The importance of rules, limits, and structure for children's development was discussed. Using recommendations and experiences from various programmes (Battistisch et al., 1989; Bierman, Greenberg, and CPPRG, 1996; Olweus, 1993; Smith and Sharp, 1994), the value of discussions about victimisation in the class and of the elaboration of a behaviour code *in collaboration with the children* was stressed. The teachers were invited to come back with the rules that they had agreed upon with the children in their classes. The usefulness of co-operation with parents was highlighted once more, and the concrete organisation of a parent meeting was given as a homework task.

Several teachers felt uncomfortable about talking about victimisation with the children, when they themselves had not directly observed systematic or harsh bullying. Therefore, many possible ways were discussed to address the issue of victimisation, including stories, books, films, etc. Several teachers chose to start the discussion with the children addressing the issue of good and bad feelings, that is, what they knew about good and bad feelings and what triggered such feelings. Our experience, also with other groups of teachers, is that children nearly automatically report on bullying experiences when they start explaining what bad feelings are.

We learned that the discussion and implementation of rules against victimisation occurred too early because teachers felt somewhat overwhelmed. Therefore, in our present work with Be-Prox, we use one additional meeting on the presentation and discussion of specific aspects of victimisation and reserve a 3-week period for the teachers to work on sensitisation of the children. We also give the teachers more time during the meeting to prepare how to discuss aggressive behaviour and victimisation with the children.

The third meeting is then reserved to work intensively on the importance of limits and rules, and the time between the third and fourth meeting is used to implement the behaviour code.

Third meeting: making use of the behaviour code

Feedback on discussions with the children and the implementation of rules was highly positive. Children were very eager to work on such rules, and produced many suggestions and drawings. In most kindergartens, the teachers then used the children's drawings to illustrate and concretise the behaviour code. Many teachers reported that the children were very proud of the behaviour code they had produced.

The topic of the third meeting was the importance of consistent teacher behaviour, positive and negative sanctions, and the use of basic learning principles. The issue of reporting on bullying behaviour or requesting help from the teacher versus tattling on peers was addressed. In fact, tattling on peers was a very sensitive issue. Many teachers were very concerned about introducing a tattling culture in their classes if children were encouraged to report on rule transgressions regarding bullying behaviour.

Myths and stereotypes regarding victims and bullies and teachers' *tendencies to excuse aggressive behaviour* because of possible inner conflicts were intensely discussed during this meeting. In addition, the role of the *teacher as socialisation agent* and many teachers' reluctance to use negative sanctions were discussed. The task for the next implementation period was to note transgressions against the behaviour code and to reflect about and describe reinforcement patterns around victims and bullies in the class.

By that time all teachers had organised meetings with the parents. They all had taken the opportunity to ask the consultants to participate in these meetings. This again shows how insecure they felt when considering telling parents about their work with the children, and particularly in soliciting parents' co-operation about the behaviour code. This, in turn, highlights the need for emphasising the importance of structure, limits, and rules in the socialisation of children today.

Fourth meeting: the non-involved children

The main focus of the fourth session was on the role and responsibility of the so-called non-involved children and bystanders. Teachers were asked to draw some kind of personality profiles of passive and aggressive victims and of bullies. Research findings on characteristics of involved and non-involved children were then discussed, and emphasis was put on the immense resources that empathic, non-aggressive, and socially competent children represent in the prevention of victimisation. The teachers also reported on their behaviour towards different children, and particularly towards bullies and victims. Their task until the next meeting was to observe the so-called non-involved children and to develop some means of involving them in the prevention of victimisation.

Fifth meeting: body awareness and concrete goals

Research-based knowledge on motor development and body awareness among pre-school children was presented. Findings from our own kindergarten study were discussed. An examination of children's self-perception of strength, of peers' perceptions of the strength of victims and bullies and of factual measures of strength and other motor characteristics of the children yielded important insights. As expected, victims perceived themselves as weaker than others. Also their peers perceived them as weak. In contrast, bullies reported being stronger than other children in their class, and this corresponded to the perception of their peers. However, analyses of the measures tapping various actual motor skills revealed no significant differences between the groups of children: passive victims, aggressive victims, bullies, and non-involved children did not differ in motor skills, such as strength (Alsaker, 2003; Valkanover, 2003).

Several possibilities of enhancing victims' awareness of their own physical competence and strength and to provide all children with a more realistic perception of the strength of bullies were discussed. Also, we addressed the importance of offering children opportunities to differentiate aggression and strength, as well as the use of physical exercises and games helping children to set limits, to define their own territory, and to increase self-assertiveness.

The teachers were asked to choose some common tasks they should work on in their classes until the next meeting. They decided to work on four major issues: empathy training using body-oriented tasks and games; active participation of the non-involved children; talks with the children about their experiences of victimisation in the class; and preparation of materials that were used with the children regarding the prevention programme and that should be presented to the other teachers at the next meeting.

Sixth meeting: consolidation through own prevention goals

Time was reserved to reflect on the goals formulated by the teachers at the beginning of the prevention programme, and the issues they had agreed upon at the end of the fifth meeting, that is especially: training of empathy and body awareness, participation and involvement of the non-involved children, and talks with the children about the situation in the kindergarten. Also, teachers had time to discuss their attitudes towards aggression, towards victims, and their expectations for kindergarten children in general.

Many teachers reported having encountered difficulties in behaving consistently in case of transgressions. Therefore, we decided to come back to this issue during the next meeting, which had been defined as 'open' in order to respond to the needs and wishes of the teachers. The task for the next implementation period was to work on the issues that still needed more attention.

Seventh meeting: 'open'

Following the wish of a majority of the teachers, sanctions in cases of transgressions and the application of learning principles, especially positive reinforcement, were discussed one more time. The teachers reported facing a dilemma between feeling intolerant and rigid, on the one hand, and behaving inconsistently, on the other. Much attention was given to the unwanted positive reinforcement of negative behaviour and strategies to avoid it.

The teachers reported that they worked intensively on the expression of emotions (e.g. using pictures of children's faces displaying various emotional states) and on the improvement of social skills. During this meeting teachers identified *individual goals* that they wanted to work on until the end of the school year.

Eighth meeting: feedback and further use of the programme

For the teachers, the last meeting was an opportunity to evaluate their own work on prevention of victimisation and to give feedback about the whole programme to the consultants. The teachers' feedback was highly positive, even if they had experienced many challenges and worked intensively on several issues. As one teacher noted: 'Sometimes it is good to have someone holding a mirror in front of you.' They evaluated the amount of time spent on the programme as suitable, but they also reported that the upper limit was reached. They were very satisfied with the combination of research-based knowledge and practical tasks.

Our experience with further use of Be-Prox, however, is that it is difficult to motivate teachers – and schools – to meet as many as 8 times, as we did in the project. On the other hand, the difficulties that these kindergarten teachers experienced, such as consistent behaviour, sanctions, and addressing difficult issues, are quite common. Therefore, we believe that it is essential to follow teachers over an extended period of time, in order to support them and to challenge them, so that they have an opportunity to experience their own competence in handling victimisation situations. I will come back to this issue at the end of the chapter.

Evaluation framework and procedures

The design was a longitudinal one. Changes over time could be confounded with natural age changes, so the interest is in differential changes between the intervention and control groups. In both groups (prevention and control), the teachers completed questionnaires and children were interviewed individually before and after the programme was implemented. Teachers' questionnaires and children's interviews included for the most part questions directly related to victimisation.

Teacher reports

Teachers rated each child, indicating the extent to which he or she was victimised and/or bullied other children. They rated 4 items on bullying and 4 items on victimisation (physical, verbal, property-related, and exclusion), using a 5-point rating scale (never, seldom, once or several times a month, once a week, or several times a week). Furthermore, a set of questions was used at both pre-test and post-test on teachers' attitudes towards victimisation, perceptions of the possibilities to prevent victimisation, readiness to contact and work with children's parents, and about the children's behaviour in the peer group when bullying occurred.

Also, the implementation of some 'easy-to-use' elements of the programme was assessed. In Switzerland, kindergarten teachers are used to keeping a logbook of their educational activities. Therefore, by the end of the school year we asked all teachers (prevention and control) to use these logbooks to complete a questionnaire about their activities against victimisation during the project period. For the evaluation, we split the period of time between the beginning of the prevention programme and the end of the school year into 3 phases of about 6 weeks. We called these 3 phases implementation, consolidation, and further use.

Child interviews

As a result of earlier experiences with interviewing children about victimisation (Alsaker, 1993a,b), efforts were made to define victimisation, including power imbalance and recurrence. The intention of being mean to others was also explicitly discussed with the children. After some open-ended questions on bullying, the interviewer explained clearly what we meant by bullying, using pictures showing physical, verbal, and property-related bullying and a situation of isolation/exclusion. The children were then asked to pick out the photographs of peers who bullied other children and to tell who were the victims of these children. Peer nominations were transformed into percentages of possible nominations (see Alsaker and Valkanover, 2001).

Results of the evaluation

Teacher ratings of children's bullying and victimisation

Due to the self-selection procedure, teachers in the prevention group were highly motivated to participate in the programme and they invested much time. Therefore, it is reasonable to assume that their answers could be biased towards improvement. However, they were also highly sensitised to victimisation and especially to subtle aggressive behaviour. Hence,

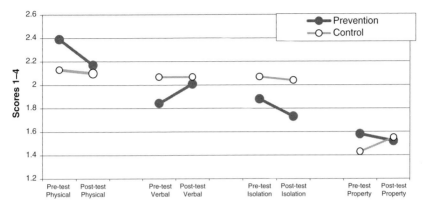

Fig. 15.2 Changes in 4 types of victimisation from pre-test to post-test according to teacher questionnaires.

we could also expect them to report much more victimisation at post-test than at pre-test. The control group had not been sensitised, but the teachers had also spent some time completing questionnaires, organising our interview visits, etc. Consequently, they could also have been motivated to show that they managed well even without our programme. Therefore, we considered teachers' data regarding reports on victimisation at post-test as somewhat problematic. The strength of our evaluation is the multi-informant design: well aware of these possible sources of error, data from the teachers are complemented with results based on children's interviews.

From the teacher data we found no changes in reported bullying behaviour for either the prevention group or the control group. Results on being victimised, however, showed significant interaction effects (a differential change in the prevention and control groups), regarding 3 of the 4 types of victimisation. In the control group, property-related victimisation had increased significantly. In the prevention group, scores on physical and indirect victimisation had dropped significantly. Verbal victimisation yielded no significant results, even though it had become slightly more frequent in the prevention group. To sum up, data from the teachers in the prevention group yielded two significant positive changes, whereas data from the teachers in the control group yielded one significant negative change (see Alsaker, 2003; Alsaker and Valkanover, 2000, 2001 for details). The findings for all four types of victimisation are illustrated in fig. 15.2.

The discrepant results obtained for bullying, on the one hand, and victimisation, on the other, as well as the concurrent drop and (non-significant) increase in different forms of victimisation in the pre-vention group, point to the absence of a general bias in the teachers' answers. The improvement in physical and indirect victimisation indi-cates some general positive effects (there is more significant improvement than aggravation of the situation in the prevention group). Our focus on non-involved children may have led to a better integration of all chil-dren in the class (leading to less exclusion and isolation). The decrease in children being regularly physically harassed corresponds to the goals of the programme. The reported slight increase in verbal victimisation in the prevention group was not significant, but may indicate some sensitisation effects. Bullying behaviour in general may have decreased, but the teach-ers could have become extremely aware of less obvious verbal aggressive behaviours. Before the prevention programme was implemented, teach-ers may have considered verbal harassment as not serious or even ignored it. Being subsequently sensitised to all forms of victimisation, they may have learned to recognise verbal harassment as such, but they might also have been over-sensitised and have interpreted some tough verbal inter-actions as harassment.

Child interviews

We transformed the peer nominations for bullies and victims, respec-tively, into percentages of nominations (on the basis of the number of children who had been interviewed in the various classes). There was no change in the prevention group as to percentage of children nominated as a bully or victim. In the control group there was a small increase in bully nominations and a larger and significant increase in victim nominations. This finding is complementary to the results obtained on the basis of the teachers' questionnaires, suggesting either a decline in victimisation in the prevention group or an increase in the control group.

On the basis of raw peer nominations as victims, we also created a dichotomous variable (0 = no or 1 nomination received, 1 = at least 2 nominations) as an indication of 'risk of victimization'. At pre-test, 88 children were assigned to the risk category in the prevention group; at post-test, 75 children met this criterion. This represents a decrease of 15%. In the control group, there were 55 children in the risk category at pre-test and 85 at post-test, an increase of 55% (fig. 15.3). We interpreted the increase reported by the children in the control group as a 'normal' pattern when nothing is done to prevent or stop bullying. When nothing was done, the risk for some children of becoming a victim was one and a half times higher by the end of the school year than in the beginning.

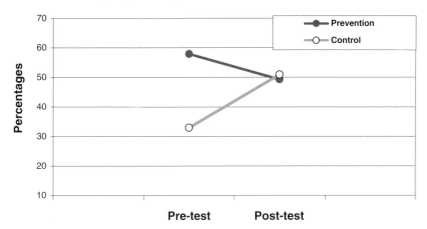

Fig. 15.3 Percentages of children nominated as victims by at least 2 of their peers at pre-test and post-test.

Teacher logbooks

Reports from the teachers' logbooks clearly showed that the teachers in the prevention group had worked according to the tasks they were assigned during the various meetings. Some interesting and sometimes paradoxical findings are described below.

First, the teachers in the control group noted during all 3 phases of the project that they had notified the children about behaviour rules in the class. The teachers from the prevention group did it only in the first phase and noted at the same time that they had discussed rules with the children. Even if the teachers from the control group reported having talked about victimisation with the children, the teachers in the prevention group had used a greater variety of methods, including body-oriented methods (particularly when teaching children to set limits) and individual talks with children. Also, the children in the prevention group reported that they had class discussions of victimisation significantly more often than children in the control group, and they were more likely to mention concrete rules against bullying than the children from the control kindergartens.

The pre-test/post-test comparisons also demonstrated that teachers in the prevention group felt more secure about how to handle bullying situations. Interestingly, teachers in the control group reported more often at post-test than at pre-test that they *told the children to report on bullying* and call for their help in case of harassment. The contrary was observed in the prevention group (see fig. 15.4). The prevention teachers also agreed more frequently with the statement *children have to learn to handle bullying*

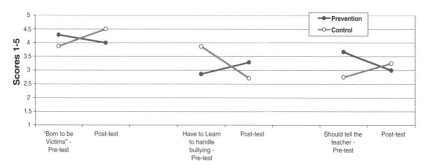

Fig. 15.4 A sample of teachers' answers regarding attitudes towards victimisation and children's opportunities to cope with victimisation.

situations at post-test, whereas the contrary was true for control teachers (see fig. 15.4). These paradoxical findings only make sense when we also know that the teachers from the prevention group reported that the children helped one another more at post-test than at pre-test. That is, they had experienced that children could be active in the prevention of victimisation and they were confident that children could learn to handle such situations.

Teachers in the prevention group agreed to a lesser extent with the statements *some children are born to be victims* (see fig. 15.4) and *victimisation always occurs behind my back* at post-test than at pre-test and less than teachers from the control group, who showed the opposite trend. Here also, their answers reflected a heightened feeling of 'being in control'. Victims can leave the victim role. Victimisation is a phenomenon teachers can be aware of and stop.

Another encouraging finding was that teachers in the prevention group developed positive attitudes towards working with the parents of the kindergarten children during the project time. They agreed almost unanimously that it was very important to work *together* with the parents and that it made sense to talk with parents. During this same period of time, teachers from the control group had become rather negative towards parents (Alsaker, 2003).

In sum, the results demonstrated that the central elements of the programme had been implemented and that children were aware of it. They also showed that important attitudes had changed in the expected direction in the prevention group, and that the increase in harassment episodes (children's reports) in the control group was accompanied by an increase in teachers' endorsement of pessimistic and self-defeating attitudes as compared with the prevention group.

At first glance, the relatively modest decrease in victimisation in the prevention group (even if significant) was somewhat disappointing. However, the similarity of the findings based on teachers' questionnaires and on children's reports indicate high reliability of the findings. Also, considering that some sensitisation effect may have influenced the results, and that teachers were much more aware of the bullying episodes in the prevention group (they agreed to a lesser extent than control teachers that bullying occurred behind their back), the results are very encouraging. In addition, the protocols from all meetings clearly indicated positive changes in teachers' handling of bullying situations. During the course of the project, the teachers became more confident in their own competence in handling these situations, they felt much more relaxed in the presence of aggressive behaviour, and they addressed the problems as soon as they occurred. Also, the fact that they made contact with parents of bullies and victims indicates that they felt much more in control of the situation and acted competently (Alsaker, 2003).

Longer term effects or evaluation of the programme

An attempt was made to do a follow-up of the intervention effects 2 years later. Unfortunately, this was at a time of industrial unrest by the teachers; and, despite efforts at various levels, further evaluation of the programme has not yet been possible.

Dissemination and impact beyond the programme schools

Several interviews in local and national newspapers as well as on radio helped to disseminate general information about the work we had done in the project kindergartens. In the meantime, some psychologists were trained to use the prevention programme and also a large number of schools (not only kindergartens) and communities have made contact with the author and her team. Teachers' organisations and parents' organisations also work intensively to give teachers an opportunity to take part in our courses. A film and a workbook for teachers are published, sponsored through the Swiss National Research Council and the Educational Ministers of around 10 of the Swiss federal states. The purpose of these two instruments is to enable teachers to work in groups (with or without supervision) following the principles that were used during the project. The workbook includes a concrete schedule for meetings, suggestions of discussions and reflection, and many examples of materials and methods used by the teachers in the project. We are currently working with parents' and teachers' organisations in several communities to set up courses for parents.

We have encountered two general problems in the implementation of Be-Prox. First, schools often have difficulties raising funds to pay professionals to supervise groups of teachers for longer periods. Second, many teachers still would like experts to come into their class and solve the problems, or endow them with a 'very-easy-to-use-technique' that would work immediately. In fact, many teachers in higher grades seem to be afraid of the reactions of their students. This, in turn, makes it difficult to believe that teachers can learn to handle victimisation situations without any supervision, some pressure, and considerably more support. Therefore, at present we are experimenting with several alternative procedures that could reduce the costs for the schools and still include some supervision.

Acknowledgements

The study presented in this chapter received financial support from the Swiss National Science Foundation (National Program on Daily Violence and Organized Crime, Grant No. 4040–45251 to Françoise D. Alsaker). I want to thank the other members of the research team, namely, Stefan Valkanover, Igor Arievich, Kathrin Hersberger, Sonja Perren, Daniel Suess, and Flavia Tramanzoli, for their contributions.

NOTE

The Bernese Programme Against Victimisation in Kindergarten and Elementary School (Be-Prox) is copyrighted. This implies certain restrictions on its utilisation and on the use of the information given here. Authorisation to use the programme with groups of teachers can be obtained upon fulfilment of a course in which the method and the contents of all meetings are discussed in detail. For more information, please write to Françoise D. Alsaker, Department of Psychology, University of Berne, Muesmattstrasse 45, CH-3000 Berne 9, Switzerland. E-mail: francoise.alsaker@psy.unibe.ch.

References

Alsaker, F. D. (1993a). *Bully/victim problems in day-care centers: Measurement issues and associations with children's psychosocial health.* Paper presented at the Biennial Meeting of the Society for Research in Child Development, New Orleans, USA.

(1993b). Isolement et maltraitance par pairs dans les jardins d'enfants: Comment mesurer ces phénomènes et quelles en sont leurs conséquences? *Enfance*, 47, 241–60.

(2003). *Quälgeister und ihre Opfer. Mobbing unter Kindern – und wie man damit umgeht* [Bullies and their victims. Victimisation among children – and how to prevent it]. Berne: Huber Verlag.

Alsaker, F. D. and Olweus, D. (2002). Stability and change in global self-esteem and self-related affect. In T. M. Brinthaupt and R. P. Lipka (eds.), *Understanding the self of the early adolescent*. New York: State University of New York Press, pp. 193–223.

Alsaker, F. D. and Valkanover, S. (2000). *Das Plagen im Kindergarten. Formen und Präventionsmöglichkeiten* [Victimisation in kindergarten. Forms and prevention]. Research report, Department of Psychology, University of Berne, Switzerland.

Alsaker, F. D. and Valkanover, S. (2001). Early diagnosis and prevention of victimisation in kindergarten. In J. Juvonen and S. Graham (eds.), *Peer harassment in school: The plight of the vulnerable and victimized*. New York: Guilford Press, pp. 175–195.

Battistich, V., Solomon, D., Watson, D., Solomon, J., and Schaps, E. (1989). Effects of an elementary school programme to enhance prosocial behavior on children's cognitive-social problem-solving skills and strategies. *Journal of Applied Developmental Psychology*, 10, 147–69.

Bierman, K. L., Greenberg, M. T., and Conduct Problems Prevention Research Group. (1996). Social skills training in the fast track program. In R. Peters and R. J. McMahon (eds.), *Preventing childhood disorders, substance abuse, and delinquency*. Thousand Oaks, Calif.: Sage. pp. 65–89.

Boulton, M. J. and Smith, P. K. (1994). Bully/victim problems in middle-school children: Stability, self-perceived competence, peer perceptions and peer acceptance. *British Journal of Developmental Psychology*, 12, 315–29.

Kochenderfer, B. J. and Ladd, G. W. (1996). Peer victimization: Manifestations and relations to school adjustment in kindergarten. *Journal of School Psychology*, 34, 267–83.

Lagerspetz, K. M. J., Björkqvist, K., Berts, M., and King, E. (1982). Group aggression among school children in three schools. *Scandinavian Journal of Psychology*, 23, 45–52.

Neary, A. and Joseph, S. (1994). Peer victimization and its relationship to self-concept and depression among schoolgirls. *Personality and Individual Differences*, 16, 183–86.

Olweus, D. (1978). *Aggression in the schools: Bullies and whipping boys*. Washington, DC: Hemisphere.

(1991). Bully/victim problems among school children: Basic facts and effects of a school-based intervention program. In D. Pepler and K. Rubin (eds.), *The development and treatment of childhood aggression*. Hillsdale, NJ: Erlbaum, pp. 411–48.

(1993). *Bullying at school. What we know and what we can do*. Oxford: Blackwell.

Slee, P. T. and Rigby, K. (1993). Australian school children's self appraisal of interpersonal relations: The bullying experience. *Child Psychiatry and Human Development*, 23, 273–82.

Sharp, S. and Smith, P. K. (1993). Tackling bullying: The Sheffield Project. In D. Tattum (ed.), *Understanding and managing bullying*. London: Heinemann, pp. 45–56.

Smith, P. K. and Sharp, S. (1994). *School bullying: Insights and perspectives.* London: Routledge.

Smith, P. K., Morita, K., Junger-Tas, J., Olweus, D., Catalano, R., and Slee, P. T. (eds.) (1999). *The nature of school bullying: A cross-national perspective.* London: Routledge.

Valkanover, S. (2003). *Aspekte der Körpererfahrung und Motorik bei aggressiven Kindern und ihren Opfern* [Aspects of body awareness and motor skills in aggressive children and their victims]. Unpublished doctoral dissertation, Department of Psychology, University of Berne, Switzerland.

16 Looking back and looking forward: implications for making interventions work effectively

Debra Pepler, Peter K. Smith, and Ken Rigby

This volume represents an unprecedented opportunity to reflect on interventions to address bullying problems at school. The contributors have been generous in their willingness to be part of this collective reflection. We benefit from their honesty in not only sharing the highlights of successful outcomes but also in providing rare glimpses of the challenges and disappointments in their well-crafted attempts to reduce problems of bullying among school children. From this vantage-point, we can look back on the efforts in many countries to address this universal problem, and look forward to sketch out intervention, evaluation, and policy strategies for a more-informed and effective collective effort to reduce bullying problems and support healthy relationships among children and youth.

With ongoing research efforts, the theoretical framework for understanding bullying is constantly being refined; however, developmental and systemic perspectives comprise its essential foundation. These perspectives relate to underlying causes of bullying which may involve individual risk characteristics of children, problems within the family, dynamics within the peer group, and problems within the classroom and larger school climate.

Developmental perspective

By considering bullying problems from a developmental perspective, we can recognise different developmental capacities, motivations, and vulnerabilities, as well as different peer-group dynamics of children at various stages. A developmental perspective also reveals that effective bullying interventions must be ongoing throughout children's school careers.

Developmental differences

There is great variability in the types of children who are involved in perpetrating bullying and being victimised. The interventions for bullying can be tailored to meet the specific developmental needs and capacities of children. At the extreme ends of the continuum, there are children with serious psychosocial problems which contribute to their involvement as bullies, victims, or both bullies and victims. These children and their families will require more intensive support from the school; however, their needs may be beyond the school's capacity and require clinical support from a community agency. Some of the programmes described in this volume, such as that of Koivisto in Finland (chapter 12) and Limber and colleagues in the USA (chapter 4), established specific links with professionals and community agencies to provide this type of additional support to children experiencing severe problems associated with, and contributing to, the problems of bullying and victimisation. The interventions provided for children must be matched to their developmental needs. As Limber and colleagues (chapter 4) note, anger-management programmes may not be suitable for most children who bully, because anger is seldom the motivation for bullying (Olweus, 2001).

Developmental timing

A developmental perspective also points to timing prevention efforts early in children's school careers. With development, both an individual child's behaviours as well as the ways in which others react to the child become increasingly consolidated and resistant to change. Research on the stability of victim-and-bully status suggests that few pupils enter into stable victim roles before 8–9 years (Kochenderfer and Ladd, 1996; Monks, Smith, and Swettenham, 2003). Intervention programmes that focus on children younger than 8 or 9 years may be able to prevent vulnerable children from developing interactional patterns of bullying or being systematically targeted and stereotyped into a stable victim role from which it may be difficult to escape. Several of the interventions in this volume focused on early prevention of bullying and victimization. Alsaker (chapter 15) found evidence for programme effects in reducing teacher ratings of victimisation with the Berne, Switzerland, anti-bullying programme in kindergarten schools. In evaluating interventions within Irish primary schools, O'Moore and Minton (chapter 14) found decreases in students' reports of bullying peers and being victimised.

A number of contributors describe interventions in both primary- and secondary-school contexts. Efforts to intervene to support healthy relationships across childhood and adolescence are important, because the children who are involved in bullying and victimisation at a serious level may be at risk for continuing these patterns into adulthood. Consistent with the developmental recommendation for early interventions, there appear to be stronger positive effects on bullying problems within primary schools, compared with secondary schools. This was found both in the Sheffield study (Smith and colleagues, chapter 6) and in the Flemish study (Stevens and colleagues, chapter 8). In the Schleswig-Holstein project (chapter 5), Hanewinkel found that students' reports of victimisation (for direct bullying) decreased less for older children after the intervention and, in fact, increased for adolescents aged 17–18 years.

Developmental characteristics of older children and organisational features of secondary schools have been suggested as explanations (Stevens, de Bourdeaudhuij, and Van Oost, 2000). Younger children are generally more willing to accept teacher authority and curriculum activities and school policies that reflect teacher influence. Therefore, the strategy to increase communication about bullying between students and teachers may sit more comfortably with younger than with older students. Older children – especially those involved in bullying and other antisocial activities – may explicitly reject teacher influence and values advocated by the school (Rigby and Bagshaw, 2003). In implementing bullying programmes, there is a challenge to develop more-effective ways of communicating with older students. The general peer climate and attitudes towards victims become somewhat more negative in early adolescence, particularly among boys (Olweus and Endresen, 1998; Rigby, 1997). In later adolescence, however, more positive attitudes towards victims re-emerge (Rigby, 1997). With the size and organisational structure of secondary schools, teachers are less likely to be familiar with individual students because they do not have opportunities to observe and interact with them throughout the school day, as is the case in primary schools. Therefore, opportunities both to detect and intervene in bullying problems are somewhat fewer in secondary than in primary schools. Secondary schools are larger and organised by year group rather than by class, making whole-school processes more difficult to promote effectively (Arora, 1994).

As new developmental stages and challenges arise, new forms of bullying require renewed attention (Connolly et al., 2000; McMaster et al., 2002). The interventions by Rosenbluth and colleagues in the USA (chapter 11) focus specifically on the emerging forms of bullying in early adolescence, such as sexual harassment and dating violence.

Gender differences

Gender is also an important consideration in developing anti-bullying interventions. Boys and girls use and experience different types of bullying: boys' bullying is more likely than that of girls to comprise physical attacks. Girls' bullying tends to be more indirect or relational, and includes social exclusion. The Sheffield project follow-up concluded that girls' experiences of being bullied may be more difficult to tackle: boys' reports of being bullied continued to fall in the follow-up assessments in 3 of 4 primary schools, but girls' reports of being bullied fell in only 1 school (chapter 6). There are difficulties in tackling relational bullying among adolescent girls (Owens, Shute, and Slee, 2000). On the other hand, Olweus (1999) found more substantial reductions in girls' than in boys' reports of bullying and victimisation, suggesting that girls are more receptive to anti-bullying interventions. Girls generally have more favourable attitudes to victims, especially in adolescence (Menesini et al., 1997; Olweus and Endresen, 1998). Girls are also significantly more willing to play an active part in challenging school bullying, for example through participation in peer-support interventions (Cowie, 2000). In programmes such as peer mediation and peer counselling, there is a gender imbalance in the peer supporters who are recruited, with about 80% being girls; the sex balance of teachers in charge of peer-support systems is similarly weighted. Policies and curriculum interventions may be able to build on the prosocial orientations of girls and target the more covert forms of indirect and relational bullying, as well as direct bullying.

Systemic perspective

The interventions described in this volume generally derive from a systemic perspective. Since the first efforts in Norway (Olweus, 1993), interventions for bullying problems have focused broadly on systemic change rather than limiting the focus to controlling a child with aggressive behaviour problems or fortifying a child who is victimised. An example of a comprehensive systemic model is that of Ortega and her colleagues in Spain (chapter 9). They developed interventions for schools and communities based on the experience of *convivencia*, learning together with a 'spirit of solidarity, fraternity, co-operation, harmony, a desire for mutual understanding, the desire to get along well with others, and the resolution of conflict through dialogue or other non-violent means' (p. 169). The systemic perspective highlights the need for changes in awareness and behaviour strategies for children, their teachers, their parents, and beyond in the broader community.

Peer processes

Against the background of research on peer processes (e.g. O'Connell, Pepler, and Craig, 1999; Salmivalli, 1999), the focus on bullying has been not only on the problem in the relationships between children involved as perpetrators and victims but also on the contingencies in the social dynamics surrounding bullying. With a recognition of the salient role of peers in bullying, interventions must be inclusive and reshape the interactions and social experiences of bullies, victims, and peers. This reshaping entails a focus on the peers who form the audience for bullying, as well as on the adults who can provide supportive interventions for the children involved. Salmivalli and colleagues' intervention (chapter 13) had a specific focus on the roles that peers play in bullying problems.

Teachers and principals

Successful school-based interventions for bullying depend on teachers and principals to create a climate that discourages bullying and encourages peer processes that support and include vulnerable children. Analyses of the implementation processes in this volume highlight the importance of teachers' and principals' commitment to the intervention. Olweus (chapter 2) notes that in the Bergen intervention teachers 'were the key agents of change with regard to adoption and implementation of the Olweus Bullying Prevention programme in school' (p. 32). The extent to which schools attended to bullying problems, through bullying-related activities, was also related to implementation. The time and resources committed to bullying problems within the school most likely represent strategic commitment and decisions made by the school principal. Alsaker (chapter 15) focused on process changes at the teacher level: kindergarten teachers who had participated in the bullying prevention programme felt more confident about handling bullying problems; had more supportive attitudes about victims; and felt more positively about working with parents regarding bullying problems. Salmivalli and colleagues (chapter 13) also found that the degree of programme implementation related to the extent of change in the indicators of bullying.

The interventions in this volume have all included opportunities for teacher training to orient them to the concerns and strategies for bullying problems. There is a pressing need for this type of education during pre-service teacher training in college education programmes (Nicolaides, Toda, and Smith, 2002). Given the essential importance of teachers in establishing a collaborative and respectful classroom climate, effective classroom management, open communication, and appropriate responses to children involved in bullying, such training cannot be left to the chance that a principal or school system will see fit to implement a programme. Pre-service teacher-training programmes can inform teachers of the complex social dynamics in children's peer relations and create awareness of the social, emotional, and educational advantages of addressing these problems. With such awareness, teachers may be able to recognise bullying more readily, and intervene early to make a difference in bullying problems before they become part of the classroom fabric.

Parents

Parents are also essential partners in addressing bullying problems at school. Parents of victims are often aware of their children's distressing experiences long before the school is. They can raise the concerns with teachers and participate in finding ways to support their children in social interactions. Parents of children who bully are also important in the interventions; however, they may not be as easy to engage. Talks with the parents of children who bully has been an essential element of the initial Bergen programme (Olweus, 1993), as well as many others.

Community

Although bullying problems unfold most frequently within the school system, they are not just school problems. Therefore, efforts to extend an understanding of bullying and strategies to address bullying problems into the broader community may enhance the potential for change. The original Bergen intervention, led by Olweus, was part of a nationwide campaign. Some of the interventions described in this volume, such as those by Hanewinkel in Schleswig-Holstein (chapter 5) and Limber and colleagues in South Carolina (chapter 4), were part of large-area campaigns. Other projects, such as those described by Pepler in Toronto (chapter 7) and Alsaker in Berne (chapter 15), focused on a few schools or a few classes in a local area. Large-scale comprehensive programmes can benefit from more support and resources and from associated media publicity. Nevertheless, while the success of the Bergen project may have been influenced by participation in a nationwide Norwegian campaign, other large-scale studies modelled on it, in South Carolina and Schleswig-Holstein, had less successful outcomes. The intervention in Andalucia described by Ortega and colleagues (chapter 9) did not have the foundation of a nationwide campaign, but the results reported were similar to those in Bergen.

A final comment with respect to the systemic nature of interventions relates to the socio-cultural sensitivity of the approach to bullying. Some of the interventions have been implemented in regions with diverse and multi-cultural populations. The concern for racial bullying may also be addressed through bullying interventions that promote respect for differences among all children.

Intervention strategies

A consistent response to bullying and harassment problems within the school serves several purposes: it signals support for the child or youth being victimised or harassed; it highlights the need for interventions to support the individual who has been harassing; and it conveys a public message that bullying and harassment will not be tolerated within the school or organisation, with the aim of promoting a positive and safe climate. At this stage in the development and refinement of bullying interventions, the research is not at the point where we can reliably point to specific elements of interventions that are known to be the active and essential elements associated with change. It is with caution, therefore, that we provide a summary of the common elements of the interventions which specifically focus on the problems of children who bully, children who are victimised, classmates who are likely to be the peer bystanders in bullying, parents, and broader school initiatives. In adopting any of these elements for a bullying-prevention programme, the reader is advised that there remains a need for further evaluation of the effectiveness of the various components.

What to do with children who bully

It is a challenge to shift the motivations and behaviours of children who bully because their bullying behaviours can afford them a position of power and status among some peers, albeit through antisocial means. The interventions described in this volume employed a wide variety of strategies to shift the aggressive behaviour of children who bullied, ranging from providing support, redirection, and formation through to rules, consequences, zero tolerance, and suspension.

Interventions also vary in intensity. The least-intensive step is to educate students about bullying and the impact of their aggressive behaviour on others. This can be accomplished through talks with individual students who bully, as advocated, for example, by Olweus (chapter 2), Limber (chapter 4), and Hanewinkel (chapter 5). Alternative approaches which also involve working with groups of children who have bullied others are the Pikas Method of Shared Concern (see chapters 5, 6, 9, 12, and 13) and the No Blame or Support Group approach (see chapters 5, 9, and 13).

If the education approach is insufficient in shifting the behaviours of children who bully, then the intensity of intervention strategies can be increased. Counselling and support may be the next level of intervention provided. Additional interventions may still be required to reduce students' aggressive behaviours. Schools can turn to behaviour-management approaches, applying non-punitive sanctions such as withdrawing privileges (Olweus, chapter 2). These can be accompanied by some form of intervention that enhances the student's understanding of the problem (e.g. perspective-taking skills and empathy) and use of appropriate non-aggressive behaviours (Pepler and Craig, 2000). The intensity of the interventions will depend on the severity of the student's psychosocial problems. For the most seriously involved students, referral to a community clinic for child and family counselling may be indicated. When the school has established formal links with community agencies, these types of referrals are more readily accomplished.

Punitive steps at the far end of the continuum of intervention strategies have not been recommended within any of the interventions described in this volume. They are, however, part of some jurisdictions' educational policies. Zero-tolerance policies that employ exclusion responses, such as expelling students from the educational system or placing them in homogeneous classes of aggressive students, should be seen as a last resort. They may protect other children in the original school they are expelled from, but exclusion not only fails to provide opportunities to develop the relationship capacity that these children lack but also may place them at increased risk for association with similarly aggressive peers. Rather than promoting the goals of education for responsible social engagement, these contexts can promote problem behaviours through deviancy training (Dishion, McCord, and Poulin, 1999).

What to do with children who are victimised

In several of the interventions, the rates of victimisation showed a greater improvement than the rates of bullying. This may be attributable to the motivation of victimised children to protect themselves from this form of peer abuse by making use of the help being offered. It is critical to provide protection and support for children who have been victimised, with care and attention being paid to integrating and not further isolating the child. It is necessary to monitor and follow through the effectiveness of such interventions.

One set of strategies involves structuring peer-group experiences to provide supportive peer contexts. These include 'circles of friends', designated groups of same- or mixed-age students who provide a support group of peers to work with a vulnerable pupil (Newton and Wilson, 1999); and befriending or buddying, in which a pupil or pupils are assigned to 'be with' or 'befriend' a peer (Cowie and Sharp, 1996).

Some form of social-skills interventions may be indicated for victimised children who lack the social skills to build friendships, integrate into peer activities, and speak out for themselves. Assertiveness training has been recommended as one way of helping victimised children to cope in non-passive, but also non-aggressive, ways. These techniques can be taught to pupils and appear to provide some advantage (Smith and Sharp, 1994; Ross, 2003). Working with parents of victimised children, it may be possible to identify a couple of prosocial children in the class who could be invited individually to visit with the child for an interesting activity; in this way, the teacher and parents can collaborate to provide some support for the victimised child to develop friendship skills (Pepler and Craig, 2000).

Additional supports may be required for children who are bully-victims or provocative victims. These students, who are caught up in both being aggressive and being victimised in the peer group, are most at risk in terms of psychosocial-adjustment problems (Craig, 1998; Schwartz, Proctor, and Chien, 2001). Similar to children with serious bullying problems, these children may require more support than most educational systems are able to provide. Hence, the links with communities are critical in ensuring the appropriate level of counselling support for at-risk children and their families.

What to do in classrooms

A consistent theme through many of the chapters is that the implementation depends on teachers' commitment to an anti-bullying programme. Several researchers have included measures of teachers' involvement in the process of programme delivery. The importance of teachers' commitment to the programme and concern for issues of bullying has been highlighted in the process analyses by a number of contributors to this volume, such as Alsaker, Olweus, Salmivalli, and Smith.

Beyond the teachers' commitment to the process, their abilities to create a warm and inclusive class climate are also seen as important to efforts to reduce bullying. The SAVE intervention (chapter 9) placed a major focus on promoting a collaborative class climate to develop attitudes and values that were supportive of victimised children. One of the success indicators for this programme was the improvement in attitudes against bullying and for supporting victimised peers. Galloway and Roland (chapter 3) highlight the substantial differences among Norwegian classes and schools in levels of bullying and victimisation, pointing to differential effectiveness in teachers' classroom management. They found that the quality of classroom management (that is, teacher–pupil relationships) and the social structure of the class (that is, pupil–pupil relationships) substantially predict rates of reported victimisation (Roland and Galloway, 2002).

There is much still to be learned about the specific role of teachers and the most effective classroom strategies to reduce bullying. Several studies have taken classroom effects into account through hierarchical modelling. We may be able to learn more through analyses that focus on processes that differentiate classes on levels of bullying and victimisation.

The interventions in this volume suggest a variety of measures at the classroom level. In general, these strategies are designed to engage students in addressing problems of bullying when they see them, and to encourage action by the majority of pupils who do not like bullying. One derived from Olweus (chapter 2) is to develop a set of rules together with the children that will shape and guide behavioural expectations in the class. Others are co-operative approaches to classroom learning (Cowie et al., 1994), and regular classroom discussions, often structured as circle time, during which classes address relationship issues such as fighting and bullying (Mosley, 1996). Teaching basic relationship values can be integrated into many aspects of primary- and secondary-school curricula. If this integration is accomplished, both teachers and students may recognise that addressing bullying problems is integral to the school climate rather than a short-lived additional programme.

What to do with bystanders, and peer support

Cowie has been instrumental in developing active-listening or counselling-based approaches, which employ pupil helpers trained and supervised to use active-listening skills to support peers in distress. These peer-based strategies within the school were an important element in the SAVE programme (chapter 9). Such methods hold promise, and evaluations to date find that peer supporters themselves benefit and that the school climate improves generally; however, specific benefits for victims of bullying remain to be proven (Cowie, 2000; Cowie and Wallace, 2000). Where peer helpers are not regularly supervised, where there are not enough peer supporters to tackle the problem, or where the problem is particularly severe the system is less likely to be effective (Cowie and Olafsson, 2000).

What to do at school level

Some programmes, such as that by Alsaker (chapter 15) and Cross and colleagues (chapter 10), target specific grades for the intervention (kindergarten, and grades 4 and 5, respectively). Other programmes have involved all grades within a school in the intervention efforts, with the understanding that bullying occurs within various systems within the school and that all members of the school community must be aware of bullying problems and be responsive to them. Some specific interventions, such as conflict resolution or mediation programmes, use a structured process wherein a neutral third party assists voluntary participants to resolve their dispute.

Drawing from the work of Smith and colleagues (chapter 6) in the Sheffield project, some programmes developed a whole-school policy as a starting-point for the bullying intervention. A whole-school policy is a written document that sets out the school's aims in relation to bullying behaviour, together with a set of strategies to be followed. The document is supported by systems and procedures within the school to ensure that its aims and strategies are effectively implemented, monitored, maintained, and reviewed. The policy is often developed by a committee consisting of teachers, students, and parents. The whole-school approach usually emphasises the democratic involvement of all school members in devising and maintaining the policy, and has the potential advantage of integrating numerous components of an anti-bullying strategy (Suckling and Temple, 2002; Thompson and Sharp, 1999). Leadership by the principal or headteacher in the school has been identified as critical in this process.

What to do at a broader community level

Although bullying is a problem that unfolds most frequently at school, it can occur in other aspects of children's lives. Therefore, the success of transforming the social interactions of children at risk for bullying and victimisation, as well as the social dynamics around bullying, may depend on the extent to which this problem is understood and dealt with outside the school context, in families and community settings. Some of the programmes had evening meetings to inform parents about the problem of bullying and about programme plans (Limber and colleagues, chapter 4; Pepler and colleagues, chapter 7). Although parent involvement is an important step in extending the conversation of bullying beyond the schools, attendance at parent meetings tends to reflect only a small portion of the school community; the audiences may have an over-representation of parents of victimised children and an under-representation of parents of children who bully.

A number of programmes had specific strategies for outreach to engage parents. Limber and colleagues (chapter 4) sent home a bullying newsletter several times a year. The newsletters developed by Rosenbluth and colleagues (chapter 11) highlighted the issues of concern in bullying, the elements of the programme that students were involved in at school, and strategies for parents who recognised that their children were involved either in perpetrating bullying or in being victimised.

Some of the outreach to communities extended beyond the home. In the original Norwegian nationwide campaign, there was associated media coverage. Many of the programmes described in this volume were accompanied by some media attention, even if it was not a specifically planned media campaign. Other programmes extended the contact to community agencies and professionals, who could provide ancillary support for the schools' efforts. The problems of bullying are greater than can be addressed by the school, which is an essential, but single, system in children's lives. As networks are established among the important systems for children, the support that can be provided to them and their families will be strengthened.

Controversies in intervention strategies

There has been an ongoing debate in the field of bullying interventions as to whether consequences and sanctions are the most appropriate interventions or whether educative and supportive strategies, such as the No Blame approach or the Method of Common Concern, are more appropriate to reduce bullying problems. The choice of methods depends, in part, on one's perception of the problem. If one considers bullying to be a problem that resides primarily within the aggressive behavioural patterns of perpetrators, then a specific focus on providing consequences for transgressions might be indicated. Conversely, if one considers bullying to be a problem that arises not only from an individual child's propensity to be aggressive but also from the dynamics in peer groups, then this suggests an approach that alters the behaviours of many children involved in the dynamic of bullying. This ongoing debate does reflect deep philosophical differences relating to perceived developmental needs of children and how to change behaviour; in practice, any resolution most likely lies between the two extreme camps. Research that evaluates not only the effectiveness of the method but also the match of the method to the nature of the problem may help to untangle this dilemma.

There are still important questions as to whether intervention efforts should focus on addressing cases of bullying directly or whether it is more effective to emphasise less-direct means of reducing bullying through universal strategies that improve classroom climate, increase supervision, and enhance children's understanding and behaviours regarding social relations, prejudice, and interventions in bullying (chapter 3). These are essential issues for future intervention evaluations.

Finally, there is some debate about the best means to support interventions within schools. There is no question that it is a challenge to create and sustain commitment for an anti-bullying intervention with school staff who are already overwhelmed with responsibilities. In future interventions, it will be important to determine effective ways of motivating school staff and supporting them to maintain a concern for bullying problems among their students. At this point, the jury is out on whether additional support from outside experts, such as university researchers, is important and effective. On the one hand, it has been suggested that the much greater apparent success of the nationwide Norwegian campaign in Bergen, as compared to Stavanger, may have been due to the researchers' visits to the Bergen schools to give feedback and discuss further work (Smith and Ananiadou, 2003). On the other hand, the Flanders' assessment (chapter 8) suggests that a high level of engagement by researchers in the programme may not improve outcomes and can reduce the feeling of autonomy and the commitment of school staff. The approach in Sheffield (chapter 6) of having some elements in an intervention mandatory, such as producing a policy document, and some optional elements represents a compromise.

Research and methodology: Issues for the future

We now know that intervention programmes to reduce bullying can produce some positive results. A major challenge at this point, however, lies in determining what elements should be included in anti-bullying programmes and how programmes should be implemented. This requires the use of research designs that enable one to identify in a systematic way the effects of specific elements. It would be useful to shed light on the controversy about interventions with children who bully. Are interventions that rely primarily on the application of rules and consequences for breaking rules more effective in reducing bullying than those that rely on problem-solving approaches or focus upon effecting positive changes to classroom climate? It might be found that the appropriateness of the procedure depends upon the age level and the gender of the students.

Another issue relates to where the effectiveness of the intervention lies. Is it primarily in shifting the perceptions and behaviours of the majority of students, or in addressing the needs of the high-risk children involved in bullying or victimisation? Identifying differential effectiveness in changing students' behaviours and attitudes is difficult with an analytic approach that relies on central tendency data, such as changes in mean scores over time or across cohorts. Longitudinal designs in which a person-oriented approach can be used will help to elucidate the different patterns of change or stability among students. This type of analysis, such as a mixture model or group-based modelling (Nagin and Tremblay, 2001), can reveal the different developmental pathways that children follow through the course of an intervention.

For example, among students initially identified as bullies (or victims), there may be some who do not deviate from their initial role; others who quickly decline in risk; and yet others who waver – moving in and out of roles over time. The elegant feature of these analytic techniques is the ability to identify risk variables that are related to continuity along a bullying or victimisation pathway, compared to protective variables associated with moving off into a less-troubled social dynamic. According to the developmental-systemic framework, we should expect these risk and protective processes to lie not only within the child's individual make-up but also within the systems in which that child interacts. For example, children may be at risk for continued victimisation if they have an anxious temperament but also if they are isolated and unsupported within the classroom peer group. Once the risk and protective processes are identified, intervention strategies can be implemented to reduce the exposure to risk and to promote opportunities to experience protective processes. Through this dynamic assessment and iterative intervention design, we can become increasingly strategic in providing for children's developmental needs within relevant social systems.

These research designs with person-oriented analyses, however, require specific methodologies which are present in several of the intervention studies within this volume but absent in others. There must be some method to track individual children over time, which cannot be done with anonymous surveys. There is evidence from intervention research projects with longitudinal designs that students can be reassured about confidentiality. In evaluation studies, students can be encouraged to complete sensitive questionnaires that are encoded with an encrypted identification number which masks their identity.

Some broader issues remain in the research methodologies used to evaluate bullying interventions. Currently, inquiry is hampered by a lack of consensus on how the possible effects of bullying can be most reliably assessed. Programmes can have differential effects on different kinds of bullying behaviour, so this should be reflected in the choice of outcomes (behaviours and attitudes) targeted. Ideally, multiple sources of data should be used, drawing upon nominations or ratings of peers provided by fellow-students, the judgements of teachers and parents, as well as reports from students completing anonymous questionnaires (Pellegrini and Bartini, 2000). Longitudinal designs and repeated testing is needed to identify long-term as well as short-term effects.

Important issues centre on the practicalities of implementation of programmes in schools. Several studies have shown that the extent to which schools implement a programme is a significant factor determining outcomes. A thorough implementation is often difficult for schools, in part because of the inroads it makes upon staff time, with teachers confronted by other priorities. Reports from researchers frequently indicate that schools dropped out of a study after having agreed to be involved. Hence, much attention needs to be given to motivating schools to continue their participation and to implement programmes as fully as possible. This may require that schools are given less direction but more encouragement in the implementation of a programme, so that they come to own it and become committed to it.

There are also issues relating to how data for the studies are obtained and how the outcomes are evaluated and reported upon. Investigating bullying behaviours between students is clearly a sensitive matter and methods of acquiring relevant data, for example through the use of peer nominations of bullies, can, in some countries, raise ethical questions that need to be addressed. There are issues concerning the adequacy of intervention assessments (chapters 1, 2). Interventions in this book vary considerably; while all except chapter 3 report pre-test and post-test data, some have experimental and comparison groups, some do not; and some have a straightforward longitudinal design, others use age-matched controls. Finally, it is evident that evaluations of interventions have generally been conducted by the initiators of the programme, with a consequent possibility of experimenter bias. By minimising the degree of subjectivity in the data upon which judgements are based and involving external evaluators, the credibility of the findings can be enhanced.

Policy

Those who work in the field of bullying have no doubt that this is an essential issue in the development and well-being of children and youth, but this perspective is not held by all. Despite the strong evidence of negative effects of severe and long-term victimisation (chapter 1), some people still hold to myths about bullying: 'It is just kids being kids', 'They will grow out of it', and 'It prepares you for life' (even though some bullying results in death through suicide). There is still work to be done to convince educators, parents, policy-makers, and children themselves that this is a central concern for development and education. At this point, the solutions are getting closer. We need to find ways of linking current social policies to the extant research. There is also a need and an opportunity to continue learning about the nature of bullying across cultures, and the effective strategies for addressing the problems in various regions of the world (Smith et al., 1999). This volume represents another step in building bridges to strengthen cross-cultural exchanges and advances in addressing bullying problems among children and adolescents.

The international interventions have generally provided evidence that bullying can be reduced. Achievements to date, however, have been modest in scale, most substantially below the 50% mark, with some projects showing negligible improvements. Even though there has been only modest progress, intervention efforts and associated evaluations must continue to provide a foundation for identifying effective strategies and developing strong social policies to promote broad-based change.

To promote change, researchers will need to participate actively in the knowledge-transfer process. To stimulate broad-based concerns for bullying, it is important to share our understanding about the short-term and long-term effects associated both with perpetrating bullying and being victimised. From an evaluation standpoint, it is incumbent on us to measure outcomes that are relevant to the educational system as it now exists. Principals and teachers are pressed to ensure that their students meet academic standards. Those of us who work in the field of bullying have no doubt that these negative interactions impact on academic performance.

At this point, we have not been comprehensive in our evaluation strategies. Successful education requires the success of all students, even those who are marginalised. Measurements of school attendance, engagement, motivation, and academic attainment for the at-risk students might provide convincing evidence for bullying interventions. It is the role of society to educate all children to ensure they develop positive attitudes and behaviours and avoid using their power to bully or harass others. This societal function is the responsibility of parents, teachers, and other adults in the community who are in contact with children and youth. With a focus on social relations as they provide the essential foundation for learning within the school and other contexts in children's lives, we may be able to elicit a broader view of education that supports children's healthy development and protects their welfare at home, at school, and in their communities.

References

Arora, C. M. J. (1994). Is there any point in trying to reduce bullying in secondary schools? *Educational Psychology in Practice*, 10, 155–62.

Connolly, J., Pepler, D. J., Craig, W. M., and Taradash, A. (2000). Dating experiences of bullies in early adolescence. *Child Maltreatment*, 5, 299–310.

Cowie, H. (2000). Bystanding or standing by: Gender issues in coping with bullying in English schools. *Aggressive Behavior*, 26, 85–97.

Cowie, H. and Olafsson, R. (2000). The role of peer support in helping the victims of bullying in a school with high levels of aggression. *School Psychology International*, 21, 79–95.

Cowie, H. and Sharp S. (1996). *Peer counselling in schools: A time to listen*. London: David Fulton.

Cowie H., Smith, P. K., Boulton, M., and Laver, R. (1994). *Co-operation in the multi-ethnic classroom*. London: David Fulton.

Cowie, H. and Wallace, P. (2000). *Peer support into action*. London: Sage.

Craig, W. (1998). The relationship among bullying, victimization, depression, anxiety, and aggression in elementary school children. *Personality and Individual Differences*, 24, 123–30.

Dishion, T., McCord, J., and Poulin, F. (1999). When interventions harm: Peer groups and problem behavior. *American Psychologist*, 54, 755–65.

Kochenderfer, B. and Ladd, G. (1996). Peer victimization: Cause or consequence of school maladjustment? *Child Development*, 67, 1305–17.

McMaster, L., Connolly, J., Pepler, D., and Craig, W. (2002). Peer-to-peer sexual harassment among early adolescents: A developmental perspective. *Development and Psychopathology*, 14, 91–105.

Menesini, E., Eslea, M., Smith, P. K., Genta, M. L., Giannetti, E., Fonzi, A., and Costabile, A. (1997). A cross-national comparison of children's attitudes towards bully/victim problems in school. *Aggressive Behavior*, 23, 245–57.

Monks, C., Smith, P. K., and Swettenham, J. (2003). Aggressors, victims and defenders in pre-school: Peer, self and teacher reports. *Merrill-Palmer Quarterly*, 49, 453–69.

Mosley, J. (1996). *Quality circle time in the primary classroom: Your essential guide to enhancing self-esteem, self-discipline and positive relationships*. Cambridge: Learning Development Aids.

Nagin, D. S. and Tremblay, R. E. (2001). Analyzing developmental trajectories of distinct but related behaviors: A group-based method. *Psychological Methods*, 6, 18–34.

Newton, C. and Wilson, D. (1999). *Circles of friends*. Dunstable: Folens.

Nicolaides, S., Toda, Y., and Smith, P. K. (2002). Knowledge and attitudes about school bullying in trainee teachers. *British Journal of Educational Psychology*, 72, 105–18.

O'Connell, P., Pepler, D., and Craig, W. (1999). Peer involvement in bullying: Issues and challenges for intervention. *Journal of Adolescence*, 22, 437–52.

Olweus, D. (1993). *Bullying at school: What we know and what we can do*. Oxford: Blackwell.

(1999). Sweden. In P. K. Smith, Y. Morita, J. Junger-Tas, D. Olweus, R. Catalano, and P. Slee (eds.), *The nature of school bullying: A cross-national perspective*. London: Routledge, pp. 7–27.

(2001). Olweus' core program against bullying and antisocial behavior: A teacher handbook. Available from the author.

Olweus, D. and Endresen, I. M. (1998). The importance of sex-of-stimulus object: Age trends and sex differences in empathic responsiveness. *Social Development*, 3, 370–88.

Owens, L., Shute, R., and Slee, P. (2000). 'Guess what I just heard!' Indirect aggression among teenage girls in Australia. *Aggressive Behavior*, 26, 67–83.

Pellegrini, A. D. and Bartini, M. (2000). An empirical comparison of methods of sampling aggression and victimization in school settings. *Journal of Educational Psychology*, 92, 360–66.

Pepler, D. J. and Craig, W. M. (2000). Making a difference in bullying. *LaMarsh Report* 59. Toronto: York University.

Rigby, K. (1997). Attitudes and beliefs about bullying among Australian school children. *Irish Journal of Psychology*, 18, 202–20.

Rigby, K. and Bagshaw, D. (2003). Prospects of adolescent students collaborating with teachers in addressing issues of bullying and conflict in schools. *Educational Psychology*, 23, 535–46.

Roland, E. and Galloway, D. (2002). Classroom influences on bullying. *Educational Research*, 44, 299–312.

Ross, D. (2003). *Childhood bullying and teasing: What school personnel, other professionals and parents can do.* 2nd edn. Alexandria, Va.: American Counseling Association.

Salmivalli, C. (1999). Participant role approach to school bullying: Implications for interventions. *Journal of Adolescence*, 22, 453–59.

Schwartz, D., Proctor, L. J., and Chien, D. H. (2001). The aggressive victim of bullying: Emotional and behavioral dysregulation as a pathway to victimization by peers. In J. Juvonen and S. Graham (eds.), *Peer harassment in school: The plight of the vulnerable and victimized.* New York: Guilford Press, pp. 147–74.

Smith, P. K. and Ananiadou, K. (2002). The nature of school bullying and the effectiveness of school-based interventions to reduce school bullying. *Journal of Applied Psychoanalytic Studies*, 5, 189–209.

Smith, P. K., Morita, Y., Junger-Tas, J., Olweus, D., Catalano, R., and Slee, P. (eds.), (1999). *The nature of school bullying: A cross-national perspective.* London and New York: Routledge.

Smith, P. K. and Sharp, S. (eds.) (1994). *School bullying: Insights and perspectives.* London: Routledge.

Stevens, V., de Bourdeaudhuij, I., and Van Oost, P. (2000). Bullying in Flemish schools: An evaluation of anti-bullying intervention in primary and secondary schools. *British Journal of Educational Psychology*, 70, 195–210.

Suckling, A. and Temple, C. (2002). *Bullying: A whole-school approach.* London and Philadelphia: Jessica Kingsley.

Thompson, D. and Sharp, S. (1999). *Improving schools: Establishing and integrating whole school behaviour policies.* London: David Fulton.

Author index

Subject index